Charles Adolphus Row

Christian evidences viewed in relation to modern thought : eight lectures preached before the University of Oxford in the year 1877

Charles Adolphus Row

Christian evidences viewed in relation to modern thought : eight lectures preached before the University of Oxford in the year 1877

ISBN/EAN: 9783337263447

Printed in Europe, USA, Canada, Australia, Japan

Cover: Foto ©Lupo / pixelio.de

More available books at **www.hansebooks.com**

CHRISTIAN EVIDENCES

VIEWED

IN RELATION TO MODERN THOUGHT.

CHRISTIAN EVIDENCES

VIEWED

IN RELATION TO MODERN THOUGHT.

EIGHT LECTURES PREACHED BEFORE THE UNIVERSITY OF
OXFORD IN THE YEAR 1877 ON THE FOUNDATION
OF THE LATE REV. JOHN BAMPTON, M.A.,
CANON OF SALISBURY.

BY THE
REV. C. A. ROW, M.A.,
PEMBROKE COLLEGE, OXFORD; PREBENDARY OF ST. PAUL'S CATHEDRAL.

LONDON:
FREDERIC NORGATE,
17, BEDFORD STREET, COVENT GARDEN:
WILLIAMS & NORGATE, 20, FREDERICK STREET, EDINBURGH.

—

1877.

LONDON:
G. NORMAN AND SON, PRINTERS, MAIDEN LANE,
COVENT GARDEN.

EXTRACT
FROM THE LAST WILL AND TESTAMENT
OF THE LATE
REV JOHN BAMPTON,
CANON OF SALISBURY.

——"I give and bequeath my Lands and Estates to
"the Chancellor, Masters, and Scholars, of the University
"of Oxford for ever, to have and to hold all and singular
"the said Lands or Estates upon trust, and to the intents
"and purposes hereinafter mentioned; that is to say, I
"will and appoint that the Vice-Chancellor of the Univer-
"sity of Oxford for the time being shall take and receive
"all the rents, issues, and profits thereof, and (after all
"taxes, reparations, and necessary deductions made) that
"he pay all the remainder to the endowment of eight
"Divinity Lecture Sermons, to be established for ever
"in the said University, and to be performed in the
"manner following :—

"I direct and appoint, that upon the First Tuesday
"in Easter Term, a Lecturer may be yearly chosen by the
"Heads of Colleges only, and by no others, in the room
"adjoining to the Printing-House, between the hours of
"ten in the morning and two in the afternoon, to preach
"eight Divinity Lecture Sermons, the year following, at
"St. Mary's in Oxford, between the commencement of the

"last month in Lent Term, and the end of the third week
"in Act Term.

"Also I direct and appoint, that the eight Divinity
"Lecture Sermons shall be preached upon either of the
"following subjects—to confirm and establish the Chris-
"tian faith, and to confute all heretics and schismatics—
"upon the divine authority of the holy Scriptures—upon
"the authority of the writings of the primitive Fathers,
"as to the faith and practice of the primitive Church—
"upon the Divinity of our Lord and Saviour Jesus Christ
"—upon the Divinity of the Holy Ghost—upon the
"Articles of the Christian Faith, as comprehended in the
"Apostles' and Nicene Creed.

"Also I direct, that thirty copies of the eight Divinity
"Lecture Sermons shall be always printed, within two
"months after they are preached; and one copy shall be
"given to the Chancellor of the University, and one copy
"to the Head of every College, and one copy to the
"Mayor of the city of Oxford, and one copy to be put
"into the Bodleian Library; and the expense of printing
"them shall be paid out of the revenue of the Land or
"Estates given for establishing the Divinity Lecture Ser-
"mons; and the Preacher shall not be paid, nor be
"entitled to the revenue, before they are printed.

"Also I direct and appoint, that no person shall be
"qualified to preach the Divinity Lecture Sermons unless
"he hath taken the degree of Master of Arts at least, in
"one of the two Universities of Oxford or Cambridge;
"and that the same person shall never preach the Divinity
"Lecture Sermons twice."

CONTENTS.

LECTURE I.

THE ORDER OF THE CHRISTIAN ARGUMENT, ITS NATURE AND EXTENT.

Introduction, 1. The Christian revelation progressive according to the analogy of the divine working in nature, 3. Necessity of accommodating our evidential position to our increasing light, 6. The question—What constitutes the inner life of Christianity, as distinct from the vehicle through which it has been communicated, considered, 7. The essence of the Christian revelation consists not in a body of formulated dogmatic truth, but in a personal history, 12. The bearing of this on the limits of the Christian argument, 14. The relation in which theology stands to revelation, 16. Various points which are eagerly discussed among theologians extraneous to the Christian argument, 20. The moral miracles of Christianity constitute the most important attestation to its divine character, 25. Facts capable of verification ought to be placed in the forefront of the Christian argument, 29. Reasons for assigning a primary place to the argument from the moral aspects of Christianity, and a secondary one to that from miracles, 30.

SUPPLEMENT I.

THE EVIDENCE AFFORDED BY THE WRITINGS OF THE NEW TESTAMENT THAT THE ESSENCE OF THE CHRISTIAN REVELATION CONSISTS IN THE OBJECTIVE FACT OF THE INCARNATION.

The affirmations of St. John in his first epistle, 39. Those in his Gospel, 41. Our Lord's direct assertions on the same subject, 42. Further proof from the numerous incidental references made to it by St. Paul, 44. St. Paul's direct assertions on the same subject, 45. Christianity not an afterthought for the purpose of repairing the failure of God's creative plan, 47. The effects of the incarnation not limited to the human race, 49. The views propounded on this subject in the epistle to the Hebrews, and in the Apocalypse, 50. The testimony of the epistle of St. Peter, and of the Acts of the Apostles, 51. The views of the writers of the Synoptic Gospels in strict harmony with those of the other writers of the New Testament, 53.

Supplement II.

The Conception of a Miracle involves neither a Suspension of the Forces, nor a Violation of the Laws of Nature.

The confusion which has been introduced into the controversy about miracles by the use of ambiguous terms, 54. The distinction between the laws and the forces of nature, 57. The *modus operandi* of God in the performance of a miracle ought not to form a portion of its definition, 59. The question, whether, under the term nature, man and his free agency are meant to be included, all-important in this controversy, 61. Man capable of modifying the order of nature by imparting a new direction to its forces, 63. The laws of nature not violated, nor its forces suspended by the performance of a miracle, 65. The distinction between God's *modus operandi* in his ordinary providence and in performing miracles, unknown in the Old Testament, 68. The New Testament does not represent the forces of nature as suspended during the performance of miracles, 69. The theism of the Bible represents God not only as standing external to the universe, but as immanent in its forces, 71.

Lecture II.

The Superhuman Action of Jesus Christ verifiable in the History of the Past and the Facts of the Present.

The principles on which the argument is based, 73. The self-evidencing character of Our Lord's person the highest evidence of his divine mission, 75. Our Lord's direct affirmations on this subject as reported in the fourth Gospel, 76. Similar principles underlie his teaching in the Synoptics, 80. Large numbers of his miracles not performed for purposes directly evidential, 81. The views propounded in the epistles of St. John and St. Paul as to the self-evidencing character of Our Lord's divine person, 82. The evidential value assigned to miracles in the Acts of the Apostles, and in the epistle to the Hebrews, 83. Certain classes of miracles wrought rather for providential than for evidential purposes, 85. The supernatural gifts, how far evidential, 86. General summary of results, 88. The superhuman action of Jesus Christ in history a fact capable of verification, 89. The argument concisely stated, 90. Christianity based on a personal history—the unique character of this fact, 92. The mighty influence which this history has exerted on mankind, 93. The source of this influence, 95. The testimony of history to the solitary grandeur of Jesus Christ—Mr. Lecky's admissions, 96. Jesus Christ the solitary character in history who for eighteen centuries has inspired the hearts of men with an impassioned love, 98. He is the one Catholic man capable of acting on every condition of human nature, 99. He alone is the embodiment of holiness in his human life, and its perfect example, 101. Not only so, but he alone of men is capable of exerting a moral and spiritual power mighty for the regeneration of mankind, 102. His energetic action in the moral and spiritual worlds testified to by the history of the past, and the facts of the present, 104. The Church amidst its corruptions has found in the person of its Founder an ever enduring principle of regeneration, 106. The alternative propounded by unbelief to the acceptance of Christianity, 108.

SUPPLEMENT I.

THE EVIDENTIAL VALUE OF MIRACLES AS AFFECTED BY ANSWERS TO PRAYER.

The analogy between special providences and miracles, 109. The difficulty of discriminating between miracles, and answers to special prayers, which involve modifications in the action of the forces of the material universe, 110. A series of such answers in favour of a particular person would constitute a σημεῖον, 111. The case of the Bristol Orphan Asylum, 112. How far such answers to prayer affect the value of miracles as the sole attestations of a divine Revelation, 115.

SUPPLEMENT II.

MIRACLES WROUGHT IN THE PHYSICAL UNIVERSE NOT THE EXCLUSIVE ATTESTATION OF OUR LORD'S DIVINE MISSION.

Brief statement of the views propounded in the Lecture on this subject, 116. The opposite view which affirms that certain doctrinal statements contained in the New Testament can only be accepted as true, on the evidence of physical miracles, 118. The positions of Professor Mozley considered, 119. Our Lord's affirmations respecting himself to be accepted on the ground of his perfect truthfulness, and the adequacy of his knowledge, 122. While such assertions would have been incredible on the simple affirmation of an ordinary man, Our Lord was not an ordinary man, but his human life contained throughout a manifestation of the divine, 124. Our Lord's appeal to his sinlessness as an evidence of his veracity, 125. The change in the value of miracles as evidential to a divine Revelation through our inability to witness them, and the consequent difficulties with which their proof is attended, 126. The Mission of John the Baptist affirmed to have been divine, yet destitute of a miraculous attestation, 127.

LECTURE III.

THE CONTRAST BETWEEN THE TEACHING OF CHRISTIANITY AND THAT OF THE PHILOSOPHERS VIEWED EVIDENTIALLY.

The truth of Our Lord's affirmation that he is the Light of the World, and the Light of Life, verified by eighteen centuries of history, and verifiable in the facts of the present, 130-132. The continuity of the moral world— its changes take place in conformity with moral laws, 133. The teaching of Christianity involves a break in the continuity of the chain of moral causes, 134. Such a break in continuity a proof of the presence of the superhuman, 136. The condition of thought out of which Christianity must have been evolved if it owed its origin only to the ordinary forces energizing in man, 137. The ability of man to discover moral truth without the aid of revelation, instead of constituting a difficulty, confirmatory of this argument, 138. The moral teaching of Christianity, 141. First contrast between its teaching and that of the philosophers—its earnestness, method, and aim, 141. Its appeal to the entire moral nature of man contrasted with the method of the philosophers, 143. Second contrast—its freedom from all attempts at political legislation, 144. Yet Jesus Christ professed to be the founder of a kingdom—contrasted in this respect with all previous lines of thought, 147. The mode in which Christianity deals with great social questions, 149. Third contrast—Jesus Christ the founder of the everlasting religion of humanity, 148. Fourth contrast—the all-comprehensiveness and self-determinative character of the Christian law of duty, and the basis on which it is erected, 149-151. Duty measured by the love of self, 151. Duty measured by love to Jesus Christ, 152. The teaching of Christianity incapable of evolution out of the atmosphere of Jewish thought by the forces energizing in man, 154. Fifth contrast—the importance which Christianity assigns to the milder virtues compared with the political and heroical ones, 154. The mild and heroic virtues combined in the person of Jesus Christ, 157. Philosophy wrong in its preference of the heroic virtues, and Christianity right in assigning the first rank to the milder ones, 158. Sixth contrast—the views taken by Jesus Christ and the philosophers of their respective missions, 159. Jesus Christ the originator of all attempts to ameliorate the condition of the masses of mankind, 160. Seventh contrast—Christianity the Creator of a mighty moral and spiritual power, 161. The philosopher deeply conscious of his inability to operate on the masses of mankind, 162. The weakness of the moral forces at his command to struggle with the violence of passion, 163. The principle of habit, the only moral force recognized by philosophy, impotent to effect the regeneration of the human race, or the individual, 165. The political character of the ancient, and several modern systems of Ethics, 167. The New Testament propounds the principle of faith in contradistinction to that of habit as capable of effecting the regeneration of mankind, 170. The mode of its action corresponds to the necessities of man's moral constitution, 172. The religious principle in man in its bearing on moral action, 173. The results of the contrast of the teaching of Christianity with that of the philosophers viewed evidentially, 174. The concessions of Mr. Mill, 176.

LECTURE IV.

THE UNITY OF THE CHARACTER OF CHRIST A PROOF OF ITS HISTORICAL REALITY; AND THE LOGICAL VALUE OF THE ARGUMENT FROM PROPHECY.

The principle of verification recognized by the writers of the New Testament, 178. While the evangelists have given us no formal delineation of the character of Jesus Christ, its presence in their pages is a patent fact, 179. It has been created by the simple juxta-position of the materials which compose the Gospels, 180. This character is as deeply impressed on the miraculous narratives of the Gospels as on the remaining portions of their contents, 181. The character delineated in the Gospels is an essential unity, 182. Any theory which attempts to account for the origin of the miraculous narratives is invalid, unless it can also account for the unity of the character, 183. The mythic and legendary theories fail to account for the unity of the delineation, 185. The four Evangelists present us with four portraitures of the same historical reality taken from different points of view, 187. The argument unaffected by the question whether the Gospels were composed by the aid of written documents, or out of traditional reminiscences, 188. The absurdity of the supposition that a number of mythologists, acting independently, can have excogitated a number of legends impressed with the same lofty moral ideal, 189. Statement of the various points in which the mythologists must have concurred in their delineations, 191. Contrast presented by the delineations in the apocryphal Gospels, 194. The theory of tendencies equally inconsistent with the facts and phenomena of the Gospels, 197. The meaning of the writers of the New Testament when they affirm that the prophetic and typical delineations of the Old have been fulfilled in Jesus Christ, 200. The logical value of the argument from prophecy unaffected by various questions respecting the date and authorship of various books of the Old Testament, 206. A common idea underlies the books of the Old Testament, such as can be found in no other set of writings which extend over an equal space of time, 208. The nature and character of its predictive elements, 209. Its typical prophecies, 211. Their evidential value dependent on the degree in which they converge in a common centre, 215. Jesus Christ was the ideal of the institutions of the Old Testament, 216. And of the aspirations which underlay its entire system, 218. The force of the prophetic argument, 219.

Supplement I.

THE IDENTITY OF THE PORTRAITURE OF THE JESUS OF THE FOURTH GOSPEL WITH THE JESUS OF THE SYNOPTICS.

The allegation that the Jesus of the Fourth Gospel differs from the Jesus of the Synoptics considered, 221. Points in which the two delineations form an essential unity, 221. The Johannine discourses the counterpart of the Synoptical delineation, 223. Points where the two delineations exactly coincide, 224. A perfectly human character ascribed to Our Lord in the Fourth Gospel, 226. The Johannine and the Synoptical delineations of the Passion compared, 227.

Supplement II.

THE MESSIANIC ELEMENTS OF THE OLD TESTAMENT INADEQUATE AS A MODEL TO IDEOLOGISTS FOR THE DELINEATION OF THE CHRIST OF THE NEW TESTAMENT.

The materials which were open to mythologists to aid them in the delineation of an ideal Christ, 234. The Jesus of the Evangelists not manufactured out of the Messianic delineations of the book of Enoch, 235. Nor of those of Esdras, 239. Nor of Daniel, 240. Nor of that of the Servant of Jehovah, 242. Nor from the other Messianic delineations in Isaiah, 245. Nor from the other Messianic prophecies of the Old Testament, 246. Nor from its typical characters, 247.

LECTURE V.

THE EVIDENCE AFFORDED BY THE WRITINGS OF THE FATHERS, WHO FLOURISHED BETWEEN A.D. 90 AND A.D. 180, THAT THE CHURCH WAS IN POSSESSION OF AN ACCOUNT OF THE ACTIONS AND TEACHING OF OUR LORD ANALOGOUS TO THAT WHICH IS CONTAINED IN OUR PRESENT GOSPELS.

Mr. Mill's positions respecting the evidence necessary to establish the truth of miracles, as set forth in his *Logic* and his posthumous Essays, accepted as the foundation of the present argument, 249. Miracles require a stronger attestation than ordinary facts, 252. The *à priori* difficulties removed by the considerations adduced in the preceding Lectures, 254. Paley's work the model of modern evidential treatises; its defects, 256. While martyr testimony is a perfect guarantee against fraud, it is by no means equally efficacious as a safeguard against delusion, 257. Paley's proof that we are in possession of the testimony of the original witnesses imperfect as against the positions taken by modern unbelief, 261. His position, that miracles constitute the only adequate evidence of a revelation, renders it necessary not only to prove the truth of the Christian miracles but the falsehood of all others, 262. The difficulties with which this is attended, 263. The necessity which the form of his argument imposes on him of proving by the testimony of the Fathers that the Gospels were the work of the persons whose names they bear; and the imperfection of his method, 266. State of the patrisitic argument, 267. The Gospels fully recognized by the great Church writers who flourished at the conclusion of the second century, 268. The fact that Marcion's Gospel was a mutilated edition of our present Luke clearly established, 269. The value of the testimony of Papias, 270. The Clementine homilies render it nearly certain that their author used one of our present Gospels, 272. While the writings of Justin Martyr render it very highly probable that he used one or more of our Gospels, the evidence comes short of a moral demonstration, 273. The same is true of the earlier extra canonical writings, 275. The importance of proving that the Fathers actually quoted our Gospels has been over-estimated by both sides in this controversy, 277. While the writings of Justin only afford a high probability that his "Memoirs of the Apostles" contained one or more of our Gospels, they afford a moral demonstration that they contained an account of the actions and teaching of Our Lord which for all the purposes of history was identical with them, 278. The larger the number of his authorities, the more complete is the guarantee of the truth of the facts, 280. The testimony of the earlier Fathers affords a moral demonstration that the account current in the Church was substantially the same as that contained in our Gospels, 281. The accounts of Our Lord's ministry originally handed down by the Church in an oral form, of which the Synoptics are three different versions, 282. No legendary matter, invented between A.D. 80 and A.D. 180, has been incorporated into the Gospels, 283. The existence of the Church as a corporate society a guarantee of the accurate transmission of the events of its Founder's life such as is possessed by no other, 284. Such transmission was a necessary condition of its existence, 286. The impossibility of imposing a mass of fictions on the Church in place of the real events during the interval in question, 287.

LECTURE VI.

THE NATURE AND VALUE OF THE PAULINE EPISTLES AS HISTORICAL DOCUMENTS; AND THE EVIDENCE THEY AFFORD THAT THE ACCOUNT OF OUR LORD'S ACTIONS AND TEACHING WHICH WAS ACCEPTED BY THE CHURCH BETWEEN A.D. 30 AND A.D. 90 WAS IN ITS MAIN OUTLINES SIMILAR TO THAT IN OUR GOSPELS.

The sixty years which follow the Crucifixion lie completely within that period during which traditionary reminiscences possess the utmost freshness, 289. During this interval it would have been impossible for the real facts of the ministry of Our Lord to be superseded by myths and legends, 292. The entire period is covered by the testimony of St. Paul's epistles, 293. The genuineness of the four great epistles admitted by an overwhelming majority, and that of four more by a considerable number of learned unbelievers, 294. The historical value of the other writings in the New Testament, 295. The shortness of the interval which separates these letters from the events of Our Lord's ministry, 297. The value of original letters as affording materials for history, and the special value attaching to those of St. Paul, 298. They afford incontestable proof of his sincerity, and of the calmness of his judgment, 299. The value of incidental allusions as affording testimony to historic facts, 302. The existence in the Churches to which these epistles are addressed, of parties strongly antagonistic to St. Paul, renders their incidental allusions invaluable as testimony to facts, 303. These letters prove beyond question that St. Paul was firmly persuaded that he was in the habit of working miracles during the entire course of his ministry, 305. This fact fatal to the legendary theory, 308. They likewise prove that St. Paul and his opponents were persuaded that a number of supernatural endowments habitually manifested themselves in the Church from its foundation, 309. The epistles prove the presence in Christianity of a mighty regenerating power, 313. The direct allusions in these epistles to events in Our Lord's ministry—their nature and value, 314. The indirect references to it very numerous,—their character, and historical value, 317. They presuppose that the Church was in possession of a well-known account of the chief events of Our Lord's ministry analogous to that contained in the Gospels, 320. And prove that it was the same as that which was handed down by the primitive followers of Jesus, 321. The proof furnished by them that the Church was reconstructed on the basis of the Resurrection immediately after the Crucifixion, 322. The strength of the belief in the Resurrection in the Corinthian Church proved by St. Paul's peculiar mode of reasoning, 326. Summary of results, 328. The facts of the epistles leave only two alternatives—that the Resurrection was an objective fact, or that the belief originated in some form of mental hallucination, 329.

SUPPLEMENT.

THE INCIDENTAL ALLUSIONS IN ST. PAUL'S EPISTLES TO THE ACTIONS AND TEACHING OF OUR LORD.

The proof afforded by the epistles that the Christ who was accepted alike by St. Paul and his opponents was a superhuman Christ, and a worker of miracles during his earthly ministry, 330. The fact that the Christology of the epistles is not formulated proves that in its chief outlines it was accepted by the various parties in the Church, including St. Paul's opponents, 334. The incidental allusions to this Christology, 335. The Christology of St. Paul's opponents represents that of the primitive followers of Jesus, 339. The Gospel which was "another Gospel," and yet not another, 340. Additional proof furnished by the epistle to the Philippians, 341. The evidence furnished by the Apocalypse, 342. Proof furnished by the epistles that the account which the Church possessed of the actions and teaching of Our Lord must have been one of considerable fulness, and analogous to that contained in the Gospels, 344. Proved by the indirect allusions with which the epistles abound, 347. Proof furnished by the exhortations to follow Christ as an example, 349. The facts of Our Lord's ministry formed an habitual subject of Christian instruction in the Apostolic Churches, 351. And especially to converted heathen, 353. Further incidental allusions, 354. The assumption of the truth of the Resurrection underlies every portion of the epistles, 356.

LECTURE VII.

THE THEORY OF VISIONS CONSIDERED AND REFUTED.

The historical facts which must be accounted for by those who deny the objective reality of the Resurrection, 358. The solution propounded by the theory of visions, 361. The state of mind of the disciples of Jesus on the days which followed the Crucifixion, the starting-point of our inquiry, 362. Assumptions necessary to impart plausibility to this theory, 364. Not only is it necessary that it should account for the belief in the Resurrection, but for the reconstruction of the Church on the basis of this belief, 366. The inadequacy of the three principles of fixed idea, prepossession, and expectancy, to effect this result, 367. The theory that Mary Magdalene mistook a vision of the risen

Jesus for an external reality, considered and refuted, 368. The fact to be accounted for is not only that single persons mistook such visions for realities but that the disciples did so in bodies, 370. The difficulties with which such a supposition is attended, 372. The importance of the existence of the Church as a visible institution as a testimony to the reality of the Resurrection, 374. The objection that Mahometanism is a great institution which has been founded on a visionary delusion considered, 375. Further difficulties with which this theory is encumbered, 377. Objections urged from the standpoint of Dr. Carpenter's explanations of the phenomena of spiritualism, and other kindred delusions considered, 379. Answer to these objections, 383. The state of mind of the followers of Jesus during the days which followed his Crucifixion the opposite of that which would have caused them to see visions of him risen from the dead, and to mistake them for realities, 387. The points in which the evidence of the Resurrection is contrasted with that of all visionary appearances which have been mistaken for realities, 389. Solution of the difficulty that Our Lord was not easily recognized by his disciples after his resurrection, 392. The theory that Our Lord did not die from the effects of crucifixion, but slowly recovered, and that his recovery was mistaken for a resurrection considered, 393. This theory unknown to the Jewish and Pagan opponents of Christianity, 394. Its inherent difficulties, 395. Presupposes that the belief in the Resurrection owed its origin to a deliberately concocted fraud, 397. Results of the foregoing reasonings, 399.

SUPPLEMENT I.

THE VALUE OF ST. PAUL'S TESTIMONY TO THE FACT OF THE RESURRECTION.

The circumstances attending the appearance of Our Lord to St. Paul different from those of his appearances to the other Apostles, 400. The theories which have been propounded by unbelievers inconsistent with the unquestionable facts of history, 403. The objection that St. Paul was incapable of distinguishing between visions and objective realities considered, 407.

SUPPLEMENT II.

DR. CARPENTER'S OBJECTIONS TO THE EVIDENCE OF THE CHRISTIAN MIRACLES CONSIDERED.

Dr. Carpenter's objections stated, 410. The fallacy of urging objections against the miracles in the Bible in a mass as though they were all equal in point of attestation and evidential value, 414. The question whether some of the miracles in the New Testament may not have had a foundation in certain natural agencies, as for example, the action of the mind on the body, 417. The influence which powerful faith is capable of exerting on our bodily frames, 240. The question of Possession, 422. The existence of numerous narratives of false miracles does not justify us in rejecting all miracles in a mass, irrespectively of the evidence on which they rest, 423.

LECTURE VIII.
POPULAR THEORIES OF INSPIRATION—THEIR RELATION TO SCIENTIFIC THOUGHT.

The important bearing of existing theories of inspiration in the controversy between Christianity and scientific unbelief, 428. The functional character of inspiration analogous to the mode of the divine action in the constitution of our ordinary faculties, 432. The real points of danger in the controversy, 433. The positions laid down by Butler respecting the nature of inspiration adequate to meet the chief difficulties, 437. Nine propositions which he has enunciated on this subject, 439. Stated generally, they affirm the invalidity of all purely à priori theories as to what must be the extent of the supernatural assistance afforded to those through whom a revelation is communicated, 441. The mechanical and verbal theories, 443. The dynamical theory, 444. "Plenary" inspiration, 445. The theory of superintendence, 446. The theory of special inspiration vouchsafed to the writers of the books of the New Testament as distinct from their ordinary inspiration, 447. All these theories invalidated by their à priori character, 449. The results to which they inevitably lead when applied to the facts of the universe: Mr. Mill's reasoning on this subject, 448. Principles which are invalid when applied to the facts of the universe, and lead to false conclusions as to the mode in which God must have acted in His creative work, must produce similar results when applied to the phenomena of revelation, 449. A careful induction of the facts and phenomena of the New Testament the only safe guide in constructing a theory of inspiration, 451. No definite theory as to the nature or extent of inspiration laid down in the Bible, 452. Our Lord's promises of supernatural assistance made to the Apostles—their extent, 455. The assertions made on this subject by the sacred writers in the Epistles, 456. The nature of the inspiration afforded by the supernatural gifts of the Spirit, 458. Application of Butler's principles to the first chapter of Genesis, 460. The alleged antiquity of man—its bearing on this question, 455. The gradual growth of civilization and language, 466. The Bible not pledged to a system of chronology, 468. The universality of the deluge—its bearing on the question of inspiration, 470. Similarly, the question of the authorship of the Sacred Books, 471. The alleged discrepancies in the Gospels, 472. Conclusion, 474.

SUPPLEMENTARY NOTE.

REMARKS ON PROFESSOR MOZLEY'S LECTURES ON "RULING IDEAS IN EARLY AGES" 475

LECTURE I.

"Jesus saith unto them, Have ye understood all these things? They say unto him, Yea, Lord. Then said he unto them, Therefore every Scribe which is instructed unto the kingdom of heaven, is like unto a man that is an householder, which bringeth out of his treasure things new and old."—MATT. XIII. 51, 52.

THE subject which it will be my duty to bring before you in the present course of Lectures, is "Christian Evidences viewed in relation to modern thought." Not only will the treatment of such a subject carry out the intention of the Founder of this Lectureship, but its careful examination is imperatively demanded by the exigencies of the times in which we live. We are all of us painfully aware, that a large number of men who are eminent in various departments of philosophy, science, and criticism, have ceased to believe in Christianity as a divine revelation. Nor is it less certain that the wide diffusion of their principles has had the effect of suggesting anxious doubts, and even of shaking the faith of a still larger number of persons who would not willingly range themselves in the ranks of unbelief. That this latter class is a very numerous one, is a fact which it is impossible to question. Such persons have a right to our utmost sympathy, especially in those cases, which I fear are numerous, where many of the difficulties which they experience have their origin in some imperfection in our mode of stating the Christian argument. Nor is it less our duty, in accordance with the emphatic warnings of our divine Master, to do our utmost to remove every stumbling-block out of the way of professed unbelievers, by placing before them in the simplest form, the grounds on which we claim their acceptance of Christianity as a divine Revelation. It is useless to close our eyes to the fact, that the progress of philosophical, scientific, and critical inquiry during the present century has suggested difficulties which were unfelt when our great defences of Christianity were composed. We need not therefore wonder that they are inadequate to meet them.

On the other hand, it is no less certain that the same causes have disclosed reasons for the acceptance of Christianity which were only imperfectly appreciated by our predecessors. This being the case, a careful reconsideration of the Christian position in relation to the requirements of modern thought is become indispensable.

I propose, therefore, as far as the conditions imposed on me by these Lectures will allow, to take a view of our position, in relation to the chief difficulties which the progress of modern thought has suggested in connection with the evidences on which we have been accustomed to rest the claims of Christianity to be accepted as a divine revelation; and to point out the nature of the ground which the new positions which have been taken by opponents, require us to occupy in its defence. In doing this it will be requisite that I should take a careful survey of those points in the Christian position which require to be defended as essential; and that I should separate from them those which, however interesting they may be in relation to several important questions of theology, are really non-essential to the defence of Christianity as a divine Revelation. It will then be my duty to examine how far our old forms of evidence are valid for the purpose of meeting the difficulties which have been suggested by modern philosophical and critical thought, and to sketch the general outline of the defence necessary to meet the exigencies of our present position. To this latter point the seven concluding Lectures of this course will be exclusively devoted.

I am deeply conscious of the responsibility which is

involved in the treatment of this subject, which renders it necessary that I should deal with several of the most critical points of modern controversy. Still it has become the plain duty of Christian men, not to hesitate to meet all difficulties honestly, fearlessly, cautiously and calmly. The time is past for propounding inadequate solutions or for attempting to hold ground which is evidently untenable. Such a course can only be damaging to the Christian cause. Its abandonment, instead of weakening, will strengthen our position. If on the other hand there are important branches of evidences which have been but imperfectly recognized by our predecessors, our duty is without delay to assign them their proper place in the Christian argument. To effect this object these Lectures will be directed.

In the mode of treatment I shall take the text as my motto. It contains a profound and far-seeing truth, which theologians have been greatly prone to overlook. In it the great Teacher affirms that it is the duty of every subordinate teacher of his Gospel to bring out of his treasures things both new and old. Not the old only: for then progress would be impossible. Not the new only: for this would destroy that principle of continuity by which the works of God are linked together; but the new in union with the old, and the old in union with the new. Such a union it is the special glory of Christianity to have effected. Revelation, as it is recorded in the Bible, has not been imparted to us at the first complete and entire, as a rigid code irrespective of the over-changing conditions of humanity; but it is a plant which has grown in a succession of gradual stages until its culmination in Jesus Christ, just as the Creator has effected His work through a succession of developments, each one of which has been closely interwoven with that which preceded it, until it has culminated in man. In maintaining this analogy to the workings of God in nature Christianity stands in striking contrast to all other professed Revelations; and even to the opinions of no inconsiderable number of those who accept it as divine. Our Lord Himself affirmed that He came not to destroy the law or the prophets; but that on the contrary His purpose was to fill the ideal, of which they only contained an imperfect outline, up to the very full. Hence it has resulted that Revelation has been historical; and therefore it can be only rightly read and understood when it is contemplated in its historical aspect. Consequently Christianity does not consist of a mass of abstract doctrines or precepts, but of a body of historical facts, the proper meaning of which it is the function of theology to explain.

But while Christianity presents no break in point of continuity with former revelations, it vastly transcends them, in the same manner as man who, in respect of his bodily frame is closely allied to the inferior animal races, is raised to an immense elevation above them, both intellectually and morally. It is hardly possible to over-estimate the importance of this continuity of Revelation in relation to modern thought. The doctrine of continuity in nature is one of very recent growth; yet continuity in religion was fully accepted as the mode of the divine working by those who composed the records of the Christian Revelation. Nothing is more certain than that they have linked together a series of gradually progressive revelations, each growing out of that which preceded it, without a single break in the continuity of the historic chain. Such an analogy to what modern science affirms to have been the order of the production of the various forms of being which are possessed of life, is a very striking one; and one which at the time when the New Testament was written, would have been beyond the reach of the shrewdest guess, and to which no other religion can put in a claim. The developments of the great religions now existing in the world are developments of retrogression; Christianity alone is a development of progress. "Many prophets and kings," says Our Lord, "have desired to see the things which ye see, and have not seen them; and to hear the things which ye hear, and have not heard them."

But further, while every image employed by the great Teacher implies that the growth of His kingdom would be a slow and gradual process, it is no less clear that He felt assured that it would ultimately penetrate to the centre of humanity. If such be its character, can we wonder that the Christian revelation should contain truths, of which the fulness, like the great works of creation and providence, can only be fully recognized after the lapse of time, and as the result of careful investigation? That great reasoner, Bishop Butler, clearly perceived that it is only in conformity with the analogy of nature, that a book which has been so long in the possession of mankind as the Bible, if it contains a Revelation from God, should contain truths as yet undiscovered; and that events, as they come to pass, should open and ascertain the meaning of Scripture; and that such discoveries should be made " in the same way as all other knowledge is ascertained, by particular persons attending to, comparing, and pursuing intimations, scattered up and down in it, which are overlooked and disregarded by the generality of the world."*

* I subjoin the entire passage. "And as it is owned that the whole scheme of Scripture is not yet understood, so if it ever comes to be understood before the restitution of all things, and without miraculous interventions, it must be in the same way as natural knowledge is come at, by the continuance and progress of learning and liberty, and by particular persons attending to, comparing and pursuing intimations scattered up and down, which are overlooked and disregarded by the majority of the world. For this is the way in which all improvements are made by thoughtful men, tracing on obscure hints, as it were dropped to us by nature accidentally, or what seems to come into our minds by chance. Nor is it incredible that a book which has been so long in possession of mankind should contain many truths as yet undiscovered, for all the same phenomena and the same faculties of investigation from which such great discoveries have been made in the present and the past age, were equally in possession of mankind several thousand years before. And possibly it might be intended that events as they come to pass should open and ascertain the meaning of several parts of Scripture."—*Analogy*, Part II., chap. iii. These remarks are worthy of the deepest attention both of theologians and men of science.

Of this prediction we in the present age are witnessing the fulfilment. Science and research of every kind are throwing light on the pages of the Bible, and we are now viewing many of its supposed affirmations in an altered aspect. Astronomy alone has shown that many positions which were supposed in former times to be deduced from its phraseology, as infallibly certain, were utterly devoid of justification. Numerous others have shared the same fate. Who then can venture to affirm, with the history of the past before us, that additional light may not yet be cast on the contents of the sacred page? Nay, the great apostle affirms that the fulness of the meaning of Revelation will be only gradually unfolded during the ages of the future.*

If the knowledge of the full meaning of Revelation, like that of the created Universe, be thus slowly and gradually progressive, it is clearly our duty to accommodate our evidential position to our increasing light, instead of raising an outcry against every fresh discovery of science, as if it was fatal to the claims of Christianity to be accepted as a divine revelation. If the principles which have been laid down by the foresight of the good Bishop, more than a century ago, had been kept steadily in view by theologians, a large proportion of those disputes which are now raging between theologians and men of science would have been rendered impossible.

This power of self-accommodation to the ever-varying aspects of human thought which is possessed by Christianity has a most important bearing on the general character of our evidential position. Nay, it forms one of the strongest proofs of the superhuman insight which was possessed by its Founder, that He has not anchored his religion to the rock of the immovable, as has been done by others, but that He has founded one which is capable of adjusting itself to the entire condition of man. By doing so, he has become the Founder of the eternal religion of

* Ephesians i. 10.

human nature. Such a religion must be capable of presenting itself, not in a single and unvarying aspect, but in a manifold and varying one; and consequently the mode of exhibiting its claims which was fitted to one aspect of thought, must become unsuited to another, rendering it necessary that we should bring the new as well as the old out of our treasures.

In considering this subject, it is clear that my first duty must be to institute an inquiry into what constitutes the inner life of Christianity, as distinct from its accessories, and the vehicle through which it has been communicated—what in fact is its essence? The importance of rightly determining this cannot be over-estimated in reference to our mode of stating the Christian argument, for it is evident, whenever we undertake to defend a position, that it is essential to ascertain what portion of the ground constitutes its key; and on it to concentrate our entire force.

What then, I ask, constitutes the essence of the Christian Revelation? Is it a mass of dogmatic, or abstract truth after the manner of other religions; or of reasoned truth, as elaborated by the various philosophic schools; or is its essence to be found in its moral teaching, as numerous unbelievers are in the habit of affirming; or is it an historic life, which constitutes its inner temple, and forms its distinguishing characteristic—in fact, is it the manifestation of a divine being on the sphere of the human, who is the source of all the moral and spiritual power which it contains? This question suggests another:—Must our defence embrace the wide range of everything which is contained in the Bible, in all the multifariousness of its contents; or is there an inner temple of Christianity, which also constitutes its citadel and fortress, on which if we can maintain a firm hold we shall retain the command of the entire Christian position?

The answer to these questions will not only be of the highest importance in its bearing on our general conception of Christianity, but it will determine what must be the only correct method of conducting its defence. Our entire evidences will require to be marshalled and arranged in conformity with the views we entertain on this subject. To use a military metaphor, the extent of the ground which it is necessary to occupy, forms the most important consideration in the mode of posting the forces at our command. A garrison of five thousand men may be capable of holding a particular fortress against the most numerous army; but if the lines are carried five miles in advance, they may be broken through at every point. Precisely the same is it with the defence of Christianity. If we confine it to its central position with the forces at our command its citadel will be impregnable; but if we extend our defences over an indefinite mass of subject matter, only incidentally connected with it, and for that purpose proceed to enlist into our service reasonings of only doubtful validity, we shall thereby endanger our entire position.

The question as to what constitutes the inner life of Christianity, is one which amidst the Babel of the sects that distract the Church, each with intemperate zeal propounding its own formulated system as constituting its essence, is one which at first sight might appear difficult if not impossible to answer. Yet surely an intelligent reader of the New Testament, who perused it for the first time free from the prepossessions of theological systems would return no ambiguous reply. He would affirm as a matter of certainty that one prominent idea pervades its pages and underlies every portion of its teaching—the divine person of Jesus Christ our Lord; and that the central life of Christianity, as it is there depicted, consists neither in a body of dogmas, or precepts, but in an historic life.

This point is so obvious that it seems almost unnecessary to give a formal proof of it. Still as it is vital to my argument, and one which is so generally overlooked by popular theology, I must draw your attention to a few of its salient traits. What then are the points which would force themselves on the attention of my supposed reader? They are indisputably these. He would observe that the four most prominent treatises in the volume are four memoirs, which give a four-fold account of the actions and the teaching of Jesus Christ, by which he founded Christianity as a religion, and the Church as a Society. These evidently constitute the essence and foundation of the religion, for nothing can be more certain, than that every other portion of the New Testament presupposes the existence of this divine life as the foundation on which it rests.

Next follows another historical work, which details to us the means through which the Church was constituted a visible Institution in the world. One idea is fundamental to the entire book, that Jesus is the Christ, or in other words, that He is the Ruler of God's spiritual kingdom, on which is founded the summons consequent thereon to men to enrol themselves as His subjects. To this idea, and to this purpose, all the other details of the book are plainly subordinated.*

To these follow twenty-one writings of an historical character in the form of letters. They contain a mass of teaching, doctrinal and moral, pervaded and dominated by one idea which runs through them, that of Jesus as the personal Christ. While they contain doctrinal statements, it is worthy of particular remark that not one of them contains a formulated statement of what constitutes Christianity as a system of dogmatic or abstract truth. On the contrary, such doctrinal statements as are found in them, are wholly wanting in systematic form, and are evidently called forth

---

* This is evidently the burden of the entire book, from the first opening speech of St. Peter to the concluding one of St. Paul. The following passages are summaries of its teaching:—"And daily in the temple and from house to house they ceased not to teach and preach Jesus to be the Christ." (Acts v. 42). "This Jesus whom I preach unto you is Christ." (xvii. 3). "And when Silas and Timotheus were come from Macedonia, Paul was pressed in the spirit, and testified to the Jews that Jesus was Christ." (xviii. 5). "To whom he expounded and testified the kingdom of God, persuading them concerning Jesus." xxviii. 23).

by the special circumstances of particular communities of Christians to whom the letters are addressed.

But further, every one of them presupposes a Christianity already existing, and the obvious purpose of each letter is to explain it and to accommodate it to the state of thought and feeling as it existed in each particular Church. But throughout the entire contents of these letters, composed by six different writers, each of whom possessed marked mental peculiarities, one common idea unquestionably dominates—that of Jesus as the living personal Christ. Every doctrinal statement is made to have its focus in Him. Every moral precept has a vitality communicated to it by being referred to Him as the centre of obligation and spiritual power. Truth is propounded, but it is truth as it is in Jesus. Over all Christians he reigns by sovereign right. He is the supreme motive to holiness. He is Lord of the conscience. In Him centre all God's creative and providential acts. The manifested revelation of God is His historic life and actions. He is a great spiritual power, capable of acting on the human heart with energetic might. I fully admit that these points are brought out in different degrees and aspects by these writers. Yet one common thread runs through the entire series. It is not too much to say of every writer that the idea of Jesus as the Christ interpenetrates and modifies his entire thoughts, whether doctrinal or moral. To this even the Epistle of James, where it is least apparent, forms no exception.

Its predominance throughout these writings is no theory, but a fact, and forms the feature which distinguishes them from every other literary composition in the world. Of the dominance of this idea we have a striking example in the epistle to Philemon. In it St. Paul asks a personal favour of a Christian friend on behalf of a delinquent slave. That favour is asked in the name of Christ. There remains one other writing in the New Testament, the Apocalypse. Whatever opinion we may form of the purpose of its author, one thing respecting it is as clear as the existence of the sun in the firmanent—that the great prominent idea which penetrates it from one end to the other is that of Jesus as the Christ living and reigning. The removal of this idea from the pages of the New Testament would reduce the residuum of its contents to a shapeless chaos.

These facts then afford the most complete proof that the person of Jesus Christ constitutes the inner centre of Christianity, and underlies its entire system; and that everything else that is connected with it, occupies a position wholly subordinate to this its inner life. From this the inference is plain, that the Revelation which constitutes the essence of Christianity is not a body of dogmatic statements or precepts, but the manifestation of that divine person whose actions and teachings are recorded in the Gospels—or in other words, that the essence of Christianity as distinct from its adjuncts, consists of a number of objective facts, which have actually occurred in the history of the world. Of these facts the original followers of Jesus were the witnesses and proclaimers, and, as far as light was communicated to them by the divine Spirit, the exponents to mankind. We must be careful however to observe that in accordance with their own statements, this exposition is far from having exhausted all their meaning, for the greatest of apostolic writers affirms that a greater unfolding of it is reserved for the ages of the future.*

What then is the position occupied by the other books in the canon relatively to those which contain the objective

---

* "Having made known unto us the mystery of his will according to his good pleasure which he hath purposed in himself; that in the dispensation of the fulness of times he might gather together in one all things in Christ, both which are in heaven and in earth, even in him." (Ephes. i. 9, 10). "And to make all men see what is the fellowship of the Mystery, which from the beginning of the world hath been hid in God, who created all things by Jesus Christ, to the intent that now unto the principalities and powers in heavenly places might be known by the Church the manifold wisdom of God; according to the eternal purpose which he purposed in Christ Jesus our Lord." (Ephes. iii. 8, 9, 10.

facts which constitute Christianity? The Acts of the Apostles convey to us information how that divine Society called the Church was instituted and established in the world, as a visible institution, through whose agency these facts were to exert a mighty influence on mankind, and also inform us as to the mode in which the minds of the Apostles became gradually enlightened as to their meaning and import. The character of the Epistles is clear. They make no professions of being a dogmatic revelation; but in every case they assume the existence of a prior Christianity, which had been communicated orally to the converts, and consisting of such facts of its Founder's life as proved Him to be the Christ, and which the writers endeavour to unfold, explain, and apply in accordance with the various emergencies of the primitive societies of believers. One of these Churches, that at Corinth, is expressly reminded by St. Paul, that the essence of the Christianity which he had proclaimed among them consisted of a number of such objective facts.* These writings are, in the strictest sense of the term, letters which were called forth by the special exigencies of those to whom they are addressed; and in them the Christian revelation is unfolded, and adapted to the requirements, habits, and modes of thought of particular Churches, or individuals, who, having originally been Jews, proselytes, or pagans, had united themselves into a society, whose one bond of union was that Jesus was its Messiah and King.

My position therefore is, that like as we have a great revelation of God in the created universe, which is the manifestation of His eternal power and Godhead; as also we have a second revelation of God, made in the conscience and moral nature of man, which at the same time affords manifestations of the moral character of the Creator, and forms the foundation of moral obligation, so we have a third revelation of His innermost moral and spiritual perfections in

* 1 Cor. xv. 1-8.

the person and work of Jesus Christ our Lord. This revelation may be briefly summed up as consisting of the Incarnation and its results, by means of which the moral and spiritual perfections of God have been exhibited in the actions and teaching of a divine man; or in other words, in the life, death, and resurrection of Jesus Christ.

If this view be correct, it follows that the personal history of our Lord must constitute the citadel of Christianity, and must therefore form the key of the Christian position, on which, if we can retain a firm hold, we shall remain masters of the entire ground; and other points connected with Christianity will assume their due place and proper subordination. But if this cannot be maintained, the most successful defence of the remaining contents of the Bible will be so much wasted labour. On this point therefore the defence of Christianity must be concentrated.

It is evident if this view is correct, that the proof that the inner temple of Christianity consists in the personal manifestation of Jesus Christ in the sphere of human history, is of the highest importance in reference to the position which ought to be taken by the Christian advocate. But such a proof can only be supplied by an examination of a large number of passages in the New Testament. If I were to do so in the body of this Lecture, it would swell it to an undue length. I will therefore adduce the full proof in a Supplement; and assume for the purpose of this argument that the essence of Christianity consists neither in a body of dogmas nor of precepts, but in a personal history which constitutes a manifestation of the divine on the sphere of the human.

This being so, to prove that Christianity is a divine revelation, it will be only necessary to establish two points.

First.

That the person of Jesus Christ is not a manifestation of the ordinary forces which energise in man, but of a power which is superhuman and divine.

Secondly, that the account which the Church possesses of

His life, teaching, death, and resurrection, is not an ideal creation, but a body of historic facts.

In determining the extent of the position which must be occupied by the defender of Christianity, it is of the highest importance that we should keep clearly in view the distinction which exists between Revelation on the one hand, and inspiration and theology on the other. On this point great confusion of thought has prevailed; and the result has been that the line of our defence has become dangerously extended. The wide extent of the position, to the defence of which the Christian advocate is supposed to be committed, forms one of the strongholds of popular unbelief. It is also undeniable that theology has in former ages claimed, as its legitimate domains, whole provinces of thought, from which it has had to beat a retreat before the steady advance of scientific knowledge. It will probably have to retire further still before it occupies its rightful position. Such retreats have been attended with disastrous results; and with the experience of the past before us, I must claim the right—it is in fact our duty—to separate the defence of Christianity from every question which is not vitally connected with the Christian position, and to confine it to the historic facts, which form the foundation on which the Church has been erected, and the inner life of Christianity, as a great moral and spiritual power, is based. The consideration of the inferences deducible from these facts is the proper function, not of the Christian advocate, but of the scientific theologian. The relation in which the popular theories of inspiration stand to science, and their bearing on Christianity as a divine revelation, I shall consider in the concluding Lecture of this course; at present it will be only necessary for me to offer a few brief remarks on the distinction between Revelation and Inspiration.

I have already shown that the innermost temple of Christianity, around which the whole might of our defence must be concentrated, is the objective fact of the Incarnation, and the historical truth of the divine life, as recorded in the pages of the Evangelists. But in addition to this great fundamental revelation some of the writers of the New Testament claim to have been the subjects of special revelations, by which the meaning of the great facts which constitute the essence of Christianity was imparted to their minds. These revelations, however, differ widely from that of which I have been speaking; and it is very difficult to lay down a clear distinction between them and the gift which we commonly call inspiration. Thus St. Paul affirms that he received his knowledge of the great principles of Christianity by revelation, and that he did not derive them from any human source.* In other cases we can discover clear traces of the presence of a human element. Thus the slow and gradual influence of the Spirit unfolded to the leaders of the Church what constituted the essential principles of Christianity as distinct from the Judaism in which they had been born and educated. This we know from the history to have been brought about, not so much by a direct infusion of light and knowledge into their minds as by the leading of the events of Providence. Of this we have a remarkable illustration in the account which is given us of the mode in which the enlightenment of Peter was effected, which led to the reception of Cornelius into the Church. In it Peter's reason co-operated with the divine enlightenment. A vision was the immediate agent, of which several events of Providence suggested the interpretation. Of a

---

* Thus he writes, "But I certify you, brethren, that the Gospel which was preached of me is not after man; for I neither received it of man, neither was I taught it, but by the revelation of Jesus Christ" (Gal. i. 11, 12). Again, "How that by revelation he made known unto me the mystery, as I wrote before in few words, whereby, when ye read, ye may understand my knowledge in the Mystery of Christ" (Eph. iii. 3, 4). This latter passage implies that the two former chapters may be received as the record of this revelation. Both passages, however, definitely affirm that its subject matter was strictly limited to the communication of Christian truth, and involved no enlightenment beyond its limits.

similar character was the revelation made to St. Paul, which led to the first preaching of Christianity in Europe. This forms a remarkable illustration of the relation in which such revelations stood to the ordinary action of the faculties of those who received them. The command to pass into Europe was not one which was given in direct terms. The historian tells us that St. Paul proposed to open a mission in two other places; but that he was hindered by the Spirit. On arriving at Troas he saw a vision of a man of Macedonia standing by him, and saying, Come over into Macedonia and help us. From these circumstances the historian tells us that they assuredly gathered that the Lord had called them to preach the Gospel to them; or in other words, that it was not a direct revelation of the Spirit, but an inference from the vision, united with the fact, that they had been forbidden to preach in two other places. In this case, as in St. Peter's vision, the divine and the human elements are quite separable from one another, the duty of passing into Macedonia being a rational inference from the divine facts. How far this was the case in the other revelations spoken of by St. Paul, we have no means of judging.

Both these modes of communicating truth may be designated revelations.

Theoretically, therefore, the New Testament may be said to contain the record of two species of revelations—one, the record of those objective facts, which form God's great moral and spiritual revelation of Himself in the person of Jesus Christ—and the other, the commentary made by its authors on those facts, as far as their meaning was revealed to them by the Divine Spirit. This latter, however, is so mixed up with the question of inspiration that for all practical purposes it is inseparable from it; and must therefore be dealt with on the same principles as a branch of scientific theology.

It will now be necessary for the purpose of defining clearly the limits of our evidential position to consider the relation in which theology stands to Revelation.

If I have correctly laid down the two previous positions, that Revelation consists of the objective facts, on which Christianity is based, and in a secondary sense, of the disclosures made to Apostolic men respecting their nature and meaning, it follows that the position of theology in relation to Christianity must consist in the elaboration of a body of systematic truth out of the facts and data furnished by Revelation. For evidential purposes it is of the utmost importance to keep this distinction clearly in view, and thereby to guard against that widely-spread confusion of thought, which identifies Christianity as a revelation with Christianity as a theology, and has led to the almost indefinite extension of the position which it is supposed to be the duty of the Christian advocate to defend. As a clear perception of the nature of this distinction is of the highest importance in relation to my argument, it is necessary that I should define the position which I take with the utmost clearness.

I observe, therefore, that theology as a science must stand in the same relation to the facts of Revelation as the physical sciences do to the facts of the Universe. The function of these latter is to investigate the facts, to formulate them, and to evolve out of them the truths which they contain. Precisely similar is the function of theology to the facts of Revelation. These form its data. The duty of the theologian is to perform for them an office similar to that which the scientific investigator does for the facts of nature. This being so, the same methods of investigation must be applicable to each, as far as is consistent with their different subject-matter.

Both must involve rational processes; both will be liable to the intrusion of human error; and their successful study will be dependent on the employment of a proper method of investigation.

The distinction, therefore, between Christianity as a revelation and Christianity as a theology, becomes clear. Christianity as a revelation consists of those objective facts through which God has manifested to man his moral and spiritual character. Christianity as a theology consists of a body of formulated truths elaborated by reason out of those facts as its data.

It will be objected that, in running this parallel, I overlook the necessity of the influence of the Divine Spirit for the purpose of illuminating the heart and the understanding in the study of theology. I by no means do so. The Baconian method teaches us that physical truth can only be successfully studied by first dissipating those dark mists, and the various idola, which naturally brood over the human understanding, and its founder has elaborately described their nature and character. Precisely analogous is it with the successful study of the data furnished by Revelation. Here even darker mists enshroud our understandings, which must be dissipated before our mental powers can be successfully applied to the study of Christian truth. One of these preconditions is a willingness to do the will of God.* We all know how the progress of scientific knowledge has been impeded in the past by the prepossessions of those who devoted themselves to its study. Witness the failure of the acutest intellects of the ancient world to penetrate the arcana of the Universe. Similar prepossessions are equally fatal to the appreciation of Christian evidences and of Christian truth. The attention of many of the students of the physical sciences may not unfitly be directed to the closeness of the analogy; and they may well be asked to consider whether some of their methods of dealing with Revelation are not due to prepossessions and idola

---

* Such a precondition for the effectual appreciation of Revelation is distinctly laid down by Our Lord. "If any man will ($\theta\acute{e}\lambda\eta$ wills, is earnestly desirous of doing) do God's will, he shall know of the doctrine whether it be of God, or whether I speak of Myself" (John vii. 17). This, though pre-eminently true of religious truth, is applicable to every kind of truth, except perhaps the evidence of mathematical demonstration. The ethical readiness to accept it is a precondition of its perception.

which darken their mental vision, in the same manner as in former ages the same causes have rendered theologians insensible to the realities of physical truth.

But the dissipation of these being presupposed in both cases, it follows that in the same manner as physical science is the result of the application of our rational powers to the investigation of the phenomena of the Universe, and mental science results from their application to the facts of mind, and moral science to those of our moral nature and conscience; so theological science is the result of the application of our reason to the data furnished us by Revelation.* In each case our reason is fallible, and we are liable to draw erroneous conclusions, from which fallibility neither theologians nor scientists can claim exemption. In by-gone ages the latter have propounded erroneous systems in abundance. Can it be said that theologians have not fallen into similar errors? Or at the present day have we any right to claim an infallibility for our various theological systems, and after the manner of the sects stake the life of Christianity on their truth? Our only safeguard is so to profit by the errors of the past as to lead us to employ better methods of investigation in the future. But let it be observed that like as the errors of philosophers and scientists are unable to obscure the great truth that the Universe is a manifestation of the eternal power and Godhead of the Creator, a truth which will ever be recognized by the unsophisticated heart of man,

---

* Nothing is more dangerous to the Christian cause than the outcry which various schools of popular theology are in the habit of raising against the use of reason in religious investigations, and the mode in which it is constantly spoken of as opposed to faith. Such persons would do well to meditate on the following passage of Bishop Butler: "I express myself with caution lest I should be misunderstood to vilify reason, which is indeed the only faculty we have wherewith to judge concerning anything, even Revelation itself, or to be misunderstood to assert that a supposed revelation cannot be proved false from internal characters."—(*Analogy*, Part II. chap. iii.) Reason is not a perfect light, nor an infallible guide; but as it is the only light and guide which we possess, we shall not improve our condition by extinguishing it.

despite all the theories of atheism and pantheism, so the errors of theologians are unable to hide from us the still greater truth that the moral perfections of God clearly shine forth in the person and work of Jesus Christ our Lord.

In making these observations, I by no means wish to deny that the Apostolic epistles contain a theology in a rudimentary form. But viewed in relation to the present subject, the important point to observe is that they are a commentary on the facts of Revelation in a very unsystematic form, just as it was called forth by the exigencies of particular Churches, and that they also form our sole record of the subordinate revelations through which the meaning of the great facts of Christianity was communicated to the primitive believers.

I am aware that there is also another theory, which affirms that these revelations and their meaning have been handed down by the traditions of the Church, and secured from errors by the permanently abiding presence in it of the divine Spirit. But to discuss this question would be to enter into a controversy which has neither limits nor bounds. Its indefinite character alone must exclude it from forming a portion of Christian evidences. Christianity must on other grounds be accepted as a divine revelation before it is possible to accept the theory in question.

My position, therefore, stated generally is, Revelation is throughout essentially divine; systematized theology is a human science.

This being so, the ground which must be occupied and defended by the Christian advocate becomes clear and definite. It is not the wide range of Christian theology, nor any particular theory as to the mode in which Revelation has been communicated, nor as to the degree of inspiration which has been afforded to those by whom its record has been committed to writing; but the proof of the actual presence of a divine element in Christianity. My duty is to show not only that the facts are true, but that the divine is manifested in them. All other considerations stand extraneous to the subject-matter of these Lectures.

If this position be correctly taken, the points of controversy between those who affirm and those who deny Christianity to be a divine revelation, are brought within definite limits. We are saved from the necessity of wandering over an indefinite range of subject-matter. Numerous controversies now raging have only an indirect bearing on the real point at issue. This, I repeat, is, Have we evidence that there is a manifestation of the divine in Christianity? If this be so, it must be a divine revelation, and a matter of unspeakable importance to mankind. Under the influence of increasing light, whether derived from the study of the Universe, or as Butler has pointed out, of the facts of Revelation itself, we may have to change many of our theological positions, as inadequate exponents of its great realities; but the great fact that God has spoken, and is still speaking to man in Jesus Christ will remain untouched.

Such being the case, it will be desirable that I should enumerate a few of the questions which lie outside the position which the defender of Christianity is called upon to occupy. It is necessary to do so, because the identification of a large number of questions now eagerly debated between Christians and unbelievers with the truth of Christianity itself, not only in the popular mind, but by many earnest inquirers, is one of the chief causes by which the faith of multitudes has been shaken in the present day. This is the reason why I have been careful to lay down the distinction between Christianity as a revelation, and Christianity as a theology. If the view above taken is correct, the whole range of formulated theology, except as far as it is a matter of direct and positive revelation, is extraneous to the question whether Christianity is or is not a divine revelation. The determination whether its statements are legitimate deductions from the facts of Christianity, belongs to scientific theology, and will not affect the divine character of the facts themselves. In a similar manner, various questions connected with the origin of the books of the Old Testament, and their correct interpretation, however profoundly interesting in a theological point of view, form no portion of our evidential position. The defender of Christianity is by no means called upon to prove that they are free from philosophical, scientific, or historical errors, or even from moral imperfections. To use an illustration borrowed from Paley, it is most unwise to stake the truth of Christianity on our ability to prove that every miraculous narrative recorded in its pages must, beyond all controversy, be accepted as an historical fact. To do this, would involve the defender of Christianity in the necessity of maintaining the truth of some special theory of inspiration, against which it is impossible at the present time too earnestly to protest; for its identification with certain theories extensively popular forms one of the strongholds of unbelief. So likewise I accept Paley's general positions, that the Christian advocate is only concerned with the Old Testament so far as portions of it have received the direct sanction of Our Lord. I by no means overlook the importance of these questions as far as they bear on the elaboration of a true Christian theology; but they must not be allowed to be mixed up with the all-important question, whether Christianity contains a manifestation of the divine, or whether it has been the mere evolution of those moral and spiritual forces which energize in man. To do so is to weaken our position by indefinitely extending it; a movement which can only be profitable to our opponents.

For the same reasons a number of very interesting questions respecting the New Testament which have been made the subjects of most eager controversy form no portion of the position necessary to be maintained by the defender of Christianity as vital to its truth. It is a matter of comparative unimportance in reference to the real issue whether Lysanias was tetrarch of Abilene in the year when John the Baptist commenced his ministry; whether Cyrenius was twice governor of Syria; whether Our Lord cured one or two demoniacs at Gadara, or one or two blind men at

Jericho; or the precise mode in which Judas died. The successful solution of these and multitudes of similar questions would afford an additional confirmation of the historical accuracy of some of the writers of the New Testament. But such points are often discussed as if the life of Christianity was involved in them, whereas the only point which they really involve is the truth of a particular theory of inspiration. Nor is the question whether each Gospel was written by the person whose name it bears, nor the actual date when its contents were first committed to writing, material to the present issue. Nor is it necessary to prove that the quotations from the Old Testament in the New are accurate renderings of the meaning of the original, nor that the logic of the Epistles is always accurate, when estimated according to our scientific forms of reasoning.* These, and a number of other questions, are profoundly interesting in a theological point of view; but they have no direct bearing on the all-important questions, whether there is evidence that a superhuman power has manifested itself in Christianity; whether the great facts on which Christianity is based were historical realities; whether the Resurrection of Jesus Christ is a fact, or the belief in it originated in the

---

* I have selected several of these questions, because they are those by means of which modern unbelief directs some of its sharpest attacks on Christianity as a divine revelation. This indefinite extension of our position is simply to play into the hands of our opponents. They naturally prefer to raise side issues, instead of dealing with the centre of the Christian position. Thus nothing is more common than to raise questions about miracles generally, and the imperfection of the attestation of this or that particular miracle, instead of dealing with the one great evidential miracle of Christianity, the Resurrection, on the reality of which its truth rests. If they could prove that this was a fiction, they would force the entire Christian position. If it is a fact, Christianity will remain intact, notwithstanding all their attacks on the other miraculous narratives in the Bible. It must be confessed, however, that the defenders of Revelation have greatly encouraged them in this practice, by not insisting on confining the issue to the discussion of this one great question.

hallucination of His followers. If all these things can be firmly established, it follows that Christianity must be a divine revelation; and we can afford to wait for the solution of the minor difficulties with which it is attended. To lay down clearly the distinction between points which are essential, and those which are non-essential to the defence of Christianity, is at the present day of the highest importance; because a wide-spread opinion prevails, that many of the questions that are eagerly discussed in theological controversies are essential to its truth.

Thus ordinary Christians have been led to believe that such questions as—Whether St. Matthew was the author of the Gospel that bears his name; whether the writings of Isaiah consist of two portions, one of which was composed at an earlier, and the other at a later date; whether the Pentateuch in its present form was written by Moses; whether the commonly-received Chronology of the Old Testament is, or is not accurate; whether the book of Daniel was composed by the prophet of that name, who lived during the Captivity; whether it is possible to weave the narratives of the Evangelists into an harmonious whole; whether the references made by the earlier Fathers to events in the Evangelical history are citations from our Gospels, and not from others which must have closely resembled them—that all these, and a multitude of similar questions, are so bound up with the acceptance of Christianity as a divine revelation, that they must stand or fall together. Men hear that a vast number of accepted beliefs on these and similar subjects, have been called in question by persons of profound learning, and their faith in Christianity is shaken. What is the cause of this? The true answer is that popular theology has widely diffused the belief that a number of points which are really non-essential to Christianity as a divine revelation are vital to its defence. Unbelievers have not unnaturally accepted this position, and in consequence have loudly proclaimed that the belief in Christianity as a divine revelation is no longer tenable. The assumption that the defence of this wide extent of matter is essential to the Christian position, is unquestionably one of the causes which has led to that wide-spread shaking of belief which prevails at the present day. The whole question, however, as to the nature and validity of our popular theories of inspiration is a subject of which I must defer the consideration till my concluding Lecture.

My position, therefore, is, that the ground on which the whole of our defences must be concentrated, is the historic reality of the life of Our Lord, as it has been handed down by the traditions of His primitive followers; and that this life has exerted a unique and superhuman power throughout the last eighteen centuries of history. Before, however, I can address myself to the direct proof of this, it will be necessary to consider the relative value of the evidences themselves, the order in which they should be stated, and the modifications in the mode of treatment which are rendered necessary by the requirements of modern thought.

1. The proof of Christianity has been hitherto based on what is called its miraculous attestation. Miracles have been placed in the forefront of the Christian argument, and other evidences have occupied in it a very subordinate position. This is the line of reasoning which modern apologists have all but unanimously adopted.

An opinion however is becoming widely diffused among thoughtful men, that this mode of putting the argument is unsound. I am fully aware of the weight of the authorities who have taken the opposite view to the one which I feel it to be my duty to propound in these Lectures; and who have concurred in placing the evidence of miracles in the forefront of the Christian argument. Of these Paley may be cited as a crucial example. Subsequent writers have followed closely in his steps; and have contented themselves with adducing proof of the possibility of miracles, or with strengthening his central position. Some of them, however, have handled the moral argument far more effectually than it has been done by him; for the principles of his moral philosophy necessarily rendered his treatment of the moral aspects of Christianity inadequate.

I am not aware that any modern writer has suggested the necessity of a complete change of front in our evidential position, although many have attached a far higher value to the moral aspects of Christianity, as evidences of its truth. As however it seems to me that the whole exigencies of modern thought render such a change of front absolutely necessary, I will briefly give reasons why I consider that the moral evidences of Christianity ought to occupy the first place, and its miraculous attestation the second, in the Christian argument.

But as the three following Lectures will chiefly be devoted to the consideration of what I shall designate the moral miracles of Christianity, it will be necessary that I should briefly explain the meaning which I attach to this expression. Our evidential treatises restrict the term miracle to an occurrence in the physical universe the origin of which cannot be accounted for by the action of its ordinary forces. From such an event is inferred the presence of a power or force of a different order, capable of energizing in them, directing, controlling, and bending them in such a manner as to effect a particular purpose, and to bring about a result different from that which would have taken place from their ordinary action. Such an event we designate "a miracle;" and from it we infer the presence of a superhuman power. But why the expression should be limited to occurrences of this kind as constituting the sole divine attestation of Christianity it is difficult to say. Surely there is an order in the moral and spiritual world no less than in the material. Moral and spiritual forces act no less in conformity with moral and spiritual laws than the forces which energize in the physical universe act in conformity with physical laws. If deviations from the accustomed order of the one, or the occurrence of events which cannot be accounted for by the action of any of its known forces, prove the presence of a divine power, so must similar phenomena in the moral and spiritua worlds be manifestations of the energy of a superhuman power. Such manifestations I shall designate "moral miracles," by which I mean, events occurring in the moral and spiritual world, for the origin of which none of its known forces are sufficient to account. If I can prove that such manifestations have taken place in connection with Christianity, it will be evidence that a superhuman power has manifested itself in it. This being so, the all-important question will be, Are we able to verify in connection with it the presence of such a superhuman power in the history of the past, or in the facts of the present? If we can, I contend that it will afford a far stronger proof of its divine character than that which can be supplied by miracles wrought in the physical universe, which require a long and complicated chain of historical reasoning to establish their truth.

Much confusion has been introduced into our reasonings about miracles by the practice, which has been common to both the opponents and the defenders of Christianity, of using a number of ambiguous terms, so that it has become difficult to express oneself with precision on the subject.* A brief allusion to them is all that will be necessary in this place. Even the word "Supernatural" itself is one which it is almost dangerous for a theist to employ. When we use it to denote God's mode of action in connection with a reve-

* It is worthy of notice that a large proportion of the arguments employed by the author of "Supernatural Religion" against miracles are founded on the ambiguous senses in which the various terms employed in the Christian argument are used. To this their entire plausibility is due. The inconclusiveness of his reasoning is obvious enough to close logical thinkers; but unfortunately the great majority of the readers of such works are not such, and the large number of editions through which this work has passed proves that on them its influence has been sufficiently telling. This alone shows the importance of not allowing our strength to be wasted on a number of side issues, but of confining our defence of Christianity to its great central position.

lation, as distinguished from other modes of the divine activity, we run no little danger of making the covert assumption that God is not everywhere energizing in the ordinary forces of the Universe by which we are surrounded; a view which is not only opposed to all sound principles of Theism, but one to which the writers of the Bible are entire strangers. If one thing is more certain than another, it is that the whole series of these writers view the forces of nature as manifestations of the energies of God. In fact the modern distinction between the Natural and the Supernatural is to them unknown.*

This confusion has originated in the various senses which have been assigned to the words "Nature," "Natural," and their derivatives, and from the ambiguous use of the word "law," not only to denote the invariable sequences of events, but also the mode of the action of the forces which energize in the Universe. The all-important question on which the entire controversy turns is, What do we mean by "Nature," and what class of phenomena do we include under it? Thus if we confine the words "Nature" and "Natural" to matter, its necessary forces and laws, we denote by them a definite class of phenomena; but if we include under them man, his freedom, his intellect, and his moral and spiritual being, we mix up with the former phenomena of a wholly different class and order. But these terms have been used by both sides in this controversy, as though they had a clear and definite meaning, and thus various classes of

* This may be affirmed absolutely of the writers of the Old Testament. Thus in the Book of Psalms the energy of God is represented as being quite as much manifested in the daily course of nature as in the miracles of the Exodus. This is not quite so apparent in the New Testament, in which the references to the forces of nature are comparatively rare. But whenever Our Lord refers to nature in His teaching, He uniformly recognizes in it the presence of His Father. According to the Bible both the energies which are constantly exhibiting themselves in the Universe, and the phenomena which we designate miracles, are alike manifestations of the divine activity, the one differing from the other merely in their mode of action.

phenomena fundamentally distinct have become mixed together in hopeless confusion. A similar result has followed from the habitual use of the term "law," to denote both the invariable sequences and the forces that energize in the material Universe. Can any one wonder at the confusion of thought which has arisen in consequence? The importance of this subject will render it necessary that I should consider it more fully in a supplement to this Lecture.

This confusion of thought in which the whole question of miracles has become involved is a sufficient justification for placing what I have designated the moral miracles of Christianity in the forefront of our evidential position. But this change seems to me to be imperatively called for by the following reasons, in order that we may adapt our evidential position to the requirements of modern thought.

All its requirements point to verification as the great test of truth. The entire history of discovery has proved that theories which are incapable of being submitted to this test have failed to conduct us to the realities of things. Hence has arisen a great difficulty in the way of accepting as actual occurrences such events as, being without counterparts in the modern world, require that their truth should be established by a long and intricate chain of reasoning, owing to the danger that exists, that among its numerous links there may be flaws which have escaped our observation. The habits of reasoning which lie at the foundation of modern science have all tended to confirm the opinion that facts which can receive no kind of verification either in the realities of the present or in the palpable historical events of the past can only be accepted as true on an amount of evidence which is practically demonstrative. Whether this position be right or wrong, it is unquestionable that such is the tendency of modern thought. This has introduced a difficulty into the proof of miracles, which was little felt in former times, as from the nature of the case they cannot be subjected to any species of verification. Very different, however, will it be with those manifestations of a superhuman power energizing in the moral and spiritual worlds, which I shall claim for Christianity. I shall prove that they can be clearly traced in the history of the past, and in the facts of the present, in connection with the person of Jesus Christ, and the Church which He has founded. The facts are plain and simple, requiring no long or intricate historical proof to establish their truth, but admit of an easy verification. As their reality is indisputable, the only question that can arise is, Are they manifestations of a superhuman power, or can they be accounted for as the results of the known forces energizing in man? On this point I shall appeal to your judgment in the following Lectures. Their verifiable character alone forms a sufficient reason for placing them in the forefront of the Christian argument.

2. As miracles, in the sense in which that term is employed in evidential treatises, do not take place in the present day, the only mode of proving their occurrence in former times is by a chain of historical reasoning which involves the necessity of carefully weighing and balancing a large number of intricate probabilities which constitute our historical argument, a process which requires a special training for its due appreciation. In one point of view it must be conceded that modern thought has increased the value of miracles as evidential to a divine commission, if we could either witness them ourselves, or their occurrence could be proved by demonstrative evidence. In the present day our belief in the invariability of the forces of the material Universe, and in the continuity of nature, is of the strongest kind. We are firmly persuaded that this continuity is only capable of being interrupted by the Creator, or by one delegated by Him. To us, therefore, if an indubitable miracle could be performed before our eyes, it would have the highest evidential value, as affording indisputable proof of the intervention of a Being distinct from, and superior to, the forces of the material universe, *i.e.*, God. But very different were the ideas entertained on this subject

in former ages. The belief was then all but universal, that other beings were able to interfere with and modify its forces at their pleasure. Consequently, to persons who held such opinions, a miracle only offered evidence of the presence of a *superhuman*, and not of a *divine*, power; and its evidential value was diminished in proportion to the prevalence of this belief. As in Our Lord's days the belief was wide-spread that demons were capable of exercising this power, He habitually appealed to the moral aspect of His miracles in proof that they were wrought by the finger of God. But while the course of modern thought thus assigns a higher evidential value to miracles, on the supposition that their proof is rigid and exact, this advantage is far more than counterbalanced by the rigid exactitude of the proof which it requires. Nothing sets this difficulty in a stronger light than the prevailing tendency in modern times summarily to reject any account of the occurrence of a miracle without even deigning to inquire into the evidence on which it rests; and this feeling is far from being confined to unbelievers. The Church of Rome professes to possess a continuous miraculous attestation; but whenever we hear of a Romish miracle we set it aside at once without troubling ourselves to inquire into its evidence. This tendency is in some degree increased by the unquestionable fact that this Church has encouraged the belief in miracles which are notoriously false, and therefore stands before us in the character of a convicted impostor. Still we entertain much the same feelings with respect to all similar accounts, be they reported by whom they may.

Men would now accept the reality of a miracle only on the very strongest evidence that it was not the result of delusion or imposture. From these difficulties moral miracles are exempt.

The difficulty which was felt in resting the proof of the divine origin of Christianity on miracles alone is shown by the line of reasoning for the most part adopted by the early apologists, who lived in daily contact with the heathen, when they endeavoured to recommend Christianity to their acceptance. It is evident that with them miracles occupied a very different place in the controversy from that which has been assigned to them by modern writers. One feels a difficulty in believing that if Paley's argument had been placed before a Father of the second or third century, it would have commended itself to him as an efficient mode of persuading an unbeliever to embrace the Christian faith. With them the moral aspects of Christianity preponderate over the miraculous, as the chief means of winning the assent of the heathen to the Gospel.

3. The usual proof which is adduced for miracles in our common evidential treatises consists in marshalling a very complicated mass of historical evidence, requiring a course of special training for its due appreciation. This alone forms a sufficient reason why it should not occupy the van of the Christian position, while other evidences, capable of a more direct appreciation, are equally available. It is evident that the number of those who have either the ability, the time, or the means of sifting a body of evidence of this description, is comparatively small, and consequently all that others can do, is to take it at second-hand. For example: one of the necessary media of proof for this purpose is to establish the authenticity and genuineness of the Gospels by quotations from the Fathers. A mass of evidence of this description involves the careful balancing of a large number of probabilities, and in the case before us their complication is considerable; and of the effect of the whole the ordinary reader feels himself to be a very imperfect judge. But the whole current of modern thought is steadily moving in an opposite direction. It justly refuses to rest its religious convictions on the authority of others, and demands, on a subject of such profound importance, evidence the value of which each individual can estimate for himself.

I merely adduce this as one out of many difficulties, in

which the historical argument, as it is usually set forth, is involved; and which render it highly dangerous to rest upon it the chief weight of the defence of Christianity. The entire field of evidence, as we know, extends over a large body of literature, and fully to estimate its value requires the exercise of a practised judgment. This alone constitutes a decisive reason why, if we can adduce proof of the operation of a superhuman power in Christianity, capable of easy verification in the history of the past and in the facts of the present, we should assign to it the place which the argument from miracles now holds in our ordinary evidential treatises.*

4. The evidential value of miracles operates less strongly on a large number of minds at the present day, because we have not only to prove that those who have reported them honestly believed that they witnessed them; but that they

* It has not been sufficiently observed that evidence which may at some former period have been perfectly satisfactory as proving a divine commission to those to whom it was vouchsafed, may have lost much of its force by lapse of time. It is one thing to witness a miracle, and from it to infer the presence of a divine power, and quite another thing to believe, as the result of carefully balancing a long and complicated mass of historical testimony, that a miracle has been performed at some distant period of time. Besides, as many of the witnesses die without leaving any record of their testimony, the evidence is less powerful to us than it must have been to contemporaries, who had the entire evidence before them. It follows, therefore, even if it could be proved that miracles formed the chief attestation of Christianity in the Apostolic age, that it is by no means a necessary result of this that they should form its sole and all-commanding attestation eighteen centuries after they have ceased to be performed. Christianity, however, possesses this most remarkable characteristic. Precisely in proportion as its miracles have diminished in evidential value through lapse of time and the complicated methods thereby rendered necessary to prove their occurrence, the evidence derived from what I have designated its moral miracles becomes stronger and stronger, being testified to alike by the history of the past, and the facts of the present. Christianity is in fact the only religion in the world, the moral evidence of which increases by lapse of time. Contrast with this Mahometanism, the moral evidence of which, if it ever had any, is steadily diminishing.

were at the same time not labouring under any of those mental hallucinations which have unquestionably led persons under their influence to mistake the subjective creations of their own imagination for objective realities. Modern research has proved that such phenomena are not uncommon; and that they have exerted no inconsiderable influence in originating many of the delusions of the past, which were once assigned to the effect of deliberate imposture. Not only is it the case that a large number of occurrences have been reported as true, which rational men now refuse to accept as objective facts; but some of them rest on an attestation far stronger than would be necessary to establish the truth of an ordinary event. In several cases the honesty of the reporters is unquestionable. Consequently the only way of accounting for the belief in them is to assume, that under certain states of mental hallucination, the reality of which has been fully recognized by modern science, they have mistaken impressions purely subjective for external realities. The importance of this is increased, because it is a well ascertained fact that persons are capable of labouring under delusions on particular subjects, while in other respects they are mentally sound.

This principle has been applied as the explanation of some well attested narratives of miracles in past ages, the honesty of the reporters of which it would be difficult to controvert, but the reality of which it would be equally difficult to believe. But we need not wander over the ages of the past for examples of well attested miraculous narratives. At the present day the recently reported miracles in France, which, while they rest on a very high form of attestation, probably none of us accept as objective realities, are instances in point. Still more so are the phenomena of spiritualism, occurring as they are alleged to do, in the very midst of us. These latter, as far as mere attestation goes, unquestionably rest on one which is extremely strong. Their reality is affirmed, not only by large numbers of persons of every variety of mental cultivation, but by men who have been accustomed to estimate legal evidence, and by some who deservedly hold a high rank in departments of physical science, and cannot but be well acquainted with scientific processes of investigation. As their honesty is unquestionable, and on the supposition that they are not the dupes of fraud,* which in some cases is highly improbable, it follows that if the phenomena which they believe themselves to have witnessed are unreal, their belief in them must be owing to their having mistaken subjective impressions for external realities. I have selected the case of spiritualism as an illustration, because it is evident that if we view the question as one of attestation pure and simple, banishing all other considerations, some of its phenomena rest on a testimony which is unusually strong. I propose to discriminate between it and the evidence of Our Lord's resurrection when I discuss the theory of visions in my seventh Lecture. My object in noticing the subject here is to point out the difficulty and complexity which the existence of such beliefs imports into the historical argument, if we view it as a simple question of attestation.

It has now therefore become necessary to show, not only that the reporters of miracles believed that they actually witnessed them, but also that it was impossible that, in accordance with the explanations which an eminent scientific authority† has given of some well-attested spiritualistic phenomena, the belief could have originated in mistaking subjective impressions for external realities. It would be absurd to shut our eyes to the fact that the proof of miracles which have occurred in the distant past, if we view the question exclusively as one of testimony, is rendered far less convincing to a considerable number of minds by the existence of widespread delusions of this description, of which men of un-

---

* I state this on the authority of Dr. Carpenter. While he attributes a large number of these phenomena to fraud, and others to mesmeric influences, he is of opinion that there is a considerable residuum which it is impossible to refer to imposture as their cause.

† Dr. Carpenter's *Mental Physiology*.

questionable intelligence, and no small amount of scientific eminence, are a prey. Still further: it complicates the entire question by imposing on us the necessity of clearly discriminating between the evidence of the Christian miracles and those which, although they rest on a strong attestation, we reject as unrealities. These considerations alone furnish the strongest reason why the argument from miracles, as it has been usually stated, should no longer occupy the van of our evidential position, but that it should give place to one which is capable of verification, namely, the superhuman action of Christ in history.

5. Our increased acquaintance with the power of the mind to produce important results by its action on our bodily frames has tended to produce in many a distrust in the evidence of miracles alleged to have been wrought in distant ages, the precise character of which it is now impossible to submit to such a rigid scrutiny, as we would any miracles alleged to have been performed at the present day, before admitting their reality. The limits of this power are unknown; but it is unquestionably extensive and capable of producing results which to ordinary minds would seem miraculous. The eminent physiologist above referred to* has expressed his belief that the *stigmata*, alleged to have been produced on the bodies of some mediæval saints, were realities, and that a purely mental influence is adequate to produce them. On such a point I can only quote his authority; but it is unquestionable that within certain limitations, the power is a real one, and capable of producing results which in former ages would have been deemed miraculous. This being so, it places a certain class of cures in an ambiguous position, and deprives them of much of their value as evidential miracles. It is clear, however, that while some of the miracles recorded in the New Testament may be referred to influences of this kind, others lie quite beyond the power of any action of the mind on the

* "*Mental Physiology.*"

body to have effected. Still it cannot be denied that such phenomena, the belief entertained by large numbers of intelligent men in the phenomena of spiritualism, and other kindred delusions, and the existence of a considerable number of well attested miraculous narratives in the history of the past, the objective reality of which it is impossible to admit, have tended to weaken the force of the argument from miracles, and to increase the difficulty of proof, rendering it necessary, if the entire weight of the Christian argument is to be made to rest on it, clearly to discriminate between the evidence of the one set of miraculous narratives and of the other. The complexity of such an argument is, I think, a sufficient reason why we should place a body of evidence which admits of an easy verification in the forefront of the Christian position, and assign to that of miracles a collateral and subordinate one.

By way of illustration of my general position let us suppose a well informed missionary, endeavouring to win over to the acceptance of Christianity an intelligent Hindoo Theist, well acquainted with all our modern objections. Is it conceivable that he would begin by placing before him the argument from miracles, as it is set forth in our common evidential treatises? Ought he not rather to place in the forefront of his reasoning the moral and spiritual aspects of Christianity, assigning the first place to that mighty energy which eighteen centuries of history testify to be centred in the person of its Founder? To take the former course would not only render it necessary for his proposed convert to enter into the discussion of all the *à priori* difficulties with which the question of miracles is attended, but also to undertake an intricate and laborious historical investigation, not only for the purpose of estimating the value of the evidence in favour of the Christian miracles but of discriminating between them and the mass of false miracles with which history abounds. To plunge an intelligent heathen into a vast range of inquiries of this description would surely be very unlikely to result in his speedily embracing the Christian faith. But if the order in which the Christian argument is placed in our common evidential treatises would be an unwise mode of placing the claims of Christianity before an intelligent heathen, it surely cannot be a right mode of presenting it for the conviction of unbelievers, the confirmation of waverers, or the strengthening of the Christian in his faith.

In making these observations, it is by no means my intention to depreciate the argument from miracles, which I hope to show in subsequent Lectures to possess a real value when assigned to its due place, in proper subordination to that course of reasoning which the exigencies of modern thought imperatively demand. For this purpose, therefore, in conformity with Our Lord's precept, "to bring out of our treasures things both new and old," I propose in the three following Lectures to state the outlines of the argument which I contend should be placed in the forefront of our evidential position. In the next three, I propose to examine the argument for miracles with a view of strengthening those portions of it which the results of modern investigation have shown to be defective. My last Lecture will be devoted to the consideration of the value of existing theories of inspiration and the relation in which they stand to modern science.

SUPPLEMENT I.

The position which I have taken, that the essence of Christianity as distinct from its adjuncts, consists not in a mere body of abstract doctrinal statements, or moral precepts, but in the manifestation of Jesus Christ, his teaching and historic life, is so important, whether we view it in its apologetic or in its theological aspect, as to render it desirable to adduce a larger body of proof in support of it than would have been possible to bring forward in the Lecture itself. I have affirmed that the Christian revelation is not only made by Jesus Christ, but consists in his person, his actions and his teaching: in other words that he is an actual manifestation of the divine in the sphere of the human, revealing to us the innermost aspect of the moral and spiritual character of God, as far as it can be conceived of by finite intelligence. If this position is correctly taken, it has not only a most important bearing on our evidential position, but on the entire range of Christian theology. On the latter subject however I must not enter; but confine my observations to the former.

If the writings of St. John form a legitimate portion of the New Testament canon, the truth of this position must be considered as firmly established. I will therefore adduce the chief points of the evidence which they supply.

The introduction to the first epistle affirms in the most direct terms that the Christian Revelation is made in the historic life and actions of Jesus Christ; that this constitutes the truth which underlies the entire letter, and that its subsequent portions were intended to unfold it, and to form a commentary on it.

" That which was from the beginning," says he, " which we

have heard, which we have seen with our eyes, which we have looked upon, and our hands have handled, concerning the Word of life; for the life was manifested, and we have seen it, and bear witness, and show unto you that eternal life, which was with the Father, and was manifested unto us. That which we have seen and heard declare we unto you, that ye also may have fellowship with us; and truly our fellowship is with the Father and with his Son Jesus Christ. And these things write we unto you that your joy may be full."

Nothing can be more explicit than this statement. The following points are either directly affirmed in it, or deducible from it by the strictest rules of logical inference.

1. That the subject on which the author of the Epistle was going to address those to whom he wrote was "concerning the Word of life," whom he identified with the historic Jesus.

2. That this "Word of life" was from the beginning, having existed prior to the manifestation of Jesus Christ in history.

3. That this divine life which dwelt in the Logos was manifested to men in the person of Jesus Christ by the Incarnation.

4. That this divine life took so substantial a form that the Apostle had seen it with his eyes, looked upon it, and handled it with his hands. Further, he had had the testimony of his ears to the reality of this divine manifestation: for he had listened throughout the period of his ministry to its heavenly utterances.

5. That the actions and teaching of Jesus Christ constituted this divine life of the Logos, which was originally with the Father, and in Jesus Christ became manifested to men.

6. That the great end and purpose of his Apostolic ministry was to testify to the reality, the facts, and the teachings of this divine manifestation. "We have seen it, and bear witness, and show unto you that eternal life which

was with the Father, and was manifested unto us." Now the only mode in which it was possible for the Apostle to "show that eternal life" to others was by furnishing details of the actions and teaching of that person in whom it was exhibited. Consequently, as he affirms that his Apostolic ministry was a bearing witness to it, it must evidently have consisted in furnishing to those to whom he ministered details of its manifestation, and in commenting on their meaning. From this it follows that the details of this divine life which the Apostle communicated to the Church formed the essence and foundation of the Christianity which he taught.

7. The communication of what he had seen and heard, was capable of imparting to those to whom it was addressed, communion with the Father, with His Son Jesus Christ, and with one another; in other words, it formed the bond which united the Church together and the basis on which it rested.

Nothing can be more explicit than these statements. They prove that the Apostolic writer certainly viewed the Christian Revelation as consisting in the Incarnation, and the historic manifestation of the divine character and perfections in the life of Jesus Christ. "The life was manifested and we have seen it, and bear witness." This is his fundamental conception of Christianity, which forms a striking contrast to the modern popular conceptions of it which are usually designated "plans of salvation." With statements thus explicit it will be superfluous to adduce further evidence from the Epistle that such were the views of its author, for the entire writing is a commentary on it with the introduction as its text. The concluding words will be sufficient. "We know that the Son of God is come, and hath given us an understanding, that we may know Him that is true, and we are in Him that is true, even in His Son Jesus Christ. This is the true God, and eternal life." Words cannot be more explicit.

I now proceed to consider the testimony furnished by the Gospel. Its author makes the following affirmations in the prologue:—" In the beginning was the Word and the Word was with God and the Word was God. The same was in the beginning with God. All things were made by Him (πάντα δι αὐτοῦ ἐγένετο), and without Him was not any thing made that was made. In Him was life, and the life was the light of men. And the light shineth in darkness and the darkness comprehended it not." ... "And the Word was made flesh and dwelt among us, and we beheld His glory, the glory as of the only begotten of the Father full of grace and truth." ... "No man hath seen God at any time, the only begotten Son who is in the bosom of the Father, He hath declared Him."

The passage here quoted, with its context, makes it certain that the author's conception of what constituted the fundamental essence of Christianity was:

First, that all manifestations of the eternal Father were communicated through the divine Logos.

Secondly, that He was both the life and the light of men.

Thirdly, that He became man in the person of Jesus Christ.

Fourthly, that the glory which shone forth in Jesus Christ in the Incarnation was the glory of the only begotten of the Father, of whose perfections, incomprehensible to finite intelligences, He is the sole and adequate manifestation: or, to put the same thought in other words, Jesus Christ in His human manifestation is the objective revelation of the Godhead.

Fifthly, that this revelation was an objective revelation. The Apostle in his personal intercourse with Jesus Christ had beheld in Him "the glory of the only begotten of the Father," whose life and actions had been the revelation of the Father to men.

Such statements can leave no doubt that the writer of this Gospel viewed the essence of the Christian revelation as consisting in the person and work of Jesus Christ our Lord, His teaching, His life, death, and resurrection. And not only is this so, but he has represented Our Lord as affirming the same truth in the most decisive language, of which the following are instances. "Philip saith unto Him, Lord, show us the Father and it sufficeth us. Jesus saith unto him, have I been so long time with you, and yet hast thou not known Me, Philip! he that hath seen Me hath seen the Father, and how sayest thou, Show us the Father. Believe Me, that I am in the Father and the Father in Me."—John xiv. 8-11.

If these words are a real utterance of Our Lord, nothing can be more conclusive than that He claimed to constitute revelation in His own person. They form a reply to a direct request made by Philip for a revelation of the Father. "Lord show us the Father, and it sufficeth us!" Our Lord in express words affirms that He constituted such a revelation, "He that hath seen Me, hath seen the Father." "From henceforth ye know Him, and have seen Him." "Believest thou not that I am in the Father and the Father in Me." No words could convey a more direct affirmation that the apostles during their converse with Our Lord had beheld in His works and character a perfect revelation of the Father. Again, Jesus stood and cried, "he that believeth on Me, believeth not on Me, but on Him that sent Me, and he that seeth Me, seeth Him that sent Me. I am come a light into the world, that whosoever believeth in Me should not abide in darkness."—John xii. 44-46. Again, "I am the light of the world; he that followeth Me shall not walk in darkness, but shall have the light of life."—John viii. 12. "Then said they unto Him, Where is Thy Father? Jesus answered, Ye neither know Me, nor my Father, for if ye had known Me, ye should have known my Father also,"—viii. 19. "If I do not the works of my Father, believe Me not, but if I do, though ye believe not Me, believe the works, that ye may know and believe that the Father is in Me and I in Him."—(x. 37-38).

These passages all affirm the same truth, that the perfections of the Father are manifested in the person of Jesus Christ. He is the revealer of the Father; in fact, He affirms that he that sees Him, sees Him that sent Him; and that the knowledge of Him is the knowledge of the Father.

In this capacity He is the light of the world, and the light of life. These assertions, when put together, constitute a most direct affirmation that He is the objective revelation of God. The author of this Gospel also ascribes to Our Lord a number of other assertions respecting Himself and His relation to the Father, all of which presuppose the same truth, but which it will be unnecessary for me to cite.

A similar view runs through the entire writings of St. Paul. The passages which assert that Revelation is made in Christ are exceedingly numerous, and what is greatly to the purpose, the allusions are not only direct but incidental, and made in every variety of form. Of these latter I cite a few examples as showing the extent to which the conception underlies the whole range of the Apostle's thought. "God was *in Christ* reconciling the world to Himself," 2 Cor. v. 19. "For of Him are ye *in Christ Jesus*, who of God is made unto us wisdom, and righteousness, and sanctification, and redemption, that according as it is written, he that glorieth, let him glory in the Lord." 1 Cor. i. 30, 31. *In whom* we have redemption. Eph. i. 7. *In whom* we have attained an inheritance." i. 11. "The spirit of wisdom and revelation *in the knowledge of him.*" i. 17. The working of God's mighty power "is wrought *in Christ.*" i. 30. "*In Christ*, ye who sometimes were afar off are made nigh." Eph. ii. 13. "*In Him* were all things created." Col. i. 16. "*In Him* should all the fulness (*i.e.* the fulness of the divine perfections), dwell." Col. i. 19. "*In whom* are hid all the treasures of wisdom and knowledge." Col. ii. 3. "Ye are complete *in Him.*" Col. ii. 10. "The grace of our Lord was exceeding abundant with faith and love *in Christ Jesus.*" 1 Tim. i. 14. "Live godly *in Christ Jesus.*" 2 Tim. iii. 12. "The redemption that is *in Christ Jesus.*" Rom. iii. 24. "The law of the spirit of life *in Christ Jesus.*" Rom. viii. 2. "I know and am persuaded *in the Lord Jesus.*" Rom. xiv. 14. "The veil is done away *in Christ.*" 2 Cor. iii. 14. "We preach *Christ Jesus the Lord.*" 2 Cor. iv. 5. "The glory of God *in the face of Jesus Christ.*" 2 Cor. iv. 6.

All these passages in various forms affirm that Revelation was given in the person of Jesus Christ; and their incidental character proves the intense familiarity of the idea to the Apostle's mind, far more than a number of directly dogmatical assertions. They exhibit it as directly forming the basis on which his religious life was founded. They are consistent with one idea, and with one only, that Revelation was given in his person.

Equally important are some of his assertions when speaking of the progressive character of revelation, and of the purposes formed in the divine mind respecting it. These must be considered in greater detail. Thus we have the remarkable assertion in Rom. xvi. 25, 26. " Now to Him who is of power to stablish you according to my Gospel, and the preaching of Jesus Christ, according to the revelation of the mystery which was kept secret since the world began ($\dot{\epsilon}\nu$ $a\dot{\iota}\omega\nu\dot{\iota}o\iota\varsigma$ $\chi\rho\acute{o}\nu o\iota\varsigma$, in the eternal ages), but now is made manifest, and by the Scriptures of the prophets according to the commandment of the everlasting God, made known to all nations for the obedience of faith."

This passage enunciates the following truths:—

1. Revelation is no afterthought of the Divine mind, but a part of His eternal purpose, forming with creation one great harmonious plan.

2. It has been kept secret as a hidden truth ($\mu\nu\sigma\tau\acute{\eta}\rho\iota o\nu$) in the divine mind during the eternal ages, but has been manifested in the proclamation of Jesus the Messiah ($\dot{\epsilon}\nu$ $\kappa\eta\rho\acute{\nu}\gamma\mu a\tau\iota$ $'I\eta\sigma o\tilde{\nu}$ $X\rho\iota\sigma\tau o\tilde{\nu}$).

3. That this revelation is made known to all nations for the obedience of faith; and is a manifestation of the wisdom of God through Jesus Christ.

In conformity with this view the Apostle at the very commencement of the epistle declares that the subject of his writing was "concerning Jesus Christ our Lord." In Ephesians iii. 8-11 he makes the following statement:—
" Whereof (the Gospel) I am made a minister according to the gift of the grace of God given unto me, by the effectual

working of His power. Unto me who am less than the least of all saints is this grace given, that I should preach among the Gentiles the unsearchable riches of Christ, and to make all men see what is the fellowship of the mystery, which from the beginning of the world (ἀπὸ τῶν αἰώνων) has been hid in God who created all things by (ἐν) Jesus Christ, to the intent that now unto the principalities and powers in heavenly places might be known by the Church the manifold wisdom of God, according to the eternal purpose which He purposed in Christ Jesus our Lord." Similar assertions occur in chap. i. 8, "Wherein He hath abounded towards us in all wisdom and prudence, having made known to us the mystery of His will according to the good pleasure, which He purposed in Himself, that in the dispensation of the fulness of times he might gather together in one all things in Christ, both which are in heaven and which are in earth, even in Him..... That the God of our Lord Jesus Christ, the Father of glory, may give you the spirit of wisdom and revelation in the knowledge of Him ... according to the working of His mighty power which He wrought in Christ."

These passages are so important in relation to the present argument that I will enunciate in as many distinct propositions the various affirmations which they contain.

1. They affirm that the Revelation made in Jesus Christ formed one of the eternal purposes of the divine mind, coeval with those which produced his work of Creation; in fact that Creation and Redemption form portions of the same great whole, and that the latter is not a mere remedial measure superinduced in consequence of the failure of the purpose intended by the former.

2. That the Incarnation is the manifestation of this eternal purpose existing in the divine mind.

3. That unsearchable riches both of wisdom and goodness as yet undisclosed in God's creative work, were manifested in the incarnate Christ.

4. That so entirely coeval in the divine purposes are

Creation and the divine self-manifestation in Christ, that the creative work of God itself was given in Him "*Who created all things in Jesus Christ.*"

5. That the purpose and effects of the Incarnation are not limited to man, but on the contrary, it is intended to be a manifestation to "the principalities and powers in heavenly places of the manifold wisdom of God."

6. The ultimate purpose of the Incarnation is, that God might "in the dispensation of the fulness of the times gather together in one all things in Christ, both which are in heaven and which are on earth, in Him."

The views thus propounded by the Apostle stand in striking contrast to various schemes of salvation which have become widely diffused by the influence of popular theology, and which profess to give a complete rationale of redemption. Their general theory is that the revelation of God in Jesus Christ is a kind of afterthought in the Divine mind, to remedy the failure of His original creative purpose, occasioned by the Fall; in fact, a scheme devised for the mending His marred plan of Creation. Still coarser views of the divine plan in redemption have been extensively popular, exhibiting it in the vulgar form of a bargain between two independent parties, each of whom has thereby become bound to perform his part of the contract. The whole has proceeded from the assumption that it is possible accurately to represent the purposes of the Divine mind in the formularies of human thought. Such theories belong to that worst form of rationalism which makes man and his imperfections the accurate measures of the divine purposes and *modus operandi*, being closely analogous to that which in a lower stage of mental development is the parent of idolatry, and which has invested deity with some of the worst attributes of human nature, representing God as altogether such a one as ourselves. These assertions of the Apostle as to the extent of the divine purposes in Revelation are of the utmost importance in relation to the subject before us, for nothing has more damaged Christianity with thoughtful men than the idea which has been so generally adopted by various forms of popular Christianity, that those so-called schemes of salvation, not only embody the Christianity of the New Testament, but are co-extensive with the divine purpose in Revelation.

Assertions of a similar character are made by the Apostle in the Epistle to the Colossians. Thus he writes: "In whom we have redemption through His blood, even the forgiveness of sins, Who is the image of the invisible God, the First-born of every creature ($\pi\rho\omega\tau\acute{o}\tau o\kappa o\varsigma$ $\pi\acute{a}\sigma\eta\varsigma$ $\kappa\tau\acute{\iota}\sigma\epsilon\omega\varsigma$, the First-born before all creation); for in him ($\grave{\epsilon}\nu$ $a\grave{v}\tau\tilde{\omega}$) were all things created that are in heaven, and that are in earth, visible and invisible, whether they be thrones or dominions, or principalities or powers, all things were created by ($\delta\iota$ $a\grave{v}\tau o\tilde{v}$, through Him), and for Him ($\epsilon\grave{\iota}\varsigma$ $a\grave{v}\tau\grave{o}\nu$, in reference to Him); and He is before all things, and by Him ($\grave{\epsilon}\nu$ $a\grave{v}\tau\tilde{\omega}$, in him) all things consist: and He is the head of the body, the Church, who is the beginning ($\grave{a}\rho\chi\grave{\eta}$, the principle of things) the first-born from the dead, that in all things He might have the pre-eminence. For it pleased the Father that in Him should all the fulness dwell; and having made peace by the blood of His cross, through Him to reconcile all things unto Himself, through Him, whether they are things on earth, or things in heaven." Col. i. 14-20. Again: "That their hearts might be comforted, being knit together in love unto all riches of the full assurance of understanding, to the acknowledging of the mystery of God, and of the Father, and of Christ, in whom are hid all the treasures of wisdom and knowledge. As ye therefore have received Christ Jesus the Lord, so walk ye in him, rooted and built up in him and stablished in the faith, as ye have been taught, abounding therein with thanksgiving. Beware lest any man spoil ou through philosophy and vain deceit, after the tradition of men, after the rudiments of the world, and not after Christ, for in him dwelleth all the fulness of the Godhead bodily, and ye are complete in him which is the head of all principality and power." Col. ii. 2-10.

These passages make it certain that the Apostle contemplated the person of Jesus Christ as the objective revelation of the Godhead. On this point he lays down the following propositions:—

1. That the fulness of the divine perfections abides in the Incarnate person of Jesus Christ our Lord.
2. That He in His incarnate person is the image (εἰκών) of the invisible God.
3. That all creation has been constituted in Him, not only this world, but the entire Universe of Being.
4. That He is the instrumental agent (δι αὐτοῦ) through whom the creative work has been effected: that it has been formed in reference to Him; and that He had a prior existence to it.
5. That the same person who has been the source of Creation, the instrument through whom it has been effected, and the purpose towards which it tends, is He through whom the revelations of the Father have been communicated, and who has carried out the great work of Redemption.
6. That through the work of Redemption it is the divine purpose to reconcile all things unto Himself, whether things on earth, or things in heaven.

This last assertion proves that according to the views of the Apostle the effects of the Incarnation were not limited to the human race, but would be consummated by uniting to God all things in heaven and earth.

These propositions if accepted as the genuine utterances of the Apostle Paul, fully prove that according to the views entertained by him, the person of Jesus Christ our Lord constitutes the great objective revelation of God, which has manifested forth the divine character during the past and the present, and is destined still further to unfold it in the ages of the future. It is true that the genuineness of the two Epistles which contain the most definite affirmations on this point has been disputed by a number of unbelieving critics, for which one of the chief reasons is their advanced Christology. But although the statements in the other Epistles are somewhat less definite in form, the occasion and purpose of writing them not having called them forth with the same definiteness, yet there are statements, both in the Epistle to the Romans and those to the Corinthians, and even to the Galatians, which prove that the Apostle regarded the Christian revelation as centred in the person of our Lord. The reference which I have above made to these Epistles is far more than sufficient to prove that their author entertained the same views as are more formally enunciated in these latter writings. Whether Paul or any one else was the author of the Epistles to Timothy, these likewise contain a strong affirmation of the same truth. "Great," says he, "is the mystery of godliness, God (or who) was manifested in the flesh." If we suppose these Epistles to have been the work of another writer, this would prove the wide acceptance of this view of the essence of Christianity in the Church.

I have not yet referred to the opinions of the writer of the Epistle to the Hebrews, on account of the doubts as to its authorship. It is, however, important, because, if not written by the Apostle, it proves that the Pauline and Johannine views on this subject were accepted by other sections of the Christian Church; for whoever may have been its author, its early date is unquestionable. For this purpose it will be sufficient to cite the opening of the first chapter: "God, who at sundry times and in divers manners (πολυμερῶς καὶ πολυτρόπως, implying the imperfections of former revelations) spoke in times past to the fathers by the prophets, hath in these last days spoken unto us by his Son, whom he hath appointed heir (κληρονόμος) of all things, by whom (δι᾽ οὗ) also he made the worlds (τοὺς αἰῶνας ἐποίησεν, constituted the ages), who being the brightness of his glory (ἀπαύγασμα τῆς δόξης, the outshining of his glory), and the express image of his person, and upholding all things by the word of his power, having by himself purged our sins, sat down on the right hand of the majesty on high." This passage is a direct affirmation of the

Pauline positions. It declares, first, as distinct from the partial manifestations which God made of Himself in former ages in the prophets, that in these last days He has spoken to us in His Son; secondly, that the manifestation in the Son differs from that made in the prophets as the divine differs from the human, He being the inheritor of all things in whom God has constituted the ages; and thirdly, that the Son, in whom God has made this last revelation, is " the shining forth of the divine glories," the precise resemblance of the divine subsistence, the inheritor of all things, through whom the divine activities in the former ages have been manifested, and that He is the person through whom God has effected His work of providence and redemption. The whole passage therefore affirms, in the most unmistakeable language, that the divine person of Jesus Christ constitutes the objective revelation of God, a view which is consistently carried out through the entire Epistle.

It will be superfluous for me to cite passages from the Apocalypse in proof that similar views were entertained by its author, because it is the idea which underlies the entire book, and forms the groundwork of all its visions. Throughout them Jesus Christ is depicted as the only Revealer of the Father. A single instance will be sufficient. A book containing the divine decrees is represented as seen in the right hand of the Creator of all things. A proclamation is made to every creature in heaven and earth to come forward and establish such a claim of worthiness as would entitle him to take possession of the book, and unfold the divine decrees. All creation fails to establish such a claim. But no sooner does the Incarnate Lamb appear than a universal chorus of acclamation from all God's creatures pronounces Him worthy; and from henceforth He assumes throughout the whole book, which is the revelation of Jesus Christ, the office of the Revealer of the Father.

The remaining writings of the New Testament, with the exception of the Synoptic Gospels and the Acts of the

Apostles, are very brief. One of them, however, the first Epistle of St. Peter, contains an unquestionable reference to the same truth.

"Searching what, or what manner of time the Spirit of Christ which was in them did signify, when it testified beforehand the sufferings of Christ and the glory that should follow. Unto whom it was revealed that not unto themselves, but unto us, they did minister the things which are now reported unto you, by them that have preached the Gospel unto you, with the Holy Ghost sent down from heaven, which things the angels desire to look into." (i. 11, 12.)

This passage makes the definite affirmation that the angels desire to look into the things "which were reported by those who have preached the Gospel unto you." From this two inferences follow. First, that the Christian revelation forms a matter of interest to other beings than men. Secondly, that it consists of a number of objective facts in connection with our Lord's divine person, viz., "The things reported unto you by them that have preached the Gospel unto you, which things the angels desire to look into."

This last point is in strict agreement with the remaining contents of the Chapter. The Epistle of James, which contains not a single statement which can be viewed as theoretical, is without any allusion to the subject.

We now come to the Acts of the Apostles. Its subject-matter, which is to record the chief incidents in the planting of Christianity, would naturally afford to the writer little opportunity of making definite statements on the point before us. One idea, however, which is closely connected with it, runs through the entire book. The writer affirms that the one great subject of the Apostles' preaching was, that Jesus was the Christ. Such an affirmation proves that certain historic facts connected with the life of Jesus must have been regarded by them as forming the essence of Christianity. This idea is by the writer identified with Christianity itself. Thus he says of the Apostles that they daily, and from house to house, ceased not to teach and to preach Jesus the Christ.

The only portions of the New Testament requiring any further observations are the Synoptic Gospels. It will be objected that this idea is wanting in them and in the Epistle of James; and consequently that it is not an original, but a subsequent development of Christianity, due to the Johannine and Pauline parties in the Church. To which I reply,

First, that although there is only one statement on this subject in the Synoptics, equally formal with that in the fourth Gospel, it is inaccurate to assert that the idea does not underlie them. Both Matthew and Luke record an utterance of our Lord respecting Himself, which approaches very closely to the strongest affirmations of the fourth Gospel. "At that time Jesus answered, and said, I thank thee, O Father, Lord of heaven and earth, because thou hast hid these things from the wise and prudent, and hast revealed them unto babes. Even so, Father, for so it seemed good in thy sight. All things are delivered unto me of my Father; and no man knoweth who the Son is but the Father, neither knoweth any man the Father save the Son; and he to whomsoever the Son will reveal him." Into the doctrinal statements of this passage I need not at present enter. It is sufficient for my present purpose that it distinctly affirms that the Son is the one Revealer of the Father; and that in terms quite as plain as any which we read in the fourth Gospel, or in the Johannine and Pauline epistles, or in the book of the Revelation.

With this express statement another trait which underlies the whole of these Gospels is in strict agreement, and is only explicable on the supposition of the truth of the assertion in question. I allude to the habitual self-assertion of our Lord, and to the fact that He is uniformly depicted as deriving the whole of His teaching from the sole source of His own self-consciousness. When we consider the mildness, unobtrusiveness, and humility, which these Gospels uniformly attribute to Him, His self-assertion is the most striking phenomenon in all history, and if it had been assigned to any other man, however great, it would have been simply extravagant. But it fits in with exquisite harmony with all the other divine aspects of His character, and can only be explained on the principle that he felt within Him the direct self-consciousness of the presence of the divine. Hence it was that throughout His teaching He referred to no other authority than His own. As He is uniformly depicted by the Synoptics, His consciousness of the divine was immediate and direct, and He felt within Himself an inherent worthiness before which every merely human tie must yield. This trait which underlies the entire structure of the Synoptics, is not only in strict conformity with the great utterance above referred to, but pre-supposes its truth. I might easily have adduced a far larger mass of evidence on this subject; but I submit that what I have brought forward is abundantly sufficient for my purpose, and proves beyond all question that according to the views of the writers of the New Testament, the person and work of Jesus Christ constitute the very centre and essence of Christianity, and that the Christian revelation is made in His divine person.

SUPPLEMENT II.

A vast amount of confusion has been introduced into the controversy about miracles by the vague use of such terms as "Nature," "Natural," "Supernatural," "The Order of Nature," "Law," "Force," &c., without any attempt to assign to them a definite and consistent meaning. In a controversy of this kind, involving as it must a large number of abstract reasonings, it is of the utmost importance to keep the signification of the chief terms which we employ in it free from ambiguity. These terms, however, have a great variety of meaning, and yet they are habitually used as if they were terms of the utmost precision. Webster's Dictionary assigns no less than twelve distinct meanings to the word "Nature," fourteen to "Natural," and twenty-seven to "Law." The Duke of Argyll tells us that even in scientific treatises the term "law" is used in not less than five different senses, viz.:—

First,—When applied simply to an observed order of facts.

Secondly,—To that order as involving the action of some force, or forces, of which nothing more can be known.

Thirdly,—As applied to individual forces, the measure of whose operation has been more or less clearly defined or ascertained.

Fourthly,—As applied to those combinations of forces which have reference to the fulfilment of purpose or the discharge of functions.

Fifthly,—As applied to abstract conceptions of the mind, not corresponding with any actual phenomena, but deduced therefrom as axioms of thought, necessary to an understanding of them. Law in this sense is a reduction of the phenomena not merely to an order of facts but to an order of thought.

Such are the various senses in which this word is employed even by scientific men; yet the Duke is not certain that he has enumerated them all. As this term enters as one of the most important factors into the discussion about miracles, we need not wonder that its ambiguity has opened wide the gate for the introduction of a large number of fallacies.

Equally ambiguous is the term "Nature" and its compounds. As however only two or three of its various significations enter largely into this question, it will be unnecessary to enumerate the others.

First,—The term "Nature" is used to denote the material Universe, its necessary forces and laws. This is a class of phenomena definite and distinct, and if its use were confined to them it would be free from ambiguity.

But it is also used to denote another class of phenomena, separated from these by the widest interval, viz., man, his intellectual and moral nature, including his volition. Thus phenomena become complicated together under a common term, which differ from one another as widely as freedom and necessity, the material and moral worlds, with the laws which regulate their action. It is even not unfrequently used to include everything which exists.

When the same term is indiscriminately used to denote phenomena thus widely differing in character, inaccuracy of reasoning is the inevitable result. But when two terms as ambiguous as "nature" and "law" become complicated together, as is necessarily the case in this discussion, the confusion is greatly increased. The whole controversy is chiefly made up of questions respecting the Natural and the Supernatural; whether miracles are the results of a power within, or without nature; whether they are contrary to the laws of nature, or are violations, or suspensions of them, or are violations of its order; or involve the action of some higher natural law; or the introduction of a new force into nature, or whether on these or any other grounds miracles are impossible, irrational, or incredible. This being so, it is evident that if we include under the same terms things so widely different in conception as the phenomena of the material and the moral worlds, nothing but hopeless confusion of thought can be the result. The whole question in fact turns on the meaning which we attach to the terms "Nature," "Natural," "Supernatural," "Order of Nature," "Force," and "Law." This last term is constantly used to cover two conceptions which are radically distinct. The first of these is when the word is used to denote an invariable sequence of events. This is unquestionably the more correct meaning to attach to it; and if its use was rigidly limited to it, it would save both theologians and men of science no small amount of useless discussion. The term "law" in its primary meaning is only applicable to man and his actions. It denotes a rule of conduct which he is bound to obey. Hence it has been applied by analogy to the orderly sequences of events in the Material Universe, which are said to observe a certain law. This simply means, that they occur in an invariable order, which we call the law of their recurrence. But nothing is more common in this controversy than to speak of the laws of nature as if they possessed an efficient power, or in other words to introduce into the conception of law the idea of causation. Yet nothing can be more certain than that in the proper sense of the term, the laws of nature are incapable of effecting any result whatever. They simply denote the invariable sequences of natural phenomena, and nothing more. They are wholly distinct from the causes of things, and those active energies in the Universe which we designate forces. Its forces are the efficient causes; its laws, the invariable sequences of the phenomena which result from the action of its forces. Thus the force of gravitation is quite distinct from the *law* of gravitation. The force is the active energy; the law is the invariable order of phenomena.

From this simple and obvious meaning the term "law" has become complicated with the conception of cause or force, and thus the laws of nature are habitually spoken of even by scientific men as though they were efficient causes, and language is used respecting them which amounts to little short of their personification. This confusion of thought is brought about as follows:—there is a principle in our minds (how it has originated is immaterial to the subject we are now considering) which irresistibly leads us to believe in the continuity of phenomena; and that a set of sequences which have invariably occurred in times past, will recur in times future. This principle lies at the foundation of the inductive process, and its validity depends on the assumption of its truth. It has been expressed in various forms, the most simple of which is that which affirms the truth of the principle of the continuity of nature; or that like causes must produce like effects. For example, we infer because the sun has risen every day in times past, that it will rise every day in times future, and we designate the sun's rising and setting for all future time a law of nature. In this way the conception of necessity, causation, or efficiency becomes mixed up with that of law, instead of simply denoting what it really is, a succession of invariable sequences. Hence when a particular class of events is spoken of as a law of nature, the idea of necessity is superadded to that of invariable sequence.

Thus it is said to be a law of Nature that all men must die. What does such an affirmation mean? It affirms as an observed fact that all men have died; and infers on the principle of continuity that what has taken place in the past, will take place in the future. In consequence of this inference, the proposition becomes altered in form from "all men have died," to "all men *must* die;" and thus the conceptions of necessity and causation become confused with the simple one of law as an observed order of phenomena. The proposition "All men must die" involves several assumptions, among the most important of which is, that the same causes must produce like effects in the future, unless other forces interpose which are capable of modifying their action. In this manner the term "law" has been extensively employed both by theologians and men of science to denote not only a set of invariable sequences of phenomena, but the causes which produce them, and the forces which energize in them. In this way it is that great confusion of thought has been introduced into the controversy about miracles. We are told that the laws of nature have effected this or that result; that they act with irresistible power, and a multitude of similar expressions are habitually applied to them, whereas the only active energies are, not the laws, but the forces of nature, and the laws by themselves effect nothing. Thus man's mortality is said to be a law of nature; *i.e.* it is an event which has invariably happened in the past, and which on the principle of continuity, we infer, will always happen in the future. But this law does not cause the death of any one, but certain forces which energize, or which fail to energize within us. Even in the primary sense of the word, law, as a rule of human conduct, can effect nothing; the only things which are efficient are the penalties which attend its violation. What effect this confusion of terms has on the clearness and precision of scientific reasonings it would be presumptuous in me to offer an opinion; but in discussions about the possibility of miracles, involving, as they do, the most intricate questions of causation and efficiency, the only result of using the term to denote two such fundamentally distinct classes of phenomena is to invite confusion of thought.

I will now adduce a few examples of the confusion arising from this indiscriminate use of the term "Nature" in union with that of "law."

One of the moot points of this controversy is, whether miracles are contrary to nature, or involve violations, or suspensions of its laws, and it has been affirmed that it is essential to the conception of a miracle that it should do so. On the other hand the opponents of Revelation affirm that this renders them absolutely incredible. It is evident however that when such a question is raised, the all-important subject for consideration is, what nature are they alleged to be contrary to, or what are the laws which they violate. Nor is it less important that our conceptions should be clear as to what distinguishes that kind of event which we call a miracle from all other occurrences. What then do we mean by a miracle? Viewed merely as an occurrence in the physical universe, it is an event of a very unusual character, for which none of its known forces are sufficient to account. If such an event can be proved to have actually occurred, it leaves only two alternatives, either that its existence must have been due to the action of some unknown force which has manifested itself on this special occasion only, or to the energy of a Being who is able either to combine the existing forces in the Universe in such a manner as to produce the event in question; or to effect the same result by calling into existence a new force; or by the direct agency of his creative will. Viewed merely as an objective occurrence, therefore, there is no difference between a miracle and a very unusual event. The distinction is a creation of the mind, and consists in the fact that the occurrence of the very uncommon event has been subsequently accounted for by the action of the known forces of the Universe, while the other cannot.

Another important factor in the idea of a miracle is that its occurrence is ushered in by a prediction that it is going to happen, and thus it becomes a manifestation of purpose. Theologians however have greatly increased the perplexity of the entire question by introducing into their definition of a miracle some account of the mode of the divine activity by which they suppose it to have been effected. Thus miracles have been defined to be events which involve violations or suspensions of the laws of nature, or are brought about by the action of a higher law of nature on a lower one, or are contrary to nature, or are brought about by the simple energy of God's creative will. Nothing can be more unwise than to introduce such conceptions into the idea of a miracle. It would only be justifiable if we were acquainted with the *modus operandi* which God would employ in the performance of one. But of this we are from the nature of the case necessarily ignorant. It is impossible for us to have any abstract knowledge whether God would bring such an occurrence about, by a combination of existing forces, or by neutralizing the action of one force by the superior energy of another, or by the direct action of his creative will. This being so, it is hardly possible to pursue a method which can involve us in greater difficulties than to introduce into our definition of a miracle some theory as to God's *modus operandi* in its performance, since from the nature of the case we must be ignorant of the mode in which He works in the Universe, except as far as his action is manifested in its known forces; and into the higher regions of the divine activity we are utterly unable to penetrate. Yet every consistent theist must hold that God is everywhere present energizing in the forces of nature, directing them and controlling them; for if there be a God the energies of the Universe must have issued from Him, and be dependent on Him. This being so, it is absolutely beyond our power to determine by what instrumentality He would effect a miracle if it were His pleasure to work one.

Next: What is the Nature to which miracles are alleged to be contrary, and what are its laws or its order which they are said to violate? Do we include within it the material universe, its necessary forces, and the sequences which inevitably result from their activity; or man, his reason, his free agency; in a word his intellectual and moral nature; or even everything that exists? It is evident that the question whether miracles involve violations of the laws or order of nature, or suspensions of the activity of its forces, or the counteraction of one force and the superior energy of another, will entirely depend on the class of phenomena which we include under the term "Nature." If we include in it free agency and its results the view which we take of the relation in which miracles stand to it and to its order will be quite different from what it would be, if we confined it to the material universe and its necessary forces. If man is a part of nature, it is evident that a being exists within it who is capable within certain limits of exerting a control over it.

It is unnecessary, in reference to the subject under discussion, to enter into the vexed question of necessity or freedom. All that we need do is to take the facts of consciousness as we find them; and it is wholly unnecessary to enter into a discussion about their origin. As a matter of fact, therefore, it is unquestionable that the forces which energize in the material universe are necessary ones; *i.e.* they are incapable, by any inherent power, of acting otherwise than they do. If nothing external to them interferes with their action, they will go on to all eternity grinding out the same invariable results, mutually acting and counteracting on one another. The never-ending sequences which result from their energy constitute the order of the material universe, which, if it existed alone, would leave no place for such an occurrence as a miracle, which, as I have said, is an event which manifests purpose. But wholly different is it, if man and the forces which energize in him, form a part of our conception of nature. In that case it becomes certain that a being exists in nature, who is capable of controlling it and modifying its order. It is beyond dispute that man acts on nature, and that the extent and mode of this action is determined, not by the blind action of necessary forces, but by the action of forces which are under the control of intelligent volition, and are capable of manifesting purpose.

It follows, therefore, that the action of man on nature differs wholly in character from that of the blind forces of the material universe which are incapable of acting otherwise than they do, or by any self-direction, of modifying their results. This being so, nature must be made up of two widely different factors, its blind unintelligent forces, and man, who by his intelligence and volition is capable of controlling those forces for the effectuation of purpose. In this point of view a miracle, as a deviation from the order of the material Universe, can be no more contrary to, or violate nature, than those actions of man which effectuate purpose.

It has often been objected that volition is not a force, and is incapable of creating any not already in existence. But for the purpose of this argument it is unnecessary to assume that it either is a force or can create force. One thing respecting it is certain, that it is capable of imparting a direction to, and combining existing forces, and of neutralizing the action of one force by the superior energy of another; and thereby it can effectuate results entirely different from those which would have taken place from the uncontrolled action of forces destitute of self-direction.

It follows, therefore, that man is capable of modifying the order of nature, for it is certain that a wholly different order of events must have taken place, had it not been for his intervention. To this the entire surface of the globe bears witness. Yet every one of the mighty results which man has effected, has been brought about without the suspension of a single force in the universe, or a violation of its laws. It follows, therefore, that whether man be included in Nature, or excluded from it, a being exists who is capable of using its necessary forces for the effectuation of purpose. If we include him, then a being capable of modifying its order exists within it. If, on the other hand, we exclude him from nature, then a being exists outside it who can do the same, without suspending its forces, or interfering with the laws of their activity. From this a further inference is inevitable. What man can do on a limited scale, the Creator of the universe must be able to effect on a much larger one. If man can change the direction of the forces of the universe, combine them, and neutralize one by the superior energy of another in such a way as to effectuate the results of purpose, without suspending them, much more must God be able to do the same for the effectuation of His purposes; since His ability to effectuate the results of purpose without suspending the action of any existing force, or introducing a new one, must be so much the greater as He is mightier and wiser. On the same principles it is no less certain that God can answer prayer, if it be His pleasure to do so, without any such interference with the forces of the universe, as some eminent men of science have affirmed to be necessary, and have, therefore rashly pronounced that the expectation of it is irrational. It may be contrary to His will to answer many prayers which are offered to Him; but this by no means affects the general principle that He can answer them when it is His pleasure to do so, without throwing the order of the universe into confusion.

These observations are not made with the smallest intention of affirming anything as to the agency which God must adopt in the performance of a miracle, on the supposition that it is His pleasure to work one; but for the purpose of guarding against the introduction of needless difficulties into the subject, which cause us to incur the danger of running counter to the truths of science. All that I am desirous of showing is, that the practice which has prevailed of laying down that a miracle must necessarily involve a violation or a suspension of the laws of nature; or that it is effected by the introduction of a higher law to act on a lower, is not only unnecessary, but dangerous; and also that by introducing into our definition of a miracle a number of ambiguous terms, it involves us in confusion of thought. Of this we have a remarkable illustration when a miracle is said to consist in the introduction of a higher law of nature to act on a lower law.* The neutralization of the action of one force by the superior energy of another, is a thing which we witness every day. Thus the chemical forces within a certain range neutralize but do not suspend that of gravitation; and the vital forces do the same for the chemical ones; and effect results wholly different from what would have come to pass from the single action of either of them. This is what man is continually doing, and thus he brings about the results of purpose by skilfully combining those forces over which he

* "So far from this, the true miracle is a higher and purer nature, coming down out of the world of untroubled harmonies into this world of ours, which so many discords have jarred and disturbed; and bringing them back again, though it is for one mysterious prophetic moment, into harmony with that higher. . . . We should term the miracle, not an infraction of a law, but behold in it a lower law neutralized, and for a time put out of working by a higher; and of this abundant analogous examples are evermore going forward before our eyes, Continually we behold in the world around us, lower laws held in restraint by higher, mechanic by dynamic, chemical by vital; physical by moral."—Trench, *On Miracles*, p. 15. Throughout this whole passage the terms Law and Nature are used without any definite meaning.

can exercise control. But laws can effectuate nothing. To speak therefore of a miracle as the result of the introduction of a higher law on the sphere of nature, is to use words as counters and not as representatives of realities.*

Similar ambiguities result when miracles are said to be violations or suspensions of the laws of nature. The thing probably intended is that they involve suspensions of its forces. Let the question be fairly asked, What laws must a miracle violate, or suspend? Surely not the invariable sequences which are the result of the energies of its forces, as for instance the law of bodies falling in the proportion of the inverse square under the influence of the force of gravitation. Viewed as a set of sequences, there is a sense in which man may be said to produce results contrary to the laws of nature, *i.e.* of the physical universe, or, to speak more correctly, contrary to the order, which would result from the action of its forces independently of his volition, whenever by a combination of them he brings about an order of events different from that which would have happened without such a combination. This he is accomplishing every day; and thus he introduces into the Universe an order of events different from that which would have occurred without his intervention. But this is in no proper sense a violation of the order of nature. The laws of nature are consequently no more violated by the performance of a miracle than they are by the activities of man.

But it may be objected that a law of nature, viewed as an invariable recurrence of a set of observed phenomena, as for

---

* "The chemical laws which would bring about decay in animal substances still subsist, even when they are hemmed in and hindered by the salt which keeps these substances from corruption. The law of sin in a regenerate man is held in continual check by the law of the Spirit of Life; yet it is in his members still, not indeed working, for a mightier law has stepped in, and now holds it in check, but still there, and ready to work."—Trench, *On Miracles*, p. 16. Surely such assertions not only confound laws and forces, but almost personify both.

example, that "all men must die," is violated by such a miracle as that of a resurrection. The whole force of the objection arises from importing into the conception of law that of causal power or force. As far as we use the term to denote a set of phenomena which have been invariable as far as human observation has extended, the effect of the occurrence of a different phenomenon, as for instance, the case of a man's not dying, would be to render it inapplicable to the occurrences in question. But the fallacy arises from making law a causal power. The expression "it is a law of nature that all men must die" simply means that there are a set of forces in constant operation which unless their action is counteracted by some other force must cause death. But if some counteracting forces could be brought to bear on man's bodily structure by which the action of those forces which result in death could be neutralized, no violation of the laws of nature would be the result. Thus it would be with a resurrection. What takes place in death? The cessation of the action of those vital forces (be they what they may) which control and neutralize the action of those chemical forces, which, if unrestrained by the former, would cause the dissolution of the frame; and which, when death has taken place, effect that dissolution. Without making any affirmation as to the means by which a resurrection might be effected by God, one thing is clear, that it must involve the reversal of the process of dissolution; or in other words the presence of a power capable of neutralizing the forces which have resulted in death; and the presence of such a vital force as is capable of reconstructing the bodily frame and imparting a renewed activity to its organism. What force or forces may be capable of bringing about such a result, we have no knowledge; but we know that a force exists which in our ignorance of its true nature we call the vital force, which has built up our bodily frames out of a mere germ. This has been effected without the smallest violation of any law or order of nature, though in the course of its activity it has neutralized the action of other forces which would have exerted an opposite influence if left to their unrestrained action. As this process has been effected once without any violation of such order, there is no reason why the might of the Creator should not be able to effect it a second time without any violation of it. Abstractedly we should probably have deemed it impossible to construct a body in the way in which it is actually accomplished; it is therefore impossible for us to affirm that the Creator cannot reverse the process without any violation of the forces, laws, or order of nature. There is nothing in the nature of the case more difficult in the effecting of a resurrection than there is in what God has actually accomplished—the formation of our present bodies by the combination of the forces of the universe which He has under his control. Many of the forces by which the first portions of the process have been effected are hidden ones, but they are real, though they cannot be measured by any of our instruments. So may it be with a resurrection. Surely that Being who has built our bodies by means of forces actually existing in the Universe, without once violating its order, if it be His pleasure to do so, can rebuild them without introducing the smallest particle of confusion into His creative work. Ignorant as we are of the mode of the Creator's working, we can have no possible ground for affirming that the mode of His action in the performance of a miracle must differ from that of His ordinary providence. He must be a bold man who will venture to affirm that we are acquainted with all the forces of the Universe which are under His control, or all the possible combinations of them by which He may work out results in the distant ages of the future very different from man's narrow experience in the past.

It follows therefore that we are only incumbering the question with needless difficulties when we introduce into our conception of a miracle some theory as to the mode of the divine action in its performance. It is clear that there is not the smallest necessity to affirm that the performance of one must involve either a directly creative act of God, or a violation or suspension of the action of any law or force in nature. I do not mean to affirm that such may not have been the mode of the divine working, but that it is wholly unnecessary to assert that it must have been. The only thing necessary to the conception of a miracle is that it should be some manifestation of the divine activity which exhibits special purpose on the part of God, and the only thing necessary for its performance is the active operation or the combination of such forces as are adequate to accomplish it.

As on general grounds the introduction of these questions into the controversy about miracles is unnecessary, so it is without any support whatever from anything which is affirmed respecting them in the Bible. If the sacred writers had made any affirmation as to the mode of the divine action in the performance of miracles we should have been compelled to adopt it, and to abide by the consequences of doing so. Whatever difficulties we encounter on this subject are, however, entirely of our own creation, and cannot possibly be charged on Holy Scripture. I have already observed that as far as the Old Testament is concerned no distinction is made between God as the worker of miracles and God as the active agent in Providence. If a miracle is referred to as a wonder, God's operations in nature are affirmed to be wonderful; if as an act of power, still greater displays of might are ascribed to Him in His ordinary Providence; if it is referred to as a proof of the divine working, so are all the operations of the Universe. "When the waves of the sea arise," says the Psalmist, "thou stillest them." "In His hands are the deep places of the earth; the strength of the hills is His also; the sea is His, and He made it, and His hands prepared the dry land." The writers of the Old Testament were certainly without the smallest idea that God was violating the order of the Universe when He wrought miracles. I am aware that it has been urged that the writers of the Bible did not recognize any order in the Universe at all, but this objection never could have been urged if the most palpable facts had not been carelessly overlooked.* Nor is the case different with the New Testament. It contains not a single affirmation as to the *modus operandi* by which a miracle was accomplished, or a hint that it suspended either the forces or laws of the Universe. On the contrary, during the performance of some of Our Lord's miracles, the intimations that the forces of the Universe were not suspended are sufficiently definite. We may take Peter's walking on the water as a crucial example. It has been affirmed that the force of gravitation must have been suspended in his favour. But the narrative affirms the contrary, for the sacred writer tells us that the moment Peter's faith failed him he began to sink, thus proving that the power of gravitation was not suspended for a moment. The only thing necessary was the presence of some force capable of neutralizing its action on Peter's body, precisely in the same way as it is constantly neutralized by ourselves whenever we lift a weight from the ground. In whatever way the miracle was performed it is clear that the suspension of the force of gravitation formed no portion of it.

Equally gratuitous is the affirmation that the performance of certain miracles must have involved an act of creative power. As far as we have any hints in the New Testament, it is clear that its authors did not suppose that the performance of a miracle was attended by an act of creation. Thus in the miracle of turning the water into wine, the wine was not produced in the empty jars, but an express direction was given to fill them first with water, and then the water was converted into wine. Of the mode of effecting it we are not informed; but there is nothing to imply that the performance of this miracle added one ounce to the weight of the globe. The jars were filled with water, and the water became wine. God slowly produces the grape out of substances already existing, of which water is the chief, by a set of elaborate combinations of the forces

* Psalms 19, 33, 104, 111, 139, 148.

of the Universe. The grapes are gathered by man, and then subjected by him to the action of another set of forces more or less under his control, and by these are converted into wine. This process we think nothing wonderful, because we habitually witness it. In the case of the miracle He turned the water into wine in some other way, by the use of forces of which we have had no prior experience; but there is nothing to imply that in this operation He violated or suspended any force or law of the Universe, or created one particle of matter which was not already in existence. I make this last observation because it is this supposed creation of matter in certain miracles, thereby adding to the weight of the globe, which endangers our coming in collision with physical science. The same observations are applicable to the miracle of the multiplication of the loaves and fishes. All the materials were at hand, either in the earth, the air, or the water. The ordinary action of God's Providence makes bread and fish in one way: in a miracle He produces them in another. In the former case we understand some portion of the process, though the remainder is buried in profound darkness. In the latter the whole process is hidden from our view.

Another striking phenomenon in the miracles of the New Testament, pointing to a similar result, is the remarkable economy in the exercise of miraculous power displayed in them. Ordinary means are invariably had recourse to where they are sufficient to effect the end in view; and where they are adequate, miracle is never invoked. Thus, in the miracle of the resurrection of Lazarus, the stone is ordered to be removed by human hands; and after the dead man was recalled to life the grave-clothes are directed to be removed by the same agency. So again, after the miracle wrought on Jairus' daughter, Our Lord, who is described as having miraculously fed the multitudes, directs the parents to furnish her with food. Whatever was the nature of the divine intervention in these miracles it was clearly limited to the smallest possible extent. This economy in the use of miracle forms one of the remarkable characteristics which distinguish those of the New Testament from all other miraculous narratives. In the case of the resurrection of Lazarus a forger would hardly have been able to refrain from ordering the stone to roll back of itself; still less would it have occurred to such a person to direct that a child just raised from the dead should be furnished with a supply of food.

But the overwhelming majority of the miracles of the New Testament were wrought not on dead matter but on the living organism of the human body. Of the mode of action of no force which comes under human observation are we more profoundly ignorant than of the vital ones, or of the mode or extent in which mind can act on matter. In this region, therefore, it is quite clear that a Being, who is thoroughly acquainted with the vital forces, and holds them in His hand, can work miracles without any disturbance of the forces, laws, or order of nature.

In several of the Old Testament miracles the affirmation of the active presence of what have been designated second causes, or in other words the known forces of the Universe, as the means through which they were accomplished, is direct. Thus the miracle of the dividing of the Red Sea, and of the supply of quails, is asserted to have been effected through the agency of a wind blowing in a particular direction. A similar affirmation is made respecting several of the plagues of Egypt. A similar principle, though less obvious, may be detected in other miracles. All these instances prove that the introduction of a particular theory of the mode of the divine action into the conception of a miracle is entirely uncalled for by anything which is asserted in the pages of the Old or the New Testament. Nor can it be shown to be necessary on any grounds of solid reason.

The whole theory that miracles must be contrary to nature, and that their performance must involve violations or suspensions of its laws and forces, arises out of a practical denial that God is everywhere every moment energizing in nature; in fact it involves the assumption that the Universe is a huge machine, outside which the Creator, if there be a Creator at all, exists—a machine which He has once contrived and set in motion, and will go on for ever grinding out results by the never ceasing activity of its forces, without any further exercise of His power. To such a conception of the Universe a miracle becomes a special intervention of the Creator, interrupting the order of its working, and consequently an indication of His presence in that from which He had previously retired.* Such a conception of God differs wholly from the God of the Bible, which contains the only worthy theistic conception of Him, not only as the Creator of the Universe, a skilful mechanist and chemist, but the Father of those beings whom he has created. Christian theism affirms that God is not only a Being who exists independently of the Universe, but that in Him we live, and move, and exist; that the earth is the Lord's and the fulness thereof, the compass of the world and they that dwell therein; and that all its forces and energies are the manifestations of His ceaseless activity. What we designate the forces of nature, and miracles, are alike manifestations of God, the latter differing from the former not in the degree of power which they exhibit, nor in the fact that He is more present when He works a miracle than He is in the active energies of those forces in the midst of which we daily live, but in the fact that a miracle is an event fitted to awaken attention by a special manifestation of intelligent purpose, and stamped with the indications of it. As such it constitutes a σημεῖον, and possesses an evidential value.

* Such a view of the Universe (undoubtedly a very popular one at the present day among scientific men) is involved in the conception of a miracle as the effect of the introduction of a higher law. (See Mozley's *Bampton Lectures*, Lecture VI.) The whole idea involves the confusion between the conceptions of law and force which I have already referred to, as well as the mechanical view of the Universe as a bare machine in which He is not immanent, but to the action of which He stands outside.

LECTURE II.

"I am one that bear witness of myself, and the Father that sent me beareth witness of me."—JOHN VIII. 18.

AT the conclusion of the last Lecture I offered some general considerations for the purpose of showing that the argument from miracles ought to occupy a less prominent place among the evidences of Christianity, than that which has been assigned to it in our modern apologetic works. The proper function which they discharge in relation to the Christian argument is a matter of such deep importance, that before I proceed to deal with the reconstructive portion of it, I must endeavour to estimate their proper value. While doing so, I must ask you to bear in mind the distinction which I have laid down between the word, "Miracle," in its ordinary acceptation as an extraordinary occurrence in the physical Universe, and those manifestations of a superhuman power in the moral and spiritual world, which I have designated moral miracles.

I shall assume as the foundation of my argument, that it is an established philosophic truth, that the forces which energize in the moral and spiritual world, act in conformity with moral laws no less than those which dominate in the physical Universe with physical ones. As, therefore, an event which manifests purpose, for the origin of which the known forces of the physical Universe are unable to account, is a physical miracle; so an event in the moral Universe, of the origin of which the forces energizing in man can give no explanation, is a moral miracle; and is, therefore, the manifestation of the energetic presence of a superhuman power.

The moral miracle possesses this advantage over the physical one in point of evidential value. To those who believe in conformity with the theism of the Bible,* that God is energizing in all the forces of nature, there is some difficulty in laying down a clear line of distinction between miracles, and remarkable acts of His providential government, as they are both alike manifestations of a divine energy. (See Supplement I.) On the other hand, those who view the Universe as a piece of self-acting mechanism, are always able to account for the occurrence of an extra-

---

* Whatever may be said for any other species of theism, such as that which contemplates the forces of the Universe as having an objective existence, by the action of which it has been evolved, independently of the immanence in them of the Creator, of whose activity they are the manifestations, as an intellectual necessity, it evidently differs widely from the theism of the Bible. If one thing is more certain than another, it is that the Bible contemplates God as immanent in the forces of nature, and that they are the manifestations of His energies, equally as any miracle recorded in its pages. He has not retired from Creation, but is present energizing in it every moment. This is not only beyond all contradiction the theism of the Old Testament, of which the book of Psalms forms a perpetual witness, but also that of the New. Thus Our Lord not only expressly affirms that His Father works hitherto, and He in imitation of Him; but he ascribes to His energetic action the rising of the sun, the falling of rain, the beauty of the flowers, the feeding of the animal races, and a providential care over man, even to the extent that a hair does not fall to the ground without His providence. The God of the Bible is not only immanent in the Universe, and energizing in its forces, but its moral governor, and the Father of rational creatures. The God of philosophy is assumed merely as an intellectual necessity. The authors of *The Unseen Universe* lay down that it is the duty of science to banish God as far as possible into the regions of the unknowable. With them the Universe is a huge machine. The authors of the Bible affirm that it is our duty to recognize in all His creative works the manifestation of the presence and energies of Him who is our **Father.**

ordinary event, by assigning it to the action of some force which has never yet come under human observation. But as the long experience of history has made us thoroughly acquainted with the forces which energize in man, an occurrence in the moral world which transcends their power to have produced, is a direct proof of the presence of a superhuman power. Hitherto the attention of evidential writers has been almost exclusively directed to physical miracles, while the evidence afforded by moral ones has been comparatively neglected. I propose, on the contrary, to appeal to the might with which Jesus Christ has energized in history; to His whole character as it is depicted in the Gospels; and to the elevation of His teaching above the conditions which, in conformity with the laws of the moral world, were imposed on Him by the environment of thought in the midst of which He was born and educated, as constituting a proof capable of being verified by the most palpable facts of history, of the presence in Christianity of an element which is superhuman.

What then is the evidential value of miracles; and in what relation do they stand to the Christian argument? In answering this question the obvious course is not to start with a number of *à priori* assumptions, but to ascertain what views the writers of the New Testament have propounded on the subject. Have they in fact made any affirmations respecting the functions of miracles in connection with Christianity, and if so, what are they? Nothing can be more absurd than to claim for them an evidential value which was unknown to those who actually performed them.

Many modern writers have affirmed that miracles constitute the sole evidences of a revelation, and that there are truths in Christianity which would be utterly incredible unless they were thus confirmed. The question, therefore, becomes one of supreme importance—Are such opinions as to the functions of miracles borne out by the contents of the New Testament? Above all what are the grounds on which Our Lord himself rested his claims to a divine Mission? I will answer this latter question first.

It is clear that Our Lord did not rest his claim to be the Christ, nor to the acceptance of his teaching as authoritative and divine, exclusively on the miracles which he performed. Of this the text is one out of many direct affirmations, "I am one that bear witness of myself, and the Father that sent me beareth witness of me." In this passage a marked distinction is laid down between his own testimony and that of his Father to the truth of his divine mission. In what did that distinction consist? His own testimony must have been his self-evidencing divine character; the testimony of his Father, the miracles that he performed. No other distinction is possible. The same truth is brought out in another passage. "If I do not the works of my Father, believe me not, but if I do, though ye believe not me, believe the works, that ye may see and believe that the Father is in me, and I in Him" (John iv. 37, 38).

These words are important, because they are addressed by Our Lord to his opponents, and therefore they throw a clear light on my position. Our Lord affirmed that they ought to have believed in him on his own testimony, *i.e.* on the evidence afforded by his moral and spiritual character, and his entire working, which he addressed to the depths of the human spirit. If however they were incapable of appreciating this, then he appeals to his miraculous works, yet not as mere wonders or energies of power, but to their entire moral environment; nor even to them as simply evidencing a divine commission, but to their special character as proving his direct union with the Father, as he himself puts it, "that ye may see and believe that the Father is in me and I in him."

Secondly: the account of the interview between Our Lord and Nicodemus proves that the latter, even from his own low standpoint, did not view miracles alone apart from their attending circumstances as sufficient proofs of a divine commission. "Rabbi," says he, "we know that thou art a teacher come from God, for no man can do these miracles that thou doest except God be with him." Such words imply that, in the opinion of the speaker, a certain class of miracles could be wrought without the intervention of God. We are not told how he discriminated between the one class and the other, but there can be little doubt that it must have been by their moral impress. The Divine Speaker, however, rests the acceptance of His testimony on higher grounds than the attestation of miracles wrought for the purpose of confirming the truth of his assertions. "We speak that we do know, and testify that we have seen, and ye receive not our witness." He then proceeds in the remainder of the discourse to make a number of affirmations respecting His own divine character, which the whole context makes it clear that Nicodemus must have heard with profound astonishment, yet He not only works no miracle to prove the truth of His affirmations, but does not make any allusion to them as distinct from his general superhuman working.

Here it is important that I should draw attention to the term by which Our Lord throughout this Gospel designates His miracles. They are His *works* (ἔργα). By the use of such a term it is clear that He did not view them as a class of actions standing by themselves, but as portions of His divine working. His working included not only His miracles but His entire divine life, His actions, and His teaching. It is a remarkable fact that this use of the word ἔργα is almost peculiar to Our Lord, proving that He viewed His miracles, not as standing in a class by themselves, but as constituting a portion of the manifestation of the divine which dwelt within Him. The sacred writers, when they refer to miracles, usually designate them as "signs" (σημεῖα), less frequently, "mighty works" (δυνάμεις), and "wonders" (τέρατα). But Our Lord Himself never uses these terms except when He is stating the views of others respecting them; as when He addressed the nobleman of Capernaum, " Except ye see signs and wonders, ye will not believe."

Thirdly: the following utterances, even if they stood alone, would afford strong proof that Our Lord considered that He had higher evidences of His divine character than that which could be afforded by mere objective miracles, and that He appealed to these latter only when the others failed. Thus He says to the Jews, "Though ye believe not me, believe the works." But His "works" are meant to include His whole superhuman working, of which His miracles formed a remarkable portion, and were stamped with the moral perfection of His character. Thus "The works which the Father hath given me to finish, the same works which I do bear witness of me that the Father hath sent me," must embrace the whole of that divine work which He came to accomplish. A similar view is propounded in His prayer of intercession, "I have glorified thee on the earth; I have finished the work that thou gavest me to do," a work which is subsequently defined as consisting in the manifestation of His Father. So likewise in the declaration made to the disciples, "My meat is to do the will of him that sent me, and to finish his work." The working of Our Lord, in short, included the whole of His divine life and actions, in which those who witnessed it, beheld "the glory of the only begotten of the Father, full of grace and truth." Such a manifestation must necessarily have been self-evidential.

Fourthly: The entire discourse recorded in the eighth chapter definitely affirms that Our Lord laid claim to a higher class of evidence than that of mere objective miracles contemplated as "mighty acts" or "wonders" in proof of His superhuman claims. This chapter is particularly important as bearing on the present question, because throughout it Our Lord is reasoning with His opponents. It will be sufficient to cite the following passage:—"And because I tell you the truth ye believe me not. Which of you convinceth me of sin? and if I say the truth why do ye not believe me? He that is of God heareth God's words. Ye therefore hear **them not because ye are not of God."**

The entire reasoning throughout this chapter is made to turn on Our Lord's self-evidencing character. It is most remarkable that throughout the whole argument Our Lord never once refers to a miracle either in its character of a mighty work, a wonder, or even a sign. On the contrary, He rests His claim to be believed in His complete and absolute sinlessness. "Which if you convinceth me of sin?" says He, "and if I say the truth why do ye not believe me?" The perfection of his holiness, as he affirms, constituted the great proof that his teaching was worthy of all acceptation. His testimony was in fact that of an eye-witness who could not fail to know the truth of the things which He uttered by the directness of his intercommunion with God, and his perfect sinlessness was the guarantee of the truth of his assertions. "I speak," says He, "what I have seen with my Father, and ye do what ye have seen with your Father." But further: it is worthy of particular notice that immediately after making these declarations, He proceeds to make one of the strongest affirmations of His divine character which is to be found in the Gospels—"Before Abraham was I am." According to the views which have been entertained by many on this subject, Our Lord ought to have performed one of His greatest miracles in confirmation of the truth of so astounding a statement, as being the only thing which could give it credibility, yet throughout the whole discourse He never once alludes to His miracles, which He surely would have done if He had regarded them as the sole or even the chief guarantee of His veracity.

Fifthly: Another striking proof that Our Lord uniformly appealed to the self-evidencing power manifesting itself in His person is contained in His last discourse. The apostle Philip makes a definite request that He would afford them a visible manifestation of the Father, and declares that if He would do so it would be sufficient for their complete conviction. What is Our Lord's reply? "Have I been so long time with you, and yet has thou not known me, Philip? He that hath seen me hath seen the Father, and how sayest thou, Show us the Father? Believest thou not that I am in the Father, and the Father in me? The words that I speak unto you I speak not of myself, but the Father who dwelleth in me, he doeth the works. Believe me that I am in the Father, and the Father in me; or else believe me for the works' sake." Such an affirmation, even if it stood alone, would prove conclusively that the evidence afforded by the presence of the divine in Our Lord's person and working ought to occupy a very prominent place in the Christian argument. But further: Our Lord affirmed that He was the light of the world. This is equivalent to the assertion that His person and work were self-evidential; or in other words, as the best proof that the sun is shining is to turn and behold its beams, so the strongest evidence of the existence of the spiritual Sun is the light which He emits. A pretender to be the light of the world, who emits no radiance, is self-convicted of being an impostor.

Sixthly: Although no such explicit affirmations are to be found in the Synoptics, they afford abundant confirmations of the same view. They fully concur with St. John that whenever Our Lord's opponents challenged Him to work a miracle as a proof of His divine mission, He uniformly refused to do so. This seems inexplicable, if He viewed them as constituting its sole and only proof. But they inform us of the further fact, that He was deeply grieved when this demand was made on Him; that He declared that it was an evil and adulterous generation that sought after a sign of this description; and that the only sign which He would afford them would be the sign of the prophet Jonas, *i.e.* His own death and resurrection. It seems incredible that persons who have attributed to Our Lord utterances of this description could have held the views laid down in some of our modern evidential treatises that miracles form the exclusive attestation of a divine mission.

Neither the Synoptics nor St. John have once represented Our Lord as performing miracles for the purpose of proving the truth of any doctrine or moral precept uttered by Him. Whenever they mention His motive at all for performing them, they nearly uniformly ascribe it to His divine compassion, or to its being an answer to a prayer for help. The only exceptions are, when Our Lord cured the paralytic in proof that He had power on earth to forgive sins; and when He wrought several miracles in reply to the message sent Him by John the Baptist, " Art thou he that should come, or look we for another?" In his reply, he directed the messengers to report the miracles they had seen and heard, as proofs of His Messianic character.* To these may be added the miracle of the Resurrection of Lazarus, which is directly stated to have been wrought that the people which stood by might believe that the Father had sent Him. But so far were Our Lord's miracles from being performed with the direct purpose of proving either doctrines, precepts, or even His divine mission, that in no inconsiderable number of cases, He strictly charged those whom He healed to keep

* St. Luke's account is as follows:—"When the men were come unto him, they said, John Baptist hath sent us unto thee saying, Art thou he that should come, or look we for another? And the same hour he cured many of their infirmities, and plagues, and of evil spirits, and unto many that were blind, he gave sight. Then Jesus answering said unto them, Go your way, and tell John what things ye have seen and heard; how that the blind see, the lame walk, the lepers are cleansed, the deaf hear, the dead are raised, to the poor the Gospel is preached. And blessed is he whosoever shall not be offended in me" (Luke vii. 20-23). The miracles wrought on this occasion were evidently wrought for an evidential purpose; but they were not merely performed as proofs of a divine commission, but as works which were suitable for the Messiah to perform as part of His divine character. As such, several of them are directly attributed to the Messiah in the Old Testament Scriptures. It should be observed that among them, the preaching the Gospel to the poor holds an equal rank with those occurrences which we commonly designate as miracles, a reference which not only points out the fulfilment of the prediction of the prophet, but draws attention to their moral aspect. Besides, the miracles in question are all works of healing—not wonders wrought in the physical universe—being manifestations of the divine goodness which dwelt in Our Lord; and as such, proofs of His Messianic character.

the miracle secret. It is simply impossible that such miracles could have been wrought for directly evidential purposes, though all miracles, as portions of His divine working, and as manifestations of the superhuman power which dwelt within Him, were evidential in the sense so often referred to in St. John's gospel. In this point of view, they form at the same time portions of the Revelation, and of its evidence.

Such then are Our Lord's affirmations on this subject. They prove beyond contradiction that He considered His own divine character and working self-evidential; and that it formed a higher attestation to His divine mission than miracles viewed as mere wonders and mighty deeds. Also that the right view to take of the miracles which He performed is, not that they are merely marvellous acts of power, displayed in the physical Universe, but essential portions of His divine working, entirely in harmony with it, and stamped with the same moral impress. Viewed in this aspect, the perfection of His divine character and working constitutes His witness to Himself; and His miracles, bearing the impress of the same character, the testimony of the Father to His Divine Mission.

The self-evidencing power of Our Lord's divine person and working occupies a very prominent place in the Apostolic Epistles.

1. The affirmations made by St. John on this point in his first Epistle and in the prologue to his Gospel are conclusive. I have fully examined them in a supplement to the first Lecture, and, therefore, I need not adduce them here. It will be sufficient to observe that they affirm in the clearest manner that the highest form of Christian evidence consists in the manifestation of the divine, made in the person of Jesus Christ. This is in fact the burden of the entire Epistle.

2. St. Paul's mode of placing the claims of Christianity to be accepted as a divine revelation is precisely similar. With his Epistles in our hands it is impossible to doubt that the Apostle viewed the moral and spiritual power residing

in the person of Jesus Christ as the all commanding evidence of His Divine Mission. He again and again declares that this had formed the very centre and essence of his teaching; and he appeals to those to whom he wrote as witnesses of the mighty effects which it had wrought in them. That teaching which had been mighty to lay deep the foundation of the Christian Church, and had manifested the energetic power of which they were the monuments, might be summed up in two pregnant sentences—Christ, the power of God, and Christ, the wisdom of God. They make it clear that the Apostle was not in the habit of appealing to miracles as the sole or even the most conclusive evidence of Christianity. In fact, he has never once appealed to them in this light, neither in the Epistles themselves nor in his discourses as recorded in the Acts. With him the great evidential miracle of Christianity is the Resurrection; his references to other miracles wrought by Our Lord are indirect, and only three, or at most four times has he referred to any as having been wrought by himself. These he viewed not as proofs of his divine commission but as manifestations of a divine power residing in Jesus Christ, and, as such, proofs of His Resurrection. Numerous and profound as are his doctrinal statements, and vehement as was the opposition of his opponents to certain aspects of the Gospel which he preached, it never once occurred to him to work a miracle in vindication of their truth. It is clear, therefore, that he could not have regarded miracles as the necessary confirmations of his doctrines.

Portions of the Acts afford on this point strong confirmatory evidence. In dealing with Jews and Proselytes, he is uniformly described as endeavouring to prove that Jesus was the Messiah, not by working miracles in their synagogues, but by reasonings drawn from the Old Testament Scriptures. When he addressed heathen auditories, his first efforts were directed to prove the Unity and Fatherhood of God, and he concludes by referring to the Resurrection as a proof that God would render to men hereafter a righteous retribution according to their deeds. He describes his own teaching as having consisted of two things, repentance towards God, and faith in our Lord Jesus Christ, but nowhere does he intimate that miracles formed the groundwork or the chief support of his arguments. This is rendered the more remarkable because the historian tells us that he wrought miracles at Cyprus, at Lystra, at Philippi, and at Ephesus; yet neither in his discourses recorded in the Acts nor in his Epistles addressed to these latter Churches does he make a single allusion to them. One miracle, and one only, is habitually appealed to by him, the Resurrection of Our Lord.

3. It will be only necessary to notice one further affirmation made by the writers of the New Testament on this subject, the remarkable one which is contained in the Epistle to the Hebrews. Having spoken of the revelation made of the perfections of God in Our Lord's divine person the author says, "How shall we escape if we neglect so great salvation, which at the first began to be spoken by the Lord, and was confirmed unto us by them that heard him, God also bearing them witness (συνεπιμαρτυροῦντος τοῦ Θεοῦ, God also bearing a joint and additional testimony) with signs, and wonders, and with divers miracles, and gifts of the Holy Ghost, according to His own will."—Heb. ii. 3, 4.

Here the enumeration of miracles is complete in all the various aspects in which they are presented to us in the New Testament. Respecting them the author makes the following affirmations:—

1. That the great salvation spoken of in the first chapter was announced by Our Lord.

2. That it was confirmed by the testimony of eye-witnesses of the facts.

3. That the various classes of miracles which took place in the Apostolic Church formed a conjoint and additional testimony to its truth, the miracles not standing by themselves but forming a portion of the same divine working (συνεπιμαρτυροῦντος τοῦ Θεοῦ). In conformity with this, several of the miracles recorded in the Acts of the Apostles

are stated to have been wrought in proof of the Resurrection of Our Lord. As such they are affirmed to be manifestations of His living energy rather than proofs of His Divine Mission.

A few further brief remarks will be necessary, as to the nature of some of the other miraculous occurrences recorded in the New Testament.

1. A considerable number of these, while they are manifestations of a superhuman power, were certainly not performed for directly evidential purposes. Some of them were providential, as the liberation of St. Peter from prison. Others were answers to the prayer of faith, as the cures mentioned by St. James, which were effected by prayer, and by anointing the sick with oil in the name of the Lord.* These evidently partook of a semi-miraculous character, and were only evidential as being manifestations of the presence of the divine Spirit abiding in the Church.

2. Two other cases of miraculous occurrences mentioned in the history are of a very peculiar character; I allude to the cures said to have been wrought by the passing of Peter's shadow; and by garments which, during his abode at Ephesus, were brought from St. Paul's person, and applied to the sick. It seems impossible to regard these as intended for evidential purposes. The historian describes the latter as occurrences of a very unusual kind. The manifestation seems to have taken place at Ephesus alone, a city which was especially addicted to the practice of Magic. This latter circumstance must have deprived them, in

---

* The passage in St. James is as follows:—"Is any sick among you? let him call for the elders of the Church; and let them pray over him, anointing him with oil in the name of the Lord. And the prayer of faith shall save the sick ; and the Lord shall raise him up; and if he hath committed sins, they shall be forgiven him."—James v. 14, 15. The cure is here expressly described as being an answer to prayer; and it is implied that it would be gradually effected. Consequently it is impossible to appeal to it as an evidential miracle, since it forms no attestation to a Divine Mission.

the eyes of the heathen inhabitants, of any value as proofs of a divine commission. All that they could have proved, would have been the presence of some kind of superhuman agency, similar to those in which they already believed; but they could have had no means of identifying it with that of the only God. But although they could not have been in our modern sense of the word evidential miracles, there was a very important purpose which these, and others which are mentioned in the New Testament, were fitted to subserve, viz. that of arresting attention, and procuring a hearing for the Christian missionary. This purpose has been far too generally overlooked in this controversy. The difficulty which the primitive missionary must have encountered in obtaining a hearing for his message must have been extreme. He was a member of a despised race, and consequently subject to all the disadvantages attending one who belongs to an inferior civilization, when he sets himself up as a teacher of those who consider themselves his superiors. Even our modern missionary finds a difficulty in commanding the attention of his hearers, though he goes armed with all the appliances of a higher civilization, and the advantage of being a member of a dominant race. But if the primitive believers had some of those miraculous endowments which are referred to in the New Testament, such as the gifts of healing, the difficulty in question would have been greatly obviated. Such seems to have been the character of St. Paul's cure of the cripple at Derbe. To the heathen inhabitants it evidently had no evidential value, as they attributed it to a visit from their own gods. But it served a valuable purpose in procuring their attention to the teaching of two despised Jews. Such also seems to have been the purpose of many of the manifestations of superhuman power in the early Church.

3. To this class belong those numerous superhuman endowments which are described with considerable detail in

the Epistles to the Corinthians and repeatedly referred to elsewhere in the New Testament as possessed by large numbers of the primitive believers.

They are uniformly represented as being the fulfilment of the promises of supernatural assistance which were made by Our Lord to His followers, to qualify them for the work of laying deep the foundations of His Church. But with two exceptions, they differ wholly from what we now designate evidential miracles. These gifts, according to the enumeration of St. Paul, were nine in number, two of which only conferred miraculous powers; and the remaining seven, as many distinct mental endowments. The purpose of these latter was evidently providential, conferring a supernatural enlightenment within their special spheres of activity. As such they were fitted to supply the defects in the character and training of the primitive converts, taken, as large numbers of them were, from the lower strata of society, thereby qualifying them for the arduous work of setting up the Church as a visible community in the world, for which their natural powers would have been utterly unfit.* The precise distinction between the two miraculous gifts it is now impossible to determine; but we shall not greatly err, if we suppose that one of them, χαρίσματα ἰαμάτων, was the gift mentioned by St. James, and conferred on the missionary those powers which were necessary for commanding the attention of heathen audiences, just as in modern times

* The following is the complete list of them:—1. The word of wisdom. 2. The word of knowledge. 3. The gift of faith. 4. Gifts of healing, χαρίσματα ἰαμάτων. 5. The working of miracles, ἐνεργή- ματα δυναμίων. 6. The gift of prophecy. 7. That of discerning of spirits. 8. Divers kinds of tongues. 9. Interpretation. The conclusion of the chapter contains a second list of the same gifts, viewed as qualifications for special offices in the Church. Their order is as follows:—1. Apostles. 2. Prophets. 3. Teachers. 4. Miracles. 5. Gifts of healing. 6. Helps. 7. Governments. 8. Diversities of tongues. 9. Interpretation. I shall consider the nature and evidential value of these supernatural endowments more at length in the Sixth Lecture.

the union of the functions of missionary and physician is found so influential a mode of procuring attention among uncultivated people. These gifts are uniformly represented as proofs of the energetic action of Christ in the Church; and the results of His resurrection and ascension into heaven; but they are never appealed to as evidential miracles, from which they differed in their entire conception.

Such are the affirmations of the New Testament on this subject. From which I draw the following conclusions.

First, that Our Lord's divine person is self-evidential; and that the various manifestations of the divine which have been exhibited in Him, whether they are recorded in the New Testament, or subsequently manifested in history, constitute the highest evidence that He came forth from God; and therefore that they ought to be placed in the front of the Christian argument.

Secondly, that the evidential value of miracles, viewed merely as objective facts in the physical universe, is subordinate to this, and in estimating it, it is necessary to take into account the moral impress which they bear.

Thirdly, that while all miracles, as being manifestations of the divine on the sphere of the human, have an indirectly evidential value, a considerable number of those wrought by Our Lord were not performed for the purposes of proof; but stand in the same relation to Him as ordinary actions do to other men.

Fourthly, while several of the apostolic miracles were wrought for the express purpose of proving to those who witnessed them the truth of Our Lord's resurrection, and of His Messianic character consequent thereon, a very considerable number of them were wrought for merely providential purposes, and consequently were only indirectly evidential.

Fifthly, that the great evidential miracle of Christianity is the Resurrection of Jesus Christ, which, if it can be proved to have been an objective fact, will carry all the other miracles in the Gospels along with it.

Having determined what is the relative importance of these evidences it will now be my duty to lay before you a sketch of the line of argument which the exigencies of modern thought require us to place in the front of the Christian position.

We have seen that the great difficulty with which the argument from miracles is attended is the intricacy of the proof by which it is necessary to establish their occurrence, and the difficulties which have been suggested with respect to portions of that proof. The question, therefore, becomes of the highest importance, Is there any other species of evidence which will lead us to the same result by a less circuitous route? The whole course of modern thought has produced in the minds of men an urgent demand that our beliefs should be based on facts which admit of some species of verification; and a conviction that long processes of reasoning, which are incapable of being submitted to such a test, are unreliable. This being so, the method which I propose to pursue in this inquiry is one which is in strict conformity with the principles of the inductive philosophy. I shall inquire, therefore, whether we can discover either in the history of the past or in the facts of the present anything in Christianity which manifests the action of a superhuman power, and whether it is possible for those facts connected with it, the truth of which is beyond dispute, to be accounted for as the mere result of the forces that energize in man.

I shall base my reasonings only on facts which are either verifiable in the history of the past or of which we have present experience. In drawing inferences from them I shall assume such only to be valid as are in conformity with the realities of human nature and the past experience of history. This mode of inquiry is strictly analogous to that by which our discoveries in physical science have been effected. In fact it involves the application of the inductive method of investigation to the facts and phenomena of Christianity, a method which is strictly in conformity with the requirements of modern thought. I shall therefore directly put the question, Do the known forces which energize in man give any rational account of the might with which Jesus Christ has energized in history? If not, His action in history must be the manifestation of a superhuman power. If we can discern distinct manifestations of a superhuman power energizing in Christianity it will form a far more decisive proof of its being a divine revelation than the long and intricate argument from miracles.

My argument is founded on the principles of common sense. If Christianity is divine we ought to be able to discern in it the clear indications of the operation of a superhuman power. If Jesus Christ really was what the writings of St. John and St. Paul affirm Him to have been surely we ought to be able to discover in Him the action and presence of forces different from those which operate in ordinary humanity. If He is the light of the world that light must be visible to those who seek for it. If He is a living power energizing in the Church, its Governor and Head, indications must exist of that life and energy; or to put the same idea in other words, the action of Jesus Christ in history ought to have been different from that of all other men however great. If a divine attractiveness dwells within Him He ought to manifest such a power of attracting the human heart as has been manifested by none other beside Him. If Jesus Christ was a manifestation of the divine on the sphere of the human, then His entire work and teaching ought to manifest a breadth and depth which has been possessed by no other man—one which is absolutely unique —in fact His entire character, and not merely those actions which are commonly called miraculous, ought to be instinct with the presence of the divine.

The great question, therefore, for us to consider is, Are any such manifestations of the divine discoverable in connection with Jesus Christ? On these and similar points the evidence is of no doubtful character. Present facts, no less than the unquestionable testimony of history, prove that He stands on an elevation, which, among the sons of men, is solitary and alone. But if He be the one man who has no peer, His solitary greatness must be due to some cause different from those forces which have produced not only ordinary men, but all great men; for a unique effect must have a corresponding cause. If so, He must have been a manifestation of the superhuman.

My argument briefly stated will stand thus :—As an event manifesting purpose for which the action of the forces of the Material Universe is unable to account, is a physical miracle, and proves the presence of a power different from those forces, so an event in the moral and spiritual worlds, for which the forces that energize in man are unable to account, must be a moral miracle, and must prove the presence of a superhuman power. I claim on behalf of Jesus Christ, that His character and action in history constitute a manifestation of such a power, the presence of which admits of an actual verification in the history of the past and the facts of the present.

If it be objected to this line of reasoning, that we are not sufficiently acquainted with those forces that energize in man, and the laws of their action, to determine when an event is a moral miracle; and that man may possess within him a number of latent powers of which we have as yet no knowledge, my reply is, that our experience of them lies over an historical period of not less than three thousand years, during which they have had ample opportunity of manifesting themselves and proving what they can accomplish. If, therefore, Jesus Christ was the result of their activity, it is clear that during this long interval of time they must have produced other men at least approaching to His greatness.

Further, if I can establish the fact that Jesus Christ has acted on history with an energy which is absolutely unique, the proof of the miraculous actions attributed to Him in the Gospels will be rendered easy, for it would be far more improbable that such a person did not manifest a superhuman power in the Material Universe, than that he performed the miracles in question. In other words, the *à priori* difficulties attending them will disappear, and their occurrence can be proved by the evidence which is valid to establish the ordinary facts of history.

Such is my argument. My inquiry, therefore, must be directed to ascertain the following points:—What is there in Christianity, and in its action on history, which distinguishes it from every other system which man has invented in the past or in the present? Is there anything in it which stands out absolutely unique? Surely, if Christianity contains a manifestation of the superhuman, this is where we ought to be able to discover unequivocal traces of its presence. To this question there is only one possible answer—that it stands out in marked contrast to every other human institution, in that its entire system, its inner life, and its sole principle of cohesion is based on the personal history of its Founder.

I ask your deep attention to this most remarkable fact. The inner life of Christianity, as I have shown, consists not in a body of moral precepts, or of dogmas, or in a ritual, or a system of philosophy, but in a personal history. To this the entire history of man presents nothing parallel. Take a careful survey of its wide range. He has originated religions without number; and every form of political and social institution; but the inner life of not one of them is based on the personal history of its founder. Not to speak of other religions of inferior importance, three great religions, exclusive of Christianity, now existing in the world, probably number among their votaries between seven and eight hundred millions of the human family; Braminism, Buddhism and Mahomedanism. Two of these have known founders, whose memory is held in deep reverence by their votaries. Yet the essential principle of each consists in a body of dogmatic teaching, and not in a personal history. As systems of religion, the personal history of their founders might be removed out of them, and leave their fundamental principles intact. The same is true of every other religion which has existed in the past, or still exists in the present. But to take away the person of the Founder of Christianity out of His religion would be its destruction. Its doctrines and its precepts would lose all cohesion; the key-stone would be removed from its arch, and its whole superstructure would collapse.

If we take a survey of the various philosophical systems and political and social institutions that have ever existed, we shall arrive at the same result. Individuals may have founded them; but that is all. Their vitality and cohesion have never been based on their own personal histories. A common agreement in a number of dogmatic statements has formed the bond of union among all the philosophic sects which have ever existed in the ancient or the modern world. The last thing which would have occurred to the leaders of ancient thought would have been to found their systems on their own persons. So it has been with every political and social institution. A common end or purpose, not a personal history, has constituted the principle of their inner life.

But, further, although Christianity has set the example of basing itself as a religion, and the Church as a society, on a personal history, it has never yet found a successful imitator. A vast number of sects have sprung up within the Church, but the bond which has imparted to them unity and vitality, has been a doctrinal one, and never the events of an historic life. Here then we are in the presence of a fact which is absolutely unique in the history of man.

It is needless to attempt to prove that the supreme attractiveness of the person of the Founder of Christianity has imparted to the Church the whole of its vitality. To this fact all history bears witness. Nor is its testimony less certain that of all the influences that have been exerted in this earth, that of Jesus has been the most potent. Enumerate all the great men who have ever existed, whether they be kings, conquerors, statesmen, patriots, poets, philosophers, or men of science; and their influence for good will be found to have been as nothing compared with that which has been exerted by Jesus Christ. Why is this? He alone of the sons of men possesses in himself a power of divine attractiveness which can penetrate to the depths of the human heart, and exercise there a mighty moral and spiritual power. What has He accomplished? He who was in outward form a Galilean peasant, who died a malefactor's death, has founded a spiritual empire which has endured for eighteen centuries of time, and which, despite the vaticinations of unbelievers, shows no signs of decrepitude. Commencing with the smallest beginnings, His empire now embraces all the progressive races of men. Those by whom it has not been accepted are in a state of stagnation and decay. It is the only one which is adapted to every state of civilization. It differs from all other states and communities in that it is founded neither on force nor self-interest, but on persuasion, and the supreme attractiveness of the character of its Founder.* The holiest of men have bowed before Him with the supremest reverence; and have accepted Him as a king who is entitled to reign by right of inherent worthiness, and with the greater eagerness in proportion to their holiness.

Such are indisputable facts of history. Even unbelievers are not unwilling to yield to Him the highest place in their pantheon of great men among the benefactors of mankind. But this by no means satisfies the requirements of the case.

---

* I fully admit that force has been employed in the propagation of Christianity by some of its zealous but mistaken adherents. Two facts must, however, be borne in mind respecting it. First,—That this did not take place until several centuries after it had attained a firm footing in the world, when Mahomedanism had set the evil example of propagating religion by the sword. Secondly,—That its use is in direct opposition both to the letter and the spirit of the New Testament, which not only repudiates every form of violence for its propagation, but directly affirms that the kingdom of Jesus Christ is based only on persuasion. It is also an unquestionable fact that the influence of force in the propagation of Christianity has been really very inconsiderable.

History affirms that Jesus has not only been a great man among great men, or even the greatest of them, but that He stands at an immeasurable height above them, as their Lord, before whom it is becoming that the greatest of them should bow down. He is the one only catholic man, the one ideal of humanity, for whose presence in and action on history none of the known forces that energize in the moral and spiritual worlds can account. What is the necessary inference from this? I answer, that as those forces which have energized in man from the day of His appearance on this earth have failed to produce His fellow, we must be in the presence of a moral miracle.

It is all important that we should observe in what this mighty influence, or in other words, this supreme greatness of Jesus consists: It is not the mere result of either His doctrinal, or His moral teaching, nor is it simply because His human life constitutes an embodiment of the morality which he taught. Nor is it the mere result of intellectual superiority, nor of all the causes combined which by their united action make a great man in the ordinary acceptation of the term. The mighty influence of Jesus is founded on that divine life which runs through His entire character, as it is depicted by the Evangelists—not merely in those actions which we designate miracles—but in every portion of it. This attractiveness culminates in one aspect of it— the perfection of self-sacrifice manifested in His life, followed by the divinest exhibition of love displayed in His voluntary death. This is it which distinguishes the greatness of Jesus from that of all other men, and constitutes the secret of His power. Wonderful is that great utterance of His, if we view it merely as a prediction: " I, if I be lifted up from the earth, will draw all men unto me."

Who would have believed in the possibility of its accomplishment, even if we accept the date which unbelievers have assigned to the composition of the fourth Gospel as that of its utterance? What human foresight could have anticipated the fact that the crucifixion of a Galilean peasant would prove the most attractive influence which has been exerted on the heart of man during all the ages of the future? If this portion of the divine delineation was removed from the portraiture of the Jesus of the Gospels, it would exert no more influence than that of other men who have been good and great.

The testimony of history to the solitary grandeur, and to the might of the influence which has been exerted by Jesus Christ, is indisputable. I cannot better state the facts which it discloses than in the words of an historian, who does not accept Christianity as a Divine Revelation, and whose partiality as a witness cannot be suspected. Mr. Lecky, in the second volume of his *History of Morality from Augustus to Charlemagne*, writes as follows:—" It was reserved for Christianity to present to the world an ideal character, which, through all the changes of eighteen centuries has filled the hearts of men with an impassioned love, and has shown itself capable of acting on all ages, nations, temperaments, and conditions; has not only been the highest pattern of virtue, but the highest incentive to its practice, and has exerted so deep an influence that it may be truly said that the simple record of three short years of active life has done more to regenerate and to soften mankind than all the disquisitions of philosophers, and than all the exhortations of moralists. This has indeed been the well-spring of whatever has been best and purest in the Christian life. Amid all the sins and failings, amid all the priestcraft, the persecution, and fanaticism which have defaced the Church, it has preserved in the character and example of its Founder an enduring principle of regeneration" (vol. ii., p. 8.)

This passage will, I think, be admitted even by unbelievers to be a correct statement of the facts as they are presented to us by history. They all admit of the most certain verification. Jesus Christ has certainly exerted an influence such as is here described by the historian, and he is the only one of the sons of men who has done so. The only thing which can admit of discussion is—What is the legitimate deduction from the facts? Are they consistent with the theory that Christianity has originated in nothing but the action of those forces which for three thousand years of unquestionable history, and for an indefinite period which is semi-historical, have been energizing in man's intellectual, moral, and spiritual being, and have produced the results which we behold in his past developments? Or do they testify to the presence and energy of a superhuman power? The long course of history has furnished us with abundant materials for forming an accurate judgment as to what the forces which energize in human nature are capable of accomplishing. It is in vain to plead that we are here dealing with a number of unknown quantities. We know that the forces of the moral and spiritual worlds do not work at hap-hazard, but in a definite order. Here, no less than in the physical Universe, like causes must produce like effects, and different results cannot flow from the same cause. It follows, therefore, if the character of Jesus Christ and his action in history are separated by a profound interval from that of every other man, if He stands at an elevation immeasurably higher than the greatest, the wisest, and the best of men, if His influence for good not only transcends that of single great men, but of all great men united, it is utterly unphilosophical to affirm that He was the simple product of those forces that energize in humanity; on the contrary, the difference in the effect proves a difference in the cause which has produced it. If He were their simple product, how, I ask, has it come to pass that they have produced only this one great perfect man, this single ideal of human nature, and then ceased from their activity for evermore? Such a question urgently demands solution, if our beliefs are to be grounded on rational conviction. The difference in the results proves that the causes which produced them must have been different; in other words, that the greatness of Jesus Christ and His action on history cannot have been due to those forces which have produced other great men, but are manifestations of the energy of a superhuman power.

This conclusion will become more clearly established if I examine each fact as it has been stated by the historian, and place before you separately and conjointly the inferences which they justify.

1. "It has been reserved for Christianity," says Mr. Lecky, "to present to the world an ideal character, which, through all the changes of eighteen centuries, has filled the hearts of men with an impassioned love." This character, I need not say, is that of Jesus Christ, as it is depicted in the Gospels. Whether it be the creation of the imagination or an historical reality, space will not allow me to discuss in this place. I have done so in another work.* My present argument is unaffected by the question whether it be an ideal or an actual one. The great fact will remain the same, that during eighteen centuries it has inspired the hearts of men with an impassioned love, and that its power to accomplish this shows no signs of diminution.

The statement before me contains two distinct affirmations. First: The character of Jesus Christ has accomplished this result.

Secondly: that it is the only one in the history of man which has succeeded in doing so. These two affirmations, as matters of fact, rest on evidence which is so plainly written on the pages of history as to render a formal proof unnecessary.

Whence, I ask, has come this power of inspiring the hearts of men with an impassioned love, which has been exhibited by Jesus Christ for a period of more than eighteen centuries after the termination of his earthly life? Why have not other great men exerted a similarly attractive power? If they have not done so to the full extent, why have they not at least made some approaches towards it? Great men have existed in abundance; and not a few of them have been great benefactors of mankind, and to the utmost of their powers have laboured to do them good. But where is the great man, Jesus Christ

* *The Jesus of the Evangelists.*

alone excepted, who has for eighteen centuries after the termination of his earthly life been capable of exciting in the hearts of men an impassioned love? Who among them has called forth a self-sacrificing devotion of heart and life? The memory of other great men we respect and reverence; but not one of them inspires us with impassioned love. Take a careful survey of the entire history of the past. Does Socrates, or Plato, or Aristotle? does Zoroaster, or Confucius, or Sâkyamuni? does Mahomet, does even the venerable Howard? Who among the sons of men who have ever existed has kindled towards himself a self-sacrificing love in the smallest degree analogous to that which has been aroused towards Jesus Christ? Even if we assume the character of Jesus to be an ideal creation, the argument is no less cogent. Where is the ideal creation which has exerted this singular power? The interval which separates the earliest of poets from the greatest of living ones is very wide, and contains many illustrious names; yet poetic genius has been unable to create a character which could similarly inspire the hearts of men, and thereby act mightily on man's moral and spiritual being for eighteen centuries, and afford the promise of continuing to act mightily for ever. Jesus Christ alone has exerted such a power. What then is the inference? I answer that we must be in the presence of the superhuman.

2. The next fact mentioned by the historian is, that this influence has not been merely temporary or local, but has acted on all ages, nations, temperaments and conditions of men; in one word, it has been as wide as humanity itself.

The truth of this will not be far to seek; for it is everywhere stamped on the pages of history. The European, the Asiatic, the African, the aboriginal American, the native of the Polynesian Isles, notwithstanding that these races exhibit the widest divergency of intellect and character, have alike confessed its power. It has surmounted every peculiarity of temperament and of race. Men of the profoundest intellect have been penetrated by it; men of the greatest moral elevation have been raised still higher by its influences; it has touched a chord in the hearts of the uncivilized and the savage; yes, its influence has burst the trammels imposed by nationality, intellectual and moral training, and social condition. It speaks to man as man.

Is it true then that Jesus Christ is the one solitary character known to history who has exerted this influence?

We have had no lack of great men during the ages of the past; great conquerors, great philosophers and great poets—great men of various orders and degrees—who have possessed a wide range of intellectual vision; and I may add, many of whom have been animated by an earnest desire to benefit their fellows according to the light that was in them. But every one of them has been national or local, only partially able to break through the conditions imposed upon them by their birth and their moral and intellectual environment. Not one of them has been capable of speaking to all races, nations, temperaments, and conditions of mankind. No genius is perhaps more catholic than that of Shakespeare; yet compared with Jesus it is narrow. Its influence too is the influence of intellect, not of character. We may feel admiration for it; but to whom is the character divinely attractive? Who is impelled to self-sacrifice by the love of Shakespeare? Whom does it elevate to holiness? Whom has it rescued from moral degradation? None can speak to the universal heart of man but Jesus Christ.

What then is the inference? I answer, that a power must have manifested itself in Him which has burst through those bands by which the greatest of men are chained fast to that spiritual, moral, and intellectual environment in the midst of which they have been born and educated. If He is thus the only really catholic man, it proves the presence in Him of something which exists in no other man, He must be superhuman. Is it, I ask, believable that the very ideal of humanity has been produced and developed in the midst of the atmosphere of Jewish narrowness and exclusiveness, through the sole agency of those forces by which the moral and intellectual character of mankind is generated and produced? To assert its possibility is to deny the reign of law in the moral and spiritual worlds. Thistles cannot produce figs, nor brambles grapes.

3. The next fact mentioned by the historian is, that Jesus is "the highest pattern of virtue" that has ever been exhibited among mankind; in fact, the only one who can be propounded as an actual embodiment of holiness. This has been admitted by numbers of unbelievers. Mr. Mill concurs with Mr. Lecky. To these it would be easy to add a whole chorus of assenting voices. Mr. Mill goes so far as to affirm that even in these modern days the rational sceptic would do well to make Him the subject of imitation, and to live such a life as would meet with His approbation. Nay more, he treats with absolute scorn the idea which has so frequently been thrown out by opponents, that the perfection of the character can have been due to the inventions of His followers, or of the early Christians, whose whole sphere of thought was immeasurably beneath Him. The perfection of the moral character of Jesus therefore is an indisputable fact, which remains unassailed by the minute criticisms of an inconsiderable number of objectors. What the Baptist said of himself is still true of the holiest of men. They are not worthy to unloose the latchet of His sandals.

But if this be so, the question demands solution, how can we account for the moral perfection of Jesus Christ? To say that it is due to His exalted genius is simply to confess our inability to account for it. Why, I ask, is it that this exalted genius has appeared only once among men, if it is nothing more than the offspring of the forces which energize in the production of men? Has nature expended all her powers in His production; and retired ever since wearied with her work. But if one fact respecting man is more certain than another, it is this—characters of commanding moral elevation do not emerge from a hotbed of narrowness, bigotry, and fanaticism. All that great men under such circumstances can effect is to raise themselves to a moderate height above their surroundings. Yet Jesus was by birth a Jew; and His entire surroundings were those of Jewish thought and feeling such as prevailed during the century which preceded and that which followed the Advent, and respecting the character of which history gives ample evidence. Far more might we expect the forces of nature to develop by their unassisted power a venerable Howard out of one born and educated in the moral and spiritual atmosphere of a society of Kaffirs or of Bushmen, than that the perfection of the character of Jesus could be the natural outcome of the condition of Jewish thought during that period of time.

4. But the historian tells us that Jesus Christ has not only been the highest example of virtue, but the highest incentive to its practice. Here then we are in the presence of a fact, which, if true, is of the profoundest significance. Multitudes of men have in different degrees been patterns, though not perfect patterns, of virtue; but the whole course of history presents us with only one character who has been set up as the great motive and incentive to its practice; or, in other words, who constitutes in his person and history a great moral and spiritual power. This person is Jesus Christ our Lord. Some of the great teachers of religion and morality have, with various degrees of modesty, and frequently with the deepest misgivings, ventured to propound their example for the imitation of their followers; but the idea of propounding a teacher as the highest incentive to the practice of holiness, or, in other words, as the mightiest moral and spiritual power that can be brought to bear on man, is to be found in Christianity alone. The fact is, there is no other character known to history, real or fictitious, with respect to whom this would have been possible except Jesus Christ. The idea is one which is absolutely unique.

Let it be observed that to propound a man as an example of virtue, and to propound him as an incentive to its practice, are two things fundamentally distinct. All good men may be used as patterns of virtue in proportion to the degree of their holiness, and the elevation of their characters. There is also a very subordinate sense in which they may be said to be incentives to its practice, if their example is capable of exciting in others a spirit of emulation either to rival or to excel it. But such a power is very limited, nor is it in this sense that Jesus Christ is an incentive to holiness; for no man has yet been found presumptuous enough to think that he can rival or excel the holiness of Jesus. They can also exhort us, urge on us the motives to virtue; in a word, preach to us. But this is all that can be accomplished by even the holiest and the best of men.

Why is this? The answer is evident. A power which is capable of acting as an incentive to holiness, must be one that is capable of energizing on man's moral and spiritual being. It must be a power capable of exerting an attractive influence; one which can bind the conscience, profoundly stir the emotions and the affections, call into activity all that is good in them, and enable the higher portions of human nature to triumph over those which are meaner and baser. Now there is nothing in an ordinary man, however holy, which can effect this. If done at all, it can only be by the exhibition of an attractiveness capable of seizing on some affection of our moral being; and of a right which is self-assertive to rule the conscience, and make him in whom it dwells the centre of moral and spiritual obligation. Such a power implies worship, adoration, love. Our moral nature, unless debased, refuses to bow before a fellow-man, however holy. If therefore one can act on another as a power capable of impelling him to virtue, in the sense in which Jesus Christ is an incentive to holiness, it can only be by right of a superhuman superiority residing within him. Many men have inspired devotion within the sphere of their influence, as has been done by great generals both in ancient and modern times; but it is impossible to produce any man known to history, however great, who has acted as a motive to holiness.

Yet that Jesus Christ is thus presented in the New Testament is apparent from the most casual perusal of its pages.

Nor is this merely accidental to its teaching, but of the very essence of it. The Synoptic Gospels, which have been represented as depicting Him in a less divine aspect, represent Him as claiming a right to supersede every tie which binds man to man in favour of Himself; and as grounding that claim on His own inherent worthiness, even to the extent of demanding unlimited sacrifice of self as due to Him. His whole deportment as depicted in these Gospels is that of one who feels that He has an inherent right to reign; and the fourth Gospel and the Apostolic epistles do little more than unfold the idea which runs through the discourses of the Synoptics. It is impossible therefore to affirm that the idea of representing Jesus as the centre of obligation, is an aftergrowth on Christianity. Every record which we possess proves that it formed part of its primary and original conception: yet the originality of the idea is startling, for it is the one solitary attempt to do so known to history. But further: since it has been made, it has not had a single imitator.

The question of fact therefore becomes one of the highest importance. Has the attempt proved a success? Has Jesus Christ energized in history as the mightiest of moral and spiritual powers? Is the evidence clearly legible on its pages? Further, I ask, is it, or is it not a fact, that He is the mightiest incentive to holiness, and self sacrifice, which is energizing at the present hour? There can be no doubt what must be the answer. To remove the action of Jesus Christ out of the history of the last eighteen centuries would be to reduce it to a blank. Whether his character, as depicted in the Gospels, be an ideal or an historical one, does not in any way affect the fact that its energy has been mighty, and that this one solitary attempt to exhibit a character as the highest incentive to virtue and holiness, has proved a great success. I will state the answer of history in the words of Mr. Lecky. "The brief record of three short years of active life, has done more to regenerate and soften mankind than all the disquisitions of philosophers, and than all the exhortations of moralists."

Who with the history of the past in his hands can doubt the truth of this statement? Jesus Christ has stamped His impress on the entire range of modern civilization, its modes of thought, its legislation, its social customs, and its morality. If we survey the efforts that have been made for the amelioration of mankind, and the self-sacrifice by which these efforts have been carried out, it is not too much to say, that nine-tenths of it—it would probably be more correct to affirm, that ninety-nine hundredths of it—have been called forth by attachment to Him, and by this alone.

I ask you specially to observe, that this result has not been due to the mere teaching of Jesus, great as its influence has been. It has been the result of a personal influence, seated in the record of a life. To this the entire history of Christendom bears witness. This alone has made Him capable of acting as a power, mighty to inspire devotion, love, and adoration. Apart from this, His doctrines and His moral teaching would have exerted as little influence as those of the philosophers and moralists, for what mankind stand in urgent need of is, not wise precepts for the regulation of life, but a moral and spiritual power, capable of making obedience to it an actuality. Nor is His unique power seated in a mere fond reminiscence of departed worth which perishes after a lapse of time; but in self-sacrifice rendered to one who is capable of recognizing that sacrifice which He has Himself evoked.

And, I ask, is He not energizing at this moment? Although we cannot see Him with our eyes, we can verify His present power in the facts of daily experience. The noble army of self-sacrificers in the Christian Church may be counted by hundreds of thousands. Wherever Christianity exists, its rank and file may be found.* Let us put the

* It is worthy of remark that this is the case even in the most degraded forms of Christianity, and has been so in every age. The divine rays which issue from the person of its Founder succeed in penetrating those mists of darkness and superstition which have brooded over the Church. Although these have grievously obscured

question to them, What is impelling you to your self-denying exertions? They will answer with unanimous voice, We are constrained by the love of Jesus Christ, and His divine attractiveness—His self-sacrifice for us impels us to sacrifice ourselves for Him. This is a fact which each of us may verify for himself, and it is unique in the history of man. These modern times have set up a phantom called the religion of humanity, whose great moral principle is altruism, or the sacrifice of self to the idea of human nature, *i.e.*, the sum total of men and women who have existed in the past, or will exist in the future—a mere caricature of Christianity. But it is powerless! Where is its army of self-sacrificers? It stamps on the ground, but no legions appear at its bidding. All that its adherents have yet succeeded in accomplishing is to draw largely on the bank of hope.

It follows therefore, inasmuch as the idea of making an individual the centre of a great moral and spiritual power is unique in the history of man, and when tried in the person of Jesus Christ, the only being known to history in whom the experiment was possible, has as a matter of unquestionable fact, exerted a mightier influence for good than all philosophers and moralists united, that the power thus manifested in Him must be superhuman.

5. One more fact is noticed by the historian—While the Christian Church, like all other societies which have ever existed, has been infected and defaced by various corruptions, it differs from every other in that it possesses in the character and example of its Founder an ever-enduring principle of regeneration.

Here again the facts of history are indubitable. The Church has been frequently overlaid by superstition; she has sanctioned practices which her Founder expressly for-

the light, they have never been able to extinguish it. The reason of this is, that the person of Our Lord is so essential to Christianity, that even its most degraded forms cannot wholly destroy His personal influence; and wherever the bright lineaments of His character disclose themselves they are necessarily an influence for good.

bade: she has, terrible to say, unsheathed the sword, which He expressly enjoined her to put up into its scabbard. All this is true: and its truth only increases the marvellousness of the fact which the historian brings to our notice, that she has ever found in the person of her Founder an enduring principle of regeneration. There is a depth of meaning in the person and teaching of Jesus Christ, which has transcended the actual Christianity of every age—something in fact, which soars high above the discordant Babel of her sects. It has been the universal law of human institutions that their corruptions have resulted in their slow and gradual dissolution. Hence empires have passed away; institutions have become effete; religions have become corrupt. But a principle of ever-renewing vitality has been seated in the bosom of Christianity; and the effect of the unveiling of the person of its Founder before the eyes of men, just as He has been depicted by the Evangelists, free from the false lineaments in which He has been enshrouded by human folly, and human sin, ever has been, and ever will be, the source of a new life to the Church which He has founded. In this respect the Church of Christ differs from every merely human institution.

Finally: let me ask you to observe that each of these manifestations of a superhuman power shining forth in Jesus Christ, do not stand by themselves solitary and alone. Even if they did, their evidential value would be great. But the whole of this evidence, (and it is only some of the most striking portions of it which I have adduced) possesses a cumulative force. I ask you fully to estimate the weight of the whole of it taken together, centring as it does in the person of Jesus Christ. From Him issues, not a single ray of divine light, but a mass of rays all converging in a common focus. Before the brightness of the light which He emits, all other illuminations grow dim, like the stars in the presence of the sun; all other activities are feebleness. There are only two alternatives before us. I will simply state them, and leave it to yourselves to choose which is the most philosophical and rational; Jesus Christ must be either the manifestation of a superhuman power, or of the ordinary forces which act in man, which have energized only this once in His production, and then ceased from their activity for evermore.

There is, I am aware, one other alternative which unbelief propounds, but which space prevents me from discussing here. It is that the Jesus of the Gospels is an ideal character, devoid of historical reality. What does this mean? Its meaning, stripped of all disguises is, that the mightiest power which for eighteen centuries has energized for good, nay more, which at this moment is the cause of nearly every institution for good which exists in Europe, is based on a delusion. This theory, when examined in its details and tested by philosophy and fact, hopelessly breaks down. It will be sufficient here to say, that until it can be shown that some such shadowy creation has exerted a mightier influence for good during the ages of the past than the most strenuous exertions of the wisest and the best have been able to accomplish, the objection is dashed in pieces against the facts of history and the realities of human life.

But this alternative which unbelief propounds—the only one which it is able to propound—is terrible to contemplate. If it be true, human life is a delusion. It means this, and nothing less:—If the Jesus of the Gospels is an ideal creation, and not an historical reality, then a phantom and a shadow has been the centre of a mightier power, and has exerted a mightier influence for good, than all the realities which have ever existed. Good and wise men have struggled hard, but the results of their combined efforts have been as nothing compared with those which have been accomplished by this unreal creation of a number of distempered brains. If this be so, one thing is true, and one only —that man is walking in a vain shadow and disquieting himself in vain. Why then struggle for truth? for delusions are mightier than realities. Let us therefore take refuge in delusions, for their influence for good has been greater than all the self-sacrifice of the wisest and the best of men. This is the alternative which unbelief presents to us; and I say it is an alternative terrible to contemplate. If so, all is vanity: the present life is a dream; the life to come a blank; and man's only hope—shall I not rather say, his best hope—to be speedily swallowed up in that eternal silence, out of which he has come, to which he is hastening, and from which there will be no awakening. This is the prospect we are asked to accept in exchange for our Christianity and our belief in that God who is the merciful Father of our Lord Jesus Christ, whose kingdom is an everlasting kingdom, and whose dominion endureth throughout all ages; in whose presence there is fulness of joy, and at whose right hand there must be pleasures for evermore.

SUPPLEMENT I.

The question of the evidential value of miracles as necessary proofs of a revelation is in some degree complicated with that of special providences and answers to prayer. Professor Mozley allows that these are unseen miracles, only differing from actual ones in that their manifestation of special purpose is more or less imperfect. It is obvious that if a miracle be viewed simply as an occurrence in the physical Universe, it is impossible clearly to distinguish it from a special providence, because both alike involve such an interference with the order of nature, that a different order of events must have taken place but for the fact of such interference. The idea of a special providence is that the order of events has been diverted for a special purpose, and a new order of sequences introduced, which otherwise would not have existed. I use this language because it is the best that I can employ, although it is unquestionably inaccurate, since the very affirmation that God interferes with the order of the Universe in acts of his special providence amounts almost to a denial that He is always energizing in the production of its usual order; or in other words, that those events which are designated special providences are the effects of God's action in the Universe, while ordinary providences are not. Having thus pointed out the inaccuracy of the term, I may proceed to use it in its ordinary acceptation.

If special providences and miracles are alike interferences with the order of the Universe, they can only be brought about by some modification in the action of its forces; for the order of nature is nothing else than the sequences which are the results of their activity. In this respect special providences and miracles are alike; and only distinguishable from one another, as far as the one may be a more clear manifestation of purpose than the other. It follows therefore that the evidential value of a miracle as an attestation to a revelation is diminished in proportion to the difficulty of discriminating between the special purpose involved in a miracle, and that which is manifested in what is called an act of God's special providence: for it is clear that if the same event could subserve two purposes, it could no longer be the distinguishing mark of either.

But a distinction may be laid down between a miracle and a special providence, if the word "miracle" is used only to denote such occurrences as are preceded by a prediction that they are going to happen. Such a prediction would make the purpose of the event apparent as centring in a particular person, and thus constitute a special attestation to him. But here the question becomes complicated with events which are brought about as answers to prayer; and hence the difficulty of discriminating between them and miracles. A special answer to a special prayer, if the petition be for something other than the exertion of an influence on the mind, although the answer may be brought about through the agency of the existing forces of the Universe, necessarily involves some special modification of their action, because the supposition pre-supposes an order of events introduced in answer to the prayer different from that which would have happened if the petition had not been offered. But the event occurring in answer to a petition is almost as clear a manifestation of purpose as an event occurring after a prediction that it is going to happen, which we call a miracle. Both the one and the other cause the event to point to a particular person; in the one case, to the person who offers the petition and obtains the answer; and in the other, to the person who uttered the prediction on which the miracle followed as the result. In each case it would constitute an attestation to that particular individual, showing that the order of nature has been changed in his favour. Several of the Scriptural miracles are in fact described as answers to prayer; and this increases the difficulty of clearly discriminating between palpable answers to prayer, and what are usually called evidential miracles.

One distinction between them has been laid down, that to constitute an event an evidential miracle, it must be brought about instantaneously; whereas an answer to prayer may be a slow and gradual operation. I doubt, however, whether the distinction is one of real importance, because a series of definite and unquestionable answers to prayer occurring to the same person would be as clear a manifestation of purpose in reference to that individual as any miracle could be, and would prove that God marked him out for His special favour by deviating from His usual course of action at his request. A series of such answers would constitute such a special divine intervention as the Scriptures designate a sign ($\sigma\eta\mu\epsilon\tilde{\iota}o\nu$). It is true that in some of the Scripture miracles which are described as taking place in answer to prayer, a special command was given that the event should happen after the prayer had been offered, though this is not always the case, as in the resurrections wrought by Elijah and Elisha; and, in fact, many of their other miracles were unaccompanied by a prediction. It is difficult to see how a series of such answers can be distinguished as to their evidential value from a miracle.

This difficulty is increased when a person professes to

have been favoured with a long series of answers, all of which are brought about in favour of a particular institution. It is difficult to see how such do not constitute a direct divine attestation in its behalf. I cannot better illustrate my meaning than by referring to the well-known case of Mr. Müller's Orphan Asylum at Bristol. This institution has been in existence for a considerable number of years, and is one which from a small beginning has grown to very large dimensions. Its founder believes that it owes its support exclusively to the influence of faith and prayer. He disclaims the use of those means by which other religious societies are supported; he makes none of the usual appeals for funds, holds no public meetings, inserts no advertisements, and refuses to employ any organization for the purpose of obtaining pecuniary support. On the contrary, when funds are wanted, prayer is offered for them; and they are believed to come in consequence; and he affirms that this has never failed to supply them in their greatest straits.

But further; not only does Mr. Müller believe that this has supplied him with all the necessary funds for the support of his establishment, but he narrates a considerable number of occurrences as having taken place in answer to his prayers, involving not mere influences exerted on the mind, but direct interferences with the order of nature; as, to adduce a single example, the change of a north wind into a south wind, when in consequence of the failure of his warming apparatus, and the difficulty of repairing it, the children were in danger of suffering from cold. Taking the whole series of these events, and supposing them to have been brought about in the manner in which Mr. Müller believes them to have been, as definite answers to no less definite prayers, they constitute as distinct a divine attestation to the Orphan Asylum as could be given by any series of miracles.

I have cited the Orphan Asylum as a crucial example, because it is so remarkable an institution as to have attracted the attention of unbelievers. Mr. Wallace, who has some claims to be called the originator of the Darwinian theory of evolution, has referred to it in his work on Spiritualism, as a proof of the reality of spiritual influences. He pronounces a just condemnation on Sir W. Thomson's and Professor Tyndall's proposal to bring answers to prayer to an experimental test, by separating off two hospitals, one of which should receive the benefit of the united prayers of Christians, and the other should not, and testing the efficacy of such prayers by the results as manifested by the number of recoveries. Accepting the facts in connection with the Orphan Asylum, precisely as they appear to Mr. Müller's mind, he urges them on their consideration as an unquestionable proof of the efficacy of prayer. He then propounds his own theory as to their origin. He does not consider them as answers to prayer in any Christian sense of the term; but that Mr. Müller by the force of his devotions congregates around him a large number of kindred spirits, who suggest to other men and women of similar feelings, and possessing adequate means, to supply the wants of the Institution. To similar influences Mr. Wallace ascribes no inconsiderable number of the miracles recorded in the Bible, and those which are reported in Church and other histories.

On the discussion of Mr. Wallace's theories in connection with this subject, I cannot enter here. I have only to do with the facts of the Orphan Institution, as bearing on the evidential value of miracles. I have no intention to dispute the general truth of the facts as stated by Mr. Müller, although it is highly probable that they have received some colouring from his own peculiar opinions. To accept his testimony to the facts is one thing; to accept his views as to the agency which has brought them about is altogether another. If his views on this point are correct, the conclusion is inevitable that the Orphan Asylum has as definite a divine attestation in its favour as it would if its wants were supplied by the most direct form of miracle. In fact, a long series of such immediate answers to a set of definite petitions is of itself a miracle of the most unequivocal description. But it must be remembered that the person who believes himself to have been favoured by this kind of attestation for a long period of years, makes no claims to a divine commission of any kind, only to be the founder of a useful institution; nor does he lay claim to any divine illumination as directing him in its superintendence. The divine attestation, which has been given by this long series of answers to prayer, is tendered to the institution, and nothing else. If the facts as narrated by Mr. Müller are assigned by him to their true causes, the value of the testimony of miracles to a divine commission is greatly weakened by them, as in that case it is clear that a series of events, which it is impossible to distinguish from miracles, has been brought about, not for the purpose of attesting a divine commission, or anything resembling it, but for the benefit of an institution which does not differ in point of goodness from a vast number of others. This difficulty is further increased when it is remembered that the principle laid down is, that all other institutions for good might live and prosper by the use of similar means. If so, this would make a set of special interferences with the order of nature not the exception, but the rule of the divine government, thereby depriving a miracle of all evidential value as an attestation to a divine commission.

But I have not to deal with anything theoretical as to what might happen, if other institutions were to adopt similar means of supporting themselves; but with what has actually happened with respect to the Orphan Asylum. I fully concede that it is a very remarkable institution; but I believe that its growth and success can be accounted for by ordinary human causes without having recourse to the theory of special divine interventions.

I observe therefore that although its founder adopts none of the usual methods by which other societies obtain their income, it is clear that he employs means which, although highly efficacious, are nevertheless purely human. It is the single institution of its kind, and appeals to a sentiment which is particularly attractive to a large number of minds, the profession of living by faith: or in other words, of deriving its support from a set of supernatural interventions. All such persons (and their class is a numerous one), take a deep interest in the success of such an institution. Now, although its founder disclaims the use of means, such as are employed by other societies, yet he uses others equally efficacious, among which is the annual publication of a book containing an account of these special interventions during the past year, which is sent to all subscribers. This certainly constitutes an appeal of a very effective character, and one preeminently well fitted to stimulate the particular class of minds to which it is addressed, to large and frequent contributions.

But it may be objected, that however efficacious these means may be now, this will not account for the original setting up of the institution. I think that any one who will carefully investigate the account which Mr. Müller has given of its origin, will be able to assign it to a number of ordinary human causes, without invoking the aid of any special divine interventions in its favour; but to enter on a minute criticism of them would not be desirable in this place.

Many of the events narrated by him which involve special interferences with the order of nature, may be readily accounted for on the principle of coincidences, such as have occurred to each of us during our past lives; and are often of a very remarkable character, but which by no means involve the assumption that they have been brought about by special interferences with the forces of nature in our favour. But it is not my purpose in this place to discuss the abstract question, but only to consider how far such interferences as those alleged to have taken place in connection with the Orphan Asylum, affect the question of miracles, as evidential to a divine revelation. It seems to me to be impossible to distinguish between such occurrences as those above alluded to, if they are brought about in answer to definite petitions,

8 *

from evidential miracles. They would be simply marks of divine favour to particular persons and institutions; and would consequently be devoid of evidential value as proofs of the reality of a divine commission.

We know from the history of St. Paul that he habitually trusted to God's ordinary providence for the supply of his wants, rather than to special interventions.* Viewed in connection with the question of the evidential value of miracles, the whole subject of special answers to prayer requires very serious consideration, as it is evident that the analogy between them and miracles is of the closest character. When we offer special requests for special interferences with the ordinary mode of the divine acting, it is only in consonance with Christian humility to add to our prayers that God will be pleased to reject them, if we in our ignorance have asked Him to do what is not in accordance with the divine will. Surely a firm trust in His ordinary providence, and an habitual recognition that the forces of the universe in their daily operation are regulated by His wisdom, and subserving the purposes of His goodness, is quite as religious and reverential a state of mind, as that which is constantly asking Him to make special interventions on our behalf. Many of the prevailing ideas on this subject even among religious men owe their origin to their failing to recognize the teaching of the Bible, that all the forces of the universe are manifestations of the activity of God.

SUPPLEMENT II.

It will be seen that the view which I have taken in this and the preceding Lecture respecting the evidential value of miracles, and the relation in which they stand to the

* See the account of the dangers he encountered in his Missionary travels, 2 Cor. xii. St. Luke's narrative of his voyage to Rome, his shipwreck, and escape, is a striking illustration of the same habitual trust.

Christian revelation, differs very materially from that which has been propounded by Professor Mozley in his first Bampton Lecture. So important is this difference that it will be necessary to offer a few additional observations on the subject, for which it was impossible to find room in the Lecture itself.

The view propounded in the Lecture, briefly stated, is as follows :—The essence of the Christian revelation consists in Our Lord's divine person and work, which constitute Him the visible manifestation of the invisible God, and not in a number of dogmatic statements or moral precepts. His entire character is in fact a manifestation of the divine in union with the human, constituting an harmonious whole, of which the miracles form an important portion of the delineation. In one word, they are viewed as the natural outcome of the divine which dwelt within Him, and which manifested itself as much in His actions and teaching, in the spotless perfection of His character, and above all, in the divine self-sacrifice of His life and death, as in those actions which are usually designated His miracles. Further, while many of the miracles recorded in the New Testament were not wrought for directly evidential purposes (those which are directly affirmed to have been wrought for this purpose being few in number) ; yet all miracles, like all other manifestations of the divine, must have an indirectly evidential value, as indicating the presence and energy of a superhuman power. Also, while there are recorded in the New Testament a considerable number of doctrinal statements and moral precepts, it is a fact that however startling a statement may have been uttered by Our Lord, or whatever degree of opposition it called forth on the part of His opponents, or of incredulity in His disciples, He never condescends to perform a miracle in order to prove the truth of His assertions, but rests it solely on His own absolute knowledge and veracity.* Nor

* There are but two apparent exceptions to this rule, viz., that of the cure of the paralytic in proof of His " power on earth to forgive sins," and the raising of Lazarus, " that the people who stood by might believe that His Father had sent Him."

was such a thing once done by His apostles. In the same manner while He repeatedly appealed to His miracles as evidence of His divine character, He referred to them as portions of His moral working, and only appealed to them separately when the higher form of evidence failed to command assent.

This view of the subject seems to me to be rendered necessary by the most direct assertions of the sacred writers. Besides the evidence adduced in the Lecture, a large number of the passages quoted in the Supplement to the first Lecture for the purpose of proving that the essence of the Christian revelation consists in the person and work of Christ, tend equally to prove that the highest attestation to His divine Mission was His self-evidential character. So strong are the assertions on this point in those portions of the 1st Epistle and the Gospel of St. John, to which I have already referred, that any other view seems to me inconsistent with assigning to them canonical authority. The writer affirms that the life of the Logos was manifested. It was the light of men. This light was manifested in the person of Jesus Christ. It shone in the darkness, and the darkness comprehended it not. He was the true light which enlightens every man that cometh into the world. If these statements are the veritable utterances of the Apostle, they are conclusive on the subject. They make it certain that Jesus Christ must be a manifestation of the divine on the sphere of the human, the Sun of the moral and spiritual worlds, which energizes in them mightily. If this be so, it follows that the character of our evidential position must be such as I have described. First, Jesus Christ and His entire divine working, in which He bears witness to Himself. Secondly, His miracles, viewed as wonders, signs, and mighty deeds.

The entire argument of Professor Mozley rests on a different basis. He considers the essence of Christianity to consist in a number of statements of dogmatic truth, the discovery of which lies beyond the powers of human reason.

Of the truth of these statements he maintains that the miracles form the one great attestation and guarantee; or in other words, that they would be absolutely incredible but for their confirmation by miracles. His position is clearly stated in the following passage:—"There is one great necessary purpose, then, which divines assign to miracles, viz., the proof of a Revelation. And certainly if it were the will of God to give a Revelation, there are plain and obvious reasons for asserting that miracles are necessary as the guarantee and voucher of that Revelation. A Revelation is, properly speaking, such only by virtue of telling us something which we could not know without it. But how do we know that that communication of what is undiscoverable by human reason is true. Our reason cannot prove the truth of it, for it is by the very supposition beyond our reason. There must be then some note or sign to certify it, and distinguish it as a true communication from God, which note can be nothing else than a miracle."

This passage, which contains the essence of the view in question, seems to me to be based on the direct assumption of the point at issue. " A Revelation," says the Professor, "is properly speaking such only by telling us something that we could not know without it." This assumption is involved in the use of the word "Telling." It takes for granted that a Revelation, to be such, must consist in certain abstract statements of truths to be believed, and not of facts such as St. John speaks of, which he could see, hear, and bear witness to. It is in fact assumed not only that a Revelation, to be such, must be a dogmatic Revelation; but that it cannot consist of truths, which have a self-evidencing power to the heart and the conscience, and through them to the understanding. Such a view seems to me not only to contravene the express statements of the fourth Gospel, but the whole of the implied teaching of the Pauline epistles.

I by no means dispute that a Revelation, "to be worthy of the name," must communicate to us something which was previously unknown. This can certainly be done in many other ways besides in a number of dogmatic propositions. St. Paul definitely affirms that the Universe is a Revelation of God. "The invisible things of Him from the creation of the world are clearly seen, being manifested by the things that are made, even His eternal power and Godhead, so that they are without excuse. For that which is known of God is manifest in them, for God has showed it unto them." Words could hardly have been framed to affirm in a more definite manner that the Universe constitutes a revelation of the eternal power and Godhead of its Creator, and one of so distinct and definite a character that the heathen were without excuse for not attending to it. Yet in making this revelation, God has told us nothing respecting its forces or its laws, but has left them to be discovered by the use of the faculties with which He has endowed us. Of what, I ask, does this revelation consist? Evidently of an immense number of objective facts, showing forth the divine power and wisdom, and in an inferior degree His other attributes. Every creative work of God is unquestionably a discovery of a new truth, and, as such, a revelation of Himself. But it consists of a fact, manifested to man's understanding, the meaning of which he is capable of discovering; not the dogmatic affirmation of some truth previously unknown. Least of all does such a revelation require to be confirmed by a miracle wrought to attest either its reality or its truth. On the contrary it is self-evidencing, and its miracles, which are God's creative works, constitute its essence.

In a similar manner another great Revelation of God has been made in man's conscience and moral nature, by which we learn the law of duty, and that the Creator of the Universe is not only a Being who possesses wisdom and power, but that He is also a moral being.* But here again the revelation does not contain a single dogmatic statement,

* Here again St. Paul's assertions are definite and precise. "For when the Gentiles, which have not the law, do by nature the things contained in the law, these having not the law, are a law unto them-

nor is it confirmed by a single miracle, except that great one which constitutes its essence, the moral nature of man, and the greatest of all marvels, the creation of a free agent.

Again, a resurrection from the dead would constitute a real revelation; even if unaccompanied by a single dogmatic explanation. It would plainly be a discovery of at least one truth which was previously unknown, viz. that man was capable of a renewed life after he had undergone the stroke of death, and would thereby impart a certain degree of reasonableness to the expectation that others would receive the same. So again the appearance of an angel, and an actual conversation with one, would be an unquestionable revelation that there were other orders of intelligences in existence besides men. These, and a multitude of other kindred things, would in the truest sense of the term constitute revelations of truths, to which the unaided power of man's reason could never have penetrated, yet they are self-evidential, and require no miracle to confirm them. In a similar manner God's revelation of His moral perfections made in the life and death of Jesus Christ is self-evidential. In it, as St. John says, the divine life is manifested. We can see it, *i.e.* with the eye of our moral vision, and draw conclusions from it in the same manner, as we do from the other objective revelations of God.

In reply then to the question proposed by Professor Mozley, How do we know that the communication of what is undiscoverable by human reason is true?, I answer, By beholding it. Our reason cannot prove the truth of it until it has been discovered. Granted. But this forms no obstacle to our ability to recognize God in it, when He has thus revealed Himself. Such revelations require no note or sign to certify that they are true communications from God, other than themselves, when contemplated by the eye of reason. It is clear therefore that his remarks are only applicable

selves; which show the works of the law written in their hearts, their conscience also bearing witness, and their thoughts the meanwhile accusing or else excusing one another."—Rom. ii. 14, 15.

to such revelations as consist of statements of dogmatic truths which would have been undiscoverable by the unaided human intellect. But whatever connection such truths may have with the Christian Revelation, it is certain that the sacred writers affirm the presence of an objective Revelation in the person of Jesus Christ, apart from the dogmatic assertions which are found in the New Testament.

I fully agree with Professor Mozley that such assertions as some of those made by Our Lord respecting Himself would be incredible if made by one who had passed thirty-three years in converse with mankind without once exhibiting anything superhuman in his character. But it by no means follows that the only way of doing this is by the display of those marvels in the physical universe which we commonly designate miracles. Surely the presence of the divine is as clearly recognizable in superhuman holiness and loveliness as in acts of power in nature. I admit that the divine presence is manifested in the volcano and the earthquake; but it is far more so in the character of Christ our Lord as delineated in the Gospels. Every one of His actions was radiant with superhuman goodness, and surely a character which is a manifestation of superhuman goodness is a stronger guarantee of truthfulness than the performance of any number of marvellous works. Apart from such manifestations the assertions concerning Himself which are attributed to Him in the Gospel of St. John would not be rendered credible by the performance of any number of mere marvels in the physical Universe. Power is no doubt an attribute of God, but moral perfection is no less so. If anything analogous to miracles can be performed by the agency of demons, it is clear that the only means of distinguishing between the divine and the diabolical, must be the moral impress which they bear.

It follows therefore that our acceptance of Our Lord's testimony respecting himself is founded on His entire divine working, manifested during His life on earth, and not on His miracles pure and simple. Such a person could not but have known whether his statements were true or false. We therefore accept them as we do those of any other witness, on the ground of his adequate knowledge and entire veracity. Professor Mozley has more fully expressed his views on this subject in another passage of this lecture. It has been quoted somewhat unfairly by the author of *Supernatural Religion*. Still I think that the general mode of putting the case incurs a serious danger of causing misconception. As the passage is a long one, I will only quote its salient points.

"If then a person of evident integrity and loftiness of character rose into notice in a particular country and community eighteen centuries ago, who made these communications about himself, that he had existed before his natural birth, &c., &c." (here follow a number of affirmations which Our Lord actually made respecting Himself as reported in the fourth Gospel). "If this person made these assertions respecting himself; and all that was done was to make the assertions, what would be the inevitable conclusion of sober reason respecting that person? The necessary conclusion of sober reason respecting that person would be that he was disordered in his understanding. What other decision could we come to, when a man *looking like one of ourselves, and only exemplifying in his life and circumstances the ordinary course of nature*,* said this about himself, but that when reason had lost its balance, a dream of extraordinary and unearthly grandeur might be the result. By no rational being could a just and benevolent life be accepted as proof of such astonishing announcements. Miracles then are the necessary complement of the truth of such announcements, which without them are purposeless and abortive, the unfinished fragments of a design which is nothing unless it is the whole. They are necessary to the justification of such announcements, which unless they are supernatural truths are the wildest delusions. The matter and its guarantee

---

* The italics are mine.

are the two parts of a revelation, the absence of either of which neutralizes and undoes it."

This passage is misleading, because while it contains statements very closely resembling the facts of the Gospel, Dr. Mozley applies them to a condition of things wholly different from those exhibited in the life of Christ as there depicted. I fully admit that if a mere man, who differed in nothing from ordinary good men made such statements, they would be utterly incredible, and the fair inference would be that he had become suddenly insane. But the Gospels do not tell us that it was an ordinary man like ourselves who made these assertions; but one whose entire character and actions were as much a manifestation of superhuman goodness and holiness, as His miracles were of superhuman power. To assume that Our Lord before He performed His first miracle at Cana, did not differ from an ordinary man, is to beg the whole question. In fact it is simply impossible that He did not, if His own affirmations and those of the writers of the New Testament are true, that he who had seen Him had seen the Father; and that the fulness of Godhead dwelt in His incarnate person. The question is not what we should think of such assertions, if made by a man of ordinary goodness; but what we should think of them, if made by one who during the whole of his past life had been the highest manifestation of the moral perfections of God. St. Luke tells us that even at the age of twelve years Jesus astonished the Jewish doctors by His understanding and answers. Surely during the eighteen years which elapsed between this event and his public ministry, when His manhood had become fully developed, the divine rays must have shone in Him with greater brilliancy. According to Professor Mozley's position, these assertions, if they had been made by Our Lord before He had performed His first miracle at Cana, might have been justly deemed the results of insanity (we know that the Jews did subsequently affirm that he was mad); but they would have been rendered credible by its performance. Surely such a position is untenable. The error has originated in the incorrect assumption that Our Lord did not differ from an ordinary man until He manifested that difference by the performance of miracles.

But the Professor continues, "Would not a perfectly sinless character be a proof of a revelation? Undoubtedly that would be as great a miracle as any that could be conceived; but where is the proof of perfect sinlessness? No outward life and conduct, however just, benevolent, and irreproachable, could prove this, because goodness depends on the inward motive, and the perfection of the inward motive is not proved by the outward act." . . . "We accept Our Lord's perfect goodness then on the same evidence upon which we admit the rest of His supernatural character; but not as proved by the outward goodness of His life, by His character, sublime as it was, as it presented itself to the eye."

First. This affirmation is a very unfortunate one, because it directly traverses one made by Our Lord Himself as reported in the Fourth Gospel, "which of you convinceth me of sin; and if I say the truth, why do ye not believe me?" Surely Our Lord here affirms that the inability of any one to convince Him of sin was an adequate proof that His moral character was perfect. He demands to be believed in virtue of His inherent truthfulness; and on the strength of it He proceeds to make the affirmation of His pre-existence, "Before Abraham was, I am." He certainly here distinctly lays down that His absolute sinlessness was a sufficient ground for His affirmation being entitled to the fullest credence.

Secondly. But, says the Professor, how could this sinlessness be known? It is impossible that we could know that any man was sinless unless we could penetrate to his motives, and this we cannot do. Surely this is hypercritical. A being whose entire outward life was a manifestation of absolute moral purity, must have been equally pure in his inward character. "The tree," says Our Lord, "is known by its fruits." A being whose actual life is moral perfection, while his inward life is corrupt, must possess a superhuman power of hypocrisy. My answer, therefore, to the question, "How could the perfection of Jesus be proved?" is, By His perfect life. It was a question, not of theory, but of fact. I fully admit " that we accept Our Lord's perfect goodness on the same evidence on which we admit the rest of His supernatural character," *i.e.* by its manifestations. But here let it be observed, the proof of the manifestations of his superhuman power derived from His miracles is dependent on a complicated chain of historical proof; that of His divine working in the history of the past and the facts of the present is patent to the ordinary student of history.

It may be urged that large numbers of the Jews would not have any evidence that His character was morally stainless; and consequently to such persons it would be no sufficient guarantee of the truth of his assertions. This I fully admit. The same observation is equally true with respect to those who did not witness His miracles; and we know, as matter of fact, that even many who did, ascribed them to demoniacal agency. But it was far more difficult to ascribe His manifestations of divine goodness to such an influence than His miracles, when viewed separately from their moral environment. Both His moral perfection and His miracles could only be evidential as far as He afforded evidence of their reality.

But the character of the evidence has become widely different in the present day from what it was in Our Lord's. Then the miracles could be witnessed; now they cannot. Then their reality could be tested; now it cannot; now they can only be accepted on the testimony of those who witnessed them. Then the only alternative, if they were accepted as true, was between their being wrought by the finger of God or by Satanic agency. This latter alternative would weigh little now; but we are embarrassed by the length of the chain of the historic proof, and other difficulties peculiar to modern times, which considerably overbalance this advantage. Those who came into direct contact with Jesus were able to behold the divine radiance of His character. This we cannot do; but we have eighteen centuries of experience of the superhuman working of this character in history, and of the laws which regulate the evolution of ordinary men. This furnishes us with materials for judging whether a superhuman power manifested itself in Jesus Christ of which His contemporaries were destitute. We have also the character depicted before our eyes in the pages of the Evangelists. The only question is, whether it is possible that this character can be an ideal one, and of this our means of judging are ample. If any one will set himself thus carefully to balance our losses and our gains, I think that the conclusion at which he will arrive must be that the evidences of the divine mission of Jesus Christ which we now possess are of equal, if not of greater weight, than those which were enjoyed by those who lived in the apostolic age. It is true that we witness no physical miracles now; but we witness mightier moral ones. The moral miracles we can behold and verify: these being established, render our proof of the physical ones comparatively easy, which, when dissevered from that of the moral ones, becomes a balance of intricate probabilities.

The history of John the Baptist fully confirms the positions laid down in the Lecture, that miracles are not the one indispensable proof of a divine mission. The divine mission of John is directly affirmed by Our Lord. "Among those that are born of women," he says, "there has not arisen a greater prophet than John the Baptist." These words, if taken strictly, affirm that he was a greater prophet even than Moses. Yet not only do the Synoptics record no miracle as having been performed by him, but the fourth Gospel expressly affirms that he wrought none, while at the same time it attributes to him several dogmatical assertions respecting the superhuman greatness of Our Lord. If it be urged that a miracle was wrought on the occasion of the descent of the divine Spirit on Our Lord at his baptism, I reply, though the special mark to John by which the presence of the Messiah was indicated, and to him in the highest sense evidential, yet it was not so to others. As far as the people are concerned, the evidence of the fourth Gospel is incontestable, "John did no miracle, but all things which John spake of this man were true."

If it be urged that while miracles may not be necessary to prove a divine mission, yet they are necessary to prove the truth of a revelation, and that John had no revelation to communicate, I reply, that it is equally true that neither Elijah nor Elisha introduced a new revelation, yet the Old Testament ascribes to them a number of miracles. Nor is the affirmation that he had no revelation to communicate strictly accurate: for he was far more a communicator of one than any of the former prophets, in that he pointed out the Messiah as actually come; and authoritatively affirmed that Jesus was He. It is true that the Synoptics describe him rather as a preacher of repentance; but St. John's Gospel not only affirms that he gave distinct testimony to Jesus as the actual Messiah, but that he made several remarkable statements as to the divine character of His person, one of them being an affirmation referred to by Dr. Mozley, as requiring to be substantiated by miracle, that "He was the Lamb of God who takes away the sin of the world;" and if we accept the conclusion of the third chapter as an utterance of the Baptist, and not a meditation of its author, he must have announced yet profounder truths respecting His divine character. Although utterances of this kind are not directly mentioned by the Synoptics, yet they make it certain that John must have given a very clear and well known testimony to the Messiahship of Jesus, for they inform us that after Our Lord had performed the high Messianic act of cleansing the temple, and the Sanhedrim demanded His authority for doing so, He replied by asking their opinion as to the divine mission of John the Baptist; and that after consulting among themselves, they declined to return an answer, on the ground that if they affirmed its reality, Our Lord would fall back on His testimony to Himself as the Messiah; and if they denied it, they were afraid of a serious loss of reputation among the people, who believed in John as a prophet. If miracles are the necessary confirmation of a revelation, it is difficult to understand how a prophet who had a direct divine commission to point out Jesus as the Messiah, was not armed with the power of working them, while that power was so largely possessed by prophets with a mission so inferior as that of Elijah or Elisha. According to the theory which has been commonly accepted, when John the Baptist pointed out Jesus as the Messiah, and declared Him to be "the Lamb of God, who takes away the sin of the world," and that "he that believed on Him had everlasting life," he ought to have wrought a miracle to prove that such extraordinary assertions were true. It is impossible for me to enter here on a discussion of the grounds on which John rested the truth of his divine mission. I am only concerned with it in this place as showing that the affirmation that miracles are indispensable for the proof of its reality, and that certain truths are incredible unless they are attested by them, is not borne out by the statements of the New Testament. I am far from wishing to deny their value as a portion of the attestation given to Jesus as the Messiah, but this is a very different thing from affirming that they constitute the sole attestation, or are absolutely necessary to prove the truth of His utterances. The fact is, that neither abstract nor moral truths can be attested by miracles, viewed merely as marvels or exhibitions of power. As mere exhibitions of power, the greatest miracles recorded in the Bible are transcended by the daily workings of God in Creation and Providence. If we cannot attain to the knowledge of certain truths by the use of our reason, we can only accept them on the testimony of a witness whom we know to be veracious and to possess adequate means of information.

LECTURE III.

"I am the light of the world; he that followeth Me shall not walk in darkness, but shall have the light of life."—JOHN VIII. 12.

Is this light clearly shining in the spiritual and moral firmament? Can we behold its beams? Do the rays of the spiritual Sun generate vitality and life in the moral World? These are questions not of theory but of fact, which can be verified in the experience of the past and of the present. The text affirms not only that Jesus Christ is the great illuminator of the moral and spiritual worlds, but that the light which He emits communicates also a vital influence. He is *the Light of Life*. Such an assertion was a bold one, for it removes His pretensions out of the regions of the abstract and the theoretical, and brings them to the test of fact. If we can discover neither in the history of the past nor in the facts of the present clear and unmistakable signs of an illuminating and vital power issuing from Jesus Christ, then the author of the Fourth Gospel has placed in His mouth words which make Him bear false witness of Himself, and He thus becomes convicted of imposture. But if, on the other hand, He has proved during eighteen centuries the great source of man's spiritual illumination, then the writer has either reported a true utterance of Jesus, or, if a forger, he must have been possessed of a superhuman insight into the history of the future.

This inference will be equally certain, whether we accept

the Gospel as the veritable work of the Apostle John, written near the conclusion of the first century, or adopt the theory so dear to modern unbelievers, that it is the production of an unknown author some seventy or eighty years afterwards. In either case the assertion that an obscure Jewish carpenter would be the great illuminator of the most civilized and energetic races of mankind; that he would be the creator of a new moral and spiritual life; that he would indelibly stamp the impress of his action on all the progressive races of mankind—nothing, I say, could have been more unlikely in the year 170, than that such a saying would be realized. No human foresight could have anticipated the fact that this obscure carpenter would exert this mighty influence on history, and would distance the combined efforts for good of the wisest and the best of men. Such an utterance, if made by an ordinary man, could have only been attributed to madness. The question is, Have this and similar utterances which this Gospel has attributed to Jesus been verified in fact ? If they have, not only is the assertion that Jesus is the Light of the World, and the Light of Life, proved on indisputable evidence to be true, but the further conclusion is inevitable, that a spirit of the profoundest prophetic insight must have dwelt in Him who gave utterance to it—or, in other words, that it proves in Him the presence of a superhuman power.

The evidence that Jesus Christ has exerted this mighty influence, as the illuminator of the world, and the introducer of a new principle of moral and spiritual life, is so complete and overwhelming, that I need not further discuss it. It is written on every page of history from the year 315 downwards.* I have pointed out its evidential value in the

---

* I take the date of the conversion of Constantine as the starting point, because it is clear that from that time to the present Christianity has been the mightiest influence which has acted on the history of the Western world. From that time its action emerges into the clear light of history. Previously it had been comparatively obscure; Mr. Lecky's observation is worthy of deep attention, that nothing is

last Lecture. Look at the modern world. Is it not everywhere present in its institutions, its legislation, its forms of thought, its morality, its language, and its social life? The unbeliever cannot dispute the fact that the whole course of modern civilization has been deeply imbued, if it has not been actually created by Christianity. Let the experiment be tried of striking out of the history of the last eighteen centuries every event which has been affected by its influence, and we shall empty our historical libraries.

It follows then that the assertion that Jesus Christ is the light of the world, and the light of life, is not only capable of being verified in the history of the past, but is visibly receiving its accomplishment before our eyes in the facts of the present. What is the inevitable inference? I answer: Either Jesus Christ has been the manifestation of a superhuman power, or all this influence has been exerted by an obscure carpenter, whose entire moral and intellectual character must have been fashioned and developed in the narrow atmosphere of Jewish thought. If it be objected that a large portion of mankind are still unillumined by him, I reply that Christianity obeys the laws of the moral world in exerting an influence which is slowly and gradually progressive, and that its Founder distinctly stated that such would be its mode of operation.*

I now pass on to consider the evidence afforded by the moral teaching of Christianity to the presence of a superhuman power in Jesus Christ. I will first state the conditions of the argument, and point out what it is valid to prove.

more remarkable than the unconsciousness of pagan writers of the second and third centuries of the power that was growing up among them, prior to the hour of its triumph. This being so, we need not wonder at the inconsiderable notice it received from the heathen writers of the first.

* This is the idea which underlies those parables of Our Lord which draw their imagery from the processes of nature. Among them, those of the sower, the wheat and the tares, the mustard seed, and the leaven, stand out conspicuously.

First, I assume as an established scientific truth that the forces which energize in the moral world, act in conformity with moral laws;* that the long course of human history has enabled us to ascertain what these forces are, and the laws of their action; that each successive stage of the moral world has grown out of that which preceded it; and that its changes are not sudden, nor violent, but follow a law of gradual evolution. This being so, it follows that there are no violent breaks in the developments of man; but, on the contrary, that the entire atmosphere of thought and feeling of any one particular period, has grown out of that which preceded it, and has only slowly elevated itself above it.

Such is a brief statement of the law of human progress, as confirmed by the universal voice of history, and accepted by modern philosophy. It is now an established truth that man presents no great gaps in the course of his intellectual and moral development, so long as he is only acted on by the forces which energize within him.†

* The difference between the forces that act in the material and the moral Universe is precisely this. Material forces possess no power of self-determination. Moral forces energize in a being who possesses such a power. This we designate freedom, or free agency. Necessitarians, while denying its existence theoretically, are compelled to admit it practically; *i.e.*, human nature is in reality so constructed, whatever account may be given of its origin, that not only is the existence of a power of self-determination one of the most certain facts of consciousness, but we cannot help acting on it as a practical truth. This power, which man is capable of exerting within a limited sphere, is perfectly consistent with the great truth that moral forces act in conformity with moral laws. Necessitarians are constantly in the habit of charging their opponents with assuming positions which exclude law from the moral Universe; and that the assertion of a self-determining power in man is equivalent to affirming that confusion, not order, reigns within it. This subject is far too large to admit of discussion here, but it is not too much to affirm, that such a charge is simply a caricature of the views of those who hold in conformity with the principles of the inductive philosophy, that self-determination in man is as much a phenomenon of the moral Universe, as the absence of it is of the forces which dominate in the material one.

† The principle of production by evolution has been looked upon by

It has been objected to this form of the argument that the elevated moral teaching of Christianity was due to the lofty genius of Jesus. To this I reply, that history proves that no human being, however exalted may have been his genius, has been able wholly to emancipate himself from the conditions imposed on him by his birth, and the moral and spiritual atmosphere in which he was educated; While it is true that we are ignorant of the laws which regulate the production of genius, and of the precise extent of

many with great jealousy as a theory which is destructive of religion. On the value of such theories as a philosophical account of the origin of things, I would not wish to express an opinion, as having no immediate bearing on the subject of these Lectures. In fact all dogmatic assertions on this subject are evidently premature, as our inductions are as yet far too narrow to form a firm foundation for a theory so vast. But viewed as an abstract question, there is no more difficulty in conceiving that the Creator has carried on His work in conformity with some principle of evolution than by that which is designated special creation. I say this on the supposition that the theory presupposes an intelligent Creator acting on the forces of the Universe and moulding them to His purposes. Such theories are only dangerous to religion when they assume that the results which we behold in the Universe have been brought about by the action of its blind forces independently of the direction of intelligence. We know as a fact that every existing man and woman has been brought into existence by a very complicated process of evolution through a long train of ancestry, yet this is no hindrance whatever to our acceptance of the great truth, "I believe in God the Father, who made me and all the world." The outcry which has been raised against theories of evolution as destructive to religion is, to say the least of it, unwise. But I am here concerned with them only as far as they bear on the Christian argument. In this respect their importance has been far too generally overlooked by both parties in the controversy. If for the sake of argument we assume that things have been produced in conformity with a principle of evolution (and it is important to observe that this is maintained by a great majority of unbelievers), then it follows that the principle of continuity in the development of man must be a great philosophical truth; and the existence of considerable intervals between its stages an impossibility. As in conformity with the principles laid down by evolutionists, evolution is effected by a number of small and inconsiderable varia-

its action; yet the experience of history renders it certain that there are limitations imposed on it by its surroundings, which it is unable to transcend.*

This being so, it will follow, if there was nothing super-

tions, it follows that it is impossible that a man can emerge suddenly as a moral and intellectual giant above those surroundings in the midst of which he has been born and has drawn his entire moral and intellectual nourishment. This being so, a theory of evolution interposes an impenetrable barrier against the theory that Jesus Christ and His mighty action on history has been the simple creation of the ordinary forces energizing in man. The interval which separates Him not only from his own countrymen, in the midst of whom he was born and educated, but from the greatest of men, is too wide to be bridged over by any theory of evolution with which philosophy is acquainted. In this point of view the theories propounded by modern philosophy instead of weakening, impart strength to the Christian argument.

* It may be objected that I am basing my argument on the principles of the Necessitarian philosophy. I am simply appealing to the plain facts of the moral world, which I believe to be entirely consistent with the principle of self determination in man. It is impossible to deny that the characters of the majority of mankind are largely, though not exclusively, formed by their surroundings; and that such as has been the environment, such will be the man. The power of self-determination is confined within definite limits which it cannot transcend, though it may be able to effect modifications of the character within those limits. The distinction between physical and moral law is that the sequences of the former are invariable, while those of the latter are subject to modification by this principle, as in the material Universe the action of one force may be controlled by that of another. Whatever theory we may hold on these subjects, it is our duty to make them accord with the facts, and not the facts with the theories. Nothing has been more common in this controversy, whenever unbelievers are beset by difficulties, than to ascribe every fact connected with Jesus which cannot be accounted for on ordinary principles, to the influence of genius. Thus, in endeavouring to account for the mighty influence which He has exerted in history, and for the elevation of His teaching and character, it is found to be a ready way of escape from all difficulties to say that it was due to His exalted genius. This however is really equivalent to the admission that it has been due to a force for which we are unable to account, and that a power has manifested itself in Him of a character wholly different from those which energize in ordinary humanity.

human in Jesus Christ, and if the forces which manifested themselves in Him were nothing but the ordinary ones which energize in human nature, the moral teaching of Christianity must have been a natural growth out of that moral and spiritual environment in which He and his Jewish followers were born and educated, aided by such influences as may have been imported into it by St. Paul and his Grecian converts. Consequently, however exalted may have been the genius of Jesus, it would only have enabled Him to elevate Himself above those conditions in a way precisely analogous to what has been done by other great men, of whom Mahomet may be cited as an example. His case is one which bears directly on my argument. I readily concede that he must be numbered among the great men of our race; but the Koran makes it certain that his genius, great as it was, was unable to break through the conditions imposed on him by his birth, his education, and his surroundings. Its whole teaching bears the strongest impress of the Arab mind, and proves that the prophet was unable to free himself from the conditions which it imposed on him. The same truth is borne witness to by all the other great teachers of mankind. The peculiarities of the moral and spiritual atmosphere which they breathed are indelibly impressed on their respective systems. All are national, and local; Jesus Christ alone is Catholic as humanity.

From these principles I draw the following conclusions:

First. If the teaching of Jesus Christ clearly transcends the limits which were imposed on Him by His birth and surroundings, it proves the existence in Him of a force different from those which energize in ordinary humanity.

Secondly. If the moral teaching of Christianity, taken as a whole, not only transcends that of the great teachers of the ancient world, but solves problems, of which, while they recognized the importance, they found the solution impossible, it proves that it cannot have originated in that hot-bed of fanaticism and credulity which unbelievers are obliged to attribute to the followers of Jesus in order to impart plausibility to the theories they have propounded to account for the belief in His resurrection from the dead.

I shall assume as one of the bases of this argument the position which is taken by a large number of my opponents,* that the Jewish race, during the century which preceded and that which followed the advent, were to the

---

* I accept the positions laid down by unbelievers on this subject for the purposes of the argument, though there can be no doubt that they can only be received with considerable modifications. They have freely attributed to the Jewish mind at the period of the advent an enormous amount of credulity and superstition, for the purpose of enabling them to give something like a plausible account of the miraculous narratives contained in the Gospels, and above all, of the belief in the Resurrection. In taking this course it does not seem to have occurred to them that just in proportion as they heap on the primitive Christians this charge of credulity and superstition, they increase the difficulty of accounting for the moral teaching of the New Testament as the natural product of such a soil. Besides, if the entire environment of Jesus was such a mass of credulity and superstition as they assume, no amount of genius could have wholly freed him from its influences; for we know as a matter of fact that even the greatest of men have shared in the credulity and superstition of their age. Nothing is more certain than that an elevated system of moral teaching, which embodies a wide catholicity of spirit, cannot be the natural product of a soil which is deeply impregnated with these qualities. It follows therefore that the more certainly it can be proved that such was the moral and spiritual atmosphere of the primitive followers of Jesus, the stronger will be the evidence that the moral teaching of the New Testament is not of their creation. The evidence that their credulity exceeded that of the average of mankind hopelessly breaks down when tested by the facts of history—it is, in short, an hypothesis which has been invented to support a theory—still, in arguing with unbelievers, I am fully entitled to the benefit of their own assumptions, especially as their reasonings against the truth of the Resurrection owe all their plausibility to them. But the evidence of the narrow-mindedness and exclusive bigotry of the Jews of this period rests on a firm historical foundation; and this fact is alone sufficient to support the weight of the argument.

last degree exclusive, fanatical, and superstitious; and that in an atmosphere of this kind Jesus and His disciples must have been born and educated; and that a corresponding character was deeply impressed on His early followers. So much was this the case, that in the opinion of so profound a thinker as Mr. Mill it is simply incredible that the discourses attributed to him in the Synoptic Gospels can have been invented by the evangelists, or even by the Apostle Paul. This being so, it is surprising that he did not ask himself the question, Whence did this man get all this wisdom? instead of contenting himself with a vague platitude about the genius of the prophet of Nazareth?*

Further: it will be quite unnecessary for the purposes of this argument to maintain that a large amount of moral truth has not been discovered by man's unassisted reason. Many persons have argued on the principle that the more they can detract from reason, the more they strengthen Revelation. Such a position is however utterly unsound.

* On the other hand another class of unbelievers endeavour to prove that a considerable number of the moral precepts in the Gospels were the current sayings of Jewish doctors, who were Our Lord's contemporaries. The sole authority for this is the Talmud, one portion of which, the Mishna, was not committed to writing before A.D. 180 at the earliest; and the other, the Gemara, about A.D. 500. This being the case, it is impossible to say, how far any of its sayings accurately represent the teaching of Our Lord's contemporaries, or whether they may not have been borrowed from Christian sources. These writers display an unbounded trust in tradition when it can be used as a weapon against Christianity, and an equal distrust in it, when it makes in its favour. They also forget to inform their readers, that these moral gems which are scattered over twelve folio volumes are entombed in a mass of contemptible trivialities, and hair splittings, about questions of which not a single vestige can be found in the pages of the Gospels. All the evidence of which we are in possession tends to prove that Jewish teaching in Our Lord's time had fully entered on that course of casuistry, of which the Talmud is the consummation, and of which the moral teaching of Christianity is the absolute contrast. But as I shall show, objections of this kind, even if they had all the value which has been attributed to them by those who have adduced them, leave the real point of issue untouched.

To assert the inability of reason to discover moral truth, is not only to contradict the most unquestionable facts; but it is equivalent to the denial that man possesses a moral nature; for if he does, the discovery of a large amount of moral truth must be possible. To adopt this course is in fact to sacrifice one of our strongest arguments. On the contrary, my position is, that as far as portions of the teaching of the New Testament are in agreement with that of the most enlightened teachers of the ancient world, it proves that the persons by whom it has been elaborated must have been emancipated from the narrow-mindedness of the Jew of the Apostolic age; and consequently that it could not have been evolved by any natural process out of such a moral and intellectual atmosphere. Further; if Jewish peasants and fishermen have succeeded in accomplishing what all the masters of ancient thought, after all their efforts, failed to effect, it proves the presence in Christianity of an insight which is more than human.

It has been objected against this line of reasoning, that some of the moral precepts which are contained in the New Testament can be found elsewhere ;* and that if reason can

* Of the first of these objections we have some remarkable examples in Mr. Buckle's *History of Civilization*. He not only charges the writers of the New Testament with borrowing largely from heathen sources, but he goes the length of affirming that it is a fact well known to every scholar that several of its most elevated moral precepts are quotations from heathen authors. When we consider that the quotations from such sources are only three in number, it is incomprehensible how a man of Mr. Buckle's extensive erudition can have committed so extraordinary a blunder. I am aware that it has been inferred from some passages in St. Paul's writings that he was acquainted with the Greek tragedians. But of this the evidence amounts to little, or nothing. Nothing can be more absurd than to affirm, because two sets of writings contain a few moral precepts which bear a close affinity to one another, that the one must have been derived from the other, when the resemblance can be sufficiently accounted for by the fact that both writers drew from the dictates of that moral nature which is common to man. The bare perusal of St. Paul's epistles ought to be sufficient to convince any reader of the

discover moral truth, a revelation is unnecessary. But how, I would ask, can the fact that some of its precepts are to be found scattered up and down in detached aphorisms, in the writings of ancient moralists, be valid against its originality taken as a whole? The objection would only have weight, if some one of them had succeeded in elaborating its entire system. Nor does it follow, that because reason can discover a considerable amount of moral truth, it can discover all that is necessary for the well-being of man. But above all; it is founded on the assumption that the chief end and aim of Christianity is to propound a body of ethical truth, instead of what it affirms to be its great purpose, to communicate to man a great moral and spiritual power of which he was previously destitute. The real point for our investigation is, Are there specialities in Christianity, which

vast difference between his teaching, taken as a whole, and the entire system of Pagan ethics; nor can the smallest trace of such an influence be found in that of Jesus Christ. But Mr. Buckle, in common with nearly every unbeliever who has touched on the moral teaching of Christianity, persistently ignores the fact that the most striking characteristic of the teaching of the New Testament consists in its bringing the principle of faith to bear on the human mind as a great moral and spiritual power. In fact they habitually speak of it as a mere system of ethical doctrine. Of the second objection, the writings of Mr. F. W. Newman contain many remarkable examples. He has even gone the length of affirming that a revelation of moral truth is an impossibility. In giving utterance to such a paradox, he has laid himself open to a severe retort which constitutes in fact its best refutation. As a writer on moral subjects it is clear that he must consider himself able to impart information to those who are less informed than himself; or in other words, that he has some revelation of moral truth to impart to them. Hence it follows, if his views are correct, that what is impossible to God is possible to himself. Numerous affirmations made by both these writers constitute a remarkable proof that high mental powers form no safeguard against the blinding effects of inveterate prejudices. Of this a short work of the latter entitled *On the Defective Morality of the New Testament*, forms a singular example, the blunders in reasoning being such that if it did not bear the author's name on the title-page, it would have been scarcely credible that it could be the product of his pen.

all the wisdom of the ancient world was unable to discover? Does it bring to bear on man's moral being, a regenerating power, of the want of which the philosopher was deeply conscious, but which his philosophy was unable to supply? If so, the peasants of Galilee have distanced the results effected by all the great teachers of the ancient world. Such are the conditions of the argument.

II. We must now inquire in what does the moral teaching of the New Testament consist. It naturally separates itself into three divisions.

First: a body of special precepts in a very unsystematic form, which were called forth for the purpose of meeting the particular emergencies of those to whom they were addressed; but with no pretensions to constitute a body of ethical doctrines applicable to all time.

Secondly: a number of principles which form the foundation of all moral obligation, and are as Catholic as humanity itself, embracing every conceivable form of duty in their all-comprehensive range.

Thirdly: its chief speciality consists in the revelation of a mighty moral and spiritual power which is intended to render obedience to the moral law a possibility; to elevate the holy to higher degrees of holiness, to rescue those whose powers of self-control are weak from the violence of their passions, and to recover from their degradation those who have fallen into a state of moral corruption. This principle is the power of faith in its action on the moral nature of man; and forms the great characteristic by which the teaching of the New Testament is distinguished from every other system.

III. The following are the chief points in which the teaching of the New Testament is most strikingly contrasted with that of the philosophers; and in which its authors have transcended all the great masters of ancient thought in their deep insight into the realities of things.

First Contrast. Its earnestness, method, and aim.

The first thing which strikes every reader is the intense

earnestness and reality of its teaching. He feels himself brought into contact with a power whose aim is, not to enunciate a mere set of rules for the regulation of life or to write disquisitions on the grounds of moral obligation, but to bring men into subjection to the moral law. In striking contrast to this was the teaching of philosophy. A large portion of its attention was directed to the investigation of the grounds of moral obligation. These Christianity assumes as testified to by the conscience, and therefore sufficiently known. It accepts the moral nature of man as a fact, and assumes that every one of its primary principles has a legitimate sphere of action in its proper place. This has imparted to its teaching a catholicity which is to be found in no other system. Thus, for the purpose of enforcing the practice of holiness, it appeals to every principle which acts mightily on human nature. It addresses itself to the love of God, to the love of Christ, to the principle of benevolence in man, to his self-love, to his perception of moral beauty, to his sense of truth, to his love of justice, to his appreciation of the honourable, his sense of self-respect, his love of approbation, and even to his desire of praise.* These last principles are deeply implanted in human nature; and instead of denouncing them as unhallowed or ignoble, it appeals to every one of them as holding a legitimate place in man's moral constitution.

Striking is the contrast between this and the course which has been pursued by a large number of systematic moralists. They have occupied themselves in endeavouring to ascertain a number of abstract questions respecting the nature of moral obligation; as, for example, whether regard for others or rational self-love constitutes the fundamental

---

* No less than seven of these principles are appealed to by St. Paul in one single passage, as incentives to holiness. "Finally, brethren, whatsoever things are true; whatsoever things are honest (σεμνά); whatsoever things are just; whatsoever things are pure; whatsoever things are lovely; whatsoever things are of good report; if there be any virtue, if there be any praise, think on these things."—Phil. iv. 8.

principle of virtue; and according as they have determined in favour of one or the other, they have elaborated systems based on partial principles, and in disregard of some of the great realities of man's moral constitution.* This is also the case with several of our modern systems. Some of the ancient ones in this respect even displayed a spirit of fanaticism, and preached the uprooting of some of the fundamental principles of our moral constitution as a duty. Other defects inherent in their method have stamped them with an impress which is partial, national, and local. The New Testament, on the contrary, embraces all its

* Such has been the course taken by systematizers in every age, to concentrate the mind on one or two motives as correct principles of action, and to ignore all others, however deeply seated they may be in the moral nature of man. Thus those who have taken a narrow view of Christianity have affirmed that the only motive which ought to influence the Christian is the love of Jesus Christ, and that for a Christian to act on any inferior motive, such as the desire of approbation, or the love of praise, would be almost sinful. The love of Christ is undoubtedly the highest motive appealed to by Christianity; but while the writers of the New Testament habitually place this in the forefront, they appeal to every principle in man's moral constitution which can be enlisted in the service of holiness. Thus St. Paul urges the forwardness of other Churches in making contributions to relieve the poverty of the Church in Judæa as a motive to provoke the Corinthians to additional liberality. Sectarianism would pronounce such a motive unworthy to regulate the conduct of Christian men. St. Paul however, recognizes the fact that every principle in man's moral nature has a legitimate sphere of action, and in so doing, he shows a comprehensiveness of view wholly foreign to the enthusiast or the fanatic. A similar exclusiveness has been often exhibited by philosophy. The principle of self-love is one which is deeply seated in human nature, and as such, it claims to occupy a suitable place in the philosophy of man. But a well-known school denounces the appeal to it as a principle of action, and affirms that an elevated system of morality must be founded on absolute benevolence. Yet Jesus Christ has repeatedly appealed to enlightened self-love as a principle of action. Thus the writers of the New Testament, by recognizing every principle of man's moral nature in its proper subordination, have shown themselves alike free from the exclusiveness of sectarianism and philosophy.

principles within its comprehensive range, and is as catholic as human nature. What is the necessary inference? It is this: that from whatever source its teaching has been derived, it is impossible that it can have been developed by any natural process of evolution out of that hot-bed of narrow-minded bigotry which unbelievers affirm to have constituted the moral and spiritual atmosphere which was breathed by Jesus and His early followers. To attribute such a result to the genius of Jesus is to allow that it cannot be accounted for by the action of any of the known forces energizing in man.

Second Contrast. The freedom of Christianity from all attempts at political legislation.

A very remarkable contrast between the teaching of Christianity and that of philosophy is presented to us in that the former is entirely free from all attempts to deal with either political or social questions. The universal practice of the great philosophers of the ancient world was precisely the reverse. With them moral questions invariably assumed a political aspect; Ethics were in fact a branch of politics. The reason of this is obvious. Their only hope for the regeneration of man was based on the creation of sound political and social institutions, by means of which men might be trained to virtue. Hence they thought it necessary to sketch an ideal republic, which never became an actual one. The Jew on the contrary, who knew nothing of philosophy, was filled with the profoundest reverence for the Scriptures of the Old Testament. These not only propounded a system of political legislation as of divine authority, but the teaching of the prophets is addressed to Israel, not in an individual, but in a corporate or political capacity. Surely if the teaching had been the mere natural outcome of either Jewish or Gentile thought, this striking characteristic would not have been entirely wanting.

But what is still more remarkable, the great Teacher professed to be the founder of a kingdom; yet His abstinence from political and social questions is total: the kingdom which he set up was one which was diverse in character from everything which had existed in the past, being exclusively based on conviction and persuasion. Yet it has existed in full vigour for eighteen centuries; and during this long interval of time, not a single attempt to erect another on the same principles has proved successful. Jesus Christ alone at one single bound has passed from the political, the formal, and the ritual, to the individual, the spiritual, and the moral. The one single sentence of His teaching, which bears a political aspect, "Render to Cæsar the things that are Cæsar's, and to God the things that are God's," has for ever emancipated the conscience from the control of the State, assigning to each their respective limits, and establishing for ever the liberty of the individual.*

* It has often been objected that St. Paul has taught the doctrine of non-resistance to Governments, however tyrannical they may be. (Rom. xiii. 1-9.) This objection has arisen from a disregard of the important principle that the precepts in the Epistles, in the special form in which they are there enunciated, are not portions of a moral code, binding for all time, but were called forth by the special circumstances of those to whom they were addressed. The Jewish element in the Church was always turbulent, and by such persons the doctrine of the Kingdom of God easily admitted of being perverted into a treasonable principle against pagan Governments, and thus compromising the Church as a political institution. Hence it became necessary that the Apostle should carefully guard against this danger, which was so far real that the Roman Government only a short time previously had made it the pretext for expelling all Jews, and doubtless the Christians among them, from the city. Hence in the peculiar circumstances of the Roman Church these precepts of the Apostle against political turbulence are peculiarly appropriate. In them he lays down that civil government is a divine ordinance, and consequently civil obedience a duty which must be conscientiously rendered by the Christian. He then decides the question which the Jews were constantly raising as to the lawfulness of paying taxes to heathen Governments, and affirms that it is a Christian duty to do so on the ground that the end of all government is the protection of the individual, and that this was the divine purpose in its institution. It is quite true that the Apostle has given no precept as to what is the duty of

I need not draw your attention to the fact that the presence of a body of political and social legislation in the Koran constitutes the rock on which Mahomedanism is being hopelessly shipwrecked before our eyes, and utterly unfits it for being the religion of humanity. Is it possible, I ask, that any one who was born and educated under the influences by which Jesus was surrounded could have rigidly excluded all political and social questions from His teaching? With the experience of the past before Him, would any amount of foresight have enabled Him to guess that if He had prescribed a body of political legislation, the consequences would have been fatal to His religion, and would have caused the ruin of that kingdom which it was His purpose to establish. Mr. Mill considers the moral teaching of Christianity defective because it dwells so little on public duties and public virtues.* Such an opinion is not to be wondered at, when we consider that the whole school of thought to which he belongs place their hopes of man's future regeneration on improving his condition politically and socially, rather than by acting on his conscience and his heart. This most remarkable abstinence from entering on questions of this description I claim to be a striking proof that the Founder of Christianity possessed an insight which must have raised Him above all the trammels imposed on Him by His birth and His surroundings, in that while He has kept clear of all political and social questions, He has been able to enforce all the duties which they demand in the all-comprehensive principle of self-sacrifice rendered to Himself. If He had pursued the course which many eminent moderns would have suggested to Him, and commenced His work of regenerating mankind, not by appealing to the conscience of the individual, but by

---

Christians when Governments fail in the discharge of this their proper function. If he had done so he must have converted his epistle into a political treatise, and incurred the danger which under the existing circumstances of the Church he wished to avoid.

* *Essay on Liberty.*

addressing Himself to the external, the social, and the political, Christianity would never have survived the century that gave it birth.*

It will perhaps be urged that the far-seeing genius of Jesus enabled Him thus to penetrate into the realities of the distant future. But genius can only act in conformity with the laws of our intellectual and moral being. If therefore Jesus was a genius after the model of other great men, and nothing more, all this profound insight must have been generated in the solitary musings of a Jew, whose moral and spiritual surroundings were the atmosphere of narrow exclu-

* The mode in which Christianity deals with the great social question of Slavery is a remarkable instance of the profound wisdom which dwelt in the authors of the New Testament. Many modern writers would have had Our Lord and His Apostles denounce it as an unhallowed institution. What would have been the consequences if they had done so? It would have brought down the whole weight of the Roman Government on the Church as a political society whose object was to subvert the existing order of things, and thus have caused its speedy extinction. If on the other hand an anti-slavery propaganda had been instituted, and any amount of success had attended its efforts, which in the then condition of society was in the highest degree improbable, the result would have been a war of classes; and we know as a matter of fact that the previous revolts of the slaves had been attended with one result only, the production of a frightful amount of human misery, and the more firmly rivetting their chains. The course taken by Christianity in dealing with this great evil has been very different from that which modern theorisers would have suggested, but it has been an effectual one. Instead of a number of precepts directly aimed at Slavery, it has laid down certain great principles of duty obligatory towards all men, with the practice of which the existence of Slavery is impossible. These have gradually leavened the whole atmosphere of thought, and after a long and severe struggle Slavery has become extinct in every nation which professes Christianity. In this manner it has far more effectually crushed the evil than if it had openly declared war against it as a social institution. Other social evils will share the same fate in proportion as its great principles gradually leaven the entire lump of humanity. Nothing can afford a stronger proof that Christianity has not been the invention of a number of credulous fanatics than the wisdom it has shown in dealing with these and kindred questions.

siveness, and who perished at the early age of thirty-four. We may call this genius, if we please, but it must be one which manifests the presence of the superhuman.

Third Contrast. The teaching of Christianity has founded the religion of humanity.

I adduce from the Fourth Gospel another instance of the profound insight which must have dwelt in the Author of Christianity or whoever put the saying into His mouth, by which he has enthroned religion in the centre of man's moral and spiritual being. The utterance to which I allude, is the great utterance made to the woman of Samaria, " Woman, believe me, the hour is coming when ye shall neither in this mountain nor yet at Jerusalem worship the Father. . . . But the hour cometh and now is, when the true worshippers shall worship the Father in spirit and in truth, for the Father seeketh such to worship him. God is a Spirit; and they that worship Him must worship Him in spirit and in truth." John iv. 21, 24.

Mr. Mill has expressed the opinion that the utterances which the author of this Gospel has put into the mouth of Jesus (and he makes no exception in favour of the one before us), are "Poor Stuff." It was only in conformity with the principles of his philosophy, and of the atmosphere of thought in which he was nurtured from his earliest years, that he should have been incapable of appreciating their insight and their depth. M. Renan, however, affirms that in this utterance Jesus has for ever laid deep the foundations of the religion of humanity. Can there be any doubt, I ask, with respect to this great saying, that an overwhelming majority of deep thinkers will confirm his verdict. No such profound utterance had up to this time passed the lips of man.

What then are the facts before us? Jesus, or the author of this Gospel, who has put the saying into His mouth, must have been possessed of an insight so profound as to have burst through all the conditions of his environment, and in three short sentences laid deep for all ages the everlasting foundations of the temple of humanity. The repudiation of what is national, local, and outward is complete, and religion is declared to rest for evermore on the Fatherhood of God. By this act he has effected what the philosophers were unable to accomplish, the union of man's religious aspirations with his moral nature. Compare with this our modern worship of humanity, and its moral aspects. Surely those unbelievers who allow a religion to be possible must concede that the Author of this saying has placed it on a foundation which will endure for evermore. Yet the moral and spiritual atmosphere in the midst of which He was born and nurtured, was the exclusiveness of Judaism. If it be said that an insight which rose to such an elevation above its surroundings, was due to the exalted genius of the prophet of Nazareth, I shall not absolutely quarrel with the term, but it must have been a genius which manifested the presence of the superhuman.

Fourth Contrast. The all-comprehensiveness of the Christian law of duty.

I now ask your attention to the great law of duty as enunciated by Christianity, and its all-comprehensive character. The great Teacher who, if there was nothing superhuman in him, must have been a mere peasant, nurtured in the narrow exclusiveness of Judaism, has by the enunciation of three great principles, solved all the various questions of duty raised by the endless discussions of philosophers. These are:—

First. Man's duty to man, as founded on, and originating in the relation in which man stands to God.

Secondly. Man's duty to man, measured by the regard which he feels for himself.

Thirdly. Man's duty to man, measured and sanctioned by the obligations he is under to Jesus Christ.

The first of these makes the law of duty co-extensive with the human family. We are all aware that the greatest of the ancient philosophers failed to discover any law of duty which could make it co-extensive with all races and conditions of men. They did not regard duty as an obligation to man as man, but restricted it within the narrow bounds of citizenship, race, and social condition; and consequently looked upon the majority of mankind as pariahs, who stood outside the pale of obligation. Some dim conception of the universal brotherhood of mankind may be found in the later Stoic philosophy, but it exists only as a barren speculation, devoid of any substantial basis. Ancient philosophy, in short, divorced morality from religion, and thereby deprived itself of all moral and spiritual power. Jesus Christ, on the contrary, has united the two, and thereby strengthened the moral principle by all the sanctions which religion can impart. Contrast with the teaching of the illiterate Jewish peasant that of our modern Atheistic and Pantheistic systems. Instead of being able to announce a law of duty extending to all men, because all men are the children of the same gracious Father, who has made all the nations of the earth, the only bond of union they can suggest is, not that all men are the children of the same Father in heaven, but that they are the common descendants of some primeval savage.*

* All modern systems of anti-Christian philosophy find it impossible to propound any principle which can form an effectual basis on which to rest the universal brotherhood of mankind. The question demands an answer—How do we know that we owe obligations to others? Why is self-sacrifice a duty? To those who admit that gratitude and a sense of justice are inherent portions of man's moral nature, and that the voice of conscience is authoritative, the answer is not difficult. The principle that we are bound to render to others what we would wish to have done to ourselves, is at once pronounced by it to be in accordance with the highest reason. The answer of Christianity on this point is clear and distinct. God is our Creator, and the Creator of all men. From Him come down every faculty and power we possess, and we are His stewards in the use of them. He has therefore a right to demand the highest self-sacrifice; and the voice of conscience asserts that His claims are just. As therefore all men are the children of God, all fall within a common bond of obligation, as members of the same family. But if the Fatherhood of God, and the principle of intuitional morality is renounced, the question Why is one man bound to an act of self-sacrifice on behalf of another, becomes incapable of solution. A system which denies that our moral

The second great principle of the teaching of Jesus renders the law of duty self-determinative, *i.e.*, it converts the individual conscience into a law to itself. Under it the question, What is my duty in this or that particular instance? is infallibly answered by another, which the questioner may put to himself, What would I have done to me, if I were in that man's place? Obedience may be hard, but the answer will certainly be unmistakably distinct.

The third great principle carries the law of duty to its extremest limits. The love of Jesus Christ to man is made both the measure and the motive of the love of man to man. It has been objected (I think absurdly) that the divine rule, " Thou shalt love thy neighbour as thyself" (obedience to

perceptions of right and wrong are intuitional, is compelled to resolve all moral distinctions into mere questions of expediency; or, in other words, into the principle of self-love. If it be affirmed that the sacrifice of self for others is a duty merely because it is conducive to our own highest happiness, the difficulty is, to prove it. In fact there are cases of unquestionable duty, where the highest forms of self-sacrifice, even that of life itself, are demanded of us, where such proof becomes impossible. Atheistic and Pantheistic systems of thought have no resource but to base moral obligation on expediency. If this be its only foundation, it is clear that each man must be a measure of obligation to himself only as far as he is capable of perceiving that a particular line of conduct is conducive to his own happiness. I am aware that this principle is affirmed to mean the greatest happiness of the greatest number, and not merely the greatest happiness of the individual. But the question immediately arises, How do we know that it is obligatory on us to pursue the greatest happiness of the greatest number except as far as the realization of it is conducive to our own? It is quite conceivable that the pursuit of the greatest happiness of the greatest number may involve a degree of self-sacrifice which is inconsistent with the pursuit of our own individual good. The fact is, that all theories which refuse to rest duty on some intuitional basis resolve it into a question of accurate calculation; and the best man will be he who possesses the clearest head. The Fatherhood of God being renounced, and the intuitional perception of any moral principle denied, Atheistic and Pantheistic philosophy are able to announce no principle binding on the conscience which will bring all mankind within the range of obligation.

which would certainly go far to convert this world into a heaven), sets up a selfish standard of morality. Those who have made the objection, if they had looked a little further, would have found in the last great precept of Jesus Christ, which he designates his "new Commandment," a rule which would have gratified their most unselfish wishes; "Love one another, *as I have loved you.*" This removes the ideal of duty out of self; and measures and sanctions it by the divine self-sacrifice of Christ our Lord. Surely this is one beyond which it is impossible for human thought to pass. On this is founded the great Christian duty of self-sacrifice, which underlies the whole moral teaching of the New Testament, and which embraces within its comprehensive range all other possible duties, whether they be individual, social, or political. Every duty which man owes to man in every situation in life in which he is placed, he is bound to render as a grateful sacrifice to Christ his Lord, whom he is bound to glorify alike in life and death. I earnestly draw your attention to this principle, because its existence is overlooked by the various classes of unbelievers who treat of the moral teaching of Christianity, and pronounce it defective.* A popular school of modern thought has made the charge against Christianity of not having made adequate provision for the discharge of those duties which man owes to the public. Surely those who have made this charge must have read the New Testament with blinded eyes, for nothing can be clearer than that its great fundamental

---

* I am not aware that Mr. Mill has once recognized the fact that the great Christian duty of sacrifice of self as due to Christ our Lord; nor the equally comprehensive one that the Christian in every position in society in which he is placed as God's steward, is bound to use every gift with which he is entrusted to God's glory, as a fundamental principle, which underlies the moral teaching of the New Testament. His philosophy was no doubt very adverse to its recognition. Yet surely it is absurd to discuss the value of any system, above all, to pronounce it inadequate to meet the requirements of advancing civilization, when we neglect to include its most fundamental principles in our survey of it.

principles of our being stewards of God, and our duty of sacrifice of self, measured by the self-sacrifice of Christ, must include every social duty which man can owe to man.*

* The New Testament lays down another principle which has a most important bearing on the obligation of the Christian to the faithful discharge of all the various duties which he owes to the public. It teaches that every mental gift which he possesses, and the position in society in which he is placed are a stewardship intrusted to him by God, for the right discharge of which he is responsible. The overlooking of these two great principles has caused many unbelievers to charge the moral teaching of Christianity with imperfection. It is clear that if the position in society in which a Christian is placed is a stewardship intrusted to him by God, he is bound by the strongest considerations to the diligent discharge of the various duties which it imposes on him. If he possesses wealth, he is bound to administer it, not merely as he pleases, but under a direct feeling of responsibility to God who has intrusted him with it. The same is true of every mental endowment, and of all the political and social influence he possesses. Christianity, in short, is ignorant of the distinction so commonly laid down between religious and secular duties; between things sacred and the pursuits of daily life. It has made every duty which man can owe to man a religious duty. It has sanctified the whole of human life, including its pleasures and enjoyments, and claimed it for God. "None of us liveth unto himself" says the Apostle, "and no man dieth unto himself," "Ye serve the Lord Christ." The error above referred to has originated in the idea that Christianity has so directed our attention to the importance of the world to come as to divert it from the concerns of the present. This however is an evident misapprehension of its teaching. It is perfectly true that it speaks in the strongest manner of our interest in the future state; and that the interests of this world are unimportant in comparison with those of the next. But its assertions are no less emphatic that the only mode of securing our interests in the world to come is by a faithful discharge of every duty which man owes to man in the present. Thus, instead of disparaging the importance of present duties, it imparts the highest possible sanction to the conscientious and faithful discharge of them. The fact is, that Christianity lays down that this world is God's world; and that whatever duty man is called upon to discharge, he is to do it heartily unto the Lord, and not to man, because he is bound to glorify God in his body and in his spirit, which are God's. Such is the provision which Christianity makes for the discharge of all the duties

Striking then is the contrast between the all-comprehensive teaching of the illiterate Jewish peasant and that of the profoundest teachers of the ancient world. The one is one-sided, national and partial; the other as catholic as human nature, and as many sided as the moral nature of man. The one bears on it the impress of those by whom it was elaborated; the other has burst through every trammel which was imposed on it by its surroundings. The one discussed questions of duty with endless prolixity; the other by a few comprehensive utterances has solved all such questions for evermore. Whence then did this man derive all this wisdom? The profoundest thinkers of the ancient world with all the mass of accumulated experience at their command, were unable to approach to the comprehensiveness or the elevation of His teaching. Yet if Christianity be a mere human development, this world-wide catholicity must have been evolved out of a system of narrow-minded exclusiveness.

IV. Another contrast between the teaching of the New Testament and that of the philosophers, which probably strikes every intelligent reader, is the relative importance it assigns to the milder virtues. As no inconsiderable amount of misrepresentation has taken place on this subject, I will briefly state what are the actual facts.

Respecting the views of philosophy there can be little doubt. The political or heroical virtues occupy the first place in every system; the milder ones a place wholly subordinate; and one of them, humility, a virtue much insisted on by Christianity, has no place at all. We have only to read the Ethics of Aristotle to ascertain the fact, and the writings of the great philosopher fairly represent the views of the

we owe to the public; and I maintain that it is more comprehensive than that enjoined by any system of modern teaching, and sanctioned by the highest motives that can be brought to bear on man. If on the other hand we view the question as one of fact, it is certain that no servants of the public discharge their duties with greater faithfulness and devotion than those who are thoroughly leavened with the principles of Christianity.

ancient world. If we consider its standpoint, the case could hardly have been otherwise. Christianity on the contrary places the milder virtues in the forefront, quite as emphatically as philosophy did the political ones.* Of some of these latter, such as patriotism, it takes no direct notice. To the practice of others its exhortations are few; but so earnest is its effort to enforce the practice of the milder ones, that several of its precepts, if taken literally, and detached from the immediate circumstances which called them forth, may be said to be inconsistent with a due regard for the public rights of man.

In considering this subject it should be borne in mind that while it was the end and purpose of philosophy to propound a complete ethical code, such was wholly foreign to the aim of the writers of the New Testament. While the great principles of the latter are of world-wide comprehensiveness, their special precepts are invariably called forth

---

* I do not claim for Christianity absolute originality in assigning a more prominent place to the milder virtues. The principle is very distinctly recognized in the Old Testament Scriptures. In fact the assigning a prominent place to certain virtues, such as humility, the existence of which is scarcely recognized by pagan ethics, is inseparable from any system of theism which views God as the Creator of all things, and man as standing in a personal relation to Him as His creature. Whenever this conception receives a practical recognition, all those feelings which spring out of man's relationship to God, and from a sense of sin, are called into lively exercise. But while the Old Testament assigns to the milder virtues a very different place from that which is assigned to them in pagan ethics, most of its great characters are striking exemplifications of the predominance of the heroic ones. A few of them exhibit the former qualities, but taking the whole as a series, the sterner aspects of human nature unquestionably predominate. It is therefore quite true that it has been reserved for Christianity to bring the importance of the milder virtues into prominent light, by placing them in the forefront of its teachings; and above all, by exhibiting them as the predominant element in the divine character of Christ our Lord. The manner in which they are exhibited in Him, in the closest union with, but yet predominant over the heroical ones, constitute Him the perfect exhibition of moral loveliness.

by the special circumstances of those to whom they are addressed.* Consequently before they can be applied to other circumstances and conditions, they require to be resolved into the principles on which they are based, and then accommodated to the altered facts. They are in fact directions for practice under special circumstances; and to interpret them as though they were intended as abstract precepts binding on man for all time, is utterly to mistake their meaning. Thus a strong precept inculcating the duty of obedience to governors, might be very appropriate when addressed to a body of turbulent Jews, but would be wholly inapplicable to the free citizens of a well-ordered State. Similarly, precepts urging abnegation of the rights of property might have been very necessary when addressed to certain conditions of society, which would be absolutely pernicious if regarded as applicable to every state of civilization.† Nothing has been a

* The precepts given by St. Paul to the Roman and Corinthian Churches in reference to the duty of observing certain days, and the lawfulness of eating certain kinds of food, form a very remarkable illustration of this principle. The circumstances which called them forth have passed away: and consequently the precepts, in the form in which they were given by the Apostle, have no direct bearing on the present condition of the Church. But the underlying principles are valid for all time for the solution of a vast number of questions beyond those which came within the Apostle's immediate view. They lay down the broadest principles of toleration with respect to the differences which arise among Christians in every age; and may be truly said to constitute the "Magna Charta" of religious liberty. Would that the Church had given heed to them during the various controversies that have agitated her throughout the long period of her history! The principles of no modern philosophical system surpass them in comprehensiveness. Yet they are the utterances of one who was born and nurtured amid the narrowest Jewish fanaticism and intolerance, and who had carried out these principles by fiercely persecuting the Church.

† I allude to those which seem to condemn saving, and to enjoin indiscriminate almsgiving. There can be no doubt that if such precepts were acted on to the letter, they would not only occasion a far greater amount of misery than would be relieved by their observance,

more fruitful source of error respecting the teaching of the New Testament, than this assumption that its precepts, as distinct from its great moral principles, were intended to constitute a body of ethical doctrine applicable to all time, instead of being specially addressed to particular Churches and individuals, in reference to the circumstances in which they were placed.

On the other hand it should be observed that, although the political virtues receive but a partial recognition, they are strongly exemplified in the actions of its great characters. While there is scarcely a precept which enjoins courage or self-respect, the world contains no grander example of these two virtues than is exhibited in the Founder of Christianity and the Apostle Paul. I invite you to compare the portraiture of the Jesus of the Gospels as exhibiting the perfection of self-conscious dignity with that which has been drawn by the great author of the Ethics, of his μεγα-

---

but would be destructive of modern civilization. It has been said that such precepts are intended to embody an ideal morality, which would be fitted to a perfect state of society. I cannot attribute anything so unpractical to Our Lord and His Apostles, for it is clear that they did not anticipate the realization of a perfect state of society during the present condition of things; and when it was realized, such precepts would be unnecessary. The only correct view seems to me to be, that they are precepts enunciated in a very popular form, addressed to a state of thought and feeling in which the opposite tendencies were extremely powerful. As a general fact there can be no doubt that the benevolent impulses are the weakest in human nature, and therefore require to be called forth by having the whole weight of the religious principle thrown into the scale with them; and that those which terminate in self are so powerful as to require the strongest repression. I fully allow that these precepts (which are far fewer in number than is commonly supposed,) if carried out to the letter, amount to communism; but the great Teacher Himself has given an emphatic warning against such a mode of interpreting them, and so has the Apostle Paul (John vi. 63; 2 Cor. iii. 6). Taking the teaching of the New Testament as a whole, it is clear that while it makes the strongest effort to awaken the benevolent affections, it keeps itself wholly free from communistic principles.

λύψυχος, or magnanimous man. The comparison makes the latter seem like a burlesque. Though none of the writers of the New Testament have written direct commendations of courage, they exhibit the brightest example of it in their practice, and place it on its true foundation in the great saying, "It is right to obey God rather than man." The very men whose exhortations to the practice of the milder virtues are so strong that they almost seem to have overlooked the existence of the heroic, exhibit these latter in their practice on the grandest scale, affording them thereby the highest recognition.

I fully concede, however, that while it is an utter misrepresentation of the moral teaching of the New Testament, to charge on it the purpose of superseding the heroical and political virtues, it was its aim and purpose to reverse the order in which they stood in the estimation of the ancient world. Admitting the fact, the important question is, have they in adopting this course exhibited a deep insight into the realities of human nature? Which in fact have been right, the writers of the New Testament or the philosophers, in the relative importance they have assigned to these two classes of virtues? If this question can be decided by authority, there cannot be a doubt that since Christianity has pronounced in favour of the milder virtues, an overwhelming majority of the wisest and the holiest of men have accepted its decision as the right one. There can be no doubt that if, during the last three thousand years, the milder virtues had occupied the place which the heroical ones have held in men's estimation, the happiness of mankind would have increased a thousand-fold. Take, for example, the three great political virtues, of courage, patriotism and ambition, which have in all ages commanded the most unbounded admiration. When we calmly survey the pages of history, is it, I ask, too much to affirm that a large portion of the crimes with which it has been stained, have been due to the unrestrained action of these three qualities: qualities noble in themselves, but which become simply pernicious when uncontrolled and unregulated by the predominant influence of the milder virtues ? The political and heroical ones are highly valuable when kept in proper subordination to the milder qualities of the human mind ; but when they reign supreme and alone, as they have generally done throughout the ages of the past, the perniciousness of their influence has only been in proportion to their greatness.

I claim therefore for the writers of the New Testament, that in reversing the order of the importance of the virtues, they have shown a profound insight into the realities of human nature; and that they are right in assigning the first place to the fruits of the Spirit of God, and the subordinate one to the qualities in question. The place they have assigned to the milder virtues, and their exhibition of them in combination with the heroical ones in the person of Jesus Christ, have, in the words of Mr. Lecky, "done more to regenerate and soften mankind, than all the disquisitions of philosophers, and than all the exhortations of moralists."

Fifth Contrast. The views taken by Jesus Christ and by the philosophers of the extent of their respective missions.

The next striking contrast between the Founder of Christianity and the philosophers is His great conception of addressing His mission to the masses of mankind, while theirs was confined to a small spiritual aristocracy. In this respect the interval which separates Jesus Christ from the traditions of the past is profound. He is the founder and the leader of all the benevolent and missionary exertions in the modern world, and has made the duty of following His example an inherent portion of His system to such an extent that it is impossible for any genuine disciple to avoid making Him the subject of his imitation.

I need not in this place dwell on the exclusiveness of the great teachers of the ancient world. This was inevitable from their position. Their teaching was not a religion, but a philosophy, and their object was to form a school for its study. Hence it was that nothing could be more alien to the ideas of the philosopher than to go out into the highways and hedges of humanity, and compel the degraded to come in. The reason is obvious. Philosophy had no Gospel of good news for such. With the means at its command it could only address itself to the intellectual aristocracy of mankind. Two sentences will, I think, present the contrast between the method of Jesus and that of the philosophers in a striking light. Jesus Christ affirmed that He came not to call the righteous but sinners to repentance. Philosophy affirmed that its special mission was "to those of mankind who have a natural tendency and disposition towards virtue." The conception which Jesus Christ and the philosophers entertained of their respective missions differed as widely as the poles.

I boldly affirm that all modern attempts to ameliorate the condition of the masses have originated in this grand conception of Jesus Christ. He is the originator, the leader, and the pioneer of every self-sacrificing effort which has been made for the improvement of mankind; its example, and what is more, the motive force which has impelled all subsequent efforts. In this respect it is beyond all question that the teaching and example of Jesus has transcended that of all philosophy. Yet if the positions of unbelievers be true, the genius of a peasant, born and educated in the narrowest atmosphere of Jewish exclusiveness, has originated and carried out this grand conception. If it be so, the genius which has effected this great result must have been an inspiration from above, for it is unique in the history of mankind.*

---

* It will perhaps be urged that Socrates took a wider view of his mission than that which I have assigned to the philosophers; that he spent his whole life in endeavouring to improve his fellow-citizens in virtue; and that he died a martyr to his exertions. There can be no doubt that he took a wider view of his mission than that which was taken by the other philosophers. Still it was confined to the citizens of a single State; and these formed the intellectual aristocracy of the ancient world. The philosopher affirms in his defence that it was his fixed purpose to confine his labours to his countrymen; and in reply to all exhortations to avoid the dangers which surrounded him, by

Sixth Contrast. The creation by Christianity of a mighty moral and spiritual power, which, while philosophy confessed the need of it, it failed to discover.

This brings me to the consideration of the most striking contrast which exists between the teaching of philosophy and that of Christianity, viz. the affirmation which Christianity makes that it possesses within itself a moral and

transferring his labours to another sphere of action, declined to do so on the ground that it would prove an uncongenial soil. It is clear therefore that Socrates never entertained the idea of a mission to mankind, nor even to the Grecian race, but that his efforts were strictly confined to the improvement of his fellow-citizens. With these in the public places of resort he spent his time in arguing and discussing. Between his own conception of his mission and that of Jesus Christ, or even that of an Old Testament prophet, there is scarcely a single point of resemblance. Jesus Christ authoritatively announced a number of great truths which penetrated to the depths of the human heart. The method of the philosopher was to create a philosophy by awakening a spirit of sceptical inquiry. He declared that he could affirm nothing as certain. His whole position disqualified him to act the part of a preacher of repentance, and none would have more readily admitted than himself that he was devoid of the means of acting as the regenerator of those who were fallen into a condition of moral corruption and degradation. His views were incapable of appreciation except by those who possessed a high order of intellectual power, and a character in some degree congenial to his own. This is evident from the discourses attributed to him by his two great disciples, unless they have wholly misrepresented his meaning. It is true that he addressed himself to the citizens generally, but the mode of his address was only calculated to attract the intellectual aristocracy among them. These he endeavoured to discover in every circle of society. The result was, that his leading disciples became, not a number of missionaries who exhorted mankind to repentance and conversion, or conceived that it was their special duty to devote themselves to the improvement of the condition of degraded man, but the founders of a number of philosophic sects. There is nothing therefore in the conduct or the example of Socrates which at all affects the originality of the conception of the Founder of Christianity; but everything to impress us with a sense of the unique power with which He has acted as the regenerator and the ameliorator of the condition of mankind.

spiritual power, adequate to effect the regeneration of mankind. This power, it affirms, can elevate the holy to higher degrees of holiness, and rescue the degraded from their degradation. This portion of my subject is one of profound importance, and to it I earnestly invite your attention, for it is one which has been greatly overlooked in the entire controversy. Of the want of such a power all the ancient philosophers were profoundly conscious, but all their efforts failed to produce any permanent influence on the regeneration of mankind from their inability to discover one. The originality of the claim on the part of Christianity to have created such a power is unquestionable.

In proof of this, I adduce the whole course of ancient philosophic thought. If we read the entire remains of ancient literature, we shall arise from it with the conviction that the idea of preaching repentance and amendment to those portions of mankind who were sinking into a state of moral corruption, or who had already become degraded, was one which never entered into the heads of the philosophers. Yet it is a certain fact that from the time of Socrates onwards, man, intellectually, politically, and morally, formed the chief subject of their investigations. To their labours we are deeply indebted, for they have thrown a flood of light on what could or could not be effected by rational investigation, before the great spiritual Sun threw the radiance of his beams on the moral and spiritual world. Their expenditure of intellect on this subject was enormous. Of the tendency of man to moral corruption they were profoundly sensible, and have submitted its causes and its symptoms to a minute analysis of which we enjoy the benefit. But did this produce on their part an energetic effort to work its cure. No; they did what the Priest and the Levite in the parable did to the wounded traveller. They looked curiously and with inquiring eye on degraded man, and passed by on the other side, leaving him to perish in his degradation. Was this owing to inhumanity? No; they felt that they had no means of cure. When moral deterioration had advanced to a certain stage, philosophy contemplated it with despair. Read your Ethics. Portions of the Seventh book speak on this point in language which it is impossible to misunderstand. That passage in the Tenth book, in which the great philosopher surveys the probable results of his labours, is almost pathetic in its melancholy.* Whom did he, the spiritual physician, consider himself capable of benefiting? A small body of ingenuous youths, born with a natural tendency to what is good and noble; but as for the masses, they have no perception of the morally beautiful, and can only be operated on by the fear of punishment. Such are the views which the great philosopher, with his deep insight into human nature, took of the hopeless character of moral corruption. For it he knew no remedy. We need not wonder therefore that the Schools pronounced on the degraded multitude the ban of spiritual excommunication.

To those who are acquainted with the range of ancient philosophic thought, the reason of its impotency to deal with moral corruption will not be difficult to discover. The philosopher was profoundly conscious that there was no moral and spiritual power which he was capable of wielding adequate to cope with the violence of the passions. Reason

* Εἰ μὲν οὖν ἦσαν οἱ λόγοι αὐτάρκεις πρὸς τὸ ποιῆσαι ἐπιεικεῖς πολλοὺς ἂν μισθοὺς καὶ μεγάλους δικαίως, ἔφερον κατὰ τὸν Θέογνιν, καὶ ἔδει ἂν τούτους πορίσασθαι· νῦν δὲ φαίνονται προτρέψασθαι μὲν, καὶ παρορμῆσαι τῶν νέων τοὺς ἐλευθέρους ἰσχύειν, ἦθος τ'εὐγενὲς καὶ ὡς ἀληθῶς φιλόκαλον ποιῆσαι ἂν κατοκώχιμον ἐκ τῆς ἀρετῆς, τοὺς δὲ πολλοὺς ἀδυνατεῖν πρὸς καλοκαγαθίαν προτρέψασθαι· οὐ γὰρ πεφύκασιν αἰδοῖ πειθαρκεῖν ἀλλὰ φόβῳ, οὐδ' ἀπέχεσθαι τῶν φαύλων διὰ τὸ αἰσχρὸν ἀλλὰ διὰ τὰς τιμωρίας· πάθει γὰρ ζῶντες τὰς οἰκείας ἡδονὰς διώκουσι καὶ δι' ὧν αὗται ἔσονται, φεύγουσι δὲ τὰς ἀντικειμένας λύπας, τοῦ δὲ καλοῦ καὶ ὡς ἀληθῶς ἡδέος οὐδ' ἔννοιαν ἔχουσιν, ἀγευστοι ὄντες. Τοὺς δὴ τοιούτους τίς ἂν λόγος μεταρρυθμίσαι; οὐ γὰρ οἷόντε ἢ οὐ ῥᾴδιον τὰ ἐκ παλαιοῦ τοῖς ἤθεσι κατειλημμένα λόγῳ μεταστῆσαι. * * * Οὐ γὰρ ἂν ἀκούσειε λόγου ἀποτρέποντος οὐδ' αὖ συνείη ὁ κατὰ πάθος ζῶν· τὸν δ' οὕτως ἔχοντα πῶς οἷόντε μεταπεῖσαι; ὅλως τ' οὐ δοκεῖ λόγῳ ὑπείκειν τὸ πάθος ἀλλὰ βίᾳ.—*Ethics*, Book X. Chap. 10.

was the only principle to which he could appeal; but he was unable to produce convictions of sufficient strength to kindle into active energy the higher principles of our moral being.

Let me briefly enumerate the only forces at his command, by the aid of which he could set himself to the task of reforming a degraded character. He could appeal to the ordinary incentives to virtue, as the love of the morally beautiful, or the nobleness of self-sacrifice; but what effect could such appeals have on those in whom such perceptions were wanting? To what purpose was it to exhort a man who had entered on the downward course of vice to practise holiness because it was morally beautiful to do so? How could such an appeal aid the man who had become the slave of his appetites and passions, or even whose principle of self-control was weakened? It is clear that if such a person could be reclaimed at all, it could only be by the creation of some powerful conviction in his inmost spirit capable of energizing mightily on his entire moral being. But the creation of such a conviction was the very thing which philosophy was unable to effect. It had nothing to hold up to the eye of faith that could mightily influence the spirit of man, or awaken him from the stupor and slavery of vice. If, on the other hand, he appealed to the principle of self-love, and argued that a virtuous life was on the whole more conducive to happiness, the evidence of this was not sufficiently strong to command the assent of a degraded or even an imperfect character. On such the prospect of remote good is powerless against the violence of present impulse.

Let us suppose that a person conscious that his powers of self-control were weak, but who was desirous of returning to the practice of virtue, had consulted the philosopher as his spiritual physician, and asked him for a prescription which would restore him to moral health, what must have been his answer? Do virtuous actions, and in time you will form virtuous principles; restrain your passions, and in time you will acquire the habit of self-control. But if the diseased man had replied, how am I to be rendered capable of performing these virtuous actions, while destitute of the power of self-control; or how am I to restrain the violence of the passions, unless you can call into active energy some force which is capable of mastering them, no answer except a few platitudes from the philosopher's standpoint was possible. The reason for this is obvious. The philosopher was incapable of appealing to the conscience through the medium of religious conviction, for of such conviction he himself was destitute. His prescription would have been a mere mockery of the patient.

But there was another force with which the philosopher was acquainted, and on which his only hope of the possible regeneration of mankind was based, that of habit. The question therefore becomes one of profound importance, Is it a power capable of regenerating mankind, or reforming the individual; or must it be supplemented by a mightier influence? Now the powerful influence of habit is undeniable. To a very considerable extent it has made us what we are. While it is an unquestionable fact that man possesses a principle of volition which within definite limits is capable of influencing the formation of his character, yet it is no less true that the characters of a great majority of mankind are largely affected by habits which have been impressed on them by their birth and surroundings. According to a very popular theory of modern philosophy, even those portions of our characters which we suppose to be original, are nothing else than accumulations of habits which have been handed down by our remote ancestors. As my present duty is to deal with facts, I am not called on to discuss the truth, or falsehood, of a theory of this description. I only notice it, because, if true, it forms the strongest evidence of the powerlessness of habit to effect the regeneration of the individual, and of the slowness of its operation in the improvement of the race.

As the force of habit is the only one known to philosophy which is capable of powerfully acting on character, it becomes a matter of the highest importance to ascertain how far it is adequate to effect the regeneration of the individual or the race. On the other hand the New Testament propounds another and mightier force, which it designates faith, as alone able to effectuate this purpose. Is it philosophically right in doing so ? If it is, it has a most important bearing on our argument. I observe—

First: the operation of habit on character is necessarily slow, being in fact the accumulated result of actions constantly repeated. Consequently, the changes which take place in the moral world under its influence can only be very gradual. This alone renders it incapable of acting as a great regenerating power on the individual.

Secondly: habit can only act through materials already existing in the character, or the surroundings, but is incapable of creating a new principle of life. It is a powerful lever; but without a fulcrum on which to support itself, it is powerless. Consequently under its influences men can do little more than develop the characters which are impressed on them by their birth and surroundings. If they are good by nature, habit will cause them gradually to increase in goodness ; if bad, in vice. I fully admit that the individual has the power, if he chooses to exert it, of slowly modifying his character under the discipline of habituation; but to render this possible, he must be possessed of a considerable power of self-control; and of this, characters that are imperfect and morally corrupt are entirely destitute.* The old prophet exactly described the effects of

* The slowness of the action of habit in producing changes in the character is of itself a sufficient reason why it is powerless to effect the regeneration of an individual who is in an advanced stage of moral corruption. Whatever changes can be effected in a formed character can only be gradual. But in the case of a man who is morally corrupt, not only have evil principles to be eradicated, but good ones to be generated. The term of human life is far too short to render the regeneration of a vicious character possible in this way, even if the other conditions were favourable. I make this observation on the supposition that a man is attempting the work of self reform by the sole aid of the principle of habituation. As a matter of fact

habit when he said, "Can the Ethiopian change his skin, or the leopard his spots; then may they do good who are accustomed to do evil." Philosophy itself says plainly that it can only exert an influence for good, where there is a large substratum of goodness on which to commence its operations.

Thirdly. The only mode in which habit can be used as a means of strengthening the character of one in whom the principle of self-control has been weakened is by bringing to bear on him some external power of coercion. This results from the fact that virtuous principles can only be formed and strengthened by doing virtuous actions. But how can a man do them who is a prey to the violence of his passions? It is evident that the only mode of enabling him to do them is by bringing to bear on him a power of external coercion sufficient to restrain him until he has acquired the habit of self-control.

From this has resulted the political character of all the ancient and several of the modern systems of Ethics. The philosopher saw plainly that he could do little or nothing in the way of regenerating the individual who had become habituated to evil. Hence his only hope of improving mankind lay in founding a society in which men should be trained to virtue, or, if necessary, coerced into it by a system of discipline. Of the effects of such a training he saw some remarkable examples in some of the small States of antiquity, which existed under very peculiar conditions. He hoped therefore that if he could obtain the power of legislation he could produce important results in a select number of citizens in favour of virtue. Mr. Mill has even given utterance to the opinion that what was done on a small scale by a particular system of training may be done on a larger one on mankind in

we know that nothing is more difficult to uproot than a confirmed habit of vice. Every act of self-indulgence weakens the power of self-control; and the moment the temptation presents itself, the old habit re-asserts its power.

general. If the name of Sparta could elicit the sacrifice of the individual to the State, why may not the conception of humanity be made to call forth the same self-sacrifice for the interests of mankind? I reply, that the conditions are so widely different that there is no parallel between the two cases.* The possibility, however, need not be discussed,

* The position taken by those who affirm that the enthusiasm for humanity may be made a substitute for a religion is this. Several of the ancient republics, of which Sparta and Rome are conspicuous examples, succeeded by means of a careful system of training in evoking on the part of the individual a profound feeling of the duty of self-sacrifice to the interests of the State. This was carried to such an extent that large bodies of citizens were prepared to sacrifice even life itself sooner than bring dishonour on their country. Hence it has been argued that what was practicable on a small scale, must be capable of being realized on a large one, and that under a suitable system of training, the same spirit of sacrifice of the individual may thus be elicited for the general interest of mankind as that which was displayed by the citizen of old for the State of which he was a member. One objection against this view is obvious; it is a theory which contradicts all the facts with which we are acquainted. The spirit of patriotic self-sacrifice has always been the strongest in small communities. It is no theory, but a fact, that it burnt with a far stronger flame in the small states of antiquity, which consisted of a few thousand citizens, than in our modern kingdoms, which number their subjects by millions. Thus it was strong in Rome while the privileges of citizenship were limited to a comparatively small class, but when she became an empire, and it was necessary to extend the privileges over an ever-increasing surface, patriotism gradually died out. The same is true of party spirit and sectarianism. The self-sacrifice of the individual for his party or his sect is elicited just in proportion to their narrowness. The reason is obvious. It is necessary, in order to create a strong spirit of patriotic self-devotion, that the individual should feel that his own interests and those of the community are one; and that what is injurious to the State is likewise injurious to himself; in other words, that the glory of the State is the gain of the individual. The feelings which inspired the patriotic self-devotion in the citizen of an ancient State are graphically placed before us in the funeral oration which Thucydides has put into the mouth of Pericles, over those Athenians who perished in the first year of the Peloponnesian War; and if we admit that the historian has accurately described them, it is evident that no system of training would be adequate to call them

for there is one insuperable difficulty which ever has and ever will prevent this philosophic speculation from becoming a fact—the inability of the philosopher to create a State in which his principles can be worked out in practice. Of this the necessary data are a body of virtuous governors and a body of subjects willing to submit themselves to their guidance. This is a state of things which has never yet succeeded in emerging from the ideal into the actual.

These considerations, therefore, prove that the only agency with which the philosopher was acquainted was impotent in his hands to effect the regeneration either of the individual or the race. Even its most eminent modern advocates, while

forth in favour of the abstract conception of humanity. In the small states of antiquity the close binding up of the interests of the individual with those of the community was capable of a very distinct realization. They in some respects resembled a joint stock company, in which the interest of each individual in the common weal is a definitely appreciable quantity. If it be urged that this will not account for the readiness of the individual to sacrifice his life in the service of the State, I reply, that not only is this accounted for by the love of posthumous glory which is inherent in a large number of mankind; but in many of the ancient States the penalties attached to cowardice were so severe, that death was far preferable. The feelings which prompt a man to surrender his life in battle are of a very varied character, and are probably never wholly due to a simple desire for the good of the community, nor altogether separate from the love of posthumous fame, the feeling of revenge, or the dread of disgrace, all of which are principles ultimately terminating in self. From these considerations it follows that those principles which kindled the patriotic self-devotion of the citizens of ancient states would be utterly inadequate to create that enthusiasm for the abstract idea of humanity which a certain school of modern unbelief invites us to accept as a substitute for those great principles of Christianity which have created a mighty army of self-sacrificers in the cause of Jesus Christ, and through Him, on behalf of the entire family of man. Even according to the opinions of those who have propounded this theory, the era of its realization must be delayed to the remote ages of the future, after thousands of generations of men have become silent in their graves. Such is the phantom which unbelief exhibits before the eyes of those who, conscious of the evil which dwells within them, are sighing for moral and spiritual regeneration.

expressing themselves in terms of hope, are compelled to adopt what is practically the language of despair. This regeneration, if possible at all, will be only so at some indefinitely remote period of the future. For the present we must be content to console ourselves with the assurance that man is slowly but steadily progressing for the better notwithstanding that the experience of the past proves that not a few races of mankind have entered on a course of gradual retrogression.* The only message of good news which a popular gospel of unbelief at the present day is able to announce, though certainly not very consoling to man in his degradation, is "The fittest shall survive." To a man impotently struggling with the violence of the passions, "the survival of the fittest" means "destruction." Such an announcement is the "ministration of death" to all the degraded races of mankind.

Such was the impotence of philosophy. To do them justice, ancient philosophers felt and confessed it. Contrast with this the teaching of Jesus Christ. He has not only pronounced man's regeneration possible, but has put into execution a plan for making it a reality, and has actually succeeded in recovering to holiness a multitude of imperfect and fallen men, whom no man can number. He has created a moral and spiritual power capable of stirring the hearts of men to their inmost depths. This power the New Testament designates faith. He has likewise created the greatest of Societies—the Christian Church—in which the subjects of His spiritual kingdom may be trained to holiness. The philosophers' principle of sanctification was,

---

* This is unquestionably true of a very large numerical majority of mankind. Witness the races in which Buddhism, Braminism, and Mahomedanism prevail, including not less than seven hundred millions of the human family. What prospect, I ask, have these races of a future, apart from the influence of Christianity? To these must be added the Negro race, which as far as history goes, has never had a Past ; and unless it can be regenerated by the aid of external influences, never will have a Future.

Begin with the outward and penetrate to the inward by means of habit: that of Jesus Christ is, Begin with the inward, and penetrate to the outward by means of faith. While He did not overlook the power of habit, the idea of effecting man's regeneration by means of faith is His exclusive discovery; and experience has proved that it is the only possible method.

It is superfluous to prove that the use which the New Testament makes of faith as the great power of sanctification in man constitutes the most striking characteristic of its moral teaching, and most distinguishes it from every other system which has been elaborated before or since. There is scarcely a page in it in which the principle of faith is not appealed to as a great moral and spiritual power. Yet the observations which not a few eminent unbelievers have made on the moral teaching of Christianity completely overlook the fact that this constitutes its inner life. They have assumed that its essence lies in its ethical precepts or in its moral principles, and have entirely ignored this, its great underlying element, which imparts vitality both to its precepts and its principles. The oversight is one which may well fill us with surprise, for it is professedly to treat a subject and to leave unconsidered its most important element.

Nor are we ourselves without blame in this particular. We are in urgent need of a system of moral philosophy which places Christ and the specialities of Christianity in the centre of its teaching. I fear that I am speaking correctly when I say that a system of philosophy which points out the harmony of the great principles of Christianity with the moral nature of man, does not exist except in very partial forms. Instead of elaborating a system which assigns to Christianity its proper place in philosophy, we have handed over the study of the science to men whose sympathies with revealed religion are small, and in whose systems Christianity can find no place. Need we wonder if the result has been eminently unsatisfactory. I would speak with the deepest respect for the great writers of antiquity. To them our debt of gratitude is great, for the light they have thrown on many of the aspects of human nature, quite independently of any influences derived from Revelation; but from the time when I first studied them in this University I have felt an ever-deepening conviction that their philosophy affords no adequate place for the great principles of Christianity. Why has not a philosophy been elaborated which has assigned an adequate place to the great principles which Christianity has brought to bear on human nature, and shown their harmony with our moral constitution? Heathen Ethics have done what they could—the wonder is that they have done so much—but surely there is something in Christianity high above them, and systems derived from them, which, if true, ought to receive a recognized place in our philosophy, unless a divorce is to take place between reason and religion, Christianity and modern thought. If Christianity is true, it must have a legitimate place in the philosophy of man. Our inability to assign such a place to the specialities of Christian teaching has propelled many a thoughtful mind downwards to unbelief.

But to return to the argument. We have shown that the principle of habit, the only moral and spiritual force at the command of philosophy, was unable to effect the regeneration of the morally degraded. All that it could do was to strengthen those who had a tendency to virtue in their virtuous character. It therefore left the degraded to perish in their degradation from pure inability to help them. Where philosophy hopelessly failed is precisely the point at which Christianity steps in. The great Teacher has proclaimed Himself the centre of a moral and spiritual power, which is not only adequate to strengthen the holy in their holiness, but to regenerate the morally corrupt. This power He not only claims to possess, but has actually exerted during eighteen centuries. Who, I ask, can deny the fact that Jesus Christ has exerted an influence which has rescued multitudes from their degradation, and has restored them to holiness and to God? It is a fact verifiable in the history of the past. Countless numbers of sinners have had their hearts melted by the divine power which resides in Him, and in the words of the Apostle, "have been washed, sanctified, and justified in the name of the Lord Jesus, and by the Spirit of our God." Who else has exerted a similar influence?

Let us now inquire how does Christianity accomplish this great result? I answer by producing a conviction in the innermost spirit of man respecting the eternal realities of things. This is faith,* which the New Testament affirms to be the great principle which can purify the heart. The only mode by which the regeneration of a morally corrupted man is possible is by the introduction of a new idea into the mind, which from the understanding passes into the heart, and awakens principles which were previously dormant. Unless some profound conviction respecting truth previously unrecognized can be produced, it is evident that a man morally corrupt must continue in his old groove. Such a conviction has been proved to be capable of revolutionizing our entire moral and spiritual being, and consequently of becoming the centre of a new life. It becomes the evidence of things not seen.

How then does Christianity seek to effectuate this result? I answer by concentrating on the conscience the whole force of the religious principle in man, so as to produce a profound conviction respecting the realities of moral and spiritual truth. It then presents to him the person of Jesus Christ in the divine attractiveness of His life and death, the perfect embodiment of all that is pure, holy, and lovely, in God or man, as the centre of a new spiritual life. By doing so it

---

* The faith of the New Testament ranges through various stages of conviction, and is powerful in its operation on our moral and spiritual being in proportion to its intensity. Its limits lie between the fulness of knowledge spoken of by St. Paul and St. John and the imperfect conviction of the father of the demoniac child, expressed in the words, "Lord, I believe; help thou mine unbelief," and include both.

has restored to holiness multitudes of degraded men which no man can number, and has elevated every holy man who has come under its influence to yet higher degrees of holiness.

Of the principle of faith or conviction as a regenerating power the philosopher was ignorant. How could it be otherwise? His philosophy created no profound convictions; it was the mere region of probabilities. Moreover, he was destitute of real religious beliefs; he justly despised those of the vulgar, but he was unable to replace them by any which amounted to real conviction. This being so, he was utterly unable to grapple with the conscience; he had no image of divine attractiveness to present to the awakened spirit—all he could do was to appeal to cold reason; and this would awaken no emotions, or summon into existence a force capable of grappling with the violence of the passions. It may perhaps be urged that the Platonic philosophy contains a nearer approach to the Christian conception. Viewing the question abstractedly, I fully admit that the contemplation of the $\tau\grave{o}$ $\mathring{a}\gamma a\theta\grave{o}\nu$ or the abstract idea of good is so. But where was it to be found? The words of the Apostle may be applied to it with entire fitness, "Who shall go up into heaven to bring it down from above?" How were the morally degraded to raise themselves to its lofty height? On the contrary, so far was the great philosopher from viewing it as a principle mighty to effect the regeneration of mankind, that with him it was the reward of a long and profound study of philosophy, which was to be the special privilege of the members of his spiritual aristocracy.

Let us pause for one moment to contrast this the highest achievement of philosophy with what has been effected by the Jewish peasant. Plato in his speculations conceived of the contemplation of the abstract idea of the good as one which might elevate to higher holiness the most advanced students of philosophy. Christianity has unfolded this divine idea of goodness in the person of Jesus Christ in a form which is capable of acting on every member of the human family. What the philosopher could only dream of in his study as the privilege of the select few, Jesus Christ has manifested in His life as the property of all. Marvellous has been the fulfilment of the philosopher's anticipations (although that fulfilment has been brought about in a manner which he utterly failed to conceive) by Him who uttered those ever-memorable words, "I, if I be lifted up from the earth will draw all men unto me." Philosophy in groping after truth, stumbled on speculations which Christianity has realized.

So also has it been with the ideal republic of the philosopher. His investigations led him to the conclusion that if men were ever to become virtuous they must be trained to it. He therefore sighed after some institution in which man might be habituated to the practice of virtue. Such an institution, though the subject of his constant speculations, he was powerless to create. Jesus Christ formed the idea of the kingdom of God as the great training institution for holiness. But with Him it has been no mere idea. He has instituted the Catholic Church, which of all human institutions has exerted the mightiest influence for good.

Thus the Jewish peasant has not only realized, but surpassed the results of the highest reason of the ancient world.

Let me now briefly sum up the results of this argument. The philosophers after the deepest study of the moral nature of man, confessed their inability to discover any spiritual power capable of effecting the regeneration of the morally degraded. Jesus Christ has acted on them mightily; and after the lapse of eighteen centuries, He is still the most powerful regenerating influence acting on mankind. The one discussed intellectual problems, the other appealed to the conscience and the heart. The one contemplated the masses of mankind with despair, and would have viewed the idea of devoting an entire life to their elevation as the phantasm of a disordered brain; the other has been the founder, and the impelling motive of the efforts which during eighteen centuries have been undertaken for the amelioration of mankind. The one coldly bade men become virtuous by performing virtuous actions, but could impart to them no power to render their performance possible; the other has breathed into man's inmost spirit a power mighty to effect his spiritual regeneration. The one ignored religion as a principle to act on the conscience; the other concentrated its entire force on man's moral and spiritual nature, and placed Himself in its centre as the perfect image of divine attractiveness. The one descanted on the duty of contemplating the divine idea of goodness as a means of moral elevation, but pronounced it undiscoverable by the multitude; the other has presented an incarnation of it in his human life. The one speculated in his study on ideal republics; the other has created the Catholic Church. Nor has philosophy in these latter days even with Jesus and His teaching for its model, succeeded better. It can reach neither the conscience nor the heart. What then is the only possible inference? I answer that the Galilean peasant must have possessed a greatness above that of all the great men of the past and of the present united; that He stands in a position among men which is unique; or, in other words, that a superhuman power must have manifested itself in Him.

Let us listen to the conclusion to which the study of the Synoptic Gospels has led so profound a sceptical philosopher as the late J. S. Mill. He is of opinion that they contain beyond all doubt an actual delineation of the character and teaching of Jesus, and that it is impossible that either the one or the other can have been an invention of His followers. He affirms therefore that it is quite consistent even for the rational sceptic to believe that Jesus Christ was all that He said that He was,—not God, for Mr. Mill thinks that He nowhere affirmed Himself to be divine,—but one with a special commission to lead men to the practice of holiness and virtue. But if the discourses in these Gospels are his veritable utterances, it is impossible to stop at this conclusion, for He affirmed Himself to be much more than this. He declared that He was the Christ; that He is the supreme legislator in the Kingdom of God; that His utterances are oracles from heaven; that He has power on earth to forgive sins; that He possesses a peculiar and exclusive knowledge of the Father; that all things are committed into His hands; that He possesses claims on the self-sacrifice of His followers more powerful than can be asserted by any earthly ties; that He will be the Judge of quick and dead; that in this capacity He will accept works of love done to others as having been rendered to Himself; that He can open the gates of Paradise; and, finally, that He came to give His life a ransom for many. All these things and much more besides He certainly claims, and who can venture to affirm that the claims of Him who during eighteen centuries has afforded verifiable proof that He has been the light of the world, and the light of life, are not just?

LECTURE IV.

"Philip findeth Nathanael; and saith unto him, We have found him of whom Moses in the law and the prophets did write, Jesus of Nazareth, the son of Joseph. And Nathanael said unto him, Can any good thing come out of Nazareth. Philip saith unto him, Come, and see."—JOHN I. 45, 46.

A FAR profounder truth underlies this passage than we are commonly in the habit of recognizing in it. It takes for granted the principle on which the arguments of the preceding Lectures have been founded, viz., that a law of continuity reigns in the moral world. Its affirmations are based on what we now know to be a great truth of mental science, that within certain limitations, such as has been the environment in which a man has been born and educated, such will be the man. Many prejudices may have existed in Nathanael's mind; still it is a great truth, that such a person as the Messiah of Old Testament prophecy could not have been evolved in the moral and spiritual atmosphere of Nazareth, by the mere action of those forces by which our characters are formed. No less pertinent is the reply of Philip, " Come, and see," *i.e.*, verify for yourself, and draw your own conclusion. This course of testing theories by facts was adopted, and the result was that Nathanael recognized in Jesus the presence of a superhuman person; "Rabbi, Thou art the Son of God, Thou art the King of Israel." I feel assured, if we apply a similar process to the Jesus of the Gospels, we shall arrive at a similar conclusion.

I adopt as the basis of the reasoning of this Lecture a fact which each of us can verify for himself, namely, that the Gospels, whether we suppose their narratives to be an account of actual occurrences, or according to the views of critical unbelief, to consist chiefly of a mass of legendary and fictitious matter, contain a portraiture of the divine character of Jesus Christ our Lord. There is the character plainly and palpably before us. It is the grandest character known to history. Not only have all the greatest and best of men bowed before it in humble adoration; but a large number of eminent unbelievers have confessed its greatness and perfection. Even those who deny its historical reality cannot help allowing that it is the greatest ideal creation of the human mind. Equally certain is it, that whether the character be an ideal or an historical one, it has proved for eighteen centuries the mightiest influence for good which has been exerted on mankind.

The following question therefore urgently demands solution:—If a large portion of the Gospels consists of myths and legends, how has the delineation got into their pages?

Another fact, apparent on the surface of the Gospels, has a most important bearing on this question. Of this great character they present us with no formal delineation. Nothing is more common than for ordinary historians to furnish us with formal portraitures of the characters of the persons whose actions they narrate, and to render them the meed of praise or blame. All this is totally wanting in the pages of the Evangelists. Not one of them has attempted to depict the character of his Master. Yet so conspicuously does it stand forth in them that it is obvious to every reader and produces a more distinct impression than the most elaborate delineation.*

* The almost entire absence of praise or blame assigned to the different agents in the scenes which they depict is a most striking feature in the Evangelists. The absence of the expression of any personal feeling on the part of the writers seems almost like coldness.

12 *

Of what then does it consist? To this question there can be only one answer. It is the result of the sum total of the narratives and discourses which compose our Gospels. These by being simply placed in juxta-position, by their combined effect, form the portraiture of the divine Christ. I say that this result has been produced by the simple juxta-position of the materials, because the most cursory perusal of the Gospels must convince every reader that nothing was farther from the intention of their authors than to delineate a character by an artificial arrangement of their parts. Their obvious aim and purpose was to furnish such a selec-

They have not one word in commendation of the absolute self-sacrifice manifested in their Master's life; nor of His unwearied labours in doing good; nor of His benevolence; His holiness, or His humility; or any one of the striking traits of His character. They must have viewed His death as the most atrocious of murders; yet not one word have they uttered for the purpose of heightening the effect of His cruel sufferings, or even of drawing our attention to His patient endurance. The whole account of the Crucifixion is a remarkably matter-of-fact one, in some respects it is even meagre; and not one word is added for the purpose of giving pathos to the scene. Equally remarkable is their entire absence of any expression of surprise or admiration at any miracle which Our Lord performed, and the want of dramatic colouring in their relation of them. The authors of the Gospels are exclusively occupied with the facts which they narrate; and trusted to them alone to produce the effect which they desired. In one word, all four Evangelists write like men who were utterly unconscious that they were delineating the greatest character in history. It is very remarkable that even with respect to the imme-diate agents in Our Lord's death there is an absence of denunciation, the hardest term which they employ being that by which they designate Judas as the Traitor, softened in three out of the four into the expression, "he who delivered Him up (ὁ παραδιδούς instead of ὁ προδότης). This absence of remark is not a peculiarity of any one of the Evangelists, but alike distinguishes the four. When we consider that their attachment to their Master was profound, it constitutes a most surprising trait, and is utterly inconsistent with the idea that any portion of the delineation has been worked up for the purpose of producing effect. Yet it has produced one which has utterly distanced the mightiest creations of genius.

tion of the actions and teaching of Jesus Christ as would be adequate to teach the great principles of Christianity. Yet out of what I may call a chance combination of their materials the delineation of this great character has emerged, which in the words of Mr. Lecky "has done more to regenerate and soften mankind than all the disquisitions of philosophers, and than all the exhortations of moralists." The question, Of what does the great character consist? will be best answered in his own words: it consists "in the simple record of three short years of active life," and I may add, composed extremely inartificially.

Another fact requires to be carefully considered. A large portion of the Gospels consists of a miraculous narrative, and of events so closely interwoven with it, that in point of credibility they must stand or fall together. So likewise is it with respect to the discourses in the Synoptic Gospels, which many eminent unbelievers allow to have been the veritable utterances of Jesus. Several of these presuppose the miraculous narrative, and others contain utterances which assume in Him the consciousness of a superhuman greatness, and which it is impossible to believe him to have spoken, if that consciousness was unreal. Now as the delineation of the character is the result of the mere juxtaposition of the contents of the Gospels, it is clear that the miraculous narratives must form an essential portion of the delineation, and the effect of their removal as unhistorical would be that the residuum would lose all cohesion and the destruction of the character be the result.

But another fact connected with the miraculous narrative has a most important bearing on the argument. The character delineated in it bears the same moral impress as that which is delineated in those parts which are not miraculous. Both are embodiments of precisely the same ideal conception, and constitute an harmonious whole as far as its ideal conception is concerned; it is impossible to imagine the miraculous portions to be the coinage of one mint, and the non-miraculous of another. Both are stamped with the same impress, and bear the clearest indications of having issued from the same die.*

I also assume that it is a fact palpable to every reader, that the great character delineated in the Gospels is an essential unity. All the parts of which it is composed fit into one another with a perfect harmony. It should be especially observed that this is equally true of the miraculous actions attributed to Our Lord, and of the other aspects of

* Mr. Mill, in the last of his posthumous essays, lays down the following position, " It is no use to say that Christ, as exhibited in the Gospels, is not historical ; and that we know not how much of what is admirable has been superadded by the tradition of His followers. The tradition of His followers suffices to have inserted any number of miracles, and may have inserted all the miracles he is reported to have wrought. But who among His disciples, or among their proselytes, was capable of inventing the sayings ascribed to Jesus, or of imagining the life and character revealed in the Gospels? Certainly not the fishermen of Galilee, certainly not St. Paul, and still less the early Christian writers, in whom nothing is more evident, than that the good which was in them was all derived, as they all professed that it was, from a higher source." This is certainly a most remarkable testimony, coming from so profound a reasoner, with such antecedents as those of Mr. Mill, to the great truth which I am labouring to establish, that it is impossible that the followers of Jesus, or their disciples, can have invented the great character depicted in the Gospels. While, however, he justly pronounces this idea utterly untenable, he expresses the opinion that all the miraculous narratives recorded in them may be their invention. It is clear therefore that he cannot have observed the fact pointed out in the text, that these narratives bear the same moral impress as the other portions of the character ; or, to say the strict truth, that some of its finest traits form portions of the miraculous narratives, or are found in those discourses in which the superhuman aspects of His character are depicted. A striking instance of this is found in the parabolic representation of the last judgment recorded in the twenty-fifth chapter of St. Matthew. Here the Son of Man is delineated, as possessing the highest superhuman attributes, yet with one exception it is the most exquisite delineation of the character of Our Lord to be found in any single passage in the Gospels, combining as it does the perfection of dignity with condescension. As I have said, to take away all those portions of the delineation which involve the presence of the superhuman, will

His character. Jesus is delineated with precisely the same moral aspect as a worker of miracles, as He is in His discourses. The delineation is made up of a vast number of parts, or, in other words, of all the facts recorded in the Gospels; yet it forms, not a mere congeries of materials, but a perfect unity. This is so evident as to require no further proof; and the importance of its bearing on the argument, whether the Gospels are narratives of facts, or a confused mass of legendary matter, is unmistakable.*

The existence of the portraiture being a fact, it follows that no theory of the origin of the Gospels, or of the nature of their contents, can be valid which is inconsistent with its existence. The theory that the Gospels are in all their main outlines historical gives a philosophical account of the existence and unity of the character. The creation is fully

not produce a human Jesus, but merely destroy the divine one; and therefore on the principles of Mr. Mill, it is inconceivable that the followers of Jesus can have invented the miraculous narratives of the Gospels. Some of them may have been within their powers to invent, but taken as a series, their moral environment is, to use Mr. Mill's language, absolutely "above them." Of this, the contrast presented by the miraculous narratives in the apocryphal Gospels affords a most decisive proof.

* Objections have been made to the unity of the character on some minor points of detail, but even if they were true, it would not affect the question of the unity of all its grand features, or the harmony with which each part fits into the others. This is a fact which ought never to be lost sight of in considering this question. It has even been affirmed that the character of Jesus underwent a deterioration during the latter portion of His ministry, owing to the opposition which he encountered from His opponents, and His own disappointed expectations. Even if the allegation were true, it would not affect the question of the essential unity of the character; but the alleged deterioration is contrary to the facts, for although during the latter days of His ministry Our Lord's opponents are rebuked with the greatest sternness, yet at no period are the milder traits of His character more exquisitely brought out. Serious objections have been also taken to the severity of Our Lord's denunciations of the Pharisees, as inconsistent with the perfection of His character. The force of the objection entirely depends on the combination of qualities

explained by the fact that the contents of the Gospels are a veritable record of the actions and sayings of Jesus, taken from the life. If, on the contrary, their historical character is denied, it is incumbent on those who do so to propound a theory which gives a rational account of the creation of such a character out of a mere mass of legendary matter, put together in the manner in which it has been affirmed to have been in our Gospels. The mere assertion that miracles are impossible, and that all narratives of them must be mythic or legendary, is no solution of the unquestionable fact that their contents present us with a portraiture of Jesus Christ; and that this portraiture constitutes an harmonious whole. A theory which asserts their unhistorical character, but which can give no rational account of the origin of the great portraiture which they contain, is crushed under its own weight.

Two alternatives only are open to those who assert that the Gospels consist of a mass of legendary matter:—Either

requisite to constitute a perfect character. Those who have urged it have assumed that benevolence is the one attribute which constitutes perfection, and ignore the claims of holiness, one of the ingredients of which is indignation at wilful moral evil. But if this is an essential portion of a perfect character (and I contend that it is so), then the delineators have displayed a more accurate knowledge of perfection than the objectors. It should be observed that the severity of aspect which the Evangelists have attributed to Jesus, is not called forth by considerations personal to Himself, but by the presence of deliberate moral evil; above all, that worst form of it, hypocrisy; and even in its sternest manifestations, as in the twenty-third chapter of St. Matthew, where Our Lord denounces the hypocrisy of the Pharisees, it is accompanied by the most exquisite burst of pathos and compassion which can be found in literature—" O Jerusalem, Jerusalem, thou that killest the prophets, and stonest them that are sent unto thee, how often would I have gathered thy children together even as a hen gathereth her chickens under her wings, and ye would not." I maintain, therefore, that holy indignation at wickedness deliberately persisted in is an essential portion of a perfect character; that its absence is not perfection but weakness; and that this portion of the delineation perfectly harmonizes with every other part.

their portraiture of Jesus Christ must be an ideal creation of some kind, or it must have been the deliberate invention of one or more fraudulent impostors.

This last alternative has only to be expressed in plain language to insure its refutation. It means that a character which has proved to be the greatest incentive to holiness which has ever been brought to bear on mankind, has been the deliberate invention of conscious fraud. This is so intrinsically incredible that it has been abandoned by all the great leaders of modern unbelief. We may therefore summarily dismiss it. The only question which requires consideration is, whether it is possible that it can be an ideal creation; for if it be an historical reality, it is too clear to require argument, that He of whom it is the delineation must have been superhuman.

The theories propounded by unbelievers respecting the origin of the Gospels, and the nature of their contents, have been framed for the purpose of giving a plausible account of the origin of the miraculous narratives they contain. They vary greatly in form, but the following brief statement will fairly represent their general character. Jesus of Nazareth was a great man, who probably fell into the hallucination of supposing himself to be possessed of a divine commission, nay, that he was the Messiah of Old Testament prediction. He gathered around him considerable numbers of enthusiastic and credulous followers. It is uncertain whether he professed to work miracles; but his followers and their converts during the course of the first century innocently invented a number of legends, containing, as such usually do, a multitude of stories of supernatural and superhuman occurrences. These were gradually attributed to Jesus, and in time formed the substance of the popular beliefs respecting Him; and after a while they succeeded in completely obscuring the actual facts of His history. These legends were gradually accepted by the Church as the genuine account of its Founder's life; portions of them were slowly committed to writing, and out of a mass of materials of this kind, partly written, and partly oral, their authors, whoever they may have been, composed the Synoptic Gospels early in the second century; the fourth Gospel, which is the work of a deliberate forger of great genius, being a composition of much later date. According to this theory, the authors of the Synoptics must be viewed as the editors of a set of legends respecting Jesus, which were floating about in the Christian Society, the groundwork of which had probably been previously reduced to writing, but which they transformed and enlarged by the aid of other materials, so as to suit the views of the respective writers, or the tastes of the different parties in the Christian Church. The fourth Gospel however is fabricated out of a wholly different class of materials.

Such, in brief outline, is the alternative to the acceptance of the Gospels as veritable narratives of facts, for every ideal theory, however varied it may be in form, is compelled to have recourse to legend or deliberate invention, to account for the origin of the miraculous narrative. It will be impossible for me to point out all its inconsistencies, or to discuss its minute details in the present course of Lectures, but I have already done this in another work.* I can only deal with it here in relation to a single point, that the unquestionable unity and perfection of the character which is delineated in the Gospels, renders it impossible that it can have originated in any agglomeration of myths and legends, such as the theory presupposes.

This theory, it is true, has not been propounded for the specific purpose of accounting for the origin of the portraiture of Jesus in the Gospels, but of their miraculous narratives; as, however, the portraiture itself consists of the entire mass of facts which they record, it is clear that a theory adequate to account for the facts ought at the same time to afford a rational account of the origin of the portraiture. This fact has been almost entirely

* *The Jesus of the Evangelists.*

overlooked by the opponents, and but very imperfectly insisted on by the defenders of Christianity. The former have acted on the supposition that if they could propound a theory which would afford a plausible account of the origin of the miraculous narratives, their work was accomplished, and the basis of Christianity subverted. But this is obviously a mistake. Before this can be effected, a theory must be propounded which, on the supposition of their legendary character, will be adequate to account for the existence in them of the portraiture of the divine Christ—a portraiture which does as clearly exist in them as the miraculous narratives. It is evident, therefore, that a theory which is inadequate to account for the origin of the former must be an incorrect account of that of the latter.

It would be comparatively easy to account for the existence of this portraiture, supposing it to be an ideal one, if it was possible to assume that, like other great ideal conceptions, it was the creation of a single genius, and that the four Evangelists had used it as a common model in framing their respective delineations, which they modified to suit their own views.* But all ideas of this kind are completely negatived by the facts and phenomena of the Gospels, for the nature of the materials of which the portraiture is composed proves to demonstration that it cannot have been due to the creative powers of any single mind;

* I do not mean that it would be abstractedly easy, but that it would be easy by comparison. It has been well observed that the genius which was capable of inventing the Jesus of the Evangelists, must have been almost as great as that of the character which he has delineated. When we take into account the conditions under which he must have worked, the success of any such attempt would have been impossible. This I have endeavoured to show in the before mentioned work by examining the difficulties in detail, which must have been encountered and overcome by any such supposed idealist. It is clear however that these difficulties are immeasurably increased by the necessity which every form of a legendary theory is under, of postulating, that the legends which compose our Gospels are not the invention of a single mind, but of many.

and equally certain is it that it cannot have been due to any artificial combination of materials on the part of the authors of the Gospels. This is abundantly proved by the fact that we have not merely one single portraiture of the Christ, but four, each of which is taken from a slightly different point of view, while at the same time all the great features are identical; for the very fact that there are four delineations, each possessing a substantial unity of conception, utterly negatives the idea that the resemblance can have been due to any artificial combination of materials. Nothing, therefore, can be more certain than that each Evangelist must have found the character already existing in the materials at his command, and that the four portraitures have simply resulted from their having arranged them in four sets of memoirs.

It is a matter of indifference in reference to this argument whether the materials out of which the Evangelists have constructed the Gospels were written documents or oral traditions, or partly written and partly oral. If we adopt the theory that the Synoptic Gospels have been largely composed by the aid of previously existing documents, then it is evident that the character must have been already virtually portrayed in those documents, and the question arises, how it got there. The documents must clearly have been composed from traditions which, if the miraculous narratives in the Gospels are unhistorical, must have been a set of legendary inventions. It follows, therefore, whether we assume the Gospels to have been composed by the aid of existing documents, or that the Evangelists drew directly from tradition, that the portraiture of Jesus must have been formed out of what was once a mass of floating legends; and, as a further consequence, these legends must have had numerous inventors.

This being so, it follows that the great character delineated in the Gospels must have been the creation of the persons who originally invented the legends which compose it; and not only so, but that as many persons must have contributed to its formation, as were the inventors of the different legends, each one having delineated that portion of it which is contained in the narrative which he invented. The only other possible supposition is, that the conception of the character was so deeply impressed on their minds, that the legends which they invented became stamped with its moral impress; but such a supposition is subversive of the theory before us; for it presupposes the character to have been already in existence, and consequently an historical reality. Moreover, as the miraculous narratives in the Gospels are numerous, the number of persons who invented the legends which compose them must also have been large, and therefore equally numerous must have been those who contributed to the creation of the portraiture of the divine Christ.

All this is presupposed by the legendary theory itself. It is based on the assumption that the primitive followers of Jesus were to the last degree enthusiastic, credulous and superstitious. In such an atmosphere the legendary spirit would run riot. It is quite clear, therefore, if this theory is correct, that the legends in our Gospels are only a selection from a much larger number which the primitive believers invented and attributed to Jesus. It is expressly affirmed in numerous passages in the Gospels that He performed many more miracles than are there recorded; consequently if all those were legendary, such legendary narratives must have been exceedingly numerous.

This being so, it is hardly too much to say that the legendary theory of the origin of the miraculous narratives involves a greater miracle than any of those related in the pages of the New Testament.

The following difficulties are insuperable.

First: it is inconceivable that the delineation of a character, possessing the unity of conception of the Jesus of the Evangelists, can have resulted from the fusion of a number of legends, which have been invented by a variety of minds. If it be an ideal one, it is certainly the greatest of ideal creations, and it is therefore quite as rational to imagine that one of the grandest works of art, such as a great painting, can have been produced by the selection of a number of smaller ones, the work of various artists, placed in juxtaposition on the canvas, as that the Gospel portraiture of the Christ can have originated in a similar manner. The unity of the character and the exquisite harmony of the parts are consistent with only two suppositions. It must be either the delineation of an historical reality, or the creation of a single mind. This last supposition is not only negatived by the facts of the Gospels; but it has not even been suggested by those who deny their historical character.

Secondly: the mythologists must have all concurred in inventing legends which were stamped with the same lofty moral ideal. This is proved by the fact that the Jesus of the miraculous narratives is the same elevated character as the Jesus of the non-miraculous ones. It is a fact which, with the Gospels in our hands, is undeniable, that wherever He is delineated in the superhuman aspects of His character, His moral elevation is as great, or even greater, than in the ordinary human ones. Yet all these, if there was nothing superhuman in his character, must have originated in a mass of legends.

But not only does a legendary spirit universally involve the presence of a low moral ideal (for this is the never-failing accompaniment of extreme credulity), but according to the theories widely accepted by unbelievers, these particular legends must have been the creation of a body of men who were at once narrow-minded, credulous, and I may say, fanatically enthusiastic. Such a character its propounders are compelled to attribute to the followers of Jesus in order that they may impart the appearance of plausibility to their account of the origin of the belief in the miracle of the Resurrection. Still more, according to the theories of modern unbelief the community in the midst of which the legends originated was animated by a strong spirit of party, which split it up into a number of contending sects. What effect, I ask, must this have exerted on the legends evolved by such a society? They would be deeply tinged with its moral impress, and they would bear the indubitable marks of narrow-mindedness, bigotry, and fanaticism. Each sect would have elaborated a set of legends in conformity with its own tastes; and as the Judaizing party was the predominant one among the primitive followers of Jesus, they would certainly have invented legends which were the counterparts of their own narrow-mindedness and intolerance. But as a matter of fact, no such spirit is impressed on the narrative of any one of the actions attributed to Jesus. Great therefore must have been the unanimity of the inventors, and their moral ideal pre-eminently lofty. I ask your attention to a few facts in illustration of the difficulties which a number of ideologists must have encountered and overcome before they could have succeeded in delineating this great character.

1. They must all have concurred in delineating a character which is the most perfect manifestation of benevolence, tempered with the perfection of holiness. They have at the same time invested it with an aspect of stern severity, when brought into contact with certain forms of moral evil. I draw attention to this point because the whole range of literature which bears on this subject proves that the diversity of opinion as to how these two elements are to be exhibited in combination is very wide; not a few contending that the perfection of benevolence requires the exclusion of the sterner aspects of holiness. Yet these two aspects of the character, as it is depicted by the Evangelists, weld together with an exquisite harmony, nor do the Gospels contain an indication of the existence of a single legend which portrayed Him otherwise. In this respect its unity is complete.

2. Numerous as must have been the mythologists, they have all concurred in attributing to Jesus absolute unselfishness. If we read the Gospels from one end to another, we can detect not one single selfish trait. It follows therefore

that none of the numerous legends out of which the character has been composed, could have depicted Him in an environment of narrowness or sectarianism, or once described Him as stirred to anger by a sense of personal injury. Still anger is not unfrequently ascribed to Him; but it is invariably aroused by the extreme forms of moral obliquity. But further: nowhere is this unselfishness more strongly exhibited than in the miraculous narratives, which according to the theory I am combating, must have been pure legendary inventions.

3. Equally unanimous must they have been in attributing to Our Lord the highest degree of self-assertion, united with the most perfect humility. This feature of self-assertion is such as has been exhibited in no other man.* Yet at

* This self-assertion of Our Lord is unique in history; and if it had been put into the mouth of any other character would have been positively offensive. It pervades the Synoptics, as well as the fourth Gospel, though in the latter it appears in a somewhat more dogmatic form. Thus the Synoptics are unanimous in representing Him as basing his teaching on no other authority than His own. This is conspicuously exhibited in the Sermon on the Mount, where He exercises the right of explaining and modifying utterances, which both He and His hearers esteemed to be oracles from heaven, on the simple basis of "I say unto you." Yet all the former prophets had uniformly referred their utterances, not to any inherent light possessed by themselves, but to one coming to them from an external source, always using a formula equivalent to the words, "Thus saith the Lord." Such a formula is never once attributed to Jesus throughout the entire Gospels. Precisely similar is His mode of performing miracles, the reference being made solely to Himself, uniformly denoted by the words "I say unto thee," or "I will." In a similar manner He is depicted throughout with a consciousness of supreme worthiness, before which every bond that unites man to man, even the highest recognized by God's law, must yield. Equally uniform is His aspect of self-conscious dignity. Viewing these utterances as those of a mere man, however great, they are simply extravagant; and the extravagance is greatly increased by the humble position of the utterer. Yet all this is united with an inexpressible sweetness and mildness of character, a humility which is perfectly natural, because it is never obtrusive, and a most unwearying patience. Now nothing

the same time it is blended with the profoundest humility; both fit into each other with an exquisite harmony, and are pre-eminently conspicuous in his miraculous actions. This is a trait the fine touches of which defy all power of imitation, and underlies the entire structure of the Gospels. The most accomplished idealist would have found the delineation of this portion of the character a work of the greatest difficulty. Yet if the legendary theory be true, not only must the numerous mythologists of primitive Christianity have been unanimous in attributing this exquisite trait of character to Jesus, but they have succeeded in delineating it to perfection.

4. It cannot fail to be observed that the same moral aspect pervades the entire Gospels. We do not find one conception of it cropping up in this place, and another in that; but the ideal of morality is uniform throughout, and I ask you particularly to observe that it is equally impressed on those portions which are indissolubly united with the narratives of miracles, and on the remainder of their contents. This being so, it follows that the inventors of the legends which compose them must have been all thoroughly penetrated with the same set of moral ideas; and those too of the most elevated character.

5. Equally unanimous must they have been in attributing the ideal of moral perfection to the character they invented;

would have more tried the skill of the poet or the novelist, than to make the parts of such a character harmonize with one another. Yet the self-assertion is free from every mark of arrogance, and the humility from meanness. The harmonious union of all these traits is one which would have defied the powers of the most exalted genius; yet every reader instinctively feels that they are exquisitely blended together in the portraiture of the Jesus of the Evangelists. Of this, the 25th chapter of St. Matthew and the 13th of St. John may be cited as crucial examples. Yet if the legendary theory is a true account of the origin of the Gospels, not only must the parts of which it is composed have been the creation of a number of minds, working independently of each other, but the exquisite blending of the parts has resulted merely from their being placed in juxta-position on the canvas.

still more remarkable is it that they must have been agreed in what the ideal of moral perfection consisted. We know as a matter of fact that there has been a very wide diversity of opinion as to the mode and degree in which the various virtues ought to be combined so as to form a perfect character. Yet the delineators of the portraiture of the Jesus of the Evangelists must on this point have been unanimous. No trait of discord can be found throughout it.

If then it was the delineation of many minds (and it cannot have been otherwise, if the legendary theory be true) it is evident that they must have all concurred in working out one common conception.

I have thus adduced a few examples of the unity of conception which underlies the whole structure of the Gospels. It would be easy to multiply them indefinitely. I contend that their existence is utterly inconsistent with any theory of the origin of the Gospels, which assumes that a large portion of their contents consists of legends which were gradually evolved during the first century, and afterwards mistaken for historical realities; and that the only theory consistent with the fact that the portraiture of Jesus is harmonious throughout is, that it is the copy of an historical reality.

The suggestion that the great character of the Gospels, one which is more perfect than the greatest of all ideal conceptions, can have originated in the agglomeration of a mass of legends, the creation of a multitude of minds, is as much opposed to our reason, as the supposition that an exquisite work of art can have been produced by any mere juxtaposition of the parts which compose it. We also know as a matter of fact that the moral ideal of a society in which the mythic spirit predominates is low. In proof of this may be quoted the whole mass of legendary literature. Such literature is invariably stamped with the moral impress of its inventors. What the legendary spirit was capable of perpetrating in Christianity, we have the means of verifying for ourselves, by perusing the apocryphal Gospels, two of which in all probability date not later than the first half of the second century. These are just what we should expect that such productions would be. Their miraculous narratives are stamped with a low moral ideal. Our blessed Lord Himself is depicted in them not unfrequently as a mischievous boy, armed with superhuman power, which he exerts with the utmost capriciousness. I do not think that they contain an account of a single dignified miracle, although the miraculous stories are numerous; they are all distinguished by every possible contrast from those recorded in the Canonical Gospels. It is simply incredible that the same spirit which has created the contents of the apocryphal Gospels, could have evolved those of the Canonical ones, or *vice versâ*. The interval which separates the one from the other is enormous.*

* We cannot be too grateful for the preservation of these eighteen collections of myths and legends which still remain, and are inaccurately designated Gospels. It is deeply to be regretted that we are not now in possession of the entire body of apocryphal literature which is known to have been in existence during the early ages of Christianity. It would have made our means of instituting a comparison between it and the Canonical Gospels more perfect and thorough. If these Gospels have perished through the indiscreet zeal of friends to the Christian cause, it proves that nothing is more injurious than zeal undirected by discretion. Such as have been preserved, however, enable us to ascertain, not merely as a matter of theory, but of fact, what was the kind of creations which were effected by the legendary spirit, when it exerted itself on subjects connected with the history of the Founder of Christianity. Every person who wishes to form a definite opinion on this subject should carefully peruse these eighteen productions. I feel confident that whoever will do so, will rise from the perusal with deep conviction of the vastness of the interval which separates legendary from historical Christianity. The following will be found to be an accurate description of the contrast between these collections of legends and our Canonical Gospels. I quote a passage from the *Jesus of the Evangelists*, in which I have endeavoured to convey to the minds of those who have not read them, a correct idea of this contrast : " Our Gospels present us with the picture of a glorious Christ ; the mythic Gospels with that of a contemptible one. Our Gospels have invested Him with the highest conceivable form of

It may perhaps be objected that a large amount of legendary matter was in existence when the Gospels were composed, and that their authors have incorporated only the more dignified portions into their narratives, and thereby consigned the rubbish to oblivion. I reply that this theory contradicts all known facts.

First, it is contrary to experience that the legendary spirit has ever invented anything of the elevated moral type such as that of the miraculous narratives, and the discourses found inseparably united with them in the Gospels.

Secondly, it is incredible that several writers, nurtured in the midst of such a spirit, should have concurred in selecting all the elevated ones, and rejecting all of a contrary character.*

greatness; the mythic ones have not ascribed to Him one action which is elevated. In our Gospels, He exhibits a superhuman wisdom; in the mythic ones, an almost equally superhuman absurdity. In our Gospels, He is arrayed in all the beauty of holiness; in the mythic ones this aspect of character is entirely wanting. In our Gospels not one stain of selfishness defiles His character; in the mythic ones, the boy Jesus is both pettish and malicious. Our Gospels exhibit a sublime morality; scarcely a ray of it shines in those of the mythologists. The miracles of the one and of the other are contrasted in every point. A similar opposition of character runs through the whole current of their thought, feeling, morality, and religion." This contrast is rendered all the more remarkable by the fact that the contents of these Gospels render it certain that if their authors had not read some of our Canonical Gospels, they must have drawn from a common source of information. They are chiefly confined to two portions of Our Lord's life, His infancy and boyhood, and His passion, giving also a number of incidents respecting Mary and Joseph, but they leave the events of His ministry almost entirely unnoticed. Respecting Our Lord's infancy and boyhood, of which the accounts in the Canonical Gospels are extremely brief, the legendary ones furnish us with the most grotesque details. Portions of the account of the Passion and the Resurrection are nearly in the words of the Gospels; but they add a number of incidents of a character utterly unhistorical; and of speeches supposed to have been uttered by different persons connected with the scenes, the contents of which are simply incredible.

* The supposition at the foundation of all legendary theories of the

Thirdly; even if this had been possible, yet as the popular legendary spirit always seizes on what is wild and grotesque, this new edition of chastened legends would never have gained acceptance by the popular mind; yet it is evident from the writings of the Fathers of the two first centuries, that the accounts in our Gospels, or at any rate, precisely similar ones, had attained universal acceptance as embodying the true type of the actions which the Church attributed to its Founder. If it be urged that in accordance with the theory of the survival of the fittest, the legends of an elevated type would survive, while the rest would perish, I reply that this theory is not true in a community which is thoroughly infected with the legendary spirit. On the contrary, the grotesque, as more adapted to the popular taste, survive, while the elevated ones, if such could spring up at all in such a soil, must perish.

Nor is the theory of tendencies more successful as a

---

origin of the Gospels is that the Evangelists, or the persons who composed the documents which they employed, were themselves deeply infected with the legendary spirit. This assumption is necessary in order to account for the miraculous narratives. Unless they had been profoundly credulous, it is impossible that they could have mistaken a mass of floating legends for historical facts, at a time when their verification was not only possible, but easy. Such persons could have possessed neither the requisite taste nor judgment to enable them to select from the mass of legends then in circulation those of an elevated type, and to reject the grotesque, which from the nature of the case must have been by far the most numerous and acceptable to the popular mind. It is also clear, whatever may have been the date of the Synoptic Gospels, that a large mass of legends must have been in existence when they were composed. Equally certain is it, although the common narrative may have been derived from a common document, that each of the Evangelists has incorporated into his own Gospel matter which is peculiar to himself, and which must therefore have been derived from legendary sources of information. This being so, it is inconceivable that each of these writers should have concurred with the others in rejecting every grotesque legend from his pages, unless they had all arrived at a previous understanding to do so, which is not even alleged as affording a probable solution of the facts.

possible account of the facts. This theory has been very extensively propounded as affording an adequate ground for some of the phenomena presented by the Gospels, and the gradual formation of Catholic Christianity. According to it the primitive Church was divided into a number of discordant Sects, which elaborated a set of doctrines and fictitious stories for the purpose of realizing their own peculiar tendencies. When the sectarian spirit had risen to a dangerous height, it was found necessary to effect compromises between these discordant schools. Of this spirit St. Luke's Gospel and the Acts of the Apostles are adduced as striking examples. Both works are said to have been composed for the purpose of mediating between contending parties, and thereby creating a common Christianity. For the same purpose the author is alleged to have largely modified the materials of which he was in possession, and to have imparted a strong colouring to, if not to have actually invented, most of the miracles which are recorded in the latter book.

It is impossible for me in these Lectures to discuss the details of this theory.* It will be sufficient for my purpose

* It is important to observe that this theory, in common with every other which affirms the unhistorical character of the Gospels, is obliged to assume the existence of a legendary spirit, as that which has created their miraculous narratives. The only difference between it and other theories which account for them on this principle is that it is obliged to assume a certain amount of fraud on the part of their inventors. Thus it is affirmed of the Acts of the Apostles that a certain number of its miracles have been invented for the purpose of producing a parallel between Paul and Peter, by some disciple of the former, who was desirous of effecting a union between Petrine and Pauline Christianity. Whatever theory may be propounded on this point, it is impossible to avoid falling back on legend, or fraudulent invention, as the only means of accounting for the origin of miraculous narratives; and consequently the same line of reasoning which proves that all legendary theories are inadequate to account for the facts and phenomena of the Gospels, is equally subversive of the theory of tendencies, and of every other. This is also true of all attempts to explain the origin of the Gospel

to observe that it is absolutely negatived by the fact that the Gospels, in addition to the narratives and discourses of which they consist, contain the great portraiture of the divine Christ, for the existence of which in their pages this theory is utterly unable to afford a rational solution. I must, however, ask your attention to one remarkable assumption in it, which contradicts all the historical facts of human nature. It assumes that a number of compromises have been effected between contending parties in the Church, and that Catholic Christianity has grown up out of them. What, I ask, says the voice of history respecting the quarrels of religious sects? Do they effect compromises? Do they conclude treaties? Do mediators arise who succeed in forming out of several contending sects a united Church? On these points it returns no ambiguous answer. Party spirit in religion, instead of effecting compromises, goes on continually widening. Witness the history of the internal divisions of all the religions in the world. Where have a number of discordant sects fused in one, and out of the fusion erected a common Church? It has passed into a proverb, that nothing is more irreconcilable than religious

miracles on the theory that they are imitations of similar ones in the Old Testament. This not only breaks down by the application of the same course of reasoning, but the affirmation is inaccurate in fact; for although such similarity exists between a few of them, as far as the mere external fact is concerned, yet when they are compared together series by series, they present the most striking points of divergency, so that it is impossible that the one can have formed the model of the other. The Old Testament series consists chiefly of extraordinary events wrought on inanimate nature; that in the New Testament, of cures performed on the bodies of men. The moral environment of the two also differs widely. It is true that the Old Testament contains accounts of three miracles of resurrections; so does the New: or if we include the Resurrection of our Lord, four. But between the account of the recuscitation of a dead body by touching the bones of Elisha, and the resurrection of Lazarus, the difference is vast, not to speak of that of our blessed Lord, which rests on a strength of attestation such as can be surpassed by no fact in history.

divisions. Yet without these compromises the theory of tendencies cannot advance a step. It is one, therefore, which, while it may look plausible in the study, is hopelessly dashed to pieces against the facts of history and the realities of human nature. (See Supplement I.)

II. I must now draw your attention to the argument from prophecy. The prophecies of the Old Testament and their particular fulfilment have been already discussed by my predecessors, and into that portion of the subject I do not propose to enter. My observations will be confined to the consideration of the character and logical value of the prophetic argument, and the freeing it from the needless difficulties with which it has been encumbered. I shall confine my observations to the Messianic prophecies, for unless their fulfilment in the person, work, and Church of Jesus Christ proves a superhuman prescience, we shall in vain seek it in any other. The importance of a correct estimate of the value of the argument is great, because the writings of the New Testament make it certain that Our Lord and His Apostles were far more in the habit of appealing to the evidence of prophecy than to that of miracles as a proof of His Messiahship. The argument also, as far as it is valid, is one which admits of verification, because we have the Scriptures of the Old Testament in our hands, and are therefore able to compare their prophetical announcements with their alleged fulfilment in the person of Jesus Christ, and the history of the Christian Church.

In estimating the value of this argument, it is of the highest importance that we should have a clear idea of what the writers of the New Testament mean when they affirm that the Old Testament has received its fulfilment in Jesus Christ, and in the history of His Church. Are the popular ideas on this subject accurate ?* Are the prophecies of the

* The value of the prophetic argument has been greatly weakened by a number of works which have attained a very wide circulation, professing to expound the prophetic Scriptures of the Old and New Testaments. These have treated them as if they were mere vaticina-

Old Testament simply predictions and nothing more, or do they include a number of imperfect delineations, shadowy

tions, that is, predictions, which were intended to be minute descriptions of events coming in the future, and which have received an equally minute fulfilment in the facts of history. The effect of this mode of treatment has been, not only that the obvious meaning of the prophetical passages has been utterly disregarded, and the fancies of the writer substituted in its place, but that historical facts have too often been misrepresented for the purpose of accommodating them to the prophecy. This supposed necessity of tracing a minute agreement between all the minor points of the prophetic delineations and the events of history has led many writers to adopt what can only be correctly described as a number of evasions. This evil is especially exhibited in that numerous class of popular writers who have treated the books of Daniel and Revelation as though they were definite historical prophecies, predicting the chief events of the world's history between the times in which they were composed and the consummation of all things, and delineating them beforehand with the accuracy of a map. To accommodate these to the facts of history, a system of symbolical interpretation has had to be adopted, which is little better than conjecture, and even then the events cannot without violence be accommodated to the symbols. Such a theory of interpretation has been adopted by a man of no less learning than Mr. Elliott in his *Horæ Apocalypticæ*; and carried out by his numerous imitators. If this theory is correct, it is plain that a successful application of it would not only enable us to ascertain the exact point in the prophetic history under which we live, but to predict the future. Its propounders have not hesitated to predict the latter, an attempt which has invariably ended in their confusion. Thus, if Mr. Elliott's system had been correct, not only ought the Turkish empire to have perished several years ago, but the consummation of all things should be an event of the past. The remarkable thing is, that when the propounders of such systems have lived to discover that their predictions have been falsified by the facts of history, they have not been led to renounce the erroneous principles on which their predictions are based, but have endeavoured to show that the prophetic dates admit of being calculated from several different commencements, and consequently that their fulfilment may be deferred to some period of the future. The effect of this mode of handling the argument has been to induce a large number of thoughtful minds to believe that it is little better than a mere system of guesswork, and rests on a logical basis which is utterly unsound.

outlines, and aspirations, the true ideal of which has been realized in Jesus Christ? Our Lord on several occasions asserts that the writers of the Old Testament spake of Him. This He directly affirms in the fourth Gospel, respecting Moses, under whose name the entire Pentateuch is intended to be included. Yet the Pentateuch contains but a small number of passages, such as we usually designate prophecies. St. Luke also tells us that after His Resurrection, "Beginning at Moses, and all the prophets," He expounded unto two of His disciples, the things spoken in the Scriptures concerning Himself; and a little further on, referring to the recognized threefold division of the Jewish Scriptures, He makes use of the words "that all things might be fulfilled which were written in the law of Moses, and in the prophets, and in the Psalms concerning Me." Such wide references prove that He must have held that the Old Testament did not merely contain a certain number of solitary vaticinations respecting Him; but that He was that to which its entire system pointed; that is to say, that He regarded Himself as the perfect ideal of every reality which underlay the Mosaic institutions, and of all the aspirations and imperfect truths contained in the prophets and the Psalms, as well as of the express Messianic prophecies; in one word, that He was the realization of the idea to which the entire scheme of the Old Testament pointed. A similar view is involved in the use which the apostolic writers make of the Old Testament Scriptures. They regard them as something very different from mere vaticinations, or in other words, as containing in imperfect outline the ideal which was realized in Christianity.

It is important to observe that the word $\pi\lambda\eta\rho\acute{o}\omega$, by which the writers of the New Testament usually express the realization in Jesus Christ of the prophetic elements of the Old, bears a far wider signification than our modern counterpart, the English word "fulfil," in its popular acceptation. Its obvious signification is "fill up to the full," corresponding to our more philosophical form of expression, "Realize the full and complete ideal." That this is its true meaning is rendered certain by the well known passage in the Sermon on the Mount, in which Our Lord says, "Think not that I am come to destroy the law or the prophets; I am not come to destroy, but to fulfil, for verily I say unto you, till heaven and earth pass, one jot, or one tittle shall by no means pass from the law until all be fulfilled." He then proceeds to show in what sense He claimed to be the fulfilment of the Law, by dealing with some of its precepts which only contained imperfect truths, and by enunciating the great moral ideal which was implied in the true conception of them. Thus the full conception underlying the law which forbade murder was the law of love; of that which forbade adultery, was the law of purity; of that which forbade perjury, the law of truthfulness. In a similar manner He was the fulfilment of the other Scriptures of the Old Testament, inasmuch as He was the complete realization of those truths which they only imperfectly adumbrated. It is important to observe the wide sense which this word bears in the New Testament; otherwise we shall get a very imperfect estimate of the evidence which the Old Testament Scriptures bear to Our Lord's divine Mission. While the prophetic element in them contains predictions, it is a great mistake to restrict it to bare vaticinations of future occurrences. The latter contain no idea of type or symbol, or the realization of an imperfect truth in a more perfect ideal. This however constitutes the essence of by far the larger portion of the Old Testament predictions as they are referred to in the New. I fully admit the presence of a directly predictive element in the Old Testament; but to rest the entire force of the argument on the limited number of passages which contain such predictions is to overlook at least two-thirds of the evidence which Our Lord declares that Moses and the prophets render to His divine Mission. His claims go to the full extent of affirming, that not only is He the subject of direct predictions, but that all the truths which are imperfectly, and frequently very darkly shadowed forth in their pages are realized in Him as the ideal to which they pointed.

A number of very interesting questions connected with the criticism of the Old Testament, and eagerly debated among theologians, but which have no real bearing on the prophetic argument, have been imported into this question; and have thereby distracted our attention from the real point at issue, which is this, and this only : Are there in the Old Testament Messianic prophecies, and a typical, symbolical, and ritual system, of the true idea of which Jesus Christ and His Church are the realization ? This is a simple question of fact, and one quite distinct from any theories as to the date when the various books were written, or who may have been their authors.*

Amidst the endless theories that have been propounded on these subjects, one fact is unquestionable, that every one

* I by no means overlook the importance of these questions ; but I make these observations for the purpose of keeping them from being mixed up with the evidential value of the prophetic element in the Old Testament Scriptures. Thus it would very materially affect our views of Deuteronomy if it could be proved that it was a forgery got up between Jeremiah and Hilkiah, and palmed off on the simplicity of King Josiah as a genuine production of Moses. Still the great Messianic prophecy of the prophet who was to arise in the future like unto Moses would be there, and the only question would be, does it or does it not indicate a superhuman prescience ? In such a case we should have to rank Jeremiah with Balaam, a false prophet who delivered true oracles. It should be observed, however, that as far as these theories are concerned, they are but theories and nothing more ; the evidence on which they rest being little better than a foundation of sand. This is the case with a large number of the theories respecting the nature and origin of the Pentateuch, no two propounders of them agreeing in the same view ; one set of critics affirming that Deuteronomy is the later composition, and Leviticus the earlier ; while another, for reasons equally satisfactory to themselves, exactly reverse this order. The only fair conclusion is, that both endeavour to erect a pyramid on its apex. Similarly, the evidence may be quite sufficient to prove that the book of Genesis is a composite document; but when Ewald not only affirms that these documents were five in number, but authoritatively assigns each part to its respective author, and that on no other foundation than his own intuitive faculty of divination, we seem to have reached the *ne plus ultra* of dogmatical assertion. This theory is now generally rejected,

of the books of the Old Testament was in existence (with the possible exception of the book of Daniel) in the form in which we now read them, and consequently with all their Messianic prophecies in them, when the Septuagint Version was made, *i.e.* at least 180 B.C. The book of Daniel, even if we accept the latest date which has been assigned to it by the school of critical unbelief, must have been written at least 150 B.C. What more can we require for our argument? If there really exists in the Old Testament a prophetic element, which has been realized in the New, it is precisely the same for all the practical purposes of the Christian argument, whether the predictions were uttered 180 or 1800 years before the Christian era. In either case they prove a superhuman prescience in their author, unless by any possibility they could have been made the means of their own fulfilment. Thus if a writer had put forth a set of predictions, which foreshadowed the events of the French Revolution, and the career of Napoleon the first in the year A.D. 1600, it would have been as certain a proof of superhuman foresight, as if he had uttered his predictions in the reign of William the Conqueror, or Charlemagne. I fully allow the profound interest which attaches to the question of the true date of the composition of the various books of the Old Testament. Many very important questions of theology are involved in it. It may affect our view as to the character of their contents, according as it is determined in this way or in that. But as far as the question, whether a superhuman prescience presided over their composition, or whether Jesus Christ is their perfect realization, is concerned, it is a matter of indifference whether they were composed B.C. 200 or B.C. 2000.

The same is equally true of the fiercely debated question of their authorship. Whether Moses wrote the Pentateuch;

to be replaced by others erected on a basis equally unsubstantial. What we want on the part both of theologians and men of science is, not theories formed out of their own subjective consciousness, but based on facts which are capable of verification.

whether it has been made up of a number of older documents; whether the book of Deuteronomy is the work of Jeremiah; whether there was an earlier and a later Isaiah; whether the book of Zechariah is the work of several writers; whether Daniel was composed by the great prophet whose name it bears, or by a later writer; however deeply interesting such questions are, or however they may be determined, all this will not add one prophecy more or less to the Old Testament Scriptures; or, if they contain prophecies which have been actually fulfilled, detract one atom from the value of the Christian argument.

I urge these considerations on your attention because there are a multitude of questions at the present day profoundly agitating the minds of theologians, on the determination of which it is commonly supposed that the life of Christianity depends. I am far from undervaluing the importance of the questions at issue, but our duty is to contemplate this subject from an evidential point of view. As such I have only to deal with a question of fact, from which we must not allow our attention to be distracted. It is this: Do the Old Testament Scriptures contain predictions respecting a Messiah and a future Kingdom of God, and are these predictions realized in the person and Church of Jesus Christ?

If the correspondence really exists between the Messianic elements of the Old Testament and the Jesus of the New, it follows that Jesus must be the Christ, and Christianity a Divine Revelation.

As this point is one of the greatest importance, I must illustrate my position by a few examples. Nothing can exceed the eagerness of the debates respecting the date and the nature of the contents of the Book of Genesis. Yet whatever theory we adopt on this subject, it will not alter the fact that the Book was in existence before the Babylonish captivity, and contained the affirmation that in Abraham all the nations of the earth should be blessed, and the prophecy about Shiloh, whatever value may be attached to it. So with respect to the Book of Deuteronomy; whenever it was composed, it was certainly written several hundred years before Christ, and it contained the affirmation that at some future time a great prophet would arise like unto Moses; and it is no less certain that although the prophets who subsequently appeared were very numerous, the only one who possessed a real resemblance to Moses was Jesus Christ, Moses being distinguished from all the other prophets by the fact that he was a founder of a dispensation, in which respect Our Lord exactly resembled him. In a similar manner the whole system of the typical worship of the Old Testament was fully evolved long centuries before the Advent, and this is equally true whichever of the innumerable theories we may adopt as to the date or authorship of the different Books of the Pentateuch. The real question is simply one of fact: Is Jesus Christ and His Church a realization of the ideal involved in these types and shadows? Again: the date and authorship of the 22nd and other Messianic Psalms may be open to question, and what was the precise idea before the mental eye of their authors when they composed them. But this does not affect the fact that every one of them was in existence prior to the time of the Maccabees, and most of them several centuries earlier, and that Jesus Christ has precisely realized the idea which they embody, and that between his sufferings and those described in the 22nd Psalm the resemblance is marvellously exact. Illustrations of this principle might be adduced in large numbers, but space will only allow me to refer to two more. Whatever view we may take of the composite character of our present Isaiah, it cannot be denied that the former portion of it contains prophecies which are unquestionably Messianic; and whether the prophet intended them for Hezekiah or some other person, that these persons never realized their full ideal, but that this has been realized several centuries later by a Jewish carpenter. In a similar manner respecting the second portion of Isaiah. Even if its author lived as late as the time of Cyrus, still the great prophecy respecting the Servant of Jehovah and the future Kingdom of God must have been in existence more than 500 years before the Advent; and whatever might have been the ideas present in the prophet's mind at the time when he composed it, it is certain that they have only received a full realization in Jesus Christ and the Church which He has founded. The same thing is true of the Book of Daniel. Notwithstanding all the attacks which have been made on its authenticity by modern criticism, it still remains indisputable that all its great Messianic prophecies were in existence 150 years prior to the Advent, that they announce the coming of a future Kingdom of God, which would differ from every other kingdom which had been previously set up, and that Jesus Christ has actually founded such a kingdom, which has been in existence for eighteen centuries of time. The important question is, have the prophecies, the typology, the moral teaching, and the aspirations of the Old Testament received in Jesus Christ and the Church which He has founded, the realization of the ideas which they embody, or are all the resemblances mere guesses such as an exalted genius may have ventured on, and occasionally guessed right?

To aid us in determining this question, let us observe what these Old Testament books really consist of. They differ from all other prophetical books in that they are not confined to the single subject of prediction, but they constitute an entire literature. Their composition extends over a space of at least one thousand years, and they are the work of not less than forty different authors, comprising men of every condition in life, including the king, the priest, the statesman, and even the herdsman. The books themselves consist of a body of political and religious legislation, of histories, poems of the highest order, the utterances of prophets on the burning questions of the day, and gnomic maxims of proverbial wisdom. Even the writings commonly called prophetical contain a large mixture of the historical element. Most of the prophets were also statesmen; and a large portion of their writings consists of exhortations called forth by the state of public affairs, and the moral condition of the people. Yet it is remarkable that this literature, extending over so wide an interval of time, and composed by such a variety of authors, is interpenetrated by a certain number of common ideas, connected with many of the profoundest questions of human thought; among which may be numbered the announcement of a kingdom of God to be set up on a grand scale at some distant period of the future, and of the advent of a Messiah who was to be its king. If we take any similar collection of writings extending over an equal space of time, and composed by an equal number of authors, we shall find nothing like this in history. But not only are these writings distinguished by this remarkable peculiarity, but many centuries after they were written a personage called Jesus appeared, who has succeeded in realizing in Himself, and in the Church which He has founded, the true idea which underlies all the predictions, the symbolical institutions, and the aspirations which are found in this mass of literature. If we search the entire history of man, we shall find it to be true of no other person that he is the realization of the aspirations of an entire literature.

Let us now briefly consider the prophetic elements in the Old Testament, and the value of the evidence they supply. And first, its Messianic prophecies.

These are of two kinds; first, those that are unquestionably Messianic, and admit of being applied to no other person. Of these, those in Daniel, in the 37th of Ezekiel, the 23rd and 33rd of Jeremiah, several in Isaiah, and a few of the Psalms, may be cited as examples. Of a similar character are the numerous predictions of a future kingdom of God, the idea of which as it is delineated in the prophets, necessarily implies that of a Christ who was to be its king.*

* It is one of the peculiar characteristics both of Judaism and Christianity, that they alone of all the systems of ancient thought place the golden age of man in the future, rather than the past. It may be objected that the book of Genesis opens with an account of man's being placed in Paradise; but this condition, be it what it may (for

All these passages are, in the strictest sense of the word, prophecies, *i. e.*, the writers did not affirm them to be true of any person or thing then existing; but they asserted that they should receive a realization in the future. They announce, in language that cannot be mistaken, the advent of a kingdom of God, of a wholly different character from anything which had been realized in the past, which was to include both Jew and Gentile, and the end of which was to be the establishment of righteousness and peace.

the whole account is extremely meagre, and popular ideas on this subject have been far more indebted to Milton than to the Bible for anything definite which they contain), was only enjoyed by the original human pair, and apparently for a very brief interval of time. In striking contrast to this is the entire system of pagan mythology, which uniformly places the golden age of man at some indefinitely remote period of the past. The idea of a future kingdom of God, in which righteousness and peace were to reign, is quite foreign to it. The single exception to this is the fifth eclogue of Virgil, composed in adulation of the reigning family at Rome; but the language of which bears so close an analogy to that in the Old Testament respecting the advent of the future kingdom of God, that it is difficult to avoid coming to the conclusion that the one has in some way been borrowed from the other. If, however, we take mythological literature as a whole, its views respecting man, and his future prospects, are invariably dispiriting. Nor did philosophy take a more cheerful view of his destinies. In fact, there was nothing in the history or condition of the ancient world that would justify the conclusion that a future Millennium of holiness or happiness was in store for the human race. On the contrary, everywhere were present the signs of moral corruption and decay. Nor was the condition or history of the Jewish people such as to have suggested the idea to the minds of the prophets and Psalmists. On the contrary, they are full of lamentations at their degeneracy and repeated apostacies. The language of the prophetical Scriptures, as addressed to the times in which the prophets lived, may be summed up in one brief sentence, "Ye are worse than your fathers." The idea, therefore, of the future kingdom of God, and of the reign of righteousness and peace under its influences, was certainly not suggested by anything in the experience of the past, or the present; it was the result of faith in God as the righteous governor of the world, and that righteousness must ultimately prevail and flourish under His government. The idea that some Millennium awaits man at

Now it is a simple fact that a considerable number of such prophecies are to be found in the Old Testament Scriptures. No less certain is it that after the lapse of several centuries a spiritual kingdom, differing in character from every earthly institution, was actually set up, of which Jesus Christ claimed to be the King, and which has during a period of eighteen hundred years exerted the mightiest and most beneficent influence on mankind. We are in the presence therefore of two facts—First, a set of predictions uttered by various persons, and at widely different intervals of time, affirming that a kingdom of God would be manifested in the future, and a Messiah to be its king. Secondly, their realization in history after an interval of several centuries. Such a correspondence between prediction and fulfilment can be found nowhere else in the entire history of man.

Secondly: there is another body of prophetic Scriptures, of which Jesus and His Disciples claimed that He was the fulfilment, *i.e.*, that He was the ideal to which they pointed. These were spoken by the prophet either of some person who had existed in the past or who was then living, but the language used was of a far too elevated character to be strictly true of the person to whom it was immediately applied. This class of predictions may be called typical prophecies. I mean by this term, when some event or historical character was used for the purpose of portraying a future one, which was to possess similar attributes, only higher and more perfect than those exhibited in the person or event of whom they were immediately spoken. Thus many things are spoken of David and Solomon, which those

some very remote period of the future has now become widespread, even in unbelieving philosophy; but it should never be forgotten that the original conception of it was not due either to mythologists, or philosophers, but to Psalmists and prophets, in whose minds the idea sprang up, as Christians believe, under a divine influence, and who firmly clung to it notwithstanding all the disasters of the past and of the present.

14 *

kings were incapable of realizing. Divine titles are given to them by prophets who were the strictest theists, and to whom the worship of a man would have been an abomination. That such ascriptions were intended to be idealizations is proved by the fact that the later prophets were in the constant habit of speaking of a David who was to be manifested as the head of the Kingdom of God long after the historical David was silent in his grave. This David was evidently an ideal David, or in other words a Christ, in whom the promises made to the historical one were to receive their full realization. Similar idealizations are very common in the prophetic Scriptures, of which that of Israel may be quoted as an example. Many of the things there spoken were only true of an ideal Israel, and are utterly inapplicable to the Israel with whom the prophets were acquainted. Of this class of predictions Our Lord claimed to be the realization, and the correspondence to the character delineated in the Gospels and to the Church which He has founded is incontestable.*

* The mode in which this class of prophecies has been dealt with in popular treatises has tended to throw discredit on the entire argument. They are often violently wrenched from the context in which they stand, and treated as if they were prophecies pure and simple, their typical character being entirely overlooked. Thus, for example, Isaiah vii. 10-16, is frequently spoken of as though it were a direct prophecy of Jesus Christ. The reader looks into the context and finds that the sign mentioned by Isaiah was one given to Ahaz to encourage him in a war then pending between Syria and Ephraim on the one side and Judah on the other. This sign was the birth of a child of a virgin mother (as our English version renders the word) who was to receive the name of Immanuel. Then follows a particular and definite promise that before this particular child had attained the age which would enable him to judge between good and evil, the kingdoms of Israel and Syria would both be overthrown. All these facts are stated by the prophet in such a manner that it is impossible to get rid of their plain signification, except by having recourse to a mode of interpretation which, if applied to any other writing, we should designate a subterfuge. Yet this passage is frequently spoken of as a direct and palpable prophecy of Jesus Christ. I have selected it for the purpose of illus-

Portions of the Old Testament describe a person who is the greatest of sufferers, but who in the midst of his sufferings displays the most unwavering trust in God, and whose career terminates in a most triumphant issue. The description is such as not to fit the circumstances of the writer himself, of any other person known to history. Two examples of this will be sufficient to refer to, the 22nd Psalm, and the

tration, because it is one which the lower class of unbelievers are never weary of citing as a proof of the dishonesty of Christian commentators, and if the commonly accepted standpoint is correct, I think it very difficult to answer their objection. The truth is, it belongs to the class of typical, or what may be more correctly designated, ideal prophecies, and the affirmation that it is a direct prophecy of Jesus Christ involves a system of interpretation which would render it impossible to be certain of the sense of a single passage in the Bible. The child was designated "Immanuel," or "God with us," for the purpose of assuring Ahaz of the divine protection in the war in which he was engaged, and, however improbable the event might then appear, of the certainty of the overthrow of the two hostile kingdoms. But, it will be urged, the popular interpretation must be correct, because St. Matthew assures us (Matt. i. 22-23) that it was fulfilled in Jesus Christ. Undoubtedly he does, *i.e.* in the sense in which the New Testament uses the word "fulfil." Jesus Christ realizes the idea involved in the passage in its fullest and truest meaning. Nothing is more common in the New Testament than to cite a few words of a passage when the writer means to refer to the entire context. This is done, I apprehend, in the present instance, and is implied in the words of the Evangelist when he says, "All this was done that it might be fulfilled which was spoken of the Lord by the prophet," referring to all the facts previously mentioned by him. While the child's name was called "Immanuel, or God with us," as a pledge of the divine ordering of events in a manner favourable to the Jewish cause, yet the idea "God with us" was in this case only imperfectly realized. The conception was filled up to the full in the birth of Jesus Christ. The child referred to by the prophet was the pledge of a temporal deliverance within a specified period to a particular nation. The child whose birth "filled up to the full" the conception of "God with us," was a pledge of a spiritual deliverance of all mankind, by manifesting the permanent abiding of God in a human personality In the birth of Jesus Christ, the saying of the prophet was filled up full, or the true ideal received its realization.

great section of Isaiah which gives us an idealized description of "the Servant of Jehovah." With respect to the Psalm, if it was composed by David, it is incredible that it should have been intended to be a description of his own sufferings, as it is simply at issue with all the facts of his life; nor can we conceive of any other person whose case the description would suit. It must therefore have been intended to describe some ideal sufferer, and that it is a very close description of the sufferings of Jesus Christ, as they are recorded in the Evangelists extending even to minute details, is an obvious matter of fact. With respect to the "Servant of Jehovah," there can be little doubt that the whole account was intended to be an idealized description, for taking it as a whole, there has been only one historical person, with the circumstances of whose life it will fit—Jesus Christ our Lord, whose whole work, rejection, and sufferings, followed by His triumphant resurrection, are a complete realization of the entire conception. It has been affirmed that Jeremiah was the image present to the writer's mind, but the description is clearly inconsistent with the known circumstances of his life.

It follows therefore that two points are incontestable. The Old Testament contains passages which form an idealized conception of a divine sufferer; and that several centuries afterwards Jesus Christ realized this conception in His own person, and that it has been realized by none other besides Him.

It will doubtless be objected that this class of typical prophecies are ambiguous, as having a human subject to whom they have an imperfect reference, and an ideal conception which was to be realized in the future; and consequently, that their evidential value is less cogent than if they had simply in view a single object to which they would correspond. To this I answer—

First, that there are not a few prophecies of this latter description which directly predict a future kingdom of God, and the advent of a Messiah who was to be its king; and that Jesus Christ not only attempted to found such a kingdom, but has succeeded in the attempt.

Secondly, the evidential force of typical prophecies is dependent on the number of them which converge in a common centre. As in all circumstantial evidence, it would be unsafe to draw any positive conclusions from one or two cases; but when large numbers of them converge in a single person, and will fit in with the circumstances of none other known to history, the conjoint effect amounts to a moral demonstration.

I now invite your attention to another element of the Old Testament Scriptures (it is a very extensive one), of which the writers of the New affirm that Jesus Christ is the complete and perfect realization, viz. its entire sacrificial system, and its symbolical worship. This claim is also made by Our Lord himself.* It amounts to this. The rites,

* Here again the force of the argument has been greatly weakened by the frequent endeavours which have been made to evolve out of the typical Scriptures of the Old Testament an amount of Christian truth, which we can only find in them by first putting it into them ourselves. Thus treatises have been composed on Leviticus, which, if the views of the writers are correct, constitute it a far clearer revelation of Gospel truth than anything which can be found in St. Paul's Epistles. The same course has been pursued with the whole typological system of the Old Testament. Every one of its minor details has been affirmed to be not merely a shadowy, but a very substantial delineation of some form of Christian truth so definite that it is impossible to find anything of equal clearness and precision in any portion of the New Testament. Under this system of interpretation, it is easy to make the typology of the Old Testament affirm anything which the fancy of its interpreter may suggest. It has been often defended on the ground that it is edifying, and enables us to arrive at clear views of Christian truth. But certainly any system of interpretation which succeeds in evolving out of the Old Testament clearer views of Gospel truth than the direct statements of the New, is open to grave suspicion. The principle laid down is that the typical Scriptures of the Old Testament have been so framed by the divine Spirit, that with the light of the New Testament shining on them, they form perfect delineations of some of the profoundest mysteries of Redemption. Before this can be accepted,

ceremonies, and institutions of Judaism all pointed to some deep-felt want in human nature. This want they imperfectly endeavoured to satisfy; but they were in no proper sense able to do so. What the New Testament affirms is, that all these rites, symbols, and sacrifices, as far as they pointed to real wants felt by human nature, have obtained a full realization in the person, work, and history of Jesus Christ; and that so complete is the embodiment in His person of every reality to which they pointed, that they have become for ever hereafter nugatory and worthless.

Here, again, we are in the presence of a simple question of fact. The writers of the New Testament affirm that Jesus Christ is the ideal embodiment of whatever was real in the institutions of the Old; the substance of which they were the imperfect shadows. Whether this be so or not we can determine by a simple examination of the Old Testament,

it is surely necessary to lay down some principle by means of which fancied analogies can be distinguished from divine utterances; but this has never yet been attempted. No book in the New Testament so much deals with the typology of the Old as the Epistle to the Hebrews. But its author was far from thinking that it contained a hidden Gospel, which, by the aid of the imagination could be converted into a full delineation of the Covenant of Redemption. His words are worthy of attention. "The law having a shadow of good things to come, and not the very image of the things." It follows therefore that according to his views the typology of the Old Testament is not the image ($\varepsilon i\kappa \omega \nu$, the substantial resemblance) of Christianity, but only its shadow ($\sigma \kappa \iota \dot{a}$) or unsubstantial outline. It stood therefore in the relation, not of an image, but of a shadow to the reality; or in other words, it darkly pointed to the ideal which is realized in Jesus Christ. If it be confined to this, its evidential value is considerable, proving the truth of those aspirations and convictions in the heart of man, which its symbolism was only in a most imperfect manner capable of satisfying, but which pointed to a higher and diviner reality, Jesus Christ our Lord, in whose person and work they all find their perfect satisfaction. But the effect of adopting the methods of interpretation above referred to, has been the wide diffusion of a belief among thoughtful minds, that the typology of the Old Testament, with its supposed fulfilment in the New rests on so unsubstantial a basis as to deprive it of all evidential value.

and by comparing its entire system of symbolism with the reality in the New.

Of this realization, I must content myself with citing two remarkable illustrations. Nothing is more certain than that the New Testament is founded on the Old; Christianity grew out of Judaism. Unless the Old Testament had been written, not one page of the New would ever have been composed, or the claims of Jesus to be the Messiah set up. Yet Christianity claims the right to supersede its entire system on the ground that Jesus Christ is not only its complete and adequate realization, but has so realized it, as to have rendered its imperfect methods nugatory. This has been effected wherever the Christian Church has been established, and constitutes a proof that whatever was real in Judaism has been so fully satisfied by Christianity, that the shadow has become useless now that we are in possession of the substance. So complete a supercession of one system by another which is founded on it, and has grown out of it, is without a parallel in history.

Secondly: the rite of sacrifice was universal in the ancient world. The only conclusion which is consistent with this fact is, that it must have had its origin in some deep-felt want of human nature.* It formed the very essence and

---

* It has been often asserted that the practice of sacrifices originated in a divine institution. Whether this were so, or not, we have no means of arriving at a certain conclusion; for the Bible makes no affirmation on the subject. It always speaks of sacrifices as a thoroughly established portion of divine worship, and describes them as having been offered by the immediate descendants of the first man; but it affirms nothing as to whether they were instituted by God, or were a spontaneous suggestion of the human mind. It is highly probable that God may have revealed himself to mankind prior to any revelations which are recorded in the Bible; but as no record of them has survived, it is most unsafe to attempt to determine, on mere abstract principles, what must have been their contents. To do so, is to imitate the unsound practice of those historians who, when certain facts have perished, endeavour to supply the deficiency by elaborating them out of their own consciousness. One thing is certain. The

centre of Judaism. Now the writers of the New Testament affirm that Jesus Christ has performed an act which has realized the ideal which was embedded in the entire sacrificial system of the ancient world; and has thereby rendered it unnecessary and unmeaning. What, I ask, has been the verdict of mankind respecting this? Have they found in Him the reality which the old sacrifices vainly attempted to realize? There can be one only answer to this question. Wherever Christianity has been accepted, the entire sacrificial system so deeply entwined with every institution of the ancient world, has perished; and a bloody victim has never once stained the altars of the Christian Church. It still has one great sacrifice to offer to God; but it is the *sacrifice of self*.

Further: Christianity has realized the ideal of that to which the dispensation of the Old Testament pointed in its general outline, but only imperfectly realized. Thus the conception of Judaism involved that of a Church; but its institutions, strictly in conformity with the ideas of the times, limited it to the members of a single nation. Christianity has swept away all the restrictions, broken down all the walls of separation, and created the Catholic Church. The conception of Judaism was that of a theocracy; that theocracy involved a vast system of symbolical worship, and the existence of an hereditary priesthood. Christianity retains the conception of the theocracy; but it is one altogether spiritual and moral, the priesthood of which is the entire Christian community. The moral teaching of the Old Testament was one of great elevation; but was rendered imperfect by being frequently obliged to accommodate itself to the circumstances of the times, which were those of barbarism, ferocity and war. Jesus Christ in His

practice of sacrifice corresponds to a need which has been in all ages deeply felt by human nature, and is an imperfect endeavour to satisfy it. This is sufficient for my argument. Jesus Christ has so completely satisfied that want that He has superseded the practice wherever His religion prevails.

teaching has realized the conception on which it is based, and freed it from its imperfections. The great men of the former dispensation were filled with the deepest aspirations for a light which would illumine many of the dark problems in the midst of which they struggled; above all, which would throw a cheerful ray on man's destiny beyond the grave. The light which they vainly struggled after has been imparted by one of their countrymen who, to all external appearance was only a Jewish peasant. My text affirms that Jesus is He of whom Moses in the Law, and the prophets did write. If He has fulfilled them; *i.e.*, if He is the ideal to which they pointed, He must certainly be the Christ.

Let me now briefly sum up the prophetic argument, and exhibit its conjoint force. The Old Testament many centuries before the birth of Jesus Christ, announced the setting up of a future kingdom of God, and the advent of a Messiah, who was to be its king. Such a kingdom of God has certainly been set up by Jesus Christ, in which He reigns as king. It affirms that a prophet should appear in the future like unto Moses. A multitude of prophets have appeared; but the only one who bears this resemblance is Jesus Christ. It has described a person of exalted holiness, and possessing a superhuman character, as suffering for others. The full conception of such a character is fully realized in Him, and in Him alone. It announces a Messiah who was to be a royal priest. Jesus Christ has assumed this office, and nullified every other sacrifice but His own. The Jewish dispensation consisted of a mass of rites, ceremonies, symbols, and shadowy representations. Jesus Christ and His Church are the embodiment of all the reality which they contain; and have rendered them for the future as worthless and unmeaning as it would be to hold up a candle to the noon-day sun. Its great kings and prophets earnestly longed for better things to come. Those aspirations have received their satisfaction in the person, actions, and teaching of the divine man. The teaching of the Old Testament, while founded on eternal truths, bears evident marks of imperfection. Jesus Christ is the embodiment of the ideal, after which the Law and the prophets were dimly groping. The argument is spread over a large amount of space, and consists of a multitude of minor details; but such are its salient points. View them not separately, but as they converge in a common centre, in the one great Catholic Man, Jesus Christ our Lord. Is it possible that this vast concurrence of circumstances in a single person can have been the result of a number of fortunate guesses? But if it has been the result of foresight, that foresight must have been superhuman. The only plausible objection to this conclusion is, that the character of Jesus has been elaborated out of the Messianic ideas of the Old Testament, and various apocryphal writings, and falsely attributed to Our Lord. On this point I shall offer a few remarks in a Supplement.

SUPPLEMENT I.

It has been often confidently asserted that the Jesus of the Fourth Gospel differs widely in conception from the Jesus of the Synoptics. If this be so, it may be urged as an objection against the argument of this Lecture, although even if this difference were an actual fact, it would lose none of its validity as founded on the unquestionable unity of the character which is delineated in the Synoptics. Still however as I am firmly persuaded that the objection is groundless, it will be desirable to offer a few general observations in proof of the identity of the character delineated in the fourth with that depicted in the first three Gospels.

In what then does the alleged difference consist? The answer must be, that the Jesus of the Fourth Gospel is delineated as possessing far higher and diviner attributes than the Jesus of the Synoptics. This is founded on the

fact that the discourses recorded in this Gospel represent
Our Lord as ascribing to Himself a number of divine attributes which are wanting in the Synoptics.

The fact is unquestionable, that the discourses of this
Gospel represent Our Lord as making a large number of
dogmatical assertions respecting Himself, which are not
found in the other three; but that this constitutes any real
break in the unity of the delineation, I deny; in other words,
I affirm that the four portraitures are simply four delineations of the same character contemplated from a different
point of view. The difference is precisely this: The Jesus
of St. John directly affirms His divine character; the Jesus
of the Synoptics is so delineated, that the assumption that
He must possess a superhuman character is the only
adequate explanation of the delineation. The Jesus of St.
John is in fact the explanation of the Jesus of the Synoptics.
In proof of this I observe :—

1. The Gospels of St. Matthew and St. Luke contain a
deliberate affirmation on the part of Our Lord, which forms
the connecting link between the Jesus of the Synoptics
and the Jesus of the fourth Gospel. I quote from St.
Matthew :—

"At that time Jesus answered and said, I thank thee, O
Father, Lord of heaven and earth, because thou hast hid
these things from the wise and prudent, and hast revealed
them unto babes. Even so, Father, for so it seemed good
in thy sight. All things are delivered unto me of my
Father, and none knoweth the Son, but the Father; neither
knoweth any the Father save the Son, and he to whomsoever
the Son will reveal him. Come unto me, all ye that travail
and are heavy laden, and I will give you rest. Take my
yoke upon you, and learn of me, for I am meek and lowly in
heart, and ye shall find rest unto your souls, for my yoke is
easy, and my burden is light."

This passage proves what has often been denied, that the
Synoptical traditions represented Jesus as making dogmatical affirmations respecting Himself. Further, that the

assertions which He is represented as making in this passage are fully on a par with anything which can be found in the fourth Gospel.

The first portion of this utterance, affirming the hiding of the fundamental elements of Our Lord's teaching from the wise and prudent, and their revelation to babes, embodies the essence of several of the thoughts contained in the great discourse which was delivered in the synagogue at Capernaum, in which He asserts the necessity of a divine influence for the appreciation of His teaching (John vi. 36-37; 41-44; 65), and also underlies the principles involved in several of his controversies with the Jews, as they are reported in this Gospel.

The second, " Even so, Father, for so it seemed good in thy sight," affirms the perfect coincidence of His own with the Father's will. Declarations of a precisely similar import are scattered widely over the discourses of the Fourth Gospel, of which John iv. 34; v. 19, 30; vi. 38; viii. 29, may be cited as examples.

The third affirms that all things are committed unto Him by the Father. The fourth Gospel reiterates again and again, that this power, which is inherent in the Father, is manifested through the Son.

The fourth affirms in direct terms that a perfect knowledge of the Son is possessed by the Father alone—" None knoweth the Son but the Father"—and that the Son in like manner possesses an equally exclusive knowledge of the Father—" Neither knoweth any one the Father, save the Son." The reader of the fourth Gospel cannot fail to observe that these assertions cover a large portion of Our Lord's dogmatical affirmations respecting Himself, which are really little more than amplifications of them.

The fifth assertion is, that He is the exclusive revealer of the Father. This is reiterated again and again in the fourth Gospel.

The whole concludes with the invitation to the weary and heavy laden to come to Him, with the promise of finding rest, and that the burden which He would lay upon them would be light. Portions of Our Lord's last discourse, in which He promised His disciples peace, and proclaimed that His service must be a service of love (John xiv. 27-31; xv. 9-17; xvi. 33), are the perfect analogue of this affirmation.

It follows therefore that a large portion of the utterances in the fourth Gospel, against which so much exception has been taken, as though they constituted a delineation of Jesus fundamentally differing from that of the Synoptics, are little more than expansions of the thoughts which are contained in this single passage. Yet as it is deliberately ascribed to Him by the Synoptics, their authors must have thought it in harmony with the traditions which they followed. From this we may safely infer that it could not have been the only one with which they were acquainted.

2. The form of the Synoptical delineation implies the existence of utterances of this description. In fact the Johannine portraiture is its direct counterpart and vindication.

The first proof of this which I adduce is that the Synoptic delineation of Our Lord's teaching invariably represents Him as resting the truth of His affirmations on no other authority than that of His own consciousness. He never speaks as though his knowledge came to Him from without; but all His assertions rest on His own ultimate authority. His utterances are in fact equivalent to oracles; but they rest on the simple basis of "I say unto you." Of this the mode in which He deals in the Sermon on the Mount with the Old Testament Scriptures (which as a Jew He must have viewed as of divine authority), explaining, enlarging, and occasionally annulling some of its precepts as defective, by no other authority but His own, may be cited as a crucial example. Without the smallest hesitation or faltering, the Jesus of the Synoptic narrative sets himself down in the seat of the chief legislator of the kingdom of God; nor can we trace in it one single indication of a misgiving on His part that He was not supremely worthy to fill it, or that His utterances were to be viewed as anything short of oracles from heaven.

But further: equally uniform is the Synoptic delineation of Our Lord as a worker of miracles. The utterances with which He announces them are as follows:—" I will, Be thou clean," and the leprosy immediately departs. " Young man, I say unto thee, arise," and the dead stands up. "Receive thy sight," and the blind man sees. " That ye may know that the Son of Man hath power on earth to forgive sins, I say unto thee, Arise, take up thy bed and walk," and the sick man carries his bed. " Come out of the Man, thou unclean spirit," and the demoniac is restored to sanity. To the waters, he says, " Peace, be still," and the storm ceases. Such is the invariable form of the Synoptical delineation, which never once represents Jesus as appealing to any power but His own, or entertaining the smallest doubt that He possessed it inherently, or even as performing a miracle after the utterance of a prayer to enable Him to do it. In this respect the delineation of the Synoptics is equally divine with that in the fourth Gospel. In one respect it even transcends it, for while the discourses of the fourth Gospel contain numerous passages which refer His miraculous works to His own concurrence in action with the Father, and describe them as the Father's testimony rendered to Him, there is not a single passage in any one of the Synoptics which makes any such affirmation, except on one occasion in a discussion with the Pharisees as to the source of His miraculous power, which they attributed to Satan, He uses the words, "If I by the finger of God cast out devils," and the affirmation made on one occasion by the author of the third Gospel, that Jesus went out "in the power of the Spirit." In a similar manner, the Johannine discourses far more definitely affirm the derivation of Our Lord's teaching from the Father, than any declaration of His own, which is recorded in the Synoptics.

It follows therefore that the utterances above commented on, and the discourses in the fourth Gospel, constitute the only adequate justification of the Synoptical delineation; and instead of the two delineations being portraitures of different characters, the one forms the direct counterpart of the other.

Equally uniform are the two delineations in attributing to Jesus the most perfect union of His own consciousness with the divine, and in carefully distinguishing it from that of other men. Of this a remarkable instance may be cited in the exactitude which both the Synoptics and the fourth Gospel attribute to Him in the use of the word "Father." They make it clear that He claimed that God was His Father in a sense different from that in which He is the Father of other men. In all four Gospels the usage in this respect is uniform. He frequently speaks of God under the character of "Father," but it is invariably "My Father" when He speaks of Him in relation to Himself; and "your Father" when He does so in relation to others. Never is the expression "Our Father" once attributed to Him in either of the Gospels, except in the prayer which He composed, not for His own use, but for that of His disciples. Such uniformity on a minute point of this description constitutes the strongest proof of identity of conception. The contrast between our Lord's view of the relationship in which He stood to God, and that in which other men stand to Him, is brought out more strongly in a passage of the Fourth Gospel, "My Father and your Father, my God and your God," and the distinction is invariably observed by all four Evangelists.

3. A claim of the most complete sacrifice of self on the part of His disciples is several times attributed to Jesus in the Synoptic Gospels. So strong is this demand that no greater amount of self-sacrifice could be rendered to Almighty God than the Galilean peasant claims for himself. Two passages in these Gospels explain the grounds of this demand, viz. His inherent worthiness, and that "He came to give His life a ransom for many." On another occasion it

is enforced by the consideration that He would deny those who denied Him, and confess those who confessed Him before the angels of God and His Father who is in heaven. Such claims, and on such grounds, were never elsewhere made by mortal man. In these respects the portraiture in all four Gospels is uniform, and the Johannine asseverations are only an expansion of those in the Synoptics, and a formal statement of the grounds on which such demands can rest.

4. While the fourth Gospel attributes to Our Lord the strong dogmatical assertions which we read in its pages respecting the dignity of His person, it delineates the other aspects of His character as being equally human with those of the Synoptics. Thus St. John describes Him as sitting near Jacob's Well, wearied with His journey; the Synoptics on several occasions represent Him as retiring to rest Himself after His day's labours. In the account of the Resurruction of Lazarus, the fourth Gospel represents Him as shedding tears of sympathy; and the whole description, while attributing to Him a very divine character, invests Him with a number of characteristics which are exquisitely human. Similarly, the third Gospel depicts Him as shedding tears and uttering the most pathethic lamentation over Jerusalem and its impending ruin. So again the whole description of the Last Supper in the Johannine Gospel delineates Him as exhibiting the same aspects of character. Its traits are even more delicately drawn than the corresponding incidents in the Synoptics. Similar also is the narrative of the betrayal, the trial, and the crucifixion. In both the Synoptics and the fourth Gospel the identity of the character is unmistakable.

Here it will be necessary to answer an objection. It has been affirmed that the author of the fourth Gospel has omitted the account of the agony in the garden because he thought it inconsistent with the divine character which he has attributed to his Master. That such an assertion can have been made in the face of the facts above referred to, and numerous others contained in this Gospel, is only one of many proofs that the enunciators of certain theories are ready to accept anything which is in accordance with their preconceived opinions on a very slender foundation of evidence. What was the reason which led the author of this Gospel to omit from his account of the passion any reference to the agony in the Garden, it is now impossible to determine; but nothing can be more certain than that it could not have been that which has been alleged by the school of critics to which I allude. This is rendered evident by the fact that while he omits the account of the agony, he alone of the Evangelists gives us an account of another perturbation of Our Lord occasioned by the prospect of His sufferings and death, which occurred only two days previously. Both delineations depict Him in an aspect equally human. It is impossible therefore that the author of this Gospel could have omitted the account of the agony because he thought it derogatory to the character which he attributed to his Master.

The following is the Johannine portraiture:

"Now is my soul troubled, and what shall I say? Father save me from this hour; but for this cause came I unto this hour. Father, glorify Thy name. Then came there a voice from heaven, I have both glorified it, and will glorify it again. The people therefore that stood by and heard it, said that it thundered; others said, An angel spake unto Him. Jesus answered and said, This voice came not because of me, but for your sakes. Now is the judgment of this world, now shall the prince of this world, be cast out. And I, 'if I be lifted up from the earth, will draw all men unto me." John xii. 27-32.

The following is one of the Synoptic delineations of the subsequent agony:—

"He said unto them (the apostles), Sit ye here, while I go and pray yonder. And He took with Him Peter and the two sons of Zebedee, and began to be sorrowful and very heavy. Then saith He unto them, My soul is exceeding

15 *

sorrowful even unto death; tarry ye here and watch with Me. And He went a little further, and fell on his face, and prayed, saying, O my Father, if it be possible, let this cup pass from Me; nevertheless, not as I will, but as Thou wilt. And He cometh unto His disciples, and findeth them asleep, and saith unto Peter, What! could ye not watch with Me one hour? Watch and pray, lest ye enter into temptation: the spirit indeed is willing, but the flesh is weak. He went away again the second time and prayed, saying, O My Father, if this cup may not pass away from me except I drink it, Thy will be done. And He came and found them asleep again, for their eyes were heavy. And He left them and went away again, and prayed the third time, saying the same words." On this follows the narrative of His voluntary self surrender into the hands of his enemies.

If the fourth Gospel is a forgery, its author must have been an adept at his art, for its delineations are almost perfect of their kind. But the idea that he invented the narrative of the perturbation, and suppressed that of the agony, for the purpose of imparting a more divine aspect to his Master's character, is only consistent with the idea that he must have been little better than a bungler; for the description in the Synoptics is the grander of the two, and the union of the will of the sufferer with that of the Father is absolute and complete. To say the least of it, the struggle as depicted in the Synoptics is Godlike and strictly in conformity with the entire scope of the Johannine delineation.

5. The identity will become more and more apparent if we compare an entire section in the Synoptics with a parallel one in the fourth Gospel. As it is longest and most complete, I will take that, which on the theory that the character is an ideal one, may not inaptly be designated the drama of the passion. It will only be necessary to notice its chief incidents.

This really commences with the anointing of our Lord at Bethany, as preparatory to His burial. It is narrated out of its proper place by the Synoptics, but it is evident that they attached a high importance to it, for it is the only event connected with His life which they represent Him as declaring that it should be proclaimed to the whole world for a perpetual memorial of the act. It is worthy of notice that this latter circumstance, which impresses on it a certain divine significance, is omitted by St. John, but in other respects the descriptions precisely correspond. To this follows the account of the triumphal entry into Jerusalem, in which all four evangelists concur in representing Him just prior to His great act of self-sacrifice, as openly assuming the character of the King Messiah. Notwithstanding several minor variations, the delineations are similar throughout, except that the Synoptics ascribe to our Lord the high Messianic act of cleansing the temple, which St. John omits to notice. At this point the narratives diverge: those of the Synoptics representing Him as being engaged during the days which intervened between His entry and the Passion in teaching in the Temple, and in discussions with the Jews, while the only incident mentioned by St. John is the interview with the Greeks and the mental perturbation above referred to. Here, however, it should be observed that the Synoptical delineations portray Our Lord in an aspect pre-eminently divine in the scene immediately preceding the account of the Passion, which is wholly unnoticed in the fourth Gospel; I allude to the prophecy which they ascribe to Him of the destruction of Jerusalem, His final advent, and the supplemental parable of the Last Judgment attributed to Him by St. Matthew, who is allowed to be the greatest authority for Our Lord's discourses. This last portion contains the grandest and most perfect delineation of Our Lord in His divine and human characters to be found in the New Testament, and is certainly not exceeded by anything which is affirmed respecting Him in the fourth Gospel.

This discourse is remarkable, as being the only one of any length in the Synoptics, except the one above alluded to, in which our Lord is described as making a number of direct assertions respecting Himself, after the manner of the fourth Gospel. Even if we take the discourse as it is recorded by St. Mark and St. Luke without the additions in St. Matthew, our Lord portrays Himself in an aspect preeminently divine, the brightest objects in nature being darkened before the manifestation of the glory of His appearance, surrounded by the Angels of His might, to take possession of His Messianic kingdom. Yet this grand delineation, perhaps the grandest in the entire Gospels, which the Synoptics have inserted immediately before their description of His lowest humiliation, is left altogether without notice in the Fourth Gospel. This is simply inconceivable if its author was a forger who invented his fiction for the sole purpose of glorifying his Master. The only incident in the Johannine narrative which supplies its place is the voice of encouragement from heaven in the account of Our Lord's mental perturbation.

The Johannine narrative of the last supper, while differing in numerous points of minor detail, which have no bearing on the present argument, from those of the Synoptics, consists of three scenes, the washing of the disciples feet, the detection and exposure of Judas, and the warning given to Peter. In each of these our Lord is delineated in an aspect exquisitely human, the perfect combination of dignity with humility, and condescending love. Its finer touches cannot be surpassed. It must be read, and carefully meditated on in order to be fully appreciated.

How stands the case with the Synoptics? It is clear that all four evangelists intended in their respective narratives to delineate our Lord in His profoundest humiliation; and it is equally certain, notwithstanding their variations, that the conception is identically the same in all four writers. The last two incidents in the Johannine account form a portion of that of the Synoptics, while the first is omitted, and in St. Luke's Gospel there is inserted in place of it the account of the unseemly contest for superiority among the disciples, immediately after the institution of the Lord's Supper, and His rebuke. The variations of detail in the four narratives only confirm the identity of the character as proving that among the various records of incidents handed down in the traditions of the different Churches, there was no real diversity of delineation.

Here the fourth Gospel again diverges from the Synoptics. Immediately after the supper, it describes our Lord as uttering a long consolatory address to the disciples, concluding with His great intercessory prayer. While this address contains a number of the most exquisite human touches, it also depicts Him in the diviner aspects of His character; the prayer of intercession being the act of self-consecration immediately before His voluntary sacrifice. There can be no doubt that the insertion of the address and prayer in this particular place, heightens the effect of His self-sacrifice, which follows; but precisely the same result is produced in the Synoptic narrative by the introduction of the great prophetic utterance, with its additions in St. Matthew, immediately before the account of the Paschal supper. In both Our Lord is described as investing Himself with superhuman greatness, immediately before His lowest humiliation; and it is impossible to affirm that the speaker, in the Gospel of St. John, has portrayed Himself in a more divine aspect than the speaker in that of Matthew. The one is in fact the counterpart of the other, only the portraiture is taken from a somewhat different point of view; but the identity is unmistakable.

We next pass on to the scenes of the arrest and trial. Here the minor details differ considerably. I need offer no further remarks on the omission of the agony in the Garden from the Johannine narrative, for amidst numerous variations in the incidents, the same fundamental conception prevails throughout all four narratives, viz. that of Our Lord's voluntary self-surrender. This is expressed in the fourth Gospel by the mode in which Jesus is represented as meeting the band at the entrance of the Garden : in the

Synoptics by the declaration that He had only to pray to His Father, and that He would immediately obtain the aid of twelve legions of angels: the Synoptics record the one, and the fourth Gospel the other. It is therefore absurd to affirm that the incident in question was invented for the purpose of heightening the effect. Both delineations are portraitures of Jesus supported by a consciousness of the divine within Him, in an act of voluntarily yielding Himself up to death. It is worthy of remark that while the Synoptics describe Him immediately before His condemnation as making a deliberate assertion of His superhuman character before the Jewish council, this incident is wholly omitted by St. John. The only thing which corresponds to it in this Gospel, if it may be really said to correspond, is His deliberate assertion of His Kingship in reply to the judicial inquiries of the Roman Governor. When interrogated by him on the question of His divine origin, He made no answer. It is clear, therefore, that in either case the character is the same, however much the incidents may vary. This variation of the incidents, while the identity is preserved, constitutes the strongest possible proof that the character is not an ideal creation, but an historical reality.

The narrative of the condemnation, and the crucifixion calls for little remark. Here again the incidents are extremely varied. But the greater the amount of variation, the greater force it imparts to my argument, for not a single variation affects the identity of the character. It is impossible to affirm that the author of the fourth Gospel has imparted a more divine, or even a less human aspect to our Lord, either before Pilate, or on the cross, than is attributed to Him in the Synoptics. If he has omitted the cry, "My God, my God, why hast thou forsaken Me?" which is attributed to him by the latter, he has inserted that of "I thirst" which they omit. Surely this is equally human with the former. Again, if he has attributed to Him the triumphant exclamation "It is finished" prior to His death, we know from the Synoptics that He uttered some cry which produced awe in the mind of the centurion; and it has its complete counterpart in St. Luke's Gospel, in the answer to the prayer of the repentant robber, that He would remember him when he came into His kingdom, "Verily, I say unto thee, to-day shalt thou be with Me in Paradise."

Nothing is easier than to raise a number of minute objections on account of the variations with which the Evangelical narratives abound; and to say that one thing has been invented, or left out for this purpose, and another for that. What was the express design of each Evangelist in making these additions, and omissions, or what was the precise amount of matter which each had before him, it is now impossible to ascertain; and if we supply our deficiency of knowledge by conjecture, we may make out any thing which falls into harmony with preconceived ideas. But amidst this divergency of incidents, one thing emerges into the clearest light, that the portraiture of the Jesus of the Evangelists constitutes an essential unity; that the separate delineations fit into one another with exquisite propriety, and that the separate parts of which each delineation is composed, adjust themselves to each other as portions of one great whole. Each Evangelist has some points in his delineation peculiar to himself, and delights to dwell on some particular aspect of the character of his Master; but all these variations amount to nothing more than that they have each contemplated the great reality from a somewhat different point of view. Identity of character arising out of great diversity of materials, points to one thing, and to one thing only—historical reality.

SUPPLEMENT II.

It has frequently been asserted that the Messianic character of the Jesus of the Gospels has been evolved out of the Messianic delineations of the Old Testament, and the Apocalyptic literature current at the time of the Advent, of which the Book of Enoch, the Second Book of Esdras, certain collections of Sybilline verses, and a few others are examples. This objection, which, if valid, would be fatal to the whole prophetic argument, has derived a certain amount of plausibility from the fact that the Messianic prophecies and the typology of the Old Testament have been frequently represented by Christian writers as being such distinct, full, and definite predictions of Christ, as to have made it comparatively easy to elaborate the Messiah of the New Testament out of the prophetic intimations of the Old. This being so, although the foregoing arguments are valid for the disproof of this particular form of the ideal theory, yet it will be desirable to offer a few additional observations for the purpose of showing that the data furnished by the Old Testament and the Apocalyptic literature in question are utterly inadequate to have afforded the materials for this grand delineation.

A large number of Christian writers in their eagerness to impart additional force to the prophetical argument, and a divine authority to doctrines which it is impossible to prove by the direct statements of the New Testaments, but which they consider to be integral portions of Christianity, have represented the Old Testament as containing a veritable Gospel. In adopting this course they have not perceived that they were cutting away the ground from under their own feet; for if the delineations of the Old Testament are thus clear and distinct, or in the language of the author of the epistle to the Hebrews, εἰκόνες, and not σκιαὶ of Christianity, it would have been comparatively easy for mythologists and inventors of fictions, to have delineated the Jesus of the Evangelists. The truth however will be found to be, that the only way of finding in the Old Testament what it has been alleged to contain, is by practising on ourselves the fallacy of first putting into it what we imagine that we find there. This mode of procedure has greatly impaired the value of the Christian argument in the eyes of thoughtful men; and put a dangerous weapon into the hands of opponents. For all evidential purposes it is as valueless, as it would be foolish in common life, to act on the assumption that a purse which we ourselves had filled, was a present made to us by a considerate friend.

In estimating the amount of light communicated by the prophetic Scriptures of the Old Testament, it is necessary to consider, not what we think that we can see in them with the light of Christianity shining upon them, but what was the only thing which any one could have seen in them who lived before Jesus Christ appeared as the realization of the ideal, towards which they obscurely pointed. In determining the question whether the Messianic conceptions of the Old Testament and the Apocalypses can have served as the model for the Jesus of the Gospels, it is our duty to contemplate them, not with the light which has been thrown upon them by the New Testament, but in the plain obvious meaning which they must have presented to the delineators themselves. In discussing this question it will be only necessary to consider the chief Messianic prophecies; for the idea that the typology of the Old Testament could have formed any portion of the model which has been employed in the delineation of the Jesus of the New, is too absurd to require serious refutation. It could only have served that purpose if it had been first put there by the delineator.

What then were the Messianic conceptions which the Old

Testament and the Apocalypses would have supplied, and how far would they have aided them in delineating the ideal Jesus of the Evangelists?

Let us suppose that such a delineator had in his hands the book of Enoch. I notice this apocalypse first, because it contains the Messianic conception in its clearest and most distinctive form. It is very doubtful whether the Messianic delineations of this book have not been inserted in it at a period subsequent to the advent, for the evidence that it is a composite work is strong. On this point, however, I will not insist, but suppose that the delineator of an ideal Christ may have been in possession of the entire book. What aid would it have afforded him in creating the great portraiture of the Gospels? He might have derived the following hints: that while the Messiah was to be divine, He was not to be invested with the attributes of absolute Deity: He is affirmed in it to have existed prior to all creation: His most usual designation is "the Elect One:" He is also repeatedly designated as the "Son of God," "the Son of Man," and once as "the Son of Woman:" He is invested with the titles of King and Judge of the world: He possesses righteousness, is gifted with wisdom, and knows all secret things: He possesses the Spirit in all its fulness, His kingdom is everlasting, and He stands highest in the acceptance of the Lord of Spirits. Although the book nowhere affirms the doctrine of an incarnation, it is unquestionably implied in the designations given to the Messiah, of "the Son of Man" and "the Son of Woman."

It is a remarkable fact, that as far as this book contains anything which may be called a portraiture of the Messiah, the character which it attributes to Him is one altogether divine. Although He is repeatedly called the Son of Man, no one trait of character strictly human is ascribed to Him. Further, it does not contain one single intimation that the Messiah was to be a sufferer; and that through His sufferings He would enter His glory, which constitutes one of the most striking features in the delineation of the Jesus of the New Testament.

The form of the book is that of a vision: and its Messianic portions are not portraitures or obscure typical outlines, but affirmations respecting Him in the most strictly dogmatic form. It is very remarkable that although He is repeatedly called the Son of Man, He is nowhere represented as exhibiting simply human characteristics.

It will be at once seen that the Messianic portions of this book are greatly in advance of anything contained in the Old Testament. Whatever view we may take of its authorship, its characteristics are very striking; and this is rendered the more so, because the reader is led by the occurrence of certain words and phrases used in common by its author and those of the New Testament, to the almost inevitable conclusion, either that the author was acquainted with some of the books of the New Testament, and derived his phraseology from them; or *vice versâ*. If we adopt the former hypothesis it is difficult to account for the absence of any delineation of the Messiah in a purely human, above all, in a suffering character. If on the contrary the Messianic portions of the work are assumed to have been in existence prior to the advent, it becomes equally difficult to account for the extremely advanced form of its dogmatical assertions, for which the remnants of Jewish literature which bear on the ideas of the times, afford no adequate vindication. The balance of probability in favour of its post-Christian date greatly preponderates; and therefore in allowing that it might have been used by some supposed delineator of the ideal of the Gospels, I give him every advantage. The question therefore arises, how far would the dogmatic assertions of this book have aided an idealist in his portraiture of the Jesus of the Evangelists?

It will immediately strike the reader, that while this book contains a number of dogmatic statements respecting the Messiah, it makes not a single attempt to give us a dramatized portraiture of Him; by which I mean, that it never embodies the attributes which it ascribes to Him in a living character. This, on the contrary, forms the very essence of our Gospels; in which Jesus not only possesses certain qualities; but actually exhibits them over a wide sphere of action, and in every variety of circumstances. It will be at once seen that between merely affirming that the Messiah was both Son of God and Son of man, and delineating Him in a career in which He is made to act both these characters with exquisite propriety, the difference is vast. In a similar manner it is easy to ascribe to such a person wisdom, holiness, benevolence, or any other virtues, or even to affirm that he will be the future judge of the world; but it is a very different thing to dramatize him as exhibiting these characteristics over an extensive sphere of action. This is what has been effected in the New Testament; but of the mode in which the Messiah was to be delineated as uniting the divine and human characters, or as exhibiting in action a number of virtues, the perfect combination of which in any single person is a matter of the greatest difficulty, the book of Enoch would not have furnished a single hint. The difference between this book and the Gospels may be summed up in the following sentence. The book of Enoch declares what attributes the Messiah in conformity with the ideas of its author ought to possess; the Gospels set before us a delineation of what, contrary to the ideas of their authors, He actually was. The one utters a number of dogmatical assertions respecting Him, the other presents us with an actual portraiture of a living Christ, exhibiting in perfect harmony the holiness of man, and the holiness of God. The one resembles a person who says to an artist, paint a magnificent picture, exhibiting certain principles; the other resembles the artist with the picture in his hands exhibiting the highest conceptions of genius, and finished in the highest style of art.

It follows therefore that although he might have learnt from this book that the Messiah was to be a person who would possess high, but not the highest form of divine attributes, that He was to be the Son of man, Son of woman, and the Son of God, that He was to be the revelation of the Lord of

Spirits, and the future Judge of the world, the delineator would not have derived a single hint as to how these characteristics were to be exhibited in action. Still more devoid of assistance would this book have left him, in depicting the human aspects of the Christ of the Gospels. The solitary hint that it would have given him would have been its assertion that He was to be the Son of man.

But as I have said, the aspect of the Messiah as a sufferer is utterly wanting. That He was to suffer, above all to die, the book does not give the smallest intimation. Its Messiah is altogether triumphant and divine. On the other hand His character as a sufferer is one of the most striking aspects of the Christ of the New Testament. A Christ in whom this portion of the Evangelical portraiture is wanting, is an utterly different one from the Christ of the New Testament, and if this was the only distinction between them, it would constitute a proof little short of demonstration, that the Messiah of Enoch could not have served as a model for the Christ of the Gospels. I need hardly say that if the suffering Jesus is an ideal creation, it must have been one of the most difficult portions of the whole character to conceive and dramatize. It follows, therefore, that apart from its seven or eight dogmatical assertions respecting certain attributes which the Messiah was to possess, the Messianic elements of the book of Enoch would not have afforded the smallest assistance to any body of idealists, who may be supposed to have imagined the Christ of the New Testament.

2. But may not another apocryphal book, that of Esdras, have supplied the deficiency, and formed the model of the suffering Jesus? Here again, great uncertainty exists respecting the date of the work. Whatever may be said of the greater part of it, there cannot be the smallest doubt, that a few passages in it are interpolations in favour of Christianity. While the book of Enoch displays a generally triumphant tone, this apocalypse is distinguished by the tone of profound melancholy which pervades it. Under its influence, it recognises the fact that

the Messiah was to die; but as with the other book, the idea of His death as a sacrifice is foreign to its contents. Its Messiah is one pre-eminently Jewish,—an aspect of thought which distinguishes the entire work. With the exception that the Messiah was to die, and the world to return to chaos before the Resurrection, it furnishes us with no fresh element of Messianic thought. If we adopt the highly improbable supposition, that this book was in the hands of some idealists, who have invented the portraiture of the Christ of the Gospels, the only possible aid it could have afforded them was the idea that the Messiah was to die; but how the conception of a dying Messiah was to be combined with the triumphant one of the other apocalypse, or how the Messiah of Esdras was to be metamorphosed into the Christ of the Gospels, it would have imparted to the idealist neither aid nor suggestion. Any one who carefully peruses this book must arise from it with a firm conviction, that it has not formed the model of the supposed delineators of an ideal Christ, who, according to any theory which does not ignore the plain facts of history, and the possibilities of things, must have been as numerous as the inventors of the legends of which the Gospels are said to be composed.

3. It being clear, therefore, that these two apocalypses have not supplied the materials out of which a number of idealogists have succeeded in delineating their Christ, it will be needless to inquire whether the remaining works of this description can have been used for the same purpose. A cursory perusal of them will be sufficient to convince the reader that they are incapable of supplying the deficiency; and it is also certain that portions of them must have been composed at a period subsequent to the Advent. This being so, it only remains to inquire what amount of aid could have been furnished by the Messianic elements in the Old Testament.

4. The book of Daniel would have furnished the conception of a Messiah who, while He was to be invested with superhuman attributes, was also to be the Son of Man.

From it they would also learn that the kingdom of God, the advent of which it announces, would differ from all other earthly kingdoms. Another prophecy of the same book would have informed them that one of the purposes of His coming would be to make an end of sin and reconciliation for iniquity, and that to effect this object the Messiah would die by a violent death. From this, when viewed in connection with the other prophecies which assign to Him a kingdom without limits and without end, it is highly probable that they would infer that it was part of the Messianic character that He should be raised again from the dead; but this could only have been an inference, for the book nowhere affirms that such would be the case. This book and that of Enoch are affirmed by those whose theories I am controverting, to have contributed largely to the formation of the Messianic conception of the Jesus of the Evangelists. It is clear however that the points above referred to form the utmost aid which it could have afforded to the supposed ideologists, but that it would have given them no hint as to the proportions in which the divine and human were to be combined in the person of the Christ, and have left them entirely in the dark as to the mode in which the character was to be delineated. In one word, as far as this book is concerned, with the exception of these imperfect hints, the entire portraiture, as it appears in the Gospels, must have been their own pure invention.

5. The Old Testament contains two distinct classes of prophecies, one of which depicts the Messiah in the divine, and the other in the human aspects of His character. These are very rarely combined in the same prediction: I mean those which speak of Him as a glorious King, and those which speak of Him as a sufferer. Ideologists therefore could only have arrived at the conclusion inferentially, that these two classes of predictions were intended to refer to the same person. If they inferred that this was to be the case, the problem how the union was to be effected, and the character dramatised over a course of action, would have proved to be

one of which each ideologist would have propounded a different solution, and thus have rendered all unity of delineation impossible.

6. Let us now turn to the greatest prophecy in the Old Testament, that of the Servant of Jehovah, in the latter section of Isaiah. It is evident that if this prophecy is not sufficiently definite to have furnished the materials for constructing the Christ of the Gospels, no other, nor the whole in combination, can have been adequate for the purpose. What then are the materials with which it could have furnished them?

Taken as a whole, it presents us with five characters, viz., that of Jehovah himself, of the Servant of Jehovah, of an ideal Israel who is often identified with the Servant of Jehovah, of the actual Israel, and of the prophet. The ideal Israel is the prophet's conception of what the historical Israel ought to have been in its covenant relation to Jehovah, as distinct from what it actually was.

Throughout the entire section which contains this delineation, Jehovah Himself is frequently introduced as a speaker, proclaiming His own omnipotence, and revealing Himself in His capacity as a Saviour. His personality and that of the Servant of Jehovah are preserved distinct throughout the entire prophecy, and there is no confusion or intermingling of the characters. It should be observed that the Servant of Jehovah forms the Messianic delineation.

The conception of the Servant of Jehovah makes its first appearance in the forty-first chapter. It is clear that he is here identified with the ideal Israel. Precisely the same conception is continued throughout the following chapter, where the Servant of Jehovah, still the ideal Israel, is invested with Messianic attributes of a very high order, which the Gospels affirm to have received their perfect realization in Jesus Christ alone. It should be observed that not only are the personality of Jehovah and that of His Servant kept perfectly distinct, but the latter is invested with no attribute which is properly divine.

The forty-third chapter opens with another ideal delineation of Israel as the Servant of Jehovah, who is described as His witness. In this chapter we are first introduced to the historical, as distinct from the ideal Israel whom Jehovah addresses in terms of expostulation.

The forty-fourth chapter again presents us with the ideal Israel as Jehovah's Servant, who receives a succession of promises, and to whom Jehovah proclaims His omnipotence. On this follows a description of the character of the historical Israel. Then the ideal Israel is again introduced with assurances of pardon, for whose sake a deliverer is raised up in the person of Cyrus, who is expressly called to his work for the sake of Israel, Jehovah's Servant, and Israel His elect.

The same imagery is continued until we arrive at the forty-ninth chapter, where a speaker is introduced who designates himself by the name of Israel, and declares himself to have been formed from the womb to be the Servant of Jehovah. He describes himself as having been discouraged at the greatness of his work, but as supported by the strength of his God. His special office is to bring the actual Israel near unto him, and he declares that though he should fail in the attempt, he would still be glorious in the eyes of Jehovah. In the fiftieth chapter he first makes his appearance as a sufferer, yet as firmly bent on the performance of his work, trusting in the aid of the Almighty.

In the fifty-second and fifty-third chapters we are introduced to the last appearance of the Servant of Jehovah, unless in the subsequent Messianic prophecies the same person is addressed, but not named. It is by far the most remarkable of them all, the well-known description of the Man of Sorrows. The Servant of Jehovah, though acting prudently, is described as having his visage more marred than any man, yet he is to sprinkle many nations, while kings shut their mouths at him. He has neither form nor comeliness; he is despised and rejected of men. He bears our griefs and carries our sorrows. He is wounded for our transgressions, smitten of God and afflicted. The Lord lays on him the iniquity of us all. He is unresisting like a lamb, and his life is cut off by a violent death, to which he submits, not for his own sin, but for that of the people. his soul is made a sin-offering; he bears the sins of many, and makes intercession for transgressors. As a reward for his sufferings voluntarily submitted to, he is not only assured of their triumphant issue, but that he himself would be satisfied with the result.

This is the most important Messianic prophecy in the Old Testament, not only on account of its length, but because the Servant of Jehovah is dramatized over a limited sphere of action. It is easy to perceive, now that the reality is come, that the Jesus of the New Testament is the perfect realization of these various shadowy delineations: but the question is, does it afford adequate materials, out of which a number of ideologists could have created the portraiture of the Christ of the Gospels.

The reader will at once perceive that the larger portion consists of doctrinal statements respecting the nature of the Messiah's work. The express delineations of his character are few. They are in fact assertions of what it was to consist of, rather than actual delineations.

Supposing a body of ideologists to have arrived at the conclusion that the Servant of Jehovah was intended to be a delineation of the Messiah, they might have learned from the fifty-second and fifty-third chapters the following facts;

First: he was to be one of the greatest of sufferers.

Secondly: he was to be despised and treated with contempt.

Thirdly: that his sufferings were to terminate in death.

Fourthly: that they were to be undergone voluntarily.

Fifthly: that he was to exhibit in his sufferings the patience of a lamb.

Sixthly: that his sufferings would terminate not only in a triumphant issue, but in a result satisfactory to himself.

Such are the materials which this prophetic delineation

would have supplied to the ideologists, to enable them to portray the suffering Christ of the Gospels. It will be at once seen how imperfect a model they would have formed on which to construct the drama of the Passion. It is important to observe that they are confined to that portion of his Messianic character alone, and would have left them entirely in the dark as to how the diviner aspects were to be combined with the human, or how the other portions of the character portrayed in the Gospels were to be delineated. The suffering Christ constitutes only a portion, though a very important one, of the great portraiture of the Gospels. The six points above referred to, would have only served as simple directions to construct a character in which these particular aspects were to be perfectly embodied: but they would have left the question unsolved as to how this was to be effected, and on the remaining portions of the delineation, as it appears in the Gospels, these two chapters would have afforded them not the smallest assistance; consequently each ideologist would have delineated his Christ according to his own imagination, which must have destroyed the unity of the conjoint work.

7. There are unqestionably other prophecies in Isaiah, which assign to the Messiah attributes of a far higher order than those attributed to him in the section which contains the description of the Servant of Jehovah. These however afford not the smallest hint as to the mode in which the divine aspects of his character were to be delineated in combination with the human. The combination of a divine with a human character is a rock on which all poets and ideologists have suffered shipwreck: and it need hardly be observed that the difficulty of effecting the union is greatly increased when it is necessary to delineate the human as a sufferer. But it is very unlikely that a number of ideologists who used Isaiah as their model, would have arrived at the unanimous conclusion that the divine and human aspects of the prophetic delineation were to be combined in a single person. It is far more probable that at least some of them

would have considered that two Christs were intended by the prophet, one of whom was to exhibit the divine, and the other the human attributes of the Messianic delineation. On such a point disagreement would have been fatal. If, on the other hand they arrived at the conclusion that both were to be combined in a single person, this would have at once launched them on the boundless ocean of conjecture as to how the union was to be effected, without rudder, compass, or star to direct their course. It is evident that the only possible result must have been the creation of as many ideal Christs as there were ideologists.

8. I need hardly pursue this subject further; for it is evident that if the Messianic delineations in Isaiah would have been incapable of furnishing the suitable materials for framing the portraiture of the Christ of the Gospels, this result could not have been accomplished by all the other Messianic prophecies in the Old Testament. In fact, the larger their number, the greater would have been the embarrassment which they would have caused as to how the various scattered rudimentary delineations were to be combined into a harmonious whole, and exhibited in the actions and teachings of a living Christ. They would have formed little more than a body of directions to construct a character who was to exhibit a certain number of attributes; but artists of every kind are painfully aware that between an order to do a thing in this or that particular way, and its realization, the interval is wide. Such must have been the position of ideologists who had nothing else to aid them in the delineation of an ideal Christ than the Messianic elements in the Old Testament. Instead of the unity of the Jesus of the New resulting from their labours, they would have constructed Christs of a wide diversity of conception. The Christian typologist has a very different task before him. He is in possession of the substance which, after he has seen and contemplated, it is comparatively easy to discern in the shadowy outline.

If it be urged that if ideologists had accepted the twenty-second Psalm as Messianic, it would have aided them in the delineation of the Passion, I fully admit that its imagery would have suggested to them the idea that the Messiah was to die by crucifixion, and that several circumstances connected with the death of Our Lord are described with remarkable precision; as the staring and insulting crowd, the limbs almost dislocated, the piercing of the hands and feet, the effects of the thirst, the parting of the garments, the offer of vinegar to drink, and the triumphant issue to which these sufferings tended. These suggestions it would unquestionably have afforded; but when the drama of the Passion is contemplated as a whole, beginning with the anointing, and terminating with the Resurrection, including the calm composure and perfect self-surrender of the sufferer, it will be seen that although the materials afforded by the Psalm would have furnished them with these facts, they would have been wholly insufficient to have enabled them to construct the grand drama of the Gospels, of which they only form an inconsiderable portion. It is also evident that as to the rest of the portraiture of the Jesus of the Evangelists they would not have furnished a single hint.

Once more: when historical characters, such as David, are idealized as typical representations of the Messiah, instead of aiding the ideologists, it would have led them astray in their delineation of the Christ of the Gospels. Now that the reality has come, we see plainly that the idealization was intended to be confined to David in his capacity of King of the theocracy. But it is hardly possible that this would have occurred to an ideologist. On the contrary, he would have been almost certain to have considered that the personal character of David was the thing intended; and consequently, instead of delineating a character who was mild and humble, he would have portrayed one of which the heroic qualities would have formed the leading characteristic. Above all, he would certainly have invested him with the character displayed by the Psalmist in the imprecatory Psalms. But between the delineation of Him who prayed, in the extremity of His agony, " Father, forgive them, for they know not what they do," and the language of the Psalmist in these Psalms, such as : " Let there be none to extend mercy unto him, neither let there be any to favour his fatherless children ;" " As he clothed himself with cursing like as with a garment, so let it come into his bowels like water, and like oil into his bones ;" " Happy shall he be that rewardeth thee as thou hast served us. Happy shall he be that taketh and dasheth thy little ones against the stones," the contrast is striking.

These brief observations will I think be sufficient to show that the prophetical Scriptures of the Old Testament would have been utterly inadequate to furnish the materials out of which the ideologists could have constructed the Jesus of the New. The more closely the materials at their command are sifted, the more firmly will this conclusion be established. If it be an ideal creation, it is certain that they must have evolved it out of their own imaginations, without a model or outline to direct them. But this supposition I have shown not only to be in the highest degree improbable, but one which is absolutely impossible.

LECTURE V.

"Prove all things; hold fast that which is good."—1 THESS. v. 21.

THE words of my text will serve as an appropriate motto to this and the following Lectures, in the first three of which I propose to examine the evidence of the miracles in the New Testament, as it is set forth in our popular evidential treatises; and to point out those additional lines of defence which the exigencies of modern thought have rendered necessary for strengthening our position where it is defective. In the treatment of this subject, I shall adhere closely to the principle laid down by Our Lord, that the Scribe who is well instructed in the things of the kingdom of heaven should bring out of his treasures things both new and old. I shall therefore adopt the old as far as it is applicable to the present aspects of thought, and strengthen it by the new whenever this is rendered necessary by the alteration in the character both of the attack and the defence.

On the *à priori* question respecting the possibility of miracles, it will be unnecessary for me to enter in these Lectures. This subject has been already so fully discussed, that after the vast amount of intellectual labour which has been expended on it, it is surely not too much to assume that some points in the controversy must be considered by all reasonable men as settled. I am therefore quite willing to accept the positions which have been laid down on this subject by Mr. Mill in his *Logic* and in his posthumous

Essays. We may do this the more readily, because unbelievers cannot dispute his competency to take a complete survey of the entire question; and all his intellectual bearings were adverse to revealed religion. The principles which I shall assume as fully established are as follows:—

1. In all reasonings about miracles it is necessary to assume the existence of a God who is a moral and personal Being. No weight of evidence can prove the performance of a miracle to any one who affirms that we have no sufficient proof of His existence. To such a person, even if a miracle were attested as a fact, it would simply be an unusual event, the occurrence of which he would ascribe to some force in nature with which he was unacquainted.

2. If the existence of a God who is a moral and personal Being, is assumed as proved, the affirmation that miracles are impossible is no longer tenable; for the very supposition itself presupposes a cause which is adequate to perform them; or, to express the same truth in other words, the idea of a miracle violates no law of causation. Theists therefore have two alternatives to choose from, viz., a supernatural, or an unknown natural agency; and in forming their judgment, a most important consideration must be, the character of God and the conformity of the supposed occurrence to that character.

3. The occurrence of an extraordinary event, such as a miracle, viewed simply as a phenomenon, can be satisfactorily certified by our senses, or by testimony. Consequently Hume's arguments, by which he endeavoured to prove that no amount of evidence can establish the performance of miracles, may be safely dismissed as either harmless truisms or exploded fallacies.*

---

* The author of *Supernatural Religion* has endeavoured to reconstruct Hume's argument against Mill; but the attempt is a hopeless failure. It is quite true that there is a sense in which miracles are contrary to experience, *i.e.* they are not ordinary occurrences; for if they were, they would lose their character as miracles; but Hume's argument, if it is valid against miracles because they are

4. That as the forces of the Universe, and the order of nature must be manifestations of the divine will, their invariability renders the occurrence of miracles highly improbable.* To overcome this improbability, it is necessary to adduce some adequate reason why the Creator has deviated from the observed course of action which, except in the specific case of an alleged miracle, prior experience proves to have been His universal rule.

5. That as the order of nature is the rule of the divine acting in the Universe, and as that order is invariable, the evidence necessary to prove the occurrence of a miracle must be far stronger than that which is required in the case of an ordinary event.

6. If adequate proof can be afforded of the existence of a

---

contrary to past experience, would be equally valid against every fresh addition to that experience, for all such additions must be facts of which men have had no prior experience.

* Two views may be taken of the forces of the Universe, which are both consistent with theism. The first considers them as directly emanating from the energy of the divine mind, and the result of God's immanence in Nature. Contemplated thus, they are manifestations of the divine activity; and their laws, or invariable sequences, of the divine will. This is the view which underlies the entire Bible, which contemplates the activities of nature as the energies of God. The second is the mechanical theory, which affirms that matter and force have been called into separate and permanent existence by the Creator, and have been so constituted by Him as to work out an infinite number of results with the precision of a machine so perfect that after it has been once constructed and set in action it will never require any fresh interference on His part to regulate its motions. The latter is the popular scientific theory of the day, and if true, it renders a miracle far more improbable than it would be on the assumption of the truth of the former. Still, even assuming the former as the true view, the fact that as far as human observation has gone, God has always energized in conformity with invariable law, lays it open to question whether it is in conformity with His character to act in any other manner, and consequently it becomes necessary that some adequate reason should be assigned why He has deviated in any particular case from His ordinary course of action, before such deviation can be rendered credible.

God who cares for man, and if we take into consideration the miserable and degraded condition in which so large a portion of the human race unquestionably are, some interference in their favour, in addition to God's ordinary providence, may be regarded as probable; and so far the antecedent improbability of miracles, if a necessary part of such an interference, is diminished. In estimating the degree of this probability, we need not accept Mr. Mill's terrific indictment against nature and against man, as a true account of the actualities of things.* If only one fourth part of it is true (and it is an undeniable fact that a large amount of physical evil, and a still greater amount of moral evil, prevails), the general principle must be considered to be established; and so far the *à priori* difficulties which lie against such special interventions as miracles, are diminished.

These points being assumed as true, the amount of proof which can be justly demanded of us for the miracles of Christianity becomes clear. It is not enough to affirm that

---

* "Man," says Mr. Mill, " viewed as a simple production of nature, has in him but one good thing, the capacity of improvement; he is naturally devoid of a sense of truth, a coward, cruel, selfish, and even a lover of dirt. The truth is," says he, " there is hardly a point of excellence belonging to human character which is not decidedly repugnant to the untutored feelings of human nature." ... " Whatever good thing man now possesses, either in himself or in his outward surroundings, he has attained not from the gift of nature, but from his having conquered and subdued her." It will be useless to quote more to a similar purport. The impression which is produced on the mind by this portion of the Essay is, that we are in the presence, not of the calm philosopher, but of one of the extremest school of Calvinistic theologians. If this statement, however, is only true to the degree which I have stated in the text, and assuming that a God exists who cares for man, it is hardly possible that the argument for some additional interference in his favour on the part of God could have been put more forcibly. Surely if man is naturally as bad as Mr. Mill represents him, the mere fact of his having succeeded in improving himself to the degree which he has, is a very near approach to a miracle.

an equally strong attestation can be adduced for them as for the ordinary facts of history. Even extraordinary events require a stronger attestation than ordinary ones. Far more must this be the case with miracles, when they are alleged as the credentials of a divine Revelation. The distinction in point of attestation which we justly require for miracles compared with ordinary events, receives a striking illustration in the history of Herodotus. His history, as we know, contains accounts of a large number of supernatural occurrences, which are closely interwoven with his narratives of ordinary events. While we readily accept the latter, we summarily reject the former, although as far as we have any means of judging, they rest on the same testimony as the facts. Thus with respect to the battles of Salamis and Mycale, we accept the chief incidents as historical, while we attribute the accounts of the supernatural ones either to legendary invention, or the excited imaginations of the combatants; although as a bare question of attestation, there can be little doubt that the historian derived his accounts of both from the same authorities.* A similar course we habi-

* Large numbers of the subordinate incidents beyond all question rest on a very inadequate attestation, and not a few of them are simply impossible. (See Cox's *History of Greece*.) This writer however carries the principles of historical scepticism to unjustifiable lengths when he claims the right of rejecting nearly every narrative as unhistorical which serves as an illustration of the theological bias of Herodotus, that a divine Nemesis rules in the affairs of men. The particular form in which it is placed before us by the historian, is no doubt a part of his theological bias; and not a few of the events narrated by him have received a colouring in conformity with it. But the principle which underlies the Greek conception of a divine Nemesis, that the overbearing arrogance of man will sooner or later receive a downfall, is part of the moral order of the Universe; and it is absurd to reject all narratives as unhistorical which illustrate it. Perhaps no better illustration of the doctrine can be found than in the career and downfall of Napoleon the First; yet if the principles on which Mr. Cox throws suspicion on several narratives are valid, the history of his rise and fall will have to be rejected by historical critics in the future as being the creation of particular theological bias, of which

tually pursue in daily life with all reputed miracles. We justly consider that the evidence requires to be submitted to a very close scrutiny, before it can claim acceptance. The necessity of this has been greatly increased by the large number of fictitious miracles with which history abounds, some of which rest on a far stronger amount of attestation than would be necessary to establish the occurrence of ordinary events. But if I have been successful in the preceding Lectures in proving the superhuman action of Jesus Christ in the history of the past and in the facts of the present, our *à priori* difficulties will not only be diminished, but will absolutely disappear, and we shall be fully justified in accepting a number of supernatural occurrences in connection with His earthly manifestation, on the same attestation as we do ordinary facts.

Let me therefore briefly state the points which I have proved in the present Lectures.

1. It is an unquestionable fact that Jesus Christ has exerted a superhuman power in the moral and spiritual worlds during the last eighteen centuries of history; and that He is exerting this power at the present moment is a fact which is also capable of verification.

2. The presence of a superhuman power in Jesus Christ is further proved by the fact that His teaching, which, if He was nothing but an ordinary man, must have been that of an uneducated Jewish peasant, brought up in the narrowest atmosphere of exclusiveness, has transcended that of all the

they are a perfect illustration. Similar principles are applied by the tendency School of critics to the New Testament, and the attempt is made to explain away its historical character on the same grounds. Mr. Cox however admits that all the great events of the history rest on an historical basis, and this is all that we require for the Christian argument. It is an unquestionable fact, however, that we reject the miraculous incidents, although they rest on precisely the same testimony as the facts which we accept as historical. This is quite sufficient to show that the observation which has been often made, that the miracles of the Bible are as strongly attested as the ordinary facts of history, does not meet the requirements of the case.

great thinkers of the ancient world in its catholicity and its breadth; and especially by His having succeeded in bringing to bear on human nature a great moral and spiritual power, of the want of which the philosophers were profoundly conscious, but which they were wholly unable to create. In one word, He has shown Himself to be the one great Catholic man, who alone has burst through all the conditions which were imposed on Him by the environment in which He was born and educated, and who has realized in His own person all the aspirations of human nature.

3. Not only does the character depicted in the Gospels stand at an immeasurable height above all other men; but its unity proves it to be the delineation of an historical reality, and not a fictitious creation.

4. That in the person and work of Jesus Christ are realized the aspirations of an entire literature, extending over a space of a thousand years. Its predictions receive in Him their fulfilment; its types their realization; He constitutes the ideal to which the whole system pointed; and not only so, but beyond the limits of the Jewish Church, realizes in His own person the inarticulate sighings and aspirations of human nature during the centuries of the past.

These things being so, the conditions of the historical argument are changed. The argument from miracles has no longer to support the entire weight of Christianity. But while it is removed from the forefront of our evidential position, the *à priori* difficulty arising from the abstract improbability of miracles is converted into a probability in their favour; in other words, it is far more probable that a person who has exerted such a superhuman influence on the moral and spiritual worlds, should have manifested a corresponding power over the forces of the material Universe, than that He should have only acted on them in the same manner as they are acted on by ordinary men. Consequently the whole question of the performance of miracles becomes one of adequate attestation.

The order of our argument therefore must be as follows:—

First: The evidence of the superhuman action of Jesus Christ in the history of the past, and in the facts of the present.

Secondly: The direct historical evidence which can be adduced in support of the events recorded in the Gospels.

III. Let us now consider what are the links in the old evidential argument which the results of modern criticism have proved to be either weak or defective. We must ascertain where the defects exist, before it is possible to strengthen the points where our position is weak.

In examining this subject I assume that Paley's argument is the model and ideal of modern evidential treatises; for not only has it been prescribed by nearly every bishop on the bench for the last half century, as a work to be studied by the candidates for holy orders, but it has occupied the chief place in the theological curriculum of our sister University during the same period. In addition to this, nearly all our other evidential treatises have been intended either to supplement, or to strengthen the line of argument which Paley has taken. This being so, the question becomes one of great importance, Is the form in which the argument for Christianity is presented in the "Evidences," adequate to enable the Christian student to grapple with the varied forms of modern unbelief?

I yield to none in my appreciation of the "Evidences." The reasoning is a model of clearness and precision; but it is directed against a wholly different form of unbelief from that with which we have at present to contend. Its chief aim was to meet the Scepticism of the last century; and consequently to prove that Christianity did not originate in an imposture. Against this form of unbelief the argument is perfect; and from this ground it has been thoroughly and completely driven, and so far we may pronounce the work to have been a great success; for no unbeliever who values his reputation, would now venture to affirm that the origin of Christianity has been due to a consciously concocted fraud. But the line of attack has since been completely changed. We have had mythic theories; legendary theories; theories of tendencies; theories of evolution, which account for the origin of Christianity as the natural result of the forces which energize in man; and the theory of visions in all its multiform aspects, backed up by all the resources of modern criticism, and a searching investigation of the documents of primitive Christianity. All these have been propounded as affording a rational account of the origin of Christianity, and of the Catholic Church of Jesus Christ.

It is no disparagement to Paley's great work to say that it is not adequate as a reply to these various theories and objections raised by modern unbelief. Further; his argument fails to meet the attacks which modern criticism has directed against the Synoptic Gospels, nor does it even touch those which are connected with the fourth Gospel. If it were otherwise its author must have been gifted with a superhuman insight into the future, for the chief of our modern difficulties were unknown when Paley wrote. The change in the line of the attack necessitates a corresponding change in that of the defence; it will therefore be necessary to particularize a few of the points where his argument is inadequate to our present needs.

The first defect which I shall notice in relation to the present aspect of the controversy between Christianity and unbelief is the undue prominence which he gives to the argument from miracles, on which the claims of Christianity as a divine revelation have been almost exclusively based. Many of the points considered in the preceding Lectures have been referred to by him, but the place which they occupy is entirely subordinate to this its main position. The principle which underlies the " Evidences," and most modern evidential works is, that the Christian Revelation consists of a number of dogmatic statements, not otherwise discoverable by reason, and of moral precepts, rather than a body of historical facts. Of such a revelation, it is evident that miracles must form the sole attestation. But as it is allowed on all hands that they have long since ceased to be performed, the only course now remaining to us for proving their occurrence, is by a long chain of literary evidence. Consequently, the evidences of Christianity resolve themselves into a literary problem, which consists in the balancing of a large number of historical probabilities.*

I have already pointed out that this line of argument is inadequate to meet the requirements of modern thought. But in addition to this, it is attended with an obvious danger. It at once brings the inquirer face to face with the whole mass of difficulties and complicated questions which have been suggested in reference to miracles, a thorough investigation of which is thereby rendered absolutely necessary as a preliminary to the acceptance of Christianity. I think that I shall not be making too strong an assertion, when I express an opinion that the solution of these difficulties in Part II. of Paley's work is inadequate to meet the objections of modern times; and that they require a far deeper handling than they have received from him.

But in addition to this, his historical argument, model of clearness as it is, really consists of a very complicated chain

* The value of miracles as the evidence of a revelation, is unquestionably weakened by lapse of time. It is one thing to witness the performance of a miracle; it is quite another thing to accept its truth as the result of carefully testing a long chain of historical testimony. Those who witnessed them could judge of their real character; we have not only to do this, but to estimate the value of the testimony on which they rest. Our position is even less favourable than that of the generation of Christians who succeeded that which witnessed them. They had means of forming a judgment, and possessed an amount of evidence which now no longer exists. It therefore by no means follows, even if it could be shown that the writers of the New Testament attached a very high importance to miracles as proofs of a divine commission, that they must have an equal value for us, when a large portion of the evidence on which they originally rested has ceased to exist. The course of time, however, has given us an ample compensation in the fulness of the evidence which it has afforded of the superhuman power residing in Christianity.

of literary evidence, demanding a far more profound sifting than it was supposed to do when first propounded by him. It even requires a considerable amount of special training to enable the student to estimate its validity; and some of the links in it modern criticism has shown to be less reliable than they were considered by Paley. It will be sufficient, if I draw attention to a few only of the weaker points.

The main stress of Paley's argument rests on the following proposition:—"That there is satisfactory evidence that many professing to be original witnesses of the Christian miracles passed their lives in labours, dangers, and sufferings, voluntarily undergone in attestation of the accounts which they delivered; and solely in consequence of their belief of those accounts; and that they also submitted from the same motives to new rules of conduct."

There can be no doubt that, if this point can be established, it forms the strongest evidence that the miracles were not the deliberate inventions of the persons who professed to have witnessed them; or, in other words, it proves the perfect sincerity of their belief in them. But unfortunately martyr testimony, although a perfect guarantee against fraud, is far from being a safeguard against delusion. On the contrary the spirit which makes a man a martyr is by no means the most favourable for the calm investigation of facts.* If we were investigating the truth or falsehood of a modern miracle, we should consider the readiness of

* It is quite clear that the spirit which makes a man a martyr is no effectual guarantee against the action of the three principles of prepossession, fixed idea, and expectancy, which Dr. Carpenter has pointed out as the originating cause of a large number of delusions, under the influence of which those subject to them have mistaken subjective impressions for external realities. It is equally certain that the readiness to encounter persecution and martyrdom in attestation of their truth would be no guarantee of their objective reality. All that it would guarantee would be the sincerity of their beliefs, but of this we have ample proof in the case of persons who have mistaken a number of mental hallucinations for objective realities.

17 *

those who declared that they had witnessed it, to attest the truth of it by their lives, as a fully satisfactory proof of their honesty. But when the question is, whether the alleged miracle be a real fact or the result of some hallucination, we should greatly prefer the judgment of twelve men, who united scientific attainments with sound common sense, to that of twelve martyrs. Now the ground which is taken by modern unbelief is, that Christianity originated, not in an imposture, but in a delusion; consequently Paley's argument, though perfectly valid as a reply to the objections which he had specifically in view, does not meet the modern affirmation, that the miracles of the New Testament, as far as they are not legends, originated in the enthusiastic temperament of the simple minded followers of Jesus, who, under the influence of certain mental prepossessions, gave a miraculous colouring to facts which were really not miraculous, in a manner somewhat similar to those which are alleged to have occurred at the martyrdom of Polycarp;*

* It is impossible to accept the occurrences which are alleged to have taken place on this occasion as objective realities. With the exception of the voice from heaven they differ wholly in character from those which are recorded in the New Testament. Stephen, the proto-martyr of the Christian Church, is described as being favoured with a vision of the risen Jesus, just before he surrendered his life as a sacrifice in his Master's cause; but no audible words of encouragement were heard either by him or by others. The Christians who were present at the martyrdom of Polycarp were no doubt in a very excited state, and their condition of mind was that which is best suited for viewing the various occurrences in the light of their subjective impressions. Of this kind are the supposed voice from heaven, which may have grown out of an exhortation addressed to Polycarp by some Christian, the account about the dove, the peculiar form taken by the flames, and their inability to consume the body, its colour, and the sweet scent which issued from it, the necessity of the executioner stabbing him (which after all might have been an act of mercy), and the extinction of the fire by the large quantity of the blood which issued from the body. All these things might easily have originated in facts which were coloured by their own heated imaginations. While they bear a close resemblance to a

above all, that the belief in the great miracle of the Resurrection originated in His followers having mistaken certain subjective impressions, the creations of their own heated imaginations, for objective realities. Against delusions of this kind, it is clear that martyr testimony is no effectual guarantee; nor is Paley's further position, " that in consequence of their belief, they submitted to new rules of conduct."

But there are several difficulties connected with the details of his argument, which modern criticism has brought to light. What the argument renders absolutely necessary is, that we should get at the actual testimony of the original witnesses (otherwise it would be impossible to form a judgment as to their competency), and prove that they exposed themselves to persecution and martyrdom, as a consequence of this belief. This imposed on Paley the necessity of establishing the authenticity of the different books of the New Testament, and above all, of the Gospels, as containing the records of the miracles, by an intricate chain of literary evidence consisting of quotations from the Fathers. How far these quotations will support the weight which the form of his argument imposes on them, I will consider presently.

Further: Paley speaks of twelve witnesses, by whom he means the twelve Apostles; but even if his proof was fully adequate to demonstrate that the Gospels were written by the persons whose names they bear, this would only put us in possession of the direct testimony of two of them; and would leave us still in the dark as to their competency to judge of the reality of the miracles recorded by them. Let it be observed that these remarks are made on the supposition that miracles constitute the sole attestation of Christianity. If this be so, it is evident, when we consider all the difficulties which modern thought has suggested in

large number of legendary miracles they differ wholly in character from those recorded in the New Testament.

connection with the subject, that the testimony of two witnesses only is insufficient for their proof.

To enable us to get at anything like the conjoint testimony of the twelve Apostles, it is necessary to adduce the strongest evidence of the historical character of the earlier chapters of the Acts of the Apostles, for it is here only that we meet with anything which can be designated their conjoint testimony to the Resurrection, of which the author informs us that they affirmed the reality, and that they encountered great dangers and sufferings in consequence of their belief in it. But if the entire weight of the Christian argument is made to rest on this, it becomes necessary to establish the authenticity of these chapters by evidence, amounting to a moral demonstration; otherwise, as far as our controversy with modern unbelief is concerned, the argument would be a near approach to a *petitio principii*. If this could be established beyond the possibility of question, it would of course prove that the Apostles testified to the truth of the Resurrection, and that the Jewish rulers did their best to suppress the belief; but even this would not settle the question as to whether the belief was not the result of some form of mental hallucination. I think it must be admitted that if we view the question simply as a matter of literary evidence, the proof which is adduced by Paley is not sufficiently strong to bear the entire weight of the Christian argument.

But this brings us into the presence of another serious difficulty.

The form of the argument, which rests the truth of Christianity exclusively on its miraculous attestation, renders it necessary, not only to prove the truth of the miracles by evidence of the highest order, but also that all other miraculous narratives rest on an inferior order of attestation. Hence the necessity of Paley's second proposition, "That there is not satisfactory evidence, that persons pretending to be original witnesses of other similar miracles, have acted in the same manner in attestation of the accounts which they delivered, and solely in consequence of their belief in those accounts."

This proposition, it is true, does not affirm the falsehood of all other miracles except those which are alleged to have been performed in proof of Christianity; all that it does is to throw discredit on them as resting on an inferior degree of evidence. But this is not enough: for if miracles are to be accepted as the sole adequate attestation of a divine revelation, it is necessary to prove, either that all other miracles are untrue, or that they bear some distinguishing mark, which proves that they could not have been wrought by the finger of God, since, if they served other purposes than such attestation, they would no longer be alone adequate to prove it. But as we have seen, martyr testimony is no guarantee against sincere delusion. Consequently this is no reply to the objection that there are other miraculous narratives, which rest on a very high form of attestation, and of the truth of which those who have reported them have been firmly persuaded, but which are nevertheless utterly devoid of all objective reality; and that the same cause which has created the belief in these, may have generated the belief in the Resurrection. I think it is undeniable, if the whole question be viewed as one of attestation pure and simple, that there are other miraculous narratives which rest on one of a very high order,* and that it is no answer to it to affirm that the

* Among these may be enumerated the long list of miracles recorded by Augustine, whose honesty cannot be called in question. One of these is the miracle alleged to have been wrought on the blind man at Milan by the relics of St. Gervasius and St. Protasius. Augustine tells us that he was present in the city at the time, and that large numbers of persons witnessed it. The truth of this miracle and of the strange circumstances attending the discovery of the Martyr's bones is also distinctly asserted by St. Ambrose, one of the chief actors in the scene, in a letter to his sister. Although it is impossible to accept the account of the discovery of the relics of the Martyrs, and of the cures effected by touching them, yet it cannot be denied, that viewing it as a mere question of attestation, it rests on one of a very high order. Either the actors in it must have been under some form of mental delusion, or if the reporters were honest, they must have been

witnesses have not confirmed their testimony by martyrdom, which after all is a proof of sincerity, but of nothing more. The fact is, that the miraculous narratives examined by Paley are not the best attested ones of their kind. It is needless however to cite examples from the past. We are at the present moment confronted by a number of similar phenomena, which as long as the question is viewed as one of simple attestation, unquestionably rest on testimony of a very high order; I allude to the phenomena of spiritualism.* The objective reality of a considerable number of phenomena, such as according to our views would constitute miracles, is not only attested by numbers of men of cultivated intellects, but even by several who have a practical acquaintance with the laws of evidence, and have occupied important judicial positions, and even by men eminent for their attain-

the victims of a carefully got up imposture. Substantial accounts of a large number of other miracles occurring within his own diocese are given by Augustine, one of which he may be said to have partially witnessed, and that he believed in their reality is beyond all question. The attestation of the existence of the Stigmata of St. Francis of Assisi is also of a very high order. St. Bernard likewise speaks of miracles as actually performed by himself. Coming nearer to our own times, we have a large number of miracles connected with the Moravians, which, as far as mere attestation is concerned, rest on a very strong one. Wesley also believed that he performed miracles; and connected with him we have a strongly attested demoniacal miracle, which occurred at his father's rectory, the evidence of which is preserved in the family letters, and is accepted by Southey as conclusive of the fact. Again: the attestation which has been given to the recent miracles in France is very strong, and to many of the phenomena of spiritualism still stronger. In most of these cases the real question is whether those who have reported them have not mistaken subjective impressions for external realities; and in some instances perhaps been imposed on by the fraud of others.

* I am aware that a large number of the most intelligent spiritualists affirm that the spiritualistic phenomena are part of the existing order of nature, and consequently are not miraculous. To persons, however, who do not hold their views, it is impossible to discriminate between them and miracles. Supposing their opinions to be correct, it would destroy the evidential character of miracles altogether.

ments in modern science, who must be fully acquainted with the principles of scientific verification, and the sincerity of whose convictions cannot be doubted. I will only refer to one of these latter—Mr. Wallace. In his work on this subject he tells us that he was once a perfect Sadducee as to his belief in a spiritual world; but that he has been led to accept the reality of its existence by the stern logic of facts.* Yet most of us will be of opinion that his belief in the objective reality of the phenomena which he is firmly persuaded that he has witnessed is the result of some species of mental hallucination. If it be urged that the spiritualistic phenomena are discredited by the large amount of fraud with which they have been united, the same is equally true of miracles, for the number of supposed miracles which have originated in fraud is very large. Cases of this kind prove that if the belief in miraculous narratives is made to rest on attestation, and nothing else, there are not a few instances in which a very high form of it is certainly not wanting, and which cannot be discredited on the simple ground that the witnesses have not sealed their testimony by their blood.

The entire history of the witch mania is also another striking illustration of the difficulty in question. Not only was the evidence sufficient to induce juries to convict and judges, among whom must be numbered so eminent a man as Sir M. Hale, to condemn to death multitudes of unfortunate persons, but many of the victims themselves confessed the reality of the crime for which they suffered. Yet few of us at the present day will be of opinion that the facts testified to were objectively real; and consequently the only mode of accounting for the belief in them is to attribute them to some form of mental hallucination.

But apart from all these considerations, the following

* Mr. Wallace's conversion to the belief in the existence of a spiritual world, has left him as far as ever from the acceptance of Christianity as a divine revelation. He even considers that many of the miracles of the Gospels are explicable on spiritualistic principles.

objection against this mode of putting the argument requires our serious consideration. It renders it necessary that the inquirer should enter on an investigation of a highly complicated character, viz. an inquiry into the validity of the evidence on which a large number of well attested miraculous narratives rest, with a view of laying down a clear line of discrimination between their attestation and that of the miraculous narratives both of the Old and New Testaments.

There is another point in which the argument, as it has been laid down by Paley, is clearly inadequate to meet the exigencies of the present controversy, if we rely on it alone, and unsupported by other considerations; I allude to that portion of it which rests the question of the authenticity of the Gospels on our ability to furnish proof of it from the writings of the Fathers, either by their direct mention of them as the works of those persons whose names they bear, or by adducing unquestionable quotations from them in the remnants of patristic literature. This opens one of the most complicated questions of modern controversy; and the form of Paley's argument, rendering it necessary as it does, to establish the authenticity of the Gospels by a mass of evidence which is purely literary, requires that our proof of it should be little short of a moral demonstration. I think we must admit that this portion of his reasoning is far from being conclusive, and that even some of the authorities referred to are of a doubtful character. Nor can we wonder that it is so; for historical criticism, even if it can be said to have been born, was only in its infancy when this work was composed. It has since grown up to become a science of the highest importance, and has applied all the resources at its command to the investigation of those documents of Christian antiquity which the ravages of time have spared, more especially to that of the writings of the Fathers of the first two centuries, the various books of the New Testament, and, above all, the four Gospels. We need not wonder, therefore, if several of the proofs relied on by him as affording unquestionable evidence of the authenticity of the Gospels are of doubtful validity. Thus it unfortunately happens that where the exigencies of modern thought require that our historical evidences should be the strongest, viz. from A.D. 30 to A.D. 180, or during the 150 years which followed the Crucifixion, is precisely the point where Paley's argument is the weakest, and where we are in urgent need of something which will supply the deficiencies of his system. For this purpose I shall endeavour to construct a line of argument from the patristic writings more efficacious than that which has hitherto been adopted. Above all, I shall appeal to the evidence afforded by the Pauline Epistles as historical documents of the highest order, and claim for the existence of the Church as a corporate Society a far higher value than has been hitherto assigned to it in our evidential treatises. All these considerations, the value of which Paley has greatly overlooked, are most important at the present time.

III. I now proceed to take a brief survey of our position as far as it respects the literary evidence which can be adduced for the authenticity of our Gospels, and then devote the remainder of this and the whole of the two next Lectures to supplementing the defects of our evidential argument. This is of the highest importance at the present time, because the utmost efforts of unbelief are directed to prove that the Gospels are compositions of a comparatively late date; and it is generally taken for granted that if this can be established, or even if it cannot be certainly proved that they were composed by the authors whose names they bear, it is destructive of the Christian position. I shall use as the groundwork of my remarks on the present state of the evidence, Mr. Sanday's recently published work, *The Gospels in the Second Century*. I take this work in preference to others because the candour and fairness with which he has treated the subject have received high commendations from several of the influential organs of unbelief in this country.

Let me first point out where the difficulty lies. In order to give full force to the argument in its existing form, we require to prove two things.

First. That the Gospels were written by the persons whose names they bear. If this can be done, it will be impossible to date the publication of the Synoptics later than the year A.D. 70; *i.e.* they must have been composed within forty years after the termination of Our Lord's ministry; and that of the fourth Gospel later than the last ten years of the first century.

Secondly. That it is impossible that the facts of the life of Jesus can have become obscured during this short interval by the introduction of a mass of legendary matter into their pages.

The proof of the first point is made to depend in our common evidential treatises on the supposed citations from the Gospels in the writings of the Fathers. It happens, however, that the alleged citations from them in the earlier Fathers are extremely inexact, and not one of our Gospels is referred to by name. Consequently this opens a literary problem of very considerable complexity, as to whether their citations and references are beyond all reasonable question made to our present Gospels, or to other documents then in circulation.

One point, however, is absolutely certain, and must, therefore, form our starting-point in this inquiry. The great Church writers who flourished towards the end of the second century—Irenæus, Clement of Alexandria, and Tertullian—not only recognized the Gospels as the compositions of the persons whose names they bear, but they referred to them as writings of canonical authority, quite as much as we do at the present day. Here, then, we are in open daylight. But this leaves an interval of not less than one hundred and fifty years between the Fathers above-mentioned and Our Lord's ministry, and nearly one hundred and twenty between it and the supposed publication of the Gospels, which it is necessary to bridge over with the requisite literary testimony as to their authorship, date, and the authority assigned to them. This constitutes our difficulty; for the testimony grows more dim in proportion as we ascend upwards, affording a very strong probability that the earlier writers read and quoted from some of our Gospels; but still, except in a few cases, and those the latest in point of date, not amounting to so complete a proof as to place the fact beyond all reasonable question.

Further. The period, which cannot be placed at less than thirty years, intervening between the publication of the Synoptic Gospels and the first Christian writing not included in the canon, viz. the first epistle of Clement, affords no attestation whatever, unless it be one or two very doubtful quotations in St. Paul's Epistles, which are inadequate to prove that he either read or cited from any one of our present Gospels.

Such is the interval of time which it is necessary to cover with literary evidence in proof that the Gospels are the works of the persons whose names they bear. Let me briefly set before you what our evidence is valid to prove.

I. Mr. Sanday has established on clear and incontrovertible evidence that the Gospel used by Marcion was a mutilated version of our present Luke; and that the latter has not been framed out of the former, as a number of persistent efforts have been made to prove. I refer with great pleasure to his masterly argument on this subject, which must be considered to have settled the question. Assuming therefore that the date of Marcion's Gospel cannot be placed later than A.D. 140, it becomes certain that St. Luke's Gospel must have been in existence early in the second century.

II. Another inference applicable to the three Synoptics, proves that their publication cannot have taken place at a later date. The citations from them in the three Fathers above referred to, prove that their text was in a condition so extremely faulty, as to render it incredible that such corruptions can have been introduced into it in a less period than sixty or seventy years from the date of their first publication, which must consequently have taken place not later than the early part of the second century. This is a very strong point of the evidence. The only difficulty respecting it is, that it requires a special course of study for its due appreciation.

III. Two Gospels bearing the same name as two of the Synoptics are directly referred to by Papias.* If this reference could be shown to have been made to our present Gospels of Matthew and Mark, it would prove that in the judgment of this Father, they were the works of the persons whose names they bear; and supposing his judgment to be trustworthy, it would prove that they were published at the date which has been usually assigned to them. But here our evidence is anything but conclusive. Not to enter on the vast controversy which has taken place over this passage, one thing respecting it is absolutely certain: The Matthew with which Papias was acquainted was according to his express statement written in Hebrew. Our Matthew is no less certainly written in Greek. Papias, it is true, has been affirmed to have been a man of small intellect; but however this may have been, it cannot have been so small that, supposing he had ever seen St. Matthew's Gospel, he was unable to distinguish between the Hebrew and the Greek character. His subsequent affirmation also, that each interpreted it as he was able, seems decisive that he could never have seen a Greek copy. To meet this difficulty, the assumption has

---

* The following is Papias's statement: — "Matthew wrote the oracles in the Hebrew tongue, and every one interpreted them as he was able. Mark as the interpreter of Peter, wrote down accurately, though not in order, all that he remembered that was said or done by Christ. For he neither heard the Lord, nor attended upon Him; but later, as I have said, upon Peter, who taught according to the occasion, and not as composing a connected narrative of the Lord's discourses, so that Mark made no mistake in writing down some things as he remembered them. For he took care of one thing, not to omit any of the particulars that he had heard, or to falsify any part of them."

been made that our present Greek Matthew is a translation from the Hebrew. Such an inference however rests on a very uncertain foundation, because our Matthew has all the appearance of being an original composition. The difficulty is also greatly increased by a careful analysis of the narrative portions. These bear few indications of being the work of an eye-witness, even less than some portions of Luke, which is confessedly a compilation, and form a striking contrast to the Gospels of Mark and John.* Candour, there-

* The Gospel of St. Mark supplies us with the best means of instituting this comparison, because so large a portion of its narratives run parallel to those in Matthew, which is not the case with the fourth Gospel. The phenomenon which strikes the reader of Matthew is that, except in a few cases, such as the accounts of the Transfiguration, the history of the woman of Canaan, the Crucifixion, and the murder of the Baptist, there is a total absence of minute detail. This is carried to such an extent in some of his narratives, such as the account of the cure of the woman with the issue of blood, as to leave us ignorant of the precise character of the facts. This is exactly reversed in Mark. His narrative is extremely rich in minute details, and in such touches as would naturally form portions of an account by an eye-witness of the scenes which he describes. It is also very remarkable that these touches are so closely interwoven with the structure of the narrative as to be inseparable from it. It is simply inconceivable that the author of our present Mark, be he who he may, had a narrative resembling that of Matthew before him, and that in composing his Gospel, he deliberately inserted those graphic touches which distinguish nearly all its narratives. Not only would the difficulty of doing this be extreme, but the idea that he has done so is totally inconsistent with the honesty of the author, for the only source from which he could have derived them must have been deliberate invention. The tradition, however, which is mentioned by Papias, that Mark derived his facts from the teaching of Peter, and consequently that his share in the composition of this Gospel was chiefly to impart to his materials their present arrangement, forms an adequate explanation of the phenomena before us; for it is a simple matter of fact that nearly in every case where we can ascertain either from this or the other Gospels, that Peter was present at an occurrence, the narrative in Mark gives us a graphic description of it, such as an eye-witness of Peter's temperament would be likely to supply. On the other hand, it is no less inconceivable that the narrative as it

fore, requires us to admit that Papias was not aware of the existence of a Greek Matthew; and that the proof that our present Matthew is a translation from the Hebrew of Papias is inconclusive. It is highly probable that it has grown out of it: but if the argument is to sustain the weight which has been imposed on it, we want something stronger than probabilities of this description, which after all are little better than mere conjectures.

The identity of the Mark of Papias with our Mark is far more probable, although it cannot be asserted positively; still I think that the probability is considerably higher than that which is assigned to it by Mr. Sanday.*

It will be unnecessary for me to pause over the other remnants of the Patristic writings, or the testimony afforded by the early heretics, which, as far as it goes, is very valuable, further than to observe that while they render it highly probable that the authors used one or more of our present

stands in Matthew can have been constructed by a person who had an outline before him at all resembling our present Mark; for in that case he must have deliberately struck out nearly all the graphic touches. Not only could no purpose have been effected by doing this, but the person who did it must have been absolutely devoid of taste. The idea which has been so often propounded, that one of these Gospels can have formed the basis on which the other has been constructed, is in direct contradiction to the phenomena which they present. One thing however must be admitted, the narrative portions of St. Matthew present few of the distinguishing traits of autoptic testimony.

* The two chief difficulties attending the identification of our present Mark with the Mark of Papias are—First: that Papias affirms that the Mark with which he was acquainted was not written in order, whereas ours follows an orderly arrangement. Secondly: it is argued from the number of cases in which Matthew and Luke are in agreement, and Mark at variance, in their use of particular forms of expression, that our present Mark cannot form one of the original documents on which our Synoptics are based, and consequently that it is not the Mark of Papias. This second reason seems to me to be inconclusive; for our Mark may be the Mark of Papias, and yet not be one of the documents which are supposed to have formed the basis of the

Gospels, they do not establish the fact beyond all reasonable question. The evidence seems very nearly conclusive with respect to the author of the Clementine Homilies, still it must be allowed that the probability, though high, is in no case so strong as to amount to a moral demonstration. The whole of the evidence, however, if taken together, may be considered as establishing beyond reasonable doubt that the Synoptics were in existence during the first twenty years of the second century.

IV. I will now offer a few remarks on the evidence furnished by the writings of Justin Martyr and the Apostolical Fathers.

The writings of Justin not only exceed in bulk all the remains of Christian literature previous to his time, but their references to the actions and teaching of Our Lord are exceedingly numerous. Assuming that his writings were composed not later than A.D. 145 to A.D. 150, and that his recollection was good for thirty years earlier, his testi-

---

Synoptic narrative. Such documents may be sought for in memoranda used by the original missionaries of the Christian Church, and which by frequent use had become thoroughly impressed upon their memories. The first objection, however, is a more serious one. Mr. Sanday justly assumes that the most natural meaning of the words " in order" is " in chronological order." Still they are applicable to any kind of orderly arrangement, as is shown by their use in the preface of St. Luke's Gospel; for it is hardly possible that its author can have meant by this expression to affirm that he has in all cases followed the strict chronological order. But there is a looseness about the expression in Papias which renders it possible to apply the words to the arrangement of the discourses which Mark has incorporated into his Gospel, rather than to the events. It is true that in the sentence where these words occur, Papias states that Mark wrote down accurately, but not in order, all that he remembered that was said or done by Christ. But in the second sentence he describes Peter, from whom he says that Mark derived his materials, as teaching according to the occasion, and " not as composing *a connected narrative of the Lord's discourses.*" A loose writer like Papias might have had these latter in view when he said that Mark had not followed an orderly arrangement in the composition of his Gospel.

mony becomes valid for the belief in the facts as it existed in the Church from eighty to eighty-five years after the termination of Our Lord's ministry. This brings us within the range of trustworthy historical tradition, Of this testimony I shall make a very important use presently. I have here only to do with it as far as it bears on the date and authorship of the Gospels.

One thing the testimony of Justin places beyond the possibility of dispute, viz. that he derived his information, not merely from oral traditions handed down in the Church, but from written documents of some kind, which he designates "Memoirs of the Apostles," and occasionally, "Gospels," and which he tells us that the Church was in the habit of publicly reading. It is also no less certain that in his time these memoirs did not stand on the same level in point of authority as the Old Testament Scriptures.* The important question is, can they be identified with our present Gospels ? If they could, this would not only afford evidence of their composition before the commencement of the second century, but it would go far to establish the fact that they were the compositions of the writers whose names they bear. In effecting this identi-

* The mode in which these "memoirs of the Apostles" are referred to by Justin renders it impossible that at the time when he wrote they could have been recent compositions. They had already attained such notoriety as to be publicly read in the Church. His mode of speaking of them justifies us in inferring that this had been the case from his earliest recollections; and that the practice was no recent innovation. It is certain therefore that they must have been published several years earlier, as it could be only by gradual steps that they could obtain the currency requisite to entitle them to this distinction. Doubtless the Christian community possessed the means of bringing a work—such a work as a gospel—into earlier notice than it could obtain under ordinary circumstances. Still a considerable interval of time must have been necessary, before a book which professed to be a "Memoir of the Apostles" could have established its reputation so firmly as to be publicly read in the Church. It is hardly possible therefore that Justin's "Memoirs" can have been published later than the last ten or fifteen years of the first century.

fication, the difficulty is caused by the inexactitude of the quotations, which it must be remembered, extends, although not in the same degree, to his unquestionable citations from the Old Testament Scriptures.

Another fact the writings of Justin establish beyond all doubt. If the memoirs of the Apostles were not our three Synoptics, they must have been writings which bore the closest possible resemblance to them.

The following is the general conclusion on which we may safely rest. The writings of Justin establish to a very high degree of probability, although not to absolute certainty, that among the documents used by him were one or more of our present Gospels. It is also very probable, but yet not absolutely certain, that he used one or more documents besides these, which are no longer extant.

V. As we ascend upwards our evidence becomes less distinct. Our materials become few and meagre. Some of the earlier writings, once accepted as genuine, and referred to as such by Paley, are now with great reason rejected as spurious. Still they are not altogether without value, for their early date is unquestionable; but the evidence to be derived from them requires for its due appreciation such an amount of skill in textual criticism as can only be acquired by a long course of special study, to which few persons have either the leisure or the inclination to devote themselves. The references, as far as they go, are to the same facts and teaching as those in our present Gospels; and only to a very inconsiderable number in which they differ from them. But whether these references are made to them, or to other documents closely resembling them, or whether the information was derived from traditions of a similar character, the inexactitude of the citations prevents us from determining with certainty. Still the balance of evidence is in favour of the assumption that these writers used one or more of our present Gospels. If we could be certain that Clement of Rome, Polycarp, or Ignatius, used our Gospels, it would go far to establish the date which has been usually assigned to

18 *

them. But as they do not directly refer to written documents, it must be admitted that their information may have been equally well derived from the traditions of the Church. As a testimony to the existence either of traditions or of documents which substantially agreed with the contents of the Synoptics, their references are invaluable, for this they establish beyond a question.

Such then is the position in which the testimony of the Fathers leaves us as to the date and authorship of the Gospels. Let me briefly summarise it.

It establishes the fact that those who flourished as late as 160 years after the events recorded in them, accepted them as indubitable authorities respecting the actions and teaching of Our Lord, and as written by the persons whose names they bear; but this leaves the question open, as to how far we can rely on their critical judgment. The evidence afforded by the earlier writers amounts only to a very high degree of probability, which diminishes in force as we ascend upwards, and will in no case carry us higher than the last ten years of the first century. But our greatest difficulty is this, that the evidence is made up of the balance of so large a number of intricate probabilities which vary greatly in weight, as to require an intellect highly trained in such studies, to estimate them at their proper value; and it is moreover a kind of evidence, which will be estimated differently by different persons. It must be conceded therefore, that our evidence that the Synoptics were written prior to the year A.D. 70, and the Gospel of St. John about A.D. 90, by the authors whose names they bear, *if we rely exclusively on the literary testimony furnished by the writings of the Fathers,* amounts not to certainty, but only to a high degree of probability.* Such a fact, I

---

* It has been affirmed by Bishop Butler that probable evidence constitutes the very guide of life. The truth of this I fully admit; but it is a kind of probable evidence which those who are guided by it are capable of weighing and judging. This renders the maxim in a great measure inapplicable to the kind of evidence which we are

think, fully justifies me in placing another kind of evidence in the forefront of the Christian argument.

Such being the position in which our purely literary evidence leaves us, it becomes a question of the highest importance whether we have made the best possible use of the historical materials which we possess? I cannot think that we have. On the contrary, I am satisfied that they can be made to afford a far more conclusive proof of the truth of the supernatural events recorded in the Gospels, than any amount of mere citations from the Fathers, and of complicated reasonings upon them. I therefore proceed to address myself to the reconstructive portion of the argument.

I observe, in the first place, that far too much importance has been attached on both sides to these citations, as if the life of Christianity depended on them. They are doubtless very interesting in reference to many important questions of theology; but with regard to the truth or falsehood of the great facts on which Christianity is based, their value has been greatly over-estimated. We have abundance of materials for proving that the general contents of the Gospels are trustworthy accounts of the traditions which were handed down

now considering. Even the great majority of educated men are very imperfect judges of its value, because a special training in this class of historical studies is necessary for its due appreciation. The ordinary class of minds can form respecting it little or no judgment of their own, and are therefore compelled to accept it, if they accept it at all, in reliance on the judgment of those who are more learned than themselves. But in this particular case, the value of the judgment of the learned is greatly weakened in the eyes of ordinary men, because those who should be guides are at issue among themselves as to the importance which they assign to the evidence in question. The whole tendency of thought in modern times is to require evidence in religious matters on which men can exercise some judgment of their own. Scientific judgments are in numerous cases accepted without this, because many of them admit of verification in our actual experience, which imparts a credibility to the assertions of eminent professors on subjects which lie beyond its range; but the case is wholly different with respect to religious truth.

by the primitive followers of Jesus, and the value of the evidence would be only slightly increased, if we could determine with certainty their genuineness and the date of publication. I do not deny that our ability to prove that they were published between the years A.D. 60 and A.D. 90, and written by the authors to whom they have been ascribed, would strengthen the evidence; but that which we possess is so strong that we can well afford to dispense with this additional confirmation. If this be so, it is surely unwise on the part of the defenders of Christianity, to rest their case exclusively on evidence which consists of a balance of intricate probabilities, when it is in our power to base it on that which amounts to a moral certainty.

Let us then for the purpose of the present argument lay aside the question whether the references to the actions and the teaching of our Lord, which are contained in the remains of the Patristic and heretical writings prior to the year 180, afford a valid proof that the authors used our present Gospels. One thing, however, these writings establish beyond all doubt, viz. that their authors used written documents of some kind, whether our Gospels or others. It is also no less certain that these documents contained an account which (whatever may have been its minor variations) was for all practical purposes the same as that which we read in the Synoptics. The actions and sayings attributed to our Lord in all the existing remains of Christian literature between A.D. 90 and A.D. 180, the complete counterparts of which cannot be found in our present Gospels, are about twelve in number. It follows, therefore, whatever the documents may have been, to which the fathers referred, or whatever traditional sources of information they may have possessed, that the facts at their command were for all the purposes of history the same as those of our present Gospels, and that the minor differences in words and language are not worthy taking into account in a controversy which is simply historical.

As the writings of Justin Martyr are by far the most

extensive of those which have come down to us, I will use them as a crucial test of the value of my position. His references to events in the Evangelical History, and to the teaching of our Lord are very numerous; and he states distinctly that he made use of documents which he designates "Memoirs of the Apostles," and occasionally "Gospels." Were they our Gospels? It is too much to affirm positively that they were. But one thing his writings prove to be an actual certainty. Whatever documents he may have used, their contents must have borne the closest resemblance to those of our present Gospels. *

Let us assume that the actual references in Justin to events in the Evangelical history, are about two hundred in number, which will be a close approximation to the truth.† Of these one hundred and ninety-six are for all practical purposes the same as those which we read in the Evangelists. The remaining four are references to some unimportant facts which we do not find in their pages; it follows therefore that the facts referred to by Justin, but not recorded in the Gospels, stand to those which are recorded, in the proportion of only two to ninety-eight. What more can be required for our purpose? What more important historical result will be arrived at, by engaging in minute discussions as to whether the references in Justin

* Such variations as the assertion that our Lord was born in a cave instead of in a stable, and the addition to the narrative of the baptism of the appearance of a bright light shining in the Jordan, &c., are really so inconsiderable as to be unworthy of serious notice. Two things are indisputable : first, that Justin's facts, with the exception of a few trifling variations of this description, are our facts; and secondly, that the teaching which he attributes to our Lord, although varied in words, is for all practical purposes identical with that in the Synoptic Gospels. The references to the Fourth Gospel are more remote and uncertain, although even here it is evident that he accepted many of its fundamental principles.

† There are more ways than one in which these references may be counted. According to some methods the number might be considerably augmented. The number stated in the text may be taken as a minimum.

do or do not prove that the documents which he used, were our four Evangelists, when it is an actual certainty that if not the same, they so clearly resembled them as to vary only to an inappreciable extent?

But I go a step further, and affirm, that even if it could be proved, that Justin made use of several documents which were not our Gospels, it would only strengthen our position. It may seem almost a paradox, but I would say, the more he used the better. Let us suppose that his "Memoirs of the Apostles," instead of being confined to our four Evangelists, were not less than twelve in number, what would follow? The more numerous the documents which he had before him, the more certain it would be that they embodied the various forms of the traditions which were current in the Church during the time in which he lived. Our knowledge of the real facts of history is far more certain when we possess several authorities than when we are obliged to trust to one only. Thus the large number of the narratives of the murder of Thomas à Becket, puts us in full possession of what were the actual occurrences, a knowledge which we should fail to obtain from any one single record.*

Let us suppose, then, that Justin had a large number of documents before him, and that his citations do not enable us positively to identify any one of them with either of our present Gospels, what would this prove? It would esta-

* Thus for our knowledge of the details of the Persian wars, we are almost exclusively dependent on the History of Herodotus, our other informants having lived at times comparatively remote from the events. With how much greater certainty should we now be able to reconstruct the history of these wars, and to solve a number of difficulties in his narrative, if twelve persons, instead of a single individual had gleaned up the different anecdotes, which were floating about in traditionary recollections of the generation which immediately followed them. All subsequent history bears witness to the inaccuracy of the accounts for which we are dependent on a single narrator. In this, above all other branches of knowledge, the old adage is true, "In the multitude of counsellors there is safety."

blish on incontestable evidence that the documents which he used must have agreed in ascribing to Jesus similar actions, and a similar teaching, to those which are attributed to Him by the Evangelists, and that the accounts then current differed from them in the proportion of two to ninety-eight. It is marvellous when we consider the nearness of the time when Justin lived to Our Lord's ministry, that he should have preserved so few incidents respecting it, which vary from those in our Gospels, rather than that those to which he has referred should present the slight variations they do; for it is an interval within which traditionary reminiscences must have possessed all their freshness. Nothing can give us a stronger sense of this than the simple reflection that the period of his distinct historical recollections was separated from the close of the ministry of Jesus by the same interval which separates us from the death of the founder of Wesleyanism. It is impossible but that traditionary reminiscences must then have been numerous. Papias even declares his preference for them as compared with written accounts. The most probable solution of the fact that Justin's references to anything outside our Gospels are so few is that he must have assigned to them a paramount authority; and this constitutes one of the strongest proofs that he actually used them.

The remarks which are true of Justin are equally so of all the earlier Christian writings which have been preserved which are not included in the Canon. Let it be granted, for the sake of argument, that the passages in them which bear a close resemblance to corresponding ones in our Gospels do not prove that their authors were acquainted with them. Still they prove beyond the power of contradiction not only that either the written documents, or the traditions of Our Lord's ministry with which their authors were acquainted, contained statements of a character precisely similar to those in the Evangelists, but that the number of the other incidents or sayings, not included in them, which they accepted as genuine, were very inconsiderable. These considerations prove that the traditions embodied in our Gospels must have been fully accepted in the Church as the groundwork of its faith, either in a written or an oral form during the last twenty years of the first century; or in other words, that they were separated from the events themselves by a period of only fifty years. With such evidence in our hands, it is simply useless to spend our time in endeavouring to determine whether the references in question prove that the Fathers were acquainted with our Gospels, and quoted from them. To represent that the proof of this is vital to Christianity is not only needless but highly dangerous.

The point at issue is a purely historical one. It is simply this: Are the accounts of the actions and the teaching of Jesus Christ as we read them in our Gospels substantially the same as those which were reported by His primitive followers and by the eye-witnesses of His ministry? If this be so, it follows that the subject which we have to consider is, not whether the Synoptic Gospels are the writings of Matthew, Mark, and Luke respectively, concerning whom our information is but scanty;* but whether their contents are truthful embodiments of the traditions of the ministry

* If we could prove that the first Gospel was written by St. Matthew, this would establish the fact that the incidents recorded in it were accepted by one of the original Apostles; but as we know nothing of St. Matthew except from the Gospel itself, it would afford no assistance in meeting the modern objection, that the belief in the miracles was the result of mistaken judgment, or of some form of mental hallucination, although it would be fatal to the belief in their legendary origin. This argument will be still more applicable to Mark and Luke, who were not original witnesses of the events which they narrate, although St. Mark's Gospel would have all the value of authentic testimony, if it could be proved that its contents represented the preaching of St. Peter. Yet even this would leave the question as to the competency of their judgment, or whether the belief in the miracles, especially that of the Resurrection, originated in mental hallucination, entirely open.

of Our Lord, as they were handed down by His primitive disciples. On this the controversy really turns. Do these Gospels practically embody these traditions, or are they made up of a number of later mythic and legendary additions, which have obscured the real history?

The nature of the case renders it certain that during the early years of the existence of the Church, the facts of Our Lord's ministry must have been handed down by His followers in an oral form. The all-important question is, not whether every one of the facts recorded in the Gospels is narrated with minute accuracy; but whether they can be relied on for the practical purposes of history, as an embodiment of these traditions. I do not say, that if we could establish this, it would prove the facts to have been actual occurrences; for it would be still open to the supposition that His followers might have been deceived as to the nature of the events which they supposed themselves to have witnessed. But it would prove that they accepted them as the veritable facts on the belief in which the Church was founded, and the question whether they were the victims of delusion must be settled on other principles.

This portion of the Patristic evidence, which is of a very simple character, and is one which the most ordinary student can easily verify for himself, establishes conclusively the following points.

First, that the traditions of the Church respecting the actions and teaching of Our Lord, whether they existed in a written or an oral form, were *at the conclusion of the first century*, substantially the same as those which we read in the Synoptics, the variations being so inconsiderable, that for historical purposes they may be safely disregarded.

Secondly: if there was a different class of traditions floating about in the Church, and modelled on the conceptions involved in the stories contained in the Apocryphal Gospels, that the writers of this early Christian literature did not attach any value to them; and that they must have accepted the one as an account of the genuine actions and teaching of their Master, and have rejected the other as a fabulous addition.

From these two conclusions it follows:—

First: that no legendary matter worthy of the notice of the historian, which was invented as late as the last ten years of the first century, has been incorporated into the narratives of the Synoptics.

Secondly; That the traditions of the same period attributed to Jesus a number of miraculous actions, nearly all of them identical, and all of them of the same character as those which are contained in our Gospels, and wholly differing in type and conception from those which are narrated in the Apocryphal ones.

Thirdly; that the religious and moral teaching, which these traditions attributed to Him, whatever slight variations it may have contained, is for all practical purposes the same as that which we read in the Synoptics.

Fourthly: that if the narrative of the Synoptics consists of a mass of legendary matter, these legends must have grown up between A.D. 30, and A.D. 90, or during the 60 years which followed the conclusion of our Lord's ministry. This interval I shall fully cover by the aid of the Pauline epistles in my next Lecture.

The importance of one element in the historical inquiry has been greatly overlooked both by the opponents and the defenders of Christianity; I mean, the existence of the Church as a visible society; and the guarantee which this affords of the accurate transmission of the facts on which it was founded, and the degree in which it renders it impossible, that the traditions of the primitive followers of Jesus should at this early period of its history, have been superseded by a set of legendary inventions, which obscured the true facts of its Founder's life. The whole question has been discussed as though it were a purely literary one, in which a complicated mass of testimony consisting of a number of minute probabilities has to be carefully estimated.

The facts of Christianity are not like the ordinary facts of history. They differ from them in this, that not only do they form the foundation on which the Church of Jesus Christ has been erected, but that a constant preservation of the knowledge of them is a necessary condition of its continued existence—they form in fact the sole principle of its cohesion as a society, and the mainspring of the religious life of its individual members. In this respect the Church differs from every human institution in that it has not only been founded by Jesus Christ, but has been built on Him, He being at the same time both its foundation and chief corner-stone.* The facts of its founder's life first brought the Society into being; an acquaintance with them was essential to that continuous growth, which it has exhibited from the first dawn of its existence to the present hour, and if they could be proved to be fabulous inventions, its destruction would be inevitable.

Another equally powerful reason for the accurate transmission of the traditions constantly in operation, was the

---

* The relation in which Jesus Christ stands to the Church, as distinct from that in which the founders of human institutions stand to the Societies which they have originated is best expressed in the words of the great Apostle "That we may grow up to Him who is the head in all things, even Christ. From whom the whole body, fitly joined together and compacted by that which every joint supplieth, according to the effectual measure of every part, maketh increase of the body, to the edifying of itself in love." Eph. iv. 15, 16. " He is the Head of the body, the Church," Col. i. 18. " As ye therefore have received Christ Jesus the Lord, so walk ye in Him, rooted and built up in Him, and stablished in the faith," Col. ii. 6, 9. " And not holding the Head, from whom all the body by joints and bands having nourishment ministered, increaseth with the increase of God," Col. ii. 19. These and a vast number of other passages which might be easily quoted from the Apostle point out in clear and unmistakable language the difference of the relation in which the Christian Church stands to its Founder from that in which the founders of human Societies stand to theirs; and the constant necessity which it was under of preserving the great facts of His life and teaching in vivid remembrance.

necessity for making converts. Consisting originally of a few hundred members, the Church has grown to its present dimensions by inducing others to join its ranks. Unless it had been thus enlarged, the century which gave it birth must have witnessed its extinction. What was the only mode in which converts could be made? Only one answer is possible. By persuading them that Jesus was the Christ. To effect this two things were necessary. First: to explain to the proposed convert the true meaning of the idea of the Christ. Secondly: to set before him such facts in the history of Jesus as were sufficient to prove that He was the Christ. This involved the necessity of keeping the record of such facts in constant remembrance. It follows, therefore, that as the Church grew with great rapidity during the first three centuries of our era, its members must have been most active missionaries, and consequently that their motive for keeping in vivid recollection the chief events of their Master's life must have been of the strongest character; and that this must have been in active operation during the entire period which elapsed between the conclusion of the ministry of Jesus Christ, and the period when I have proved from the testimony of the Fathers that the Church was in possession of an account of His actions and teaching, similar in its great outlines to that which is contained in the Synoptic Gospels.

These considerations therefore make it certain, that the knowledge of the chief events of Our Lord's ministry must have been handed down in the living recollections of the individual members of the Church in a stream of unbroken tradition; and it is immaterial for the present argument whether this was effected by the aid of written documents, by oral transmission, or by a union of both.* The importance of this fact, of which so little account is made

* I use the word "tradition" as denoting that the events were not transmitted merely by the aid of written documents; but that they must have formed a portion of the living consciousness of the entire Christian community.

in our ordinary evidential treatises, can hardly be over-estimated.

Assuming these positions to have been established, the following conclusions necessarily result from them. It would have been in the highest degree difficult, not to say, impossible, during the brief interval which separates Our Lord's ministry from the end of the first century, to have imposed on any community of Christians a mass of legendary matter, of a character wholly different from those facts, on the belief in which the existence of the Church was originally founded, and which formed the moving spring of the daily life of its individual members, and which many of them had accepted as the ground of their conversion. It is absolutely impossible that communities, like the Churches of the first century, living in a state of constant antagonism to their Jewish and pagan neighbours, and having to justify to themselves the grounds on which they had abandoned their former beliefs, could have become oblivious of those facts which had induced them to accept Jesus as the Messiah, and which had ever since formed the foundation of their religious life. From these considerations it follows that the Church must have been possessed of a machinery for transmitting an account of the chief events of its Founder's life, which was incomparably superior to that of every other form of traditionary history.

This difficulty, in itself insuperable, is greatly increased by the number of the Christian communities, and the wide extent of territory over which they were scattered. Even if we suppose such an imposition to have been possible in the members of a particular Church, it would have been impossible to extend it to any considerable number of them. But as the patristic testimony is fully adequate to prove that a body of facts similar to those recorded in the Synoptic Gospels formed the foundation of the life of the entire Church at the conclusion of the first century, it follows that they must have been substantially the same as those which the original followers of Our Lord narrated as the chief events of His ministry, and the groundwork of the Christianity of the Churches which they planted.

But in addition to these considerations, which are in themselves sufficiently weighty, the whole interval of time lies within the period of the most genuine and lively historical recollection. It is one in fact which is completely covered by the lives of the actual witnesses of the facts, and of persons who heard the reports of them from those witnesses. These various reasonings in the latter portion of this Lecture fully prove that the Synoptic Gospels do not consist of a mass of myths and legends invented between the years A.D. 80 and 170. The still more important evidence furnished by the writings of St. Paul, I shall consider in the following Lecture. In the meantime I will only press on your attention the importance of the Church as a witness to the facts of Christianity, as distinct from the mere literary evidence on which their truth has been almost exclusively rested, in the words of St. Paul, " The Church of the Living God is the pillar and ground of the truth."

LECTURE VI.

"Moreover, brethren, I declare unto you the gospel which I preached unto you, which also ye have received, and wherein ye stand; by which also ye are saved, if ye keep in memory what I preached unto you, unless ye have believed in vain. For I delivered unto you first of all that which I also received, how that Christ died for our sins according to the Scriptures; and that he was buried, and that he rose again the third day according to the Scriptures."
1 COR. xv. 1—4.

IN my last Lecture I proved

First: that the writings of the Fathers who flourished during the first sixty years of the second century afford incontestable evidence that prior to the end of the first century the Church was in possession of a body of traditions respecting the actions and teaching of its Founder, which were substantially the same as those contained in the Synoptic Gospels. From this it followed as a necessary consequence, that no legendary narrative invented subsequently to A.D. 80, can have been incorporated into their pages.

Secondly: that in the remains of the Patristic literature, the references to anything of which these Gospels do not contain a complete analogue are extremely few; and that only four or five of the incidents referred to in it belong to a type of actions differing from those which the Synoptics have attributed to Jesus. From this it followed, that not only must the traditionary reminiscences of the Church within fifty years of its Founder's death have contained the chief facts and sayings attributed to Our Lord in the Synoptics, but the whole of them must have been modelled on the same type; and further, if there were any in circulation of a different character, such, for instance, as those in the apocryphal Gospels, the Church must have rejected them as spurious.

Thirdly: that the Christian Church was not only in a more favourable position for handing down a true account of the actions and sayings of its Founder than any other Society which has ever existed, but that the peculiarity of the circumstances in which it was placed must have compelled it to do so.

These considerations afford a probability, amounting almost to a moral certainty, that during this period of fifty years, which intervenes between the termination of Our Lord's ministry and the date of the historic testimony which we have adduced, no accumulation of legendary matter can have taken the place of that genuine account, which each Church must have received from its original founders as the ground of its existence, the source of the religious life of its individual members, and the bond of its cohesion.

Further: as the different Christian communities were scattered over a wide extent of territorial space, that such a substitution, even if it could have occurred in the case of some one of the Churches, would have been absolutely impossible among any considerable number of them.

This interval is so brief that it lies far within those limits during which traditionary reminiscences are trustworthy informants respecting the important facts of history, even when unsupported by written documents. Minor details may undergo modifications according to the prepossessions of those who repeat them; but this does not affect the historical truth of the main facts. If this is true of political events, in which the interest felt by individuals is comparatively small, how much more must it have been the case with those actions and sayings of Jesus, which formed the ground of the existence of the different Christian communities, and of their daily religious life.

On the general question of the value of tradition as an historical informant, and the limits within which its testimony is to be relied on, I need not enter in this place. The whole subject has been so fully discussed by Sir G. C. Lewis in his work on *The Credibility of early Roman History*, as to render any observations of mine unnecessary.

Assuming the validity of his principles, it would follow, that even if the Synoptic Gospels were published during the first twenty years of the second century, they would still lie within the period of genuine historical tradition, within which, though variations may arise on subordinate points, the recollection of important events still remains unimpaired. But in the present case we have only to cover a period of fifty, or at most sixty years. During this period the traditionary reminiscences of the Church must have been of a most vivid character. If we assume that considerable numbers of its members who witnessed the events of Our Lord's ministry were not older than himself, and that many of them were ten years younger, according to the average duration of human life, not a few of them must have survived till the last twenty years of the first century; and several of them even longer. This being so, the numbers of those who had heard details of those facts which formed the ordinary subjects of Christian instruction, from those who had been eye-witnesses of them, must have been very considerable; and many of them must have been surviving, and in full possession of their faculties during the first twenty years of the second century. Consequently during this period of time, there must have been ample means of obtaining information of the highest order, which would have rendered it impossible, while these persons lived, that the record of the chief incidents of Our Lord's ministry could have been buried under a mass of legendary inventions.

A single illustration will place in a striking light the value of the historical traditions of the Church during this interval of time.

The last ten years of the first century are separated from the termination of Our Lord's ministry by an interval somewhat less than that which intervenes between the present year and the date of the Battle of Waterloo. Several of those who were present in it are still living; and many of those who hear me may have heard details of it, as I have myself, from those who were actually engaged in it. Precisely similar must have been the condition of the Christian Church during the last ten years of the first century as to the chief events of its Founder's life, to that in which we stand in respect to the various events connected with the return of Napoleon from Elba; while the recollections of the Church must have been far more vivid in proportion to the profound interest which was felt in them by its members. While historical recollections were thus fresh, it would have been impossible for a purely legendary Jesus to have taken the place of the actual one, and obliterated the knowledge of the real events of His life.*

* To take another illustration. A period of eighty-four years separates us from the execution of Louis XVI. This is only slightly less than that which must have separated the period of Justin's historical recollection from that of the crucifixion of Jesus. Most of us who have attained the age of sixty, have conversed with persons who took the deepest interest in that event, and who had a lively recollection of it. In France large numbers of persons must be still living who have heard details of it from those who actually witnessed some of the events connected with it. While they survive, supposing that no account of it had been committed to writing, it would be impossible that its chief occurrences, which were enacted before the public eye, could be superseded by a set of fictions. The events which took place near the scaffold were witnessed only by few; and here, as we may expect, the accounts vary considerably as to the minor details, but these variations are almost exclusively due to the prejudices of the narrators. There can be no doubt that if we were destitute of a single written or printed document, it would be quite possible to construct an accurate account of the chief facts, by the aid of the reminiscences of those who have heard them described by persons who were actually present. I have selected this event because its interest was so great that it would be certain to have impressed itself deeply on the memory of those who witnessed it,

These considerations seem decisive: but we have evidence of a far higher order, which I will now proceed to adduce, namely, the testimony of the Pauline epistles. These will enable me to cover the entire period in question; and to prove not only that the Church accepted the great facts of Christianity, as they are recorded in the Gospels, at the time when St. Paul wrote these letters; but that its belief was coeval with its reconstruction immediately after the crucifixion of its Founder. In addition to this they establish the all-important fact, that the Church was reconstructed on the basis of the belief in His Resurrection within a few days after his crucifixion.

The inconsiderable use which evidential writers have hitherto made of these epistles may well excite our surprise. They have looked upon them as a portion of the position to be defended, rather than as one of the most important elements in the historical proof. This has resulted partly from their having been viewed as the chief source of our doctrinal theology, and partly from the supposed necessity of proving the canonical authority of the various books of the New Testament, as an essential portion of the defence of Christianity. However it may have happened, it is certain that their value as historical documents has been greatly overlooked; and in consequence of this it has been found necessary to adopt long and circuitous methods of proof to establish facts of which they afford the strongest confirmation. Before however I adduce the facts which

and thereby insured its accurate transmission. Deeply interesting, however, as it was to Frenchmen, the events of Our Lord's ministry must have had a far more profound interest for the members of the Christian Church, and both the necessity and the means of transmitting an accurate report must have been far greater. It follows, therefore, that falsification of its chief events within this brief interval of time would have been impossible, even if we suppose that the recollections of individuals were not aided by written memoranda—a supposition which is not only in itself in the highest degree improbable, but in the case of Justin, and the author of St. Luke's Gospel, negatived by their express testimony.

they enable us to prove, I must draw your attention to their
high value as historical documents in connection with the
present controversy.

1. Nearly all the educated unbelievers of Europe who have
studied this question fully admit the genuineness and
authenticity of the four most important of these epistles,
viz., the two to the Corinthians, that to the Romans and the
Galatians, even while they deny that of nearly every other
writing in the New Testament. The evidence of this is of
two kinds, viz., external attestation, and internal testimony.
Both of these are of the strongest character; but the latter
is such as to put the suspicion of forgery out of the question.
In these four writings therefore we are not only in
possession of compositions of the most active missionary of
primitive Christianity, but of documents which were certainly written within twenty-eight years of the Crucifixion.
Consequently they have all the value of contemporaneous
testimony.

To these must be added four other letters, which profess
to have been written by the same Apostle, and which must
be either his, or the work of a deliberate forger, viz., the
two to the Thessalonians, and that to the Philippians, and to
Philemon. Some sceptical writers, it is true, have endeavoured to throw doubts on the authenticity of these
letters, but the greater part accept them. In fact, the
evidence in their favour is of the strongest kind; and the
objections against them are of a very trifling character,
arising chiefly from the presence of expressions and forms of
thought in them, which are alleged to be un-Pauline. Such
evidence is at best very inconclusive; but when it is weighed
against the overwhelming proof which such writings as the
epistles to the Philippians and Philemon afford of the
presence of the Pauline mind, it is worthless. We can
estimate it for ourselves if we read these two epistles and the
two to the Corinthians consecutively. I think that it is
almost inconceivable that any person who is not utterly
destitute of the power of the appreciation of character can

do so, and doubt whether the presence of the same individuality is stamped on their respective pages. Such an identity of thought and feeling utterly outweighs those minute variations which critics who possess microscopic eyes think they can detect in them when compared with those writings of the Apostle, the genuineness of which they allow. The same remarks are equally applicable to the two Epistles to the Thessalonians.

We are therefore in possession altogether of eight letters written by the greatest missionary of the Apostolic Church, the genuineness of which is beyond all reasonable question, two of which date within the short interval of twenty-five years after the termination of Our Lord's ministry. I claim the whole of these as historical documents of the highest order; but if any one is contentious, the first four, the genuineness of which is universally admitted, will furnish us with all the evidence that we require.

Against two more letters which have been ascribed to the Apostle, viz., the Epistles to the Ephesians and Colossians, I admit that more plausible objections have been urged, but they are founded on the untrue supposition that St. Paul's doctrinal views must have been stereotyped, and incapable of progress. To the Pastoral epistles, as of more doubtful authority, I shall not refer as unquestionably Pauline.

One more writing in the New Testament has a definite historical value in this controversy, viz. the Apocalypse, because unbelievers are nearly unanimous in conceding its genuineness; and according to their views, it is the only book in the New Testament which was composed by one of the original apostles of Jesus.*

---

* If the views of the unbelieving critics respecting this book are correct, its date cannot be fixed later than the year following the death of Nero, or about seven years later than the last written of St. Paul's Epistles, unless we accept the second to Timothy as a genuine production of the Apostle. Critics of this school consider that the book contains unmistakable allusions to events in the civil wars between Otho, Vitellius, and Vespasian, and to the idea that

With respect to the other writings of the New Testament, although their genuineness is denied by the majority of un-

Nero had not really perished, but had retired somewhere into the East, and to his expected return in the character of Antichrist. If their data are correct, the year when it was composed would be unquestionably fixed, and its high antiquity established. The readiness with which they have accepted the external testimony (which is certainly strong, although not stronger than that which can be adduced for other books which they summarily reject), that it is the work of the Apostle John, arises from its alleged Judaising tendencies, and the supposed opposition of the writer to Paul, whom they consider to be denounced under the character of Balaam. The whole forms a singular illustration of the class of reasoning which will satisfy some minds of the truth of theories which favour their own prepossessions. It may be briefly stated thus: We know from the Epistle to the Galatians that John was one of the pillars of the Church of Jerusalem. He must therefore have been one of the chief leaders of the extreme Judaising party in that Church. This party was violently opposed to Paul, therefore John must have been his strong opponent. Moreover, the whole imagery of the Apocalypse is essentially Jewish, therefore its author must have been an extreme Judaiser. In it he uses very strong language denunciatory of some leader of the anti-Judaising party in the Church, under the name of Balaam. Now Paul, as we learn from his Epistles, was the great opponent of Judaism in the Church. Therefore Balaam is Paul. On these grounds, therefore, we accept the traditions which affirm that the John who describes himself as the author of this book was John, not the presbyter, but the Apostle. It will be readily seen that this course of reasoning involves throughout a *petitio principii*, and has been adopted as favouring a foregone conclusion. Other internal evidence that the book is the work of John the Apostle there is none (for the Gospel and first Epistle, which contain a Christology greatly resembling that of the Apocalypse, are denied to be his), except perhaps the roughness of the Greek in which it is composed, which agrees well with the idea that it is the work of a man who had learned the language late in life. On such grounds, however, it is simply absurd to accept the genuineness of the traditions which assign the Apocalypse to the Apostle John, and at the same time to reject those which ascribe the first Epistle of Peter to the Apostle of that name, while the latter has the advantage over the former in possessing very strong indications of the presence of the Peter of the Gospels, in the various traits of the individuality of the writer, which are scattered up and down its pages.

believing critics, yet their value in an historical point of view is considerable. Their antiquity is undisputed; and although they cannot be referred to with certainty as the works of the persons whose names they bear, yet they afford unquestionable evidence respecting the opinions of those sections of the Church, in furtherance of whose views they are alleged to have been composed. Thus the Epistle of James must be considered to be an unquestionable representation of the opinions which were entertained by Jewish Christianity; and the first of Peter, of the Christianity of compromise. It follows therefore that even if we provisionally accept the views of unbelieving critics as correct, they form documents of great historical value respecting the facts of primitive Christianity; and whenever they support the Pauline letters, they furnish a most important corroboration of their testimony, proving that St. Paul's statements were not accepted merely by his own followers and disciples, but also by every section of the Church.

Such are our historical documents, which will completely cover the period in question by the highest form of contemporaneous testimony.

II. The next important consideration is their date.

The two latest of these eight letters cannot have been composed after A.D. 62, nor the next four later than A.D. 58, and the remaining two later than A.D. 55.* Conse-

* A few illustrations will place before us in a striking light the claim of these Epistles to rank as contemporaneous documents. Thus the Epistles to the Thessalonians are only separated from the termination of Our Lord's ministry by the same interval of time as that which separates us from the proclamation of Napoleon III. as Emperor of the French; the four great Epistles, by one year less than that which intervenes between the present year and the dethronement of Louis Philippe; and the latest Epistles, by that which lies between us and the repeal of the Corn Laws. These events lie within our most lively historical recollections. Equally vivid must have been the recollections of a great number of Christians of the chief events of Our Lord's ministry, when the Apostle wrote these letters, rendering it impossible that they could have been buried under a mass of myths and legends.

quently, as far as they afford testimony to the facts of primitive Christianity, they enable us to bridge over thirty-five of the sixty years which separate the testimony of the Fathers from the date of Our Lord's ministry. As far therefore as we can prove by these epistles that the same facts were accepted by the Church when the Apostle wrote them as those which are referred to by the Fathers, this forms a proof which is absolutely conclusive, that the latter could not have owed their origin to the activity of a legendary spirit during the thirty-five years which followed the composition of these letters; and that the same remark is equally true with respect to the fundamental facts recorded in the Gospels. I shall also prove that these letters contain ample materials to enable us to carry up our historical evidence to the very date of the reconstruction of the Church immediately after the Crucifixion.

III. These epistles form historical documents of the highest order.

On the general value of original letters, as far as they contain allusions to contemporary events, I need not enlarge in this place. Our historical studies prove that no materials for the composition of history are of greater value. They constitute far more reliable informants as to actual occurrences than formal documents. This is more especially the case when the allusions are incidental.* The writer in such cases is almost invariably off his guard; and we are certain

---

* In all incidental references to facts, the writer always assumes that those whom he is addressing have an accurate acquaintance with the events to which he refers, and that both he and they agree in accepting the general truthfulness of the accounts. Thus in commenting on any well-known events at the present day, we never think it necessary to give a formal account of the occurrences to which we refer, but take it for granted that the most incidental allusion is quite sufficient to recall them to the mind of the reader. This is precisely the case with the Pauline Epistles. The allusions are of a very incidental character, and therefore prove that the writer was firmly persuaded that his correspondents were both thoroughly acquainted with the facts and accepted them as true.

to get at the real facts, which in formal histories too frequently receive a colouring in conformity with the prejudices of the historian. In the letters which we are now considering, we have this additional advantage, that the indirect references greatly exceed the direct ones in number. Further, while letters addressed to opponents are carefully guarded in their statements, in those written to friends, the writer more commonly reveals to us the innermost springs of action, as far as he is acquainted with them. Both these advantages we possess in the Pauline letters, for not only had the Apostle a body of warm friends in these Churches, to whom he poured out his whole soul, but also a party of most determined opponents. The history of Rome affords a striking illustration of the value of such compositions, in the letters of Cicero, which frequently enable us to discover the secret springs of events to which they allude incidentally, and the true character of the agents. Compared with these, the statements in his orations are untrustworthy. The importance of letters composed by active participators in the events to which they refer, is now fully admitted. By their aid the disguise has been stripped from many a man who has been surrounded by a fictitious halo; and an accuracy has been imparted to the writings of modern historians of which those of their predecessors were destitute.

IV. The letters of St. Paul possess an especial value, in that they present us with a vivid picture of the entire man; and thereby enable us to judge of the worth of his assertions.

They place the sincerity of the writer beyond the power of question. The indications of this are stamped on every page. They vividly depict him in all the multiform aspects of his character. We have him before us in every alternation of feeling, in his disappointments, and in his hopes, when expostulating with opponents, and when pouring out his whole soul to friends. Probably no four letters exist in literature, which afford us so intimate a view of the character of the writer as the four great epistles of this Apostle. By their aid we can reconstruct the entire man ; and thereby form as vivid a conception of him as most readers are able to form of Dr. Johnson by perusing his life by Boswell. Not only do they afford incontestable proof of the perfect sincerity of the writer, but they let us into the innermost secrets of his heart. All these traits impart to his testimony the highest value as historical evidence, affording as strong a guarantee of its truth as if we were able to place him in the witness box, and subject him to a rigid cross-examination.

V. No less decisive is the testimony which they bear to the calmness of his judgment. This is the more important, since it has often been affirmed that his enthusiastic temperament rendered his judgment untrustworthy, especially in all matters connected with the supernatural. While nothing is more rare in such cases than the union of a highly enthusiastic temperament with soundness of judgment in the same individual, the presence of both these qualities is deeply impressed on the pages of these epistles. That the Apostle was enthusiastic none will dispute ; but his enthusiasm was under the control of one of the calmest judgments. From the numerous instances with which these epistles abound, I shall content myself with two, which have a direct bearing on the value of his judgment in relation to the supernatural.

1. The mode in which in the First Epistle to the Corinthians he discusses the supernatural gifts of the Spirit, and the rules which he lays down for the suppression of the abuse of them in this Church, constitute a striking example. This is precisely a case where we might expect that enthusiasm would run riot; yet mark the sound sense in the directions which he gives for their regulation. The whole account in the 12th, 13th, and 14th chapters requires to be carefully perused in order to its due appreciation. I question whether another person can be found in history who considered himself, and those to whom he wrote, to be the subjects of influences which both he and they were

firmly persuaded to be divine, who would have written such directions, and discussed the subject in the manner in which it is here done by the Apostle. Even those who affirm that the belief in the reality of these gifts was the result of the delusions of enthusiasm, cannot help arriving at the conclusion that it must have been an enthusiasm compatible with the soundest common sense.*

2. The directions which he gives in this epistle, and in that to the Romans, as to the forbearance to be exhibited

* I quote a few brief illustrations. In 1 Cor. xii. 3-7, the Apostle distinctly ascribes all these gifts to the operation of the Divine Spirit, and at verse 11 he makes the following definite affirmation—" But all these worketh that one and self-same Spirit, dividing to every man severally as he will." Among these gifts were those of prophecy, tongues, and interpretation, which on each mention of them he describes as being the direct result of the operation of the Spirit. The fourteenth chapter informs us that these gifts were abused by those who possessed them in the Corinthian Church; and the Apostle gives some stringent directions for the suppression of the evil. Thus with respect to the prophets he writes, "Let the prophets speak two or three, and let the other judge. If anything be revealed to another that sitteth by, let the first hold his peace; for ye may all prophesy one by one, that all may learn, and all may be comforted. And the spirits of the prophets are subject to the prophets." So again with respect to the gift of tongues, the abuse of which the Apostle describes as producing disorder in the Church, although he distinctly affirms that it was a gift due to the operation of the Divine Spirit. After having described this disorder, he gives the following rule for its suppression. "If any man speak in an unknown tongue, let it be by two, or at most by three, and that by course; and let one interpret. But if there be no interpreter, let him keep silence in the church, and let him speak to himself and to God." Rules of this kind contribute the strongest proof that the person who gave them could not have been a mere enthusiast, but must, on the contrary, have possessed strong common sense and a calm judgment. No enthusiast would have thought of imposing restrictions on the exercise of gifts which he believed to be the result of inspiration. In fact, we find it very difficult to conceive how such abuses were possible under the circumstances. Such facts, however, are highly important as bringing us into the direct presence of a state of things which was exactly fitted to excite enthusiasm to the utmost height, and consequently to overpower the judgment.

towards the conscientious scruples of weaker brethren form another striking example of the same quality. St. Paul claimed both divine illumination and apostolical authority to decide the questions which troubled the consciences of the different members of these Churches as to the lawfulness of eating certain kinds of food, and the duty of observing certain days. He gives his apostolical decision that the points at issue are utterly indifferent under the Christian dispensation; yet with a singular comprehensiveness he directs that the scruples of those who were unable to accept his judgment on these matters are to be respected. Such a spirit of toleration is without example among pretenders to a divine commission, whether they have been enthusiasts or impostors; and vastly exceeds that which the Church has since been able to realise in its practice.*

VI. The presence in these epistles of a large number of incidental allusions united with the existence in these Churches of a violent party spirit, imparts to them a value as materials for history, which is possessed by no other similar documents.

As I have observed, the incidental allusions to facts connected with Our Lord greatly exceed in number those which are direct. Their incidental form possesses this peculiar advantage. They prove not only that the writer was firmly persuaded of the truth of the facts to which he

---

* The following passages will serve as illustrations. The same man who wrote, "But meat commendeth us not to God; for neither if we eat are we the better, neither if we eat not are we the worse"— "Whatever is sold in the shambles, that eat, asking no question for conscience sake, for the earth is the Lord's, and the fulness thereof"— wrote also, "Wherefore if meat make my brother to offend, I will eat no flesh while the world standeth, lest I make my brother to offend." I know and am persuaded by the Lord Jesus that there is nothing unclean of itself; but to him that esteemeth any thing to be unclean, to him it is unclean. But if thy brother be grieved with thy meat, now walkest thou not charitably; destroy not him with thy meat for whom Christ died." Compare with such precepts the conduct of Mahomet.

refers, but also that those to whom he wrote entertained a similar persuasion. A careful perusal of the epistles cannot fail to convince the reader that there were a large number of underlying facts, which the writer, and those to whom he wrote, accepted in common as veritable realities. Allusions of this kind occurring in the Epistle to the Romans possess the highest historical value, because this Church derived its Christianity from sources which were independent of St. Paul; nor had he ever visited it. Yet he presupposes that its members accepted as the groundwork of their common Christianity the same substratum of facts as those which had been planted by himself.

But further: These epistles make it clear that in these Churches the Apostle had not only a number of devoted friends, but also a body of determined opponents. Not only were the Corinthian and Galatian Churches divided into strongly opposed parties, but one of them went the length of denying the validity of St. Paul's apostolical commission.*

* Not only is the existence of a violent Judaising party within the Church apparent on the face of the letters, but that they went the length of disparaging St. Paul in comparison with the original twelve, and of even denouncing him as a false apostle. This fact, which is of the highest importance in estimating the historical value of these epistles, has been left too much in the back-ground, owing to a desire to set up certain theories about the Apostolic Church, which the facts of the case will not warrant; but it is necessary for a right understanding of the letters themselves, and of their doctrinal statements, that the existence of this Judaising element within the Church should be fully recognized. On the other hand, the existence of an actual opposition between Paul and the original twelve is an inference for which the premises afford no authority; nor have we any other data adequate to prove it. Thus, as I have shown, the affirmation that Paul is the Balaam of the Apocalypse rests solely, as far as evidence is concerned, on its being the good pleasure of those who assert it, that it should be so. That James was the head of the Church of Jerusalem, and continued until the end of his days to practise the Jewish rites, is doubtless a fact, of which we shall do well to take account; but this proves nothing as to his opposition to Paul. Paul himself fully tolerated the observance

So formidable was this party in the Galatian Church, that they had succeeded in persuading a considerable number of his converts to embrace the principles of Jewish Christianity in opposition to his own, a fact which stirred the Apostle's soul to its inmost depths. The pages of these letters afford the strongest proof of the vehemence of the controversy; yet they were intended to be read in the presence of the very persons who denied his apostolical commission, and of Jewish rites by those Christians who were Jews by birth. He was fully aware that men cannot throw off the customs and ideas in which they have been born and educated in the same manner as they do their garments, but that it must be a work of time. According to the principles which he has laid down, there can be little doubt that if he had occupied the post filled by James, he himself would have been an observer of the Jewish rites; in fact, his assertion is express, that he did so when he lived among Jews. What St. Paul resisted was the purpose of a powerful party in the Church to convert it into a Jewish Sect, by imposing the Jewish rites on those who were not Jews by birth. It has been asserted that St. James concurred in this attempt, but the evidence of it lies in the subjective consciousness of those who make the affirmation. Its sole proof rests on an expression in Gal. ii. in which St. Paul alludes to his disagreement with Peter on this subject, and his public rebuke of his inconsistency. The words which he uses are, " Before certain came from James, Peter ate with the Gentiles; but when they were come, he withdrew and separated himself, fearing them which were of the circumcision." This is certainly a very slender foundation on which to erect a theory that these persons were sent by James for the purpose of opposing Paul. All that the passage affirms is, that they had come from James; but for what purpose we are not told. That they were Jewish Christians who held strongly to the Mosaic ordinances there can be no doubt; but there is certainly nothing to imply that they were authorised messengers of James sent by him for the purpose of opposing Paulinism. Nothing is more unsafe than such general inferences, for the whole history of religious sectarianism proves that the rank and file of a party invariably rush into extremes which its chiefs have not sanctioned. One thing the epistles fully establish, viz., that Peter, James, John, and Paul contemplated a common Christianity from somewhat different points of view, but of any trace of direct opposition to the writings of the New Testament, not even the Epistle of James affords any proof.

whom he again and again challenges to come forward and refute his positions.

This alone is sufficient to place these epistles in the highest rank as historical documents. It proves that whenever they contain allusions to facts, above all, where they are incidental, their truth must have been accepted alike by the Apostle and his opponents. To have propounded statements which he knew they would call in question in a controversy of this kind, would have indicated a degree of folly which is incredible. This particular feature therefore affords such a guarantee of the truthfulness both of the direct and indirect allusions to facts contained in these letters, as is probably possessed by no other writings in existence. I fully allow that this does not prove the truth of the facts themselves, but it renders it certain they were equally accepted by Paul, and those to whom he wrote, including his bitterest opponents. This being the case, the testimony of these latter also carries with it the belief of the Church at Jerusalem, and enables us to prove that they must have been accepted by it as the basis on which the Church was reconstructed immediately after the crucifixion of its Founder.

Such is the nature and the value of these epistles as historical documents. Let me now point out the facts which they establish.

First with respect to miracles.

1. They prove beyond the power of contradiction that the Jesus who is referred to in nearly every page, was accepted by the Apostle, and those to whom he wrote, as a superhuman Christ. It is no part of my duty here to define the degree of the divine which they assign to Him; it is quite sufficient for my argument that the Christ of these epistles possesses a highly superhuman character, and that the incidental allusions to it prove that this was not only the opinion of Paul, but of the entire Church. Nor less certain is it, that the Apostle, and those to whom he wrote, were fully persuaded that this divine Christ, who was now absent in heaven, had passed through an earthly ministry of some duration in

Judæa, with the events of which they were acquainted. The all-important question is, What was the character of this ministry? Are we justified in drawing any inference respecting it, as to whether it contained any manifestations of a superhuman power? It seems to me incredible that the Apostle, and those to whom he wrote, could have attributed to the Christ of these epistles the superhuman character with which he is evidently invested, and that the narrative of his earthly ministry, with which I shall presently prove that they were intimately acquainted, assigned to him no superhuman actions. Common sense refuses to believe that they attributed a superhuman power in heaven, adequate to the government of all things, to a man who had never performed a superhuman action in vindication of his Messianic claims while on earth. This being so, it follows that the accounts which St. Paul, and those to whom he wrote, possessed of the earthly ministry of Jesus, must have attributed to Him the performance of a number of miracles.

This point is important, because it has been alleged that St. Paul refers to no miracle as performed by Our Lord. This is true; but it is no less true that the subjects which he discusses in the epistles did not suggest a reference to them. Any direct reference to Our Lord's miracles would have been quite out of place in connection with the subjects discussed in the four great epistles, which are occupied with a wholly different set of questions. In fact, the Apostle's silence about them is a proof that their reality was undisputed in the Church. My point is, that the superhuman character presupposes the miracles, and renders their absence from the accounts which he possessed of Our Lord's personal ministry incredible.*

II. They also afford unquestionable proof that St. Paul was firmly persuaded that both himself and the other apostles were in the habit of performing miracles, and that those to whom he wrote entertained a similar belief. On this point

* See Supplement.

he makes three definite assertions in his undisputed epistles.* In the first of these he expresses his firm conviction that he had been in the habit of performing them during the whole course of his ministry. (Rom. xv. 18, 19). In the second, (2 Cor. xii. 11, 12), after making a formal enumeration of them in their threefold aspect, as they are viewed in the New Testament, viz. signs, wonders, and mighty deeds, he not only affirms that they were the signs of an apostle, but that he himself had been in the habit of performing them at Corinth. The third allusion (Gal. iii. 5) is made in a very incidental form, and therefore proves that the fact must have been accepted by those to whom he wrote. It is also particularly worthy of remark, that these two last allusions are made in those portions of the epistles which are of the most polemical character; and as he urges it in proof of his being a genuine apostle, it constitutes a direct challenge to

---

* As these passages are very important, I subjoin them. "I have therefore whereof I may glory through Jesus Christ in those things which pertain to God. For I will not dare to speak of any of those things which Christ hath not wrought by me, to make the Gentiles obedient by word or deed; through mighty signs and wonders, by the power of the Spirit of God, so that from Jerusalem, and round about unto Illyricum, I have fully preached the Gospel of Christ." Rom. xv. 17-19. The allusion here to his frequent performance of miracles is of a most incidental kind. So again in 2 Cor. xii. 11-13, "I am become a fool in glorying: ye have compelled me; for I ought to have been commended of you; for in nothing am I behind the very chiefest apostles, though I be nothing. Truly the signs of an apostle were wrought among you in all patience, in signs and wonders and mighty deeds. For what was it wherein ye were inferior to other Churches, except it be, that I myself was not burdensome to you? Forgive me this wrong." In this highly controversial passage it is evident that the Apostle fully calculated that those to whom he wrote were firmly persuaded that he had wrought miracles among them. The next allusion is brief, but it is very incidental, and in a highly controversial passage. "He therefore that ministereth to you the Spirit, and worketh miracles among you, doeth he it by the works of the law, or by the hearing of faith?" Gal. iii. 5. The context makes it evident that by the expression, "he that worketh miracles among you," he means himself.

his opponents to deny their reality if they could. But further: the argument of the epistle proves that the power of working miracles was believed to be inherent in the apostolical office; and therefore it establishes the fact that the other apostles were believed to have been in the habit of performing them.

From the foregoing facts it follows by necessary inference:

1. That it is untrue that the belief in the performance of miracles in connection with Christianity can have been due to the gradual growth of legend during the first century of our era, for these letters make it unquestionable that St. Paul believed that he was in the habit of performing them from the commencement of his work as an apostle, which cannot be dated later than A.D. 36-37; and that the other apostles were believed to have done so from a still earlier period.

2. As it is inconceivable that St. Paul could have believed that he possessed a power of which his Master was destitute, it follows that the attribution of miraculous actions to Jesus cannot have been due to the gradual growth of a legendary spirit in the Church; but that the belief that he was in the habit of working them, must have been coeval with his ministry. From this it follows that the accounts of Our Lord's ministry, which were handed down in the Church by the primitive disciples, must have contained miraculous narratives. Further, the Apostle's position as a persecutor must have rendered it incumbent on him to investigate the facts, and to make himself familiar with them.

These considerations absolutely demolish all those theories which account for the origin of the miraculous narratives in the Gospels on the ground that they were the growth of a legendary spirit in the Church, which first invented the miracles, and then gradually attributed them to Jesus, while he himself made no pretensions to perform them. On the contrary, they render it certain that he himself must have been a professed worker of them. This being so, few will doubt that he believed them to have been real. Respecting these facts the information possessed by St. Paul at the time of his conversion must have precluded the possibility of mistake. I fully allow that all this does not prove the reality of the miracles; and leaves the question still open, whether the belief in them may not have originated in some form of mental hallucination; but it does prove that the belief that they were performed by Our Lord and his Apostles was coeval with the birth of Christianity; and whether they were realities or not, they themselves were firmly persuaded that they wrought them.*

III. These letters further prove that St. Paul, and the Churches to whom he wrote, including his personal opponents, concurred in believing that not a few of their members were in possession of certain superhuman endowments, of so singular a character, as to be without parallel in the history of miraculous pretensions. The Apostle's description of them is extremely minute; and this minuteness constitutes no small portion of the evidential value of his account, as affording proof of the objective reality of the manifestation of some very extraordinary phenomena in these Churches, whatever opinion we may form of their character or origin. My space however will only allow me to notice a few of the most salient points.

1. These gifts of the Spirit are affirmed by the Apostle to have consisted of certain superhuman endowments imparted to a considerable number of the members of these

---

* These allusions also dispose of another objection which has been not unfrequently hazarded, that although many persons have expressed their belief that others have performed miracles, yet it is impossible to find a man of high character who has deliberately affirmed that he himself has wrought them. Such an assertion must have been made in oversight of the passages above referred to, and of the other allusions to the exercise of this power which are found in the epistle. It is quite true that St. Paul nowhere argues from his miracles in the same manner as our modern evidential writers; but this is nothing to the point, for it must be first shown that he accepted their position.

Churches, and conferring on them powers different from those which were imparted by their natural faculties. According to an enumeration more than once repeated, they were nine in number, two of them only conferring what we should now designate the power of working miracles. The remaining seven are described as superhuman mental endowments.

2. It is worthy of particular observation, that each of these gifts is repeatedly affirmed by the Apostle to have been distinct in function from the others.* Such a description of them is about the last thing which would have occurred to an enthusiast, and stands in striking contrast to the popular theories of inspiration which have been propounded in modern times. Such a distinction is twice asserted to have existed even between the two gifts which we now confound together under the common name of the power of working miracles, viz. ἐνεργήματα δυνάμεων, and χαρίσματα ἰαμάτων. The seven mental gifts also conferred no special illumination beyond the subject matter to which their function was limited. This is clearly shown, not only by the Apostle's express assertion and illustrations; but by the fact that a person could possess the gift of tongues, and yet be destitute of that of interpretation. Different gifts, too, were not necessarily united in the same person; and the possession of one by no means involved that of another, even when the subject matter on which they were exerted was closely allied. I draw attention to these very remarkable peculiarities, as proving not only the discriminating power of the writer of this epistle, who has been credited with such a degree of enthusiasm as to have rendered him unable to distinguish the creations of his own disordered imagination from the realities of things, but the existence of some very extraordinary phenomena in these Churches,

---

* Thus the Apostle compares their action to that of different organs of the human body, as the eye, the ear, the nose, the hand, and the feet, all of which possess distinct functions; and no one of them conveys information on the definite subject matter of another.

wholly differing in character from ordinary miraculous stories. Further: the mode of statement makes it certain that these distinctions, obscure to us, were clearly understood by the members of the Churches to whom the Apostle wrote, and that they were accepted by them as unquestionable realities, even by his opponents. No less certain is it that the writer of the letters was firmly persuaded, that he himself possessed several of these gifts, and had the power of conferring them on others. All these things indicate that we are in the presence of realities.

3. There is another circumstance connected with these gifts, of so remarkable a character, that I am bound to call attention to it. While they are all affirmed to have been imparted by the divine agency of the Spirit of God, the Apostle expressly states that they were liable to be abused, in the same manner as our ordinary faculties, for the purpose of ostentation and display. This is, I believe, without precedent in the history of those who have claimed the possession of superhuman powers. With such it has been the invariable course, along with the superhuman gift, to claim an infallible direction as to the use of it. This is so natural that we find it difficult to apprehend how it could have been otherwise. Yet the assertions of the Apostle on this point are express; and the facts to which he refers as taking place in the Corinthian Church, absolutely conclusive. Not only was the gift of tongues so abused as to incur the danger of throwing the whole Church into confusion, but the prophetic gift, the third, if not the second, in importance of the whole number, was liable to be misused by its possessor to such an extent that the prophets were in the habit of interrupting one another in its exercise. A number of stringent rules are laid down by the Apostle for the suppression of these disorders, such as could never have been propounded by a man who was labouring under mental delusion.*

* The affirmation of unbelief is that the appearance of Our Lord to St. Paul on the road to Damascus, was nothing but a subjective crea-

From these data I draw the following conclusions.

First : that these phenomena prove that we are dealing with realities of some kind, whether we explain them on the principle of a human or a superhuman origin.

Secondly : that St. Paul, who was himself the subject of these gifts, was firmly persuaded of their superhuman character.

Thirdly : that a similar persuasion was entertained by the whole Christian community, including his opponents; and that the possession of these gifts was a matter of warm emulation among its members.

Fourthly : that the belief in the presence of such manifestations was not confined to the time when the Apostle wrote his various epistles, but was coeval with the reconstruction of the Church after the Crucifixion.

Fifthly : that these gifts were believed to be the fulfilment of Our Lord's promise made to His disciples, that He would communicate to them such supernatural endowments as were necessary for building up the Church after He had ascended into heaven.

I fully admit that these points, taken alone, and apart from other considerations, do not prove that these manifestations were of superhuman origin ; but they go a great way to establish that they were so. One thing, however, they prove beyond question, namely, that both Jesus and His followers must have believed themselves to have possessed superhuman powers; and consequently, that the belief that they performed miracles is no aftergrowth of Christianity, but is coeval with its birth. From this the inference is inevitable, that Jesus Himself must have professed to have performed them. If they were unreal, it leaves us in the presence of only two alternatives; Either Jesus Himself, who on the confession of unbelievers was the greatest of the

tion of his own mind, which he mistook for an external reality. The discriminating power and sound judgment exhibited in these chapters even in matters relating to the supernatural, have a very important bearing on this question.

sons of men, must have laboured under a mental delusion on this subject; or, (with reverence be it spoken) while He Himself was the sternest denouncer of hypocrisy who has ever appeared among men, He must have concurred in the perpetration of a fraud.*

IV. These epistles afford unequivocal evidence of the existence in the Apostolic Church of another class of phenomena which were believed to have had their origin in the operation of a superhuman power, of the abiding presence of which they were the manifestation. The superhuman manifestations were not confined to mere wonders wrought in the material Universe, but the preaching of Jesus Christ acted as a mighty regenerating influence in the moral and spiritual world. Considerable numbers of those whom the Apostle addressed had been rescued from the lowest depths of Pagan vice and moral degradation, and elevated by their reception of Christianity to a life of purity and holiness. The reality and the greatness of the change was an undeniable fact, which was not only verified in its outward results, but equally so in the inward consciousness of those who had experienced it. Whatever view we may take of the cause, the reality of the change is placed by these letters beyond the power of question. I will cite a single passage out of many which bear similar testimony to this fact. In addressing the Corinthians, the Apostle was able to appeal thus to their own experience. "Know ye not that the unrighteous shall not inherit the kingdom of God? Be not deceived; neither fornicators, nor idolaters, nor adulterers, nor effeminate, nor abusers of themselves with mankind,

* Mr. Mill accepts the discourses in the Synoptics as accurate representations of the sense of the veritable utterances of Jesus, and almost treats with scorn the idea that they can have been the inventions of His followers. In taking this position Mr. Mill is in strict agreement with the course of reasoning adopted in these Lectures. But if these utterances are allowed to be genuine, two inferences necessarily follow: first, that Jesus claimed to possess a superhuman character; and secondly, that He believed Himself to be a worker of miracles. These Mr. Mill seems unaccountably to have overlooked.

nor thieves, nor covetous, nor drunkards, nor revilers, nor extortioners, shall inherit the kingdom of God. AND SUCH WERE SOME OF YOU; but ye are washed, but ye are sanctified, but ye are justified in the name of the Lord Jesus and by the Spirit of our God." 1 Cor. vi. 9-11. Can any one doubt that the Apostle is here speaking of a great reality, which must have been a patent fact? It follows therefore that the superhuman energy which these epistles affirm to have been visibly manifesting itself in the Church was not believed to confine itself to the performance of those acts which are ordinarily designated miracles, but to be a power which was equally energetic in the moral world. In this respect the supernaturalism of the Pauline epistles differs from all other miraculous narratives. The reality of its manifestation in the moral world is unquestionable. This forms a strong ground for believing that the Apostle cannot have been mistaken as to its reality in the material world.

V. The next point of which these epistles furnish unquestionable proof is, that at the time when the Apostle wrote them, the Church was fully acquainted with an outline of the actions and the teaching of Jesus Christ, which was similar in its features to that which is contained in our present Gospels. Of this the knowledge was so widely diffused as to render a number of direct references to it unnecessary; and to make the numerous indirect references with which the epistles abound thoroughly intelligible. It is immaterial to my argument whether this existed in a written or an oral form. All that we require is to prove that such an account was well known to the individual members of the different Churches; and that it formed the foundation of their daily religious life. Of all this the epistles afford indisputable evidence; and what is still more important, they not only prove its existence at the time of their composition, i.e., within twenty-eight years after the Crucifixion, but they enable us to identify it with the beliefs of the primitive followers of Jesus. This being so, it proves that all those various theories respecting the origin of the

Gospels are invalid, which affirm that a large portion of the materials of which they consist, are the production of a legendary spirit.

The direct references in these epistles to events in the history of Our Lord are few in number. The most remarkable are the statement in my text and that in which St. Paul gives the account of the institution of the Holy Communion. The last of these is in substantial agreement with those contained in the Synoptics; and is equally full. The mode in which it is introduced presupposes that the writer was in possession of a history of the Passion on an equally extensive scale. This the frequent references made to it in the other parts of these letters render absolutely certain. It follows therefore, that the Church in the year 58 was in possession of an account of the history of the Passion, which bore a close analogy to that which is contained in our Gospels.

The reference in my text (1 Cor. xv. 1-9) is a very important one, because it affirms that the Gospel which St. Paul imparted to the Corinthians consisted chiefly of facts; and both this and the former reference, prove that there was a body of facts which formed the groundwork of Christianity, and which he was in the habit of solemnly committing to the custody of the Church. Thus he says, "*I delivered unto you first of all* (ἐν πρώτοις, among matters of prime importance), *that which I also received*" (1 Cor. xv. 3). And again, "For I have received of the Lord, *that which also I delivered unto you.*" (1 Cor. xi. 23). Both these passages affirm a solemn act of reception and communication. Those which he enumerates in 1 Cor. xv., he affirms to have been among matters of prime importance. This implies that among the things which he was in the habit of committing to the Churches, there were other matters of prime importance; and that these were united with others of secondary importance. Such an account must have been analogous to that contained in our present Gospels, which consist of a number of facts of prime importance, among which the accounts of the death and resurrection of Christ occupy a very conspicuous place; and another body of facts of secondary importance, which are very closely related to them.

To another fact of prime importance which the direct evidence of these epistles proves beyond the power of question, viz. the superhuman character which the apostles and the Churches attributed to Jesus, I have already referred. This proves that the Church must have been in possession of an account of His actions, analogous to that contained in our Gospels.

These epistles contain also two other direct references to Our Lord's life. The Apostle opens his epistle to the Romans* by affirming that he was of the seed of David *according to the flesh*, thereby ascribing to him both a human and a superhuman origin; and also that he submitted to the rite of circumcision. These references prove that the apostles and the Church at Rome accepted an account of the infancy analogous to that in the Gospels of St. Matthew and St. Luke.

In like manner they contain a few direct references to the moral teaching of Our Lord, in exact conformity with the teaching which we read in the Synoptics; but on this point it will be unnecessary to enlarge, for it is too plain to require argument, that the whole of that which is contained in these epistles and in the other writings of the New Testament, is based on that which the Synoptics have attributed to Jesus Christ; and consequently that a general outline of this teaching must have been preserved among the traditions of the Church.

---

* περὶ τοῦ υἱοῦ αὐτοῦ, (τοῦ γενομένου ἐκ σπέρματος Δαβὶδ κατὰ σάρκα, τοῦ ὁρισθέντος υἱοῦ Θεοῦ ἐν δυνάμει κατὰ πνεῦμα ἁγιωσύνης, ἐξ ἀναστάσεως νεκρῶν,) Ἰησοῦ χριστοῦ τοῦ κυρίου ἡμῶν.—Rom. i. 3, 4. It seems inconceivable that any candid reader can doubt that the Apostle takes it for granted in this passage that a belief in Our Lord's supernatural conception was generally entertained in the Church; and that it was accepted by the Church of Rome, which he had never visited.

Such are the direct references.

But the indirect ones are very numerous, and prove beyond the power of contradiction that the Apostle, and those to whom he wrote, were thoroughly acquainted with an account of the actions and the teaching of Our Lord, which they accepted as the basis of their common Christianity. If I were to attempt to bring out each separate point, it would extend this Lecture to an unreasonable length. I will therefore only summarise their general character, and adduce the evidence in a Supplement.

The Apostle affirms again and again that the essence of his preaching consisted in the proclamation that Jesus was the Christ. This was addressed to men ignorant of Christianity. What does it imply? Is it consistent with the idea that the Apostle taught merely a body of doctrines or moral precepts? It is clear that his teaching must have been utterly unintelligible if it did not contain such an account of the actions of Jesus as was adequate to prove that He was the Christ.

Again: the Christ whom the Apostle preached was a superhuman Christ. He was a Christ who claimed to be "the Lord." It follows therefore that the actions which the Apostle attributed to Jesus in his preaching must have been of a superhuman character; otherwise it would have been nugatory—or in other words, it must have been similar in general type and outline to those contained in our Gospels.

The incidental character of the allusions proves that such a Christ was accepted by the different sections of the Church to whom the Apostle wrote, including the Church at Rome, which had received its Christianity from a source entirely independent of him.* From this it follows that

---

* In the absence of all definite information on the subject it is now impossible to determine the source from which the Christianity of the Church of Rome was derived. All we can do is to fall back on the probabilities of the case. Considering the constant intercourse which was taking place between Rome and the provinces, and the large number of Jews located there, the probability is, that it was directly

all these various Churches must have accepted a body of facts respecting Our Lord, which formed a portraiture of Him in entire conformity with the Christology of the Gospels.

Further, as all these Churches contained a party of Judaising Christians, whose opinions must have been in conformity with the Church at Jerusalem, it follows that the facts of the life of Christ, which formed the substratum of the Pauline Gospel, as far as they are alluded to in these epistles, must have been accepted by that Church, or in other words, by the primitive followers of Jesus.

The same result follows from the oft-repeated reference to the knowledge of Jesus Christ, as synonymous with Christianity itself. Such a knowledge necessarily implies an intimate acquaintance with an extensive body of facts respecting His life and actions . But this knowledge is described as one which was deeply influential on the heart and character, and that each individual Christian would immediately

---

derived from the Church of Jerusalem. Still the whole tone of the epistle implies that Paul was well known to the members of this Church. It is highly probable that some of them became acquainted with him at the time when Claudius expelled the Jews from Rome, when many of them would take refuge in Greece. Still the whole tenor of the epistle proves the existence of a decidedly Jewish element, which could not have been derived either from Paul or from his disciples. This is confirmed by a salutation in the last chapter. " Salute Andronicus and Junia, my kinsmen and my fellow-prisoners, who are of note among the Apostles, who also were in Christ before me." This passage proves that these two persons had joined the Christian Church before St. Paul's conversion ; and consequently, that they must already have been Christians for more than eighteen years, and, therefore, that they must have derived their Christianity direct from the Church at Jerusalem ; yet it is evident that he calculated that they would accept the chief outlines of his Christology ; and that his incidental allusions to the great facts of Christianity would be thoroughly intelligible to them. Doubts have been expressed by a certain School of critics as to the genuineness of this last chapter ; but the reasons assigned for its rejection are such that if they are valid, we may prove almost anything we wish.

recognise it as forming the groundwork of his religious life. From this it follows, that it must have consisted of a number of facts which exhibited Jesus in a light which would render Him capable of exerting such an influence. Such a delineation we possess in the Gospels. Consequently, the facts referred to by the Apostle as constituting this knowledge must have formed a portraiture closely analogous to that which they contain. Further, one effect of this knowledge was to produce towards Him a spirit of devoted love. But love can only be inspired by the presence of a lovely object. The delineation of Jesus, which was accepted by these Churches, must therefore have depicted Him as a character capable of exciting a devoted love. Here again its identification in general outline with that of the Gospels is complete.

These epistles also contain another set of indirect references which prove not only that the persons to whom they are addressed must have had an intimate acquaintance with the actions of Jesus Christ, but that these actions must have formed a vivid delineation of His character. I allude to those numerous passages in which Christians are exhorted to make Him the subject of their imitation. These exhortations are not unfrequently introduced by the words "Ye know." Such a form of expression proves that the writer was fully persuaded that those whom he addressed were in possession of such a minute account of Our Lord's actions as would enable them to use them as a model for imitation. As this is a point of some importance, I will adduce a few illustrations.

1. They are exhorted to imitate Him in various special details of conduct; and again, to "put on Jesus Christ," which can only mean that their daily life was to be an exhibition of His character. Such injunctions would be simply absurd if addressed to any but those who were known to be in possession of a detailed account of his personal character and actions.

2. Another very incidental remark of the Apostle, "Ye

have not so learned Christ," warrants us in drawing an inference considerably in advance of this. It presupposes that an account of His actions and teaching formed a regular subject of instruction in the Church, as it is described in the preface of St. Luke's Gospel, "That thou mightest know the certainty of those things in which thou hast been instructed."

3. Another similar precept adds great weight to this inference; "As ye have received Christ Jesus the Lord, so walk ye in him." The persons addressed had received Christ Jesus the Lord. How was this possible? Only by having details furnished them of His life and actions, in conformity with which they are directed to model their lives. These exhortations therefore prove not only that the account possessed by these Churches must have been of considerable detail, but that the communication of the knowledge of it was a part of the regular course of Christian instruction.

It would be easy to multiply examples of this kind, but those which I have adduced will be sufficient as illustrations. They all firmly establish the point I am seeking to prove, viz., that when the Apostle wrote these letters, the different members of the Churches were intimately acquainted, not merely with a body of doctrinal statements, or rules of conduct, which they attributed to Jesus; but with an account of His actions sufficiently minute to enable them to model their lives upon them. This is precisely what our present Gospels enable us to do. It follows therefore that whether these accounts were written or oral, they must have closely resembled them in character. Further: As the Jesus to whom St. Paul is constantly referring is not an ordinary man, but a divine one, it follows that these accounts must have attributed to him a number of superhuman actions. Here again the analogy between the account which was accepted by these Churches and that contained in our Gospels is complete.

Only one additional remark on this portion of the subject

will be necessary. When St. Paul refers to Our Lord as a model of conduct, he rarely thinks it necessary to mention any particular act as an illustration. The only exceptions are when he refers to Him as the great example of self-sacrifice. Thus when he refers to Him as the highest example of meekness, he does not quote a single instance of the exhibition of this quality. In a similar manner he speaks of it as a well-known fact, that "though He was rich, yet for our sakes He became poor," yet he mentions no special instances of His poverty or humiliation. I may say that this mode of reference is almost universal throughout the New Testament. What is the legitimate inference from it? I answer that its writers must have felt certain that those to whom they wrote were so thoroughly acquainted with the history of Our Lord's actions, as to have rendered any definite references to them superfluous.

These considerations justify the two following conclusions :—

1. As the Church was in possession of an account of Our Lord's actions, which in its great outlines was analogous to that which is contained in our Gospels, it is impossible that during the short interval between A.D. 58 and A.D. 90 a legendary Jesus can have altogether obscured the true lineaments of the Jesus of history.

2. As the recollections of the Apostle, and of a considerable number of those to whom he wrote, must have been good for at least twenty years earlier, it is impossible that a legendary Jesus can have taken the place of the historical one between A.D. 58 and A.D. 37.

3. As the incidental references in these epistles prove that the facts referred to must have been accepted by all the parties in these Churches, including those which adopted the principles of Jewish Christianity, the main outlines of these facts must have been substantially the same as that which was accepted by the Church at Jerusalem; or in other words, as that which was handed down by Our Lord's primitive disciples; and whatever differences existed

between them were not differences as to the fundamental facts of Christianity, but as to doctrinal inferences from them. The evidence therefore which is furnished by these epistles carries us up to the period of the reconstruction of the Church immediately after the Crucifixion.

I now approach a subject of paramount importance, namely, the evidence which these epistles furnish of the truth of the Resurrection of Our Lord.* It will be impossible for me to adduce within the limits of these Lectures the whole of this evidence. All I can do is to summarise the results of a careful examination of them, and of the other writings of the New Testament.

I. These epistles furnish unquestionable proof that at the time of their composition, *i.e.*, within from twenty-five to thirty years from the date of the Crucifixion, the Resurrection of Jesus Christ was accepted as a fact by every section of the Christian Church, including those Jewish opponents who denied St. Paul's apostolical commission; and the Church at Rome, which he had not planted.

II. It was not accepted, as men give credit to an ordinary occurrence, or a mere ghost story, but as an event fraught

---

* It will be evident why I do not appeal to the Gospels to establish the truth of the Resurrection, but rely exclusively on the Pauline Epistles. While the historical character of the former is denied by unbelievers, that of the four great epistles is undisputed. Therefore, in dealing with their evidence, we are resting on a foundation which is unquestionable. But before the Gospels can be made available for this purpose, we must first prove their genuineness, and that their contents embody an accurate account of the traditions of the primitive followers of Jesus. This can only be effected by the circuitous course of reasoning above referred to. In the present aspects of thought therefore, to attempt to prove the truth of the Resurrection by appealing to the testimony of the Gospels alone, and unsupported by other evidence, involves a *petitio principii* of the entire question, I therefore base the proof on documents which even unbelievers admit to be the genuine writings of the greatest Missionary of the Apostolic Church— in fact, on a species of evidence which the universal voice of modern historians affirms to be historical testimony of the highest order.

with the most important consequences. It was the foundation on which the Church was erected; it constituted the inner life of Christianity, it was felt to constitute a great moral and spiritual power;* in fact on it was based the entire claim of Jesus to be accepted as the Messiah, and his right of Lordship over the Church. From it directly flowed that duty of self-sacrifice which every believer felt to be due to his risen Master, in return for His self-sacrificing love. It was also viewed as the pledge of immortality, and formed the basis of the religious life of the Church as a community, and of its individual members.

III. The evidence furnished by these epistles, not only affords indisputable proof that the Resurrection was accepted by the entire Church as the ground of its existence, when the Apostle wrote them, but also that it was reconstructed on the basis of this belief immediately after the Crucifixion. The proof of this is of the utmost importance in reference to the historical argument, for it renders it certain that the belief in the Resurrection could not have been one which grew slowly and gradually, after the manner of marvellous stories; being made up of one addition after another, aided by distance of time and place. On this point they furnish us with the following evidence:—

1. St. Paul accepted it as a fact from the date of his conversion. He was persuaded that he had seen the risen Jesus. Whether what he believed that he saw, was an objective reality, or the result of a heated imagination, it is equally valid to prove that the belief was at that period the accepted one of the entire Church.

2. The Apostle's personal testimony enables us to prove that this belief must have originated within a few days after

---

* Between a fact which has produced no effect on the world's history and one which has exerted a mighty one, there is a wide interval. Great results are produced by realities, unrealities collapse of themselves. A phenomenon which has exerted the most powerful influence on the history of mankind affords of itself a strong presumption that it cannot have been founded on pure delusion.

the Crucifixion. He informs us that he had been one of the chief agents in the persecution of the Church. When acting in this capacity his means of ascertaining when and where the belief originated must have been ample; and as the agent of the priesthood, he must have been entrusted with their private theory on this subject. That he did not make a thorough inquiry into a point of such importance, is inconceivable. Yet he informs us that Jesus was believed to have risen on the third day after his crucifixion; and that His appearances took place immediately afterwards. It is impossible therefore to account for this belief on the principle that it originated in a mere idle story, which distance of time and place converted into a fact. Stories of this kind always require considerable intervals of time during which they consolidate themselves; but St. Paul's testimony is conclusive that the necessary interval is not to be had. If the belief in it was the result of a delusion, it must have originated then and there.

3. The Apostle's personal testimony is corroborated by the fact, that such was also the belief of the Judaising Section of the Church. The incidental form of his references proves, that on this point there was no difference of opinion between him and his opponents. Their beliefs carry with them that of the Church of Jerusalem, and of the primitive disciples of Jesus. This being so, it is impossible that they could have been ignorant when the belief originated; and whether the Church was reconstructed on its basis.

IV. These epistles also afford definite proof that Jesus Christ was believed to have been seen alive after His crucifixion on the following occasions. First by Peter. Afterwards by the entire Apostolic body, when they were assembled together. Subsequently by upwards of five hundred disciples at once, of whom more than half survived when St. Paul wrote the letter which contains the statement. Next he was seen by James. Subsequently by all the Apostles in a body. Last of all he was seen by Paul himself. The nature of this reference by no means implies that the writer meant to enumerate all the appearances with which he was acquainted.

Two incidental references in the Epistle to the Galatians will help us to verify the truth of these statements. The Apostle informs us, that three years after his conversion he paid a visit to Jerusalem of fifteen days' duration, during which he was entertained by Peter : while thus in close communication with him, it is inconceivable that he made no inquiries of him respecting his interviews with his risen Master ; this being his first meeting with any of the original Apostles of Jesus. Now in the Epistle to the Corinthians a private interview between Peter and the risen Jesus is expressly alleged to have taken place, an interview of which we have no knowledge except from an incidental reference in St. Luke's Gospel, who represents the Apostles as exclaiming, when Cleopas and his companion entered the room where they were assembled on their return from Emmaus, "The Lord is risen indeed, and hath appeared unto Simon." Can we have any doubt from whom St. Paul obtained this particular piece of information ?

In like manner the epistle informs us that on the occasion of this visit he had interviews with James. The Epistle to the Corinthians likewise informs us, that James was favoured with a private interview with his risen Master. This fact is mentioned nowhere else ; can we doubt that the source of St. Paul's information must have been James himself ? It is inconceivable that he should have had interviews with these two Apostles so shortly after his conversion, which he attributed to an appearance of the risen Jesus to himself, without making any inquiries about his appearances to them. The comparison therefore of the statements of the Apostle in the 15th of the Corinthians with those in the 2nd of the Galatians puts us in possession of the direct testimony of two of the original Apostles. This is further confirmed by the following fact.

V. St. Paul informs us in this epistle that on a subsequent

visit to Jerusalem he had a formal meeting with the heads of the Jewish Church, of whom Peter, James, and John, were the acknowledged chiefs; that on this occasion he communicated to them the most important points of that Gospel which he preached among the Gentiles; and that he received their deliberate sanction of it. Now the Epistles make it certain that one of the most important points of the Pauline Gospel was the erection of the Church on the basis of the Resurrection. It follows, therefore, that there must have been an interchange of views on this subject not only between St. Paul and the three "Pillar Apostles," but between him and the chiefs of the Jewish Church, and that they were absolutely in accordance with him. This being so, it carries with it the whole weight of the testimony of the Church at Jerusalem to the fact that they had reconstructed that Church, after the crucifixion of Jesus, on the basis of His resurrection. This fact, therefore, rests on an historical attestation, than which nothing can be stronger.

VI. The Epistle to the Corinthians furnishes us with a singular proof of the tenacity with which the belief in Our Lord's resurrection must have been clung to as fundamental to the Christian faith. Some of the members of this Church denied that there would be a resurrection of the dead. This opinion, if carried out to its logical conclusion, would have been destructive of the belief in the resurrection of Jesus. How does the Apostle deal with this question? He endeavours to convince them of their error by the following very singular argument. "If there be no resurrection from the dead, then is not Christ risen." Or, to put it in other words, "Your denial of a resurrection involves the denial of the resurrection of Christ."

Now nothing can be clearer than that the entire force of the Apostles' reasoning lies in the firmness of their belief in the reality of the resurrection of Our Lord, which they must have clung to as a fact, although they held opinions which were logically inconsistent with it. If this had not been the case, St. Paul's reasoning was obviously exposed to the following crushing answer: "We affirm that the current belief in the resurrection of Jesus is the result of some mental delusion, and therefore the argument on which you rely is worthless." Nothing can more strongly prove the tenacity with which the resurrection of Our Lord must have been accepted as a fact than the Apostle's urging it as a proof of a general resurrection to those who considered such a belief to be irrational.*

VII. These statements in the Pauline letters are fully corroborated by other portions of the New Testament, among which I would especially notice the Epistle of James, which, whoever may have been its author, presents an unquestionable portraiture of Jewish Christianity, and prove that the universal Church, without distinction of party, accepted the Resurrection as constituting the basis on which it had been erected. Further, as the Apocalypse is admitted on all sides to be the work of one of the original Apostles, it furnishes us, not with secondary, but with primary evidence on this point. Not only does it make it clear that its author was firmly convinced of the truth of the Resurrection; but

* The ground of the denial of a future resurrection would be in all probability a set of ideas respecting the impurity of matter, such as those which at a subsequent period lay at the root of the various forms of Gnosticism, viz., that matter was the source of moral evil, and was therefore a wholly unfit habitation for a purified spirit. If these were the views which formed the ground of this denial, it is strange that those who entertained them should have accepted the Resurrection of Christ as a fact; and not have attempted to explain it away in some spiritual sense. However this may have been, it forms a striking proof of the strength of the belief with which at this early period the Church must have accepted the Resurrection as an unquestionable reality. Not long afterwards these opinions were carried out to their logical conclusion; but they did not result in the denial of the reality of Our Lord's resurrection, but of his death; one party affirming that it was nothing but a phantom which suffered on the cross; and another that the Eon Christ had united himself to the human Jesus for the purpose of revealing the unknown Father; and had deserted him on his crucifixion, leaving his former companion to expire miserably on the cross.

I think that it is impossible to read it and arrive at the conclusion that the first interview which St. John believed that he had with his risen Master was the vision at Patmos.

Such are the facts which the Pauline Epistles, and the other writings of the New Testament prove with regard to the Resurrection. I will briefly summarise them.

First.

That it is an unquestionable fact that the Church, which was for the time dissolved by the Crucifixion, was reconstructed on the basis of the Resurrection.

Second.

That the belief originated on the spot within a few days of the Crucifixion, and that the fact was openly proclaimed as the new foundation on which the Church was to be erected and the Messiahship of Jesus to be set up.

Third.

That all the efforts of Paul and his fellow persecutors failed to discover that this belief was the result of fraud or delusion.

Fourth.

That the Apostolic body believed that they had two interviews with Jesus, in which they saw Him alive, after His crucifixion.

Fifth.

That two of the Apostles were persuaded that they had private interviews with Him.

Sixth.

That upwards of five hundred brethren believed that they saw Him alive after His crucifixion, when they were assembled in a body.

Seventh.

That Paul was persuaded that he had seen Him.

Eighth.

That large numbers of believers were firmly persuaded that in consequence of His resurrection they had become possessed of certain supernatural gifts and endowments.

Ninth.

That the belief in the Resurrection acted as a mighty power of moral and spiritual regeneration.

I fully admit that all this does not prove that the Resurrection was an objective reality, although it goes a long way in that direction. It is still open to the alternative, that the belief in it may have originated in mental delusion; for the idea that it was owing to a deliberately concocted fraud may be dismissed at once. Before concluding, let me briefly state what the evidence which I have adduced is adequate to prove.

1. It disposes effectually of every form of the mythic and legendary theories, as well as those of tendencies, and gradual evolution, as affording any possible account of the origin of the narratives of the Gospels.*

2. It proves that it is impossible that the belief in the Resurrection could have grown up in the gradual manner in which ordinary fictions do, *i.e.* at a considerable distance of time and place from the occurrence of the supposed events; but on the contrary, that it originated at Jerusalem within a few days after the public execution of Jesus; that it was immediately proclaimed as a fact by His followers; and the Church was reconstructed on its basis.

3. That as the truth of the Resurrection is a cause which

* It is simply marvellous that such an amount of ingenuity should have been expended in inventing theories to account for the origin of the miraculous narratives of the Gospels, on the principle that they have originated in the gradual creations of the legendary spirit, and in the other explanations which have been offered on the supposition that the belief in them has originated, not dishonestly, but in some form of delusion. It is obvious that all such attempts are futile, while the theories propounded are not adequate to account for the belief in the Resurrection. It is evident that no possible modification of any theory of myth or legend can effect this consistently with the facts which these epistles prove to have been unquestionable historical verities. The sooner that both believers and unbelievers fully recognize that the entire controversy turns on the objective reality of the Resurrection of Our Lord, the better; for it will save useless expenditure of intellectual effort. It was a belief which created the Christian Church, and not one which was evolved by it.

affords a philosophical account of all the facts of history in connection with the Christian Church, and as it has ever been put forward by the Church as the true account of those facts, and the sole ground of its existence, we are fully entitled to accept it as the true one until some other can be propounded which is equally rational.

Modern unbelief has fully admitted the necessity of some rational and philosophical solution of these unquestionable facts of history. It denies that Jesus ever rose from the dead. It affirms that the belief in His Resurrection originated in the hallucination of his followers; and in order to account for this delusion it has propounded two theories. One of these is "the Theory of Visions." The other is that Jesus did not die of the wounds he received in crucifixion, but that he recovered and retired from public view; and that this recovery and retirement was mistaken by his credulous followers for a resurrection and an ascension into heaven. How far these two theories are adequate to account for the verities of history it will be my duty to inquire in my next Lecture.

SUPPLEMENT.

The limits imposed on me by the necessity of treating this subject in a single Lecture, have allowed me to give only a summary of the chief historical facts, of which these epistles afford distinctive proof; but as the subject is one of the highest importance in relation to the Christian argument, I propose in this Supplement to adduce the evidence on which my positions rest, and to draw the conclusions which legitimately follow from it.

On estimating this evidence, it will be necessary to observe the distinction between St. Paul's express assertions and those which are made in so incidental a manner as to show that they were not only his own opinions, but were accepted by Churches which did not derive their Christianity from him, and above all, by his opponents.

But even if it were otherwise, when we consider that the date of the composition of these letters was only separated from that of Our Lord's ministry by the brief interval of twenty-eight years, and his conversion by only six or seven, his metamorphosing a perfectly human Jesus into the divine Christ of the epistles, is without a parallel in the history of deifications; and is only explicable on the assumption that he was acquainted with certain facts, which he held to justify him in depicting a man who had been publicly crucified by the chiefs of his nation, as invested with divine attributes.

But I have already shown that the four great epistles enable us to get far beyond the Pauline views on this subject. Their incidental references prove that certain of them must have been held in common with the members of the Church at Rome, which had not derived their Christianity from him; and those in the Epistles to the Corinthians and Galatians prove that even his opponents must have accepted Jesus as a superhuman Christ. Hence it is inconceivable that the accounts which they possessed of His ministry did not attribute to Him the exercise of miraculous powers.

As the Epistle to the Romans is the highest authority on this point, I will refer to it first. It opens as follows:—

"Paul, a servant of Jesus Christ, called to be an apostle, separated unto the gospel of God (which he had promised afore by his prophets in the Holy Scriptures), concerning his Son Jesus Christ, who was made of the seed of David according to the flesh, and declared to be the Son of God with power, according to the spirit of holiness, by the resurrection from the dead." (Rom. i. 1-4.) It is incredible that the Apostle should have introduced himself to a Church which he had never visited, and whose good will he was evidently anxious to conciliate by making statements such as are contained in this exordium, unless he had been persuaded that they were already fully acquiesced in by its members. His opening words, in which he affirms that the *good news* respecting the Son of God had been previously promised "through the prophets in the Holy Scriptures," prove that a large number of those whom he addressed were Jewish Christians; for such a reference would have been entirely out of place if addressed to Gentile converts, whose acquaintance with the Old Testament must have been very limited. As the epistle makes it evident that his purpose was to win their good will, it is therefore certain that he could not have entertained the smallest doubt that the Jewish party, which was a powerful one in this Church, must have accepted the statement in the exordium as a portion of their common faith. This being so, it must have constituted the faith of the Church at Jerusalem, and could not have been a mere Pauline development of Christianity.

This exordium therefore establishes the following points respecting the beliefs of the original followers of Jesus.

1. That He was the Son of God in a sense wholly different from that in which other men are the sons of God. Such a view of His character is strictly in accordance with the delineation in the Gospels, to which I have before drawn attention, and which invariably represents Our Lord as carefully distinguishing between God's Fatherhood to Himself, and His Fatherhood to other men, speaking of Him as "My Father" and "your Father," but never as "our Father." This is strongly brought out in the language of the fourth Gospel, although the distinction is invariably observed by the Synoptics, "My Father and your Father," "My God and your God."

2. That He became ($\tau o\tilde{u}$ $\gamma \epsilon \nu o \mu \acute{\epsilon} \nu o \upsilon$) according to His human birth ($\kappa a \tau \grave{a}$ $\sigma \acute{a} \rho \kappa a$) a descendant of David.

3. That He was definitely marked out ($\tau o\tilde{u}$ $\acute{o} \rho \iota \sigma \vartheta \acute{\epsilon} \nu \tau o \varsigma$) as the Son of God with power, by His resurrection.

4. That He was the Lord of the Church, and the source of grace and peace in conjunction with the Father.

From these facts it follows :—

1. The Messiah who was accepted in common by St. Paul and the Jewish members of this Church, and whom they identified with Jesus, must have been a superhuman Christ.

2. That in conformity with the statements in the Gospels Jesus was a descendant of David.

3. That He had an origin higher than His purely human one, and consequently that St. Paul and the members of this Church must have accepted an account of his superhuman birth analogous to that which is contained in our Gospels.

4. That by the Resurrection He was definitely marked out to be "the Son of God with power." Such are the views respecting the superhuman character of Jesus, which must have been held in common by St. Paul and the Jewish members of this Church, who must have derived their Christianity from some of the primitive followers of Jesus. Is it conceivable that persons who accepted such a Christ can have been ignorant of the events of his earthly ministry, and that the accounts which they possessed of it did not ascribe to him a number of miraculous actions?

II. The ninth chapter of this Epistle contains a statement closely analogous. The Apostle is speaking of the privileges of the Jews, whom he designates his kinsmen according to the flesh; and expressing his deep sorrow at their national unbelief. This portion of the Epistle is expressly addressed to that part of the Church which was of Jewish origin; he approaches them thus: "For I could wish that myself were accursed from Christ for my brethren, my kinsmen according to the flesh, who are Israelites, to whom pertaineth the adoption and the glory, and the covenants, and the giving of the law, and the service of God, and the promises, whose are the fathers, and of whom as concerning the flesh Christ came, who is over all God blessed for ever." (Rom. ix. 3-5.)

This passage taken by itself might be open to the objection that the Apostle is speaking of two kinds of fatherhood, one arising from birth, and the other spiritual, and that, as it is in the former sense that he speaks of the Jews as his kinsmen according to the flesh, it might be urged, that in speaking thus of Jesus, he refers to his earthly origin, as distinct from his spiritual character. But when we compare it with the exordium of the Epistle, no doubt can remain as to the reference intended. In like manner it has been disputed whether the words "God blessed for ever" are intended to refer to Jesus, or whether they are a doxology to God the Father. I therefore forbear to urge this passage by itself as affording a certain proof of my position; but only adduce it as a strong confirmation of that furnished by the exordium, which is open to no such ambiguity. Both passages taken together prove beyond question, that the Jewish members of the Church at Rome must have attributed to Jesus a superhuman character; and consequently that the accounts which they possessed of His ministry must have contained narratives which afforded a justification of it.

It will be needless for me to cite all the passages in this Epistle which attribute a high Christology to Jesus. The all-important question is, did the Church accept this Christology on the authority of the Apostle, or were they already believers in it independently of his testimony?

The following considerations render it certain that the latter must have been the case.

First: the Christology of the Epistle is not propounded in a formulated system, as it certainly would have been by a person who was endeavouring to set forth a body of new doctrines with which those to whom he wrote were unacquainted. On the contrary, it consists entirely of very incidental allusions. It forms a striking contrast to the mode in which the writer sets forth his doctrine of justification by faith. This is carefully formulated. Here it is evident that he felt that he was communicating something which could be only imperfectly appreciated by a considerable number of those to whom he wrote. Quite different is it with the Christology. Its most advanced statements are made for purposes pre-eminently practical. The doctrine of justification by faith is attempted to be proved. Not a single attempt is made to prove the truth of the Christology. What, then, is the legitimate inference? I answer, that the author must have been convinced that those to whom he wrote already accepted it in its great outlines.

Secondly: whenever one man urges a truth on another for the purpose of producing a practical influence on his conduct, he must necessarily do one of two things; either he must endeavour to prove it, or take it for granted that the person whom he exhorts is already persuaded of it. Thus, if we attempt to exhort a man to the practice of virtue, on the ground that it would be conducive to his highest happiness, common sense suggests that unless the person we exhort admits the truth of our principle, we must endeavour to convince him that it is so. Now the Epistle clearly shows that every reference which it contains to a Christology is made for the purpose of producing a powerful influence on the conduct of those to whom it is addressed; so that they must have already accepted one which assigned to Jesus the attributes of a superhuman Christ as fundamental to their faith. I need only subjoin a single example of the Apostle's mode of statement.

In the 14th and in the opening of the 15th chapter of this Epistle, he is discussing a question which at the time was one of the greatest interest to Christians generally, and above all, to Jewish Christians, viz., the duty of observing certain days, and the lawfulness of eating certain kinds of food. He disposes of the entire question by laying down a great principle, which involves a Christology of a high order; and as these questions were keenly debated between the two great parties in the Church, he must have felt confident that the principle thus propounded was one in which both of them would cordially acquiesce. He writes as follows:

"Who art thou that judgest another man's servant? To his own master he standeth or falleth. Yea, he shall be holden up, for God is able to make him stand. One man esteemeth one day above another; another esteemeth every day alike. Let every man be fully persuaded in his own mind. He that regardeth the day, regardeth it *to the Lord;*

and he that regardeth not the day, *to the Lord* he doth not regard it. He that eateth, *eateth to the Lord*, for he *giveth God* thanks; and he that eateth not, to the Lord he eateth not, and giveth God thanks. For none of us liveth to himself; and no man dieth to himself, for whether we live, we live *unto the Lord*, and whether we die, we die *unto the Lord;* whether we live therefore, or die, *we are the Lord's;* for *to this end Christ* died and rose, that he might be Lord both of the dead and living. For why dost thou judge thy brother; or why dost thou set at nought thy brother; for we shall all stand before the judgment seat *of Christ*. For it is written, As I live, saith *the Lord*, (Jehovah in the Prophets,) every knee shall bow *to me*, and every tongue shall confess *to God*. So then every one of us shall give account of himself *to God*." (Rom. xiv. 4-12.)

The Christology of this passage, although not formulated, is unquestionably an elevated one, and assigns a highly superhuman character to the Lord Christ. He is not only regarded as the supreme source of obligation to Christians, not only is universal Lordship attributed to Him, but the writer, in a manner which is almost unconscious, intermixes the acts done by Him, and the obligations due to Him, with those which are done by and due to God. It is impossible to conceive anything more purely incidental than the allusions of the writer to the Christology; nor can anything be more practical than the purpose for which he makes them. I infer, therefore, that he must have been firmly persuaded that the idea of Jesus as a superhuman Christ was fully acquiesced in by both sections of the Church. If so, not only does its acceptance by the Jewish section carry it up to the earliest times of Christianity, but we also learn that two members of it, Andronicus and Junia, were members of the Church before St. Paul's conversion; consequently their acquiescence carries with it that of the primitive Church at Jerusalem. This being so, it is incredible that persons who lived so near the times of Our Lord's ministry should have acquiesced in a Christology of this description, unless they were acquainted with a number of actions in which Jesus was believed by them to have manifested a superhuman power.

III. Equally valuable is the testimony furnished by the other three great Epistles. It may be objected that they are addressed to Churches which were founded by Paul, and therefore that they only represent his own opinions; but fortunately for the purpose of my argument, the Corinthian Church contained a formidable Judaising party, which was far more opposed to the views of the Apostle than the corresponding party in the Church at Rome; and in the Galatian Churches it was the predominant one. We may, therefore, safely draw the conclusion that those portions of the Pauline Christology which the structure of the Epistles proves to have been accepted by his opponents, must have been a common Christology on which the Church was erected, and similar in its features to that which was held by the primitive followers of Jesus.

Here again the introduction to the Epistle furnishes conclusive evidence that every one of the numerous parties in the Corinthian Church must have recognized Jesus as a superhuman Christ. "Paul, called to be an Apostle of Jesus Christ, through the will of God; and Sosthenes our brother, unto the Church of God which is at Corinth, to them who are sanctified in Christ Jesus, called to be saints, *with all that in every place call on the name of Jesus Christ our Lord, both theirs and ours.* Grace be unto you, and peace from God our Father, and from the Lord Jesus Christ." (1 Cor. i. 1-3.) The contents of the Epistle show that the Apostle was fully aware of the existence of a formidable party in this Church who denied the reality of his apostolical commission. It is, therefore, inconceivable that he should have opened it with the statement of a Christology of which he must have been certain that his opponents would take advantage, unless he felt sure that they agreed with him in its main outlines. As Jewish Christians they must have been deeply imbued with rigid monotheistic views, yet he speaks of them as *invoking the name of Jesus Christ;* and backs it up by a prayer invoking grace and peace from Him in conjunction with the Father. Yet the following verses prove that it was the Apostle's purpose to conciliate his opponents. This introduction, therefore, renders it certain that they must have accepted Jesus as a superhuman Christ; otherwise its reading would have been interrupted by cries of blasphemy.

But the same chapter furnishes additional evidence. At the 23rd verse he writes: "We preach Christ crucified, unto the Jews a stumblingblock, and to the Greeks foolishness; but unto them which are called, both Jews and Greeks, Christ the power of God, and the wisdom of God." (23, 24.)

The Apostle here affirms that he had been in the habit of proclaiming Christ as "the power of God, and the wisdom of God." From this it follows that he must have reported actions which justified the ascription to Him of the character of a superhuman Christ.

Other passages follow to the same purport: "But of him are ye in Christ Jesus, who of God is made unto us wisdom, and righteousness, and sanctification, and redemption: that, according as it is written, He that glorieth, let him glory in the Lord." (1 Cor. i. 30, 31.)

The passage here applied to Christ is in the Old Testament spoken of the Lord Jehovah. Nothing could have been more offensive to a Monotheistic Jew.

Again: "Let a man so account of us, as of the ministers of Christ, and stewards of the mysteries of God. Moreover it is required in stewards, that a man be found faithful. But with me it is a very small thing that I should be judged of you, or of man's judgment: yea, I judge not mine own self. For I know nothing by myself; yet am I not hereby justified: but he that judged me is the Lord. Therefore judge nothing before the time, until *the Lord come, who both will bring to light the hidden things of darkness, and will make manifest the counsels of the hearts: and then shall every man have praise of God."* (1 Cor. iv. 1-5.)

This would have been strange language to address to opponents whom the writer knew to reject the fundamental points of the Christology involved in it.

In the eighth chapter, where the Apostle discusses the lawfulness of eating food which had been offered in sacrifice to an idol, he proposes the following principle as the solution of the entire controversy :—

"For though there be that are called gods, whether in heaven or in earth, (as there be gods many, and lords many,) but to us there is but one God, the Father, of whom are all things, and we in him (εἰς αὐτὸν); and one Lord Jesus Christ, through (διὰ) whom are all things, and we through him."

This passage is conclusive. It is addressed to men with Jewish scruples for the express purpose of providing a solution of them. The writer must thenceforth have fully calculated on their acceptance of the Christology which it contains, otherwise his observations would have been nugatory.

I need only cite a single passage from the second epistle. I will therefore adduce one from the most controversial part of it, where the Apostle is distinctly grappling with those opponents who denied his apostolical authority:—" For I fear lest by any means, as the serpent beguiled Eve through his subtilty, so your minds should be corrupted from the simplicity which is in Christ. For if *he that cometh preach another Jesus,* which we have not preached, or if ye *receive another Spirit,* whom ye have not received, *or another Gospel,* which ye have not accepted, ye might well bear with him. For I suppose I was not a whit behind the very chiefest apostles." (2 Cor. xi. 3-5.)

In this passage the Apostle directly affirms in the face of his opponents that the Gospel which he preached was in its fundamental facts the same as that which was accepted by

22 *

themselves. What then was the difference? Clearly in the question whether Judaism was or was not an essential portion of Christianity. By the words, "*He that cometh*," the Apostle evidently designates his chief Jewish opponent. Yet they both proclaimed the same Jesus. This could only have been the case, by both according to Him the character of a superhuman Christ; for if they had differed on this point the affirmation that the same Jesus was accepted by both would have been untrue. It follows, therefore, that their respective Christologies must have resembled one another in their great outlines, for it is inconceivable that the Apostle should have written a statement like this, in the immediate context of which he throws down repeated challenges to his opponents to grapple with his assertions.

The Epistle to the Galatians, the most controversial of all his writings, and in which he denounces his opponents in the most vehement language, opens with the announcement of a Christology precisely similar to that which we have been considering. It is incredible that he should have adopted this course in the very opening of his letter if he had believed that his opponents, who formed the most formidable party in this Church, could have denounced it as inconsistent with that which was held by the Church at Jerusalem, his chief object being to show that the Gospel which he preached was accepted as genuine by the great pillars of the Jewish Church. Yet immediately after the introduction, in which he affirms that he derived his apostolical office from no human authority, and his usual prayer for grace and peace from God the Father, and from the Lord Jesus Christ, dropping the conciliatory tone with which he introduces his other epistles, he writes: "I marvel that ye are so soon removed from him that called you into the grace of Christ *unto another Gospel, which is not another;* but there are some that trouble you, and would pervert the Gospel of Christ. For although we, or an angel from heaven, preach any other Gospel unto you than that which we have preached unto you, let him be accursed. As I said before, so say I now again, If any man preach any other Gospel unto you than that which ye have received, let him be accursed." (Gal. i. 6-9.)

I draw attention to the very remarkable expression here used to designate the Gospel of his Judaising opponents. It was "*another Gospel, which was not another.*" How could this be possible? We have seen in the passage just cited from the Second Epistle to the Corinthians, that the Apostle distinctly affirmed that his opponents did not preach "another Jesus," "another Spirit," or "another Gospel," Yet in this passage, where he is aroused to indignation at the widespread defection which had taken place in the Galatian Churches, he designates this Judaising Gospel as "another Gospel which is not another." The only possible explanation of this expression is that both Gospels were the same in fundamental facts, but that they differed in the inferences deduced from them; in other words, that they agreed in assigning a superhuman character to Jesus; but that the Judaising Gospel differed from the Pauline in seeking to impose the observance of the Jewish rites as a condition of membership in the Church.

This conclusion is borne out by the following passage in the Epistle to the Philippians : " Some indeed preach Christ of envy and strife, and some also of good will. The one preach Christ of contention, not sincerely, supposing to add affliction to my bonds; but the other of love, knowing that I am set for the defence of the Gospel. What then ? notwithstanding every way, whether in pretence, or in truth, Christ is preached; and I therein do rejoice, yea, and will rejoice." (Phil. i. 15-18.)

Here again we are plainly in the presence of some form of this Jewish Gospel. The Apostle is evidently in a calmer state of mind than when he wrote to the Galatian Churches. So earnest is his desire that the Gospel of Jesus Christ should be proclaimed, that he rejoices at its being preached, even by Judaising opponents. It is impossible therefore that it can have been "another Gospel" in the sense in which he denounced such a Gospel, whether preached by himself, or "an angel from heaven."

From these considerations I draw the following conclusions.

1. Even if we admit that the later Epistles of St. Paul present us with a more advanced Christology than his four great Epistles, still he held even at this time one of a very advanced type; and must consequently have been acquainted with such details of the ministry of Jesus as would justify it; in other words, he was in possession of an account similar in general character to that recorded in our Gospels.

As St. Paul's opponents accepted a Christology analogous to his own, they must also have been in possession of an account of Christ's ministry which was substantially the same as that which was handed down by His primitive followers, and consequently must have ascribed to Him the character of a superhuman Christ; or, in other words, must have attributed to Him the performance of miraculous actions.

There is yet one more document in the New Testament to which I must refer, viz. the Apocalypse. Its affirmations on this point are decisive. Unbelievers not only allow that it is the work of the Apostle John, but they affirm that he was one of the pillars of the Judaising party in the Church; and the uncompromising opponent of St. Paul. This being so it must be decisive as to the opinions of the Judaising party.

Nothing can be clearer in this book than the ascription to Jesus of the character of a highly superhuman Christ. In this respect, it is fully equal to the Christology of the latest of the Pauline Epistles, and to that of the Epistle to the Hebrews; and none but critics who possess microscopic eyes, can discern any real distinction between it and the Christology of the Fourth Gospel.

It is impossible by brief quotations to give an idea of the elevated Messianic character which this book attributes to

Jesus. It will be sufficient for my purpose to observe that its author proclaims Him to be the Prince of the kings of the earth : He is the first and the last—the Living One, who was dead and is alive for evermore. He is the faithful and true witness, the beginning, *i.e.* the principle, or cause, (ἀρχή) of the creation of God. He is worshipped in heaven in conjunction with the Father, and is His sole revealer. He is King of kings, and Lord of lords. But it is needless to make further references. Yet such a superhuman character is attributed to Jesus in this book by an Apostle who was pre-eminently a Judaiser.

But it will be objected that this is an apocalypse, and the work of a dreamer. Truly, if it has been written by a dreamer, he must have been one who soared to the heights of the poetic spirit. Even in madness there is a method; and it seems impossible that any amount of mental hallucination could have induced a man who had associated with Jesus during his earthly ministry to attribute to Him the superhuman character assigned to Him in this book, unless he was firmly convinced that a number of superhuman actions had been performed by Him; and that he himself had witnessed them.

If our opponents are correct in the date which they have assigned to the composition of the Apocalypse, it is separated from that of Our Lord's ministry by an interval of only thirty-eight, or thirty-nine years. Its author would be somewhere between sixty and seventy years of age. He had followed Jesus throughout His earthly ministry; and had been intimately acquainted with Him. After an interval of thirty-eight years he writes this book, in which he arrays Him in the highest attributes of a superhuman Christ. Is it credible that he can have done this, unless he was firmly persuaded, that during Our Lord's abode on earth, he had witnessed actions which were the counterpart of the superhuman character which he has ascribed to Him ? It follows therefore that the Jewish Church, including its most extreme parties, must have accepted Jesus as a superhuman Christ;

and consequently, that they possessed accounts of His ministry, of which narratives of miracles wrought by Him must have formed a portion.

What then is the general conclusion deducible from this evidence? The narrative of the Gospels, and the Christology of the Epistles mutually corroborate each other. The miraculous actions attributed to Jesus in the Gospels presuppose the superhuman Christ of the Epistles; the superhuman Christ of the Epistles presupposes the miraculous narratives of the Gospels. The one is the natural counterpart of the other. Neither is intelligible except on the supposition of the other.

But further: a superhuman Christ, analogous to the Christ of the Epistles, was accepted not only by the Pauline Churches, but by all the sections of the Church, including the Church at Jerusalem, and the primitive believers. It follows therefore that the Christ of the Gospels, whose recorded actions form the counterpart of the Christ of the Epistles, cannot have been a legendary invention of times subsequent to Our Lord's ministry; but that the Church must have possessed a narrative of His actions similar in its chief outlines to that which we possess.

II. I proceed now to consider the evidence furnished by these Epistles as to the fulness of the narratives which were handed down in the Church respecting the ministry of its Founder.

1. We have already seen that the Epistle to the Romans contains such a reference to the supernatural birth, the Davidic origin, and the circumcision of Jesus, as to prove that they were accepted as well-known facts. It is evident therefore that the account which was handed down in the Church must have been one sufficiently copious to have made these facts intelligible, and consequently it could hardly have been less full than that which we read in St. Matthew's Gospel. The whole subject must have been one of the greatest interest to the primitive believers, and con-

sequently they would be certain to inform themselves as to the facts.

2. We further learn from the same epistle that Baptism was the acknowledged rite of initiation into the Christian Church. It follows, therefore, that it must have been in possession of an account of the institution of sufficient fulness to have been explanatory of its aim and purport.

3. Of all the direct references to events in Our Lord's ministry, St. Paul's account of the institution of the Eucharist will enable us to form the most accurate judgment as to the fulness of this primitive Gospel. It is as follows:—

"For I have received of the Lord that which also I delivered unto you, how that the Lord Jesus the same night in which he was betrayed took bread; and when he had given thanks, he brake it, and said, Take, eat, this is my body, which is broken for you. This do in remembrance of me. After the same manner also he took the cup, when he had supped, saying, This cup is the New Testament in my blood. This do ye, as oft as ye drink it, in remembrance of me." (1 Cor. xi. 23-25.)

This account in point of fulness is on the same scale as that of the Synoptics. It presupposes also that the Apostle was in possession of an account of the Last Supper and of the Passion, which he was in the habit of delivering to the Church. This probability is converted into a certainty by his assertion in the fifteenth chapter, that among the matters of prime importance which he had received of the Lord, and formally committed to the custody of the Church, was an account of His death and resurrection. We have every reason for believing, that these would be equally minute with his account of the institution of the Sacrament; which would in fact have lost nearly all its meaning, unless he had handed over with it an account of the Supper, of which it formed a portion, and of the death which it was intended to commemorate. Both accounts are described by the Apostle as having been formally committed by him to the custody of the Church as the foundation of its faith.

But the observation made in the 15th chapter that the account of Our Lord's death and resurrection was one of the matters of prime importance which he had committed to the Church, implies that there were other matters of similar importance which he was in the habit of committing to it as the foundation of its Christianity. His argument only rendered it necessary to refer to one of them, Our Lord's death and resurrection; but the whole passage makes it clear that this was not the only one, and that his object in referring to it in this brief manner, was to recall a much fuller account to their recollection. Whatever these other matters of prime importance may have been, there is no reason to believe that they were on a less extensive scale than the account of the institution of the Eucharist.

4. These epistles also clearly establish that the Church was in possession of certain well-known details of Our Lord's teaching, which could be referred to as authoritative. Thus the Apostle writes :—

"And unto the married I command, yet not I, but the Lord; Let not the wife depart from her husband; but, and if she depart, let her remain unmarried, or be reconciled to her husband, and let not the husband put away his wife." (1 Cor. vii. 10-12.)

This is evidently an allusion to a well-known account of Our Lord's teaching, of which we possess the analogue in a somewhat more condensed form in the Synoptic Gospels.

Again: "Do ye not know that they that minister about holy things live of the things of the temple, and they that wait on the altar are partakers with the altar. *Even so hath the Lord ordained*, that they which preach the Gospel should live of the Gospel." (1 Cor. ix. 13, 14.)

The reference here made to Our Lord's instructions to the Apostles and to the seventy, when He sent them on their mission, is too plain to be misunderstood. It follows, therefore, that the Church must have been in possession of an account of those instructions analogous to that which we read in our Gospels.

No less clear is it that the general moral teaching of these epistles, as for instance that which is contained in Rom. xii., is formed on the model of that which the Gospels have attributed to Jesus. The incidental mode in which it is brought out proves also that its general principles were well known and thoroughly recognized. This is equally true of every other writing in the New Testament. It follows, therefore, that these Churches must have been in possession of an outline of Our Lord's teaching bearing a close analogy to that which we read in the Synoptics.

It is needless to insist further on this point, because many eminent unbelievers allow that the discourses in the Synoptics are the veritable utterances of Jesus. This being so, the inferences follow:

First, that along with the discourses the Church must have possessed an account of His actions sufficiently full to have rendered the discourses intelligible.

Secondly: that Jesus must have professed to be a worker of miracles, because several of these discourses affirm the fact that He did so.

5. I have already shown that the reiterated assertions of the Apostle, that the great subject of his teaching had been Jesus the Christ, and that the essence of Christianity consisted in the knowledge of Christ, prove that the Church must have been in possession of considerable details respecting Our Lord's character and actions. A few quotations will suffice to show that these details must have been extensive.

Thus we read:—

"For if our Gospel be hid, it is hid to them that are lost, in whom the god of this world hath blinded the minds of them that believe not, lest the light of the glorious Gospel of Christ, who is the image of God, should shine unto them. For we preach not ourselves, but Jesus Christ the Lord, and ourselves your servants for Jesus' sake. For God, who commanded the light to shine out of darkness, hath shined in our hearts, to give the light of the knowledge of the glory of God in the face of Jesus Christ." (2 Cor. iv. 3-6.)

This passage proves the following facts:—

First: That the Apostle's preaching had been a proclamation of Jesus Christ the Lord; or, in other words, it must have contained details of his personal history.

Secondly: That this Jesus whom he preached was the image of God; and that the light of the knowledge of the glory of God, which shone forth in His face, or person, had diffused its radiance into the hearts of those to whom it had been proclaimed. Hence, it follows, that if the character of Jesus was such a manifestation of the divine perfections as to constitute the image of God, through which the knowledge of the divine glory had shone into the hearts of the Corinthians, they must have possessed an account of His life and actions in considerable detail; in other words, one which must have delineated Him as morally perfect, as He is depicted in the Gospels.

The same result follows from another passage:—"But we all, with open face beholding as in a glass the glory of the Lord, are changed into the same image from glory to glory, even as by the Spirit of the Lord." (2 Cor. iii. 18.)

Again: "Yea, doubtless, and I count all things but loss for the excellency of the knowledge of Christ Jesus my Lord, for whom I have suffered the loss of all things, and do count them but dung, that I may win Christ. That I may know him, and the power of his Resurrection, and the fellowship of his sufferings, being made conformable unto his death. (Phil. iii. 8, 10.)

It is simply incredible that the Apostle could have written passages of this description, unless he had made every effort to inform himself of the minute details of his Master's life.

Statements of this kind are not exclusively Pauline. "If these things be in you, and abound, they make you that ye be neither barren nor unfruitful in the knowledge of Our Lord Jesus Christ. (2 Pet. i. 8.) "But grow in grace, and in the knowledge of Our Lord and Saviour Jesus Christ." (2 Pet. iii. 18.)

A few more passages will suffice to show the extent to

which the Pauline Gospel must have consisted in the proclamation of a personal Christ, and the degree in which His historic life must have been the subject of constant meditation in the Apostolic Churches. "We preach Christ crucified, to the Jews a stumblingblock, and to the Greeks foolishness; but to them who are called, both Jews and Greeks, Christ the power of God, and the wisdom of God." (1 Cor. i. 23, 24.) "I determined to know nothing among you, save Jesus Christ, and him crucified." (1 Cor. ii. 2.) "For the Son of God, Jesus Christ, who was preached among you by us, even by me and Silvanus and Timotheus." (2 Cor. i. 19.) "But ye have not so learned Christ, if so be, ye have heard him, and have been taught by him, as the truth is in Jesus." (Eph. iv. 20, 21.)

Incidental allusions of this kind prove that the acquaintance with the life of Jesus which was possessed by the apostolic Churches, must have been one of considerable minuteness, and that it must have been kept in constant recollection.

6. Equally definite is the evidence afforded by those numerous incidental references which exhort Christians to follow Christ as the great example of holy practice. Of this I cite the following instance :—

The Apostle concludes his discussion of the lawfulness of eating certain kinds of food, in the following words :— "Whether therefore ye eat or drink, or whatsoever ye do, do all to the glory of God. Give none offence, neither to the Jews, nor to the Gentiles, nor to the Church of God. Even as I please all men in all things, not seeking my own profit, but the profit of many that they might be saved. *Be ye imitators* (μιμηταί) *of me as I also am of Christ.*" (1 Cor. x. 31-33; and xi. 1.)

This passage proves :—

First, that the actions and character of Paul were so well known in the Corinthian Church, that he could appeal to them as unquestionable proofs of his disinterestedness.

2. That it was possible to institute a comparison between the actions of Paul and those of Our Lord.

3. That it was the duty of Christians before they took St. Paul as the model for their imitation, to institute such a comparison, and only to imitate him as far as his conduct was in conformity with that of Christ.

Next. The Church must also have been in possession of a narrative of Our Lord's actions, which delineated Him in various special aspects of His character. Thus the Apostle writes:

"We that are strong ought to bear the infirmities of the weak, and not to please ourselves. Let every one of us please his neighbour for his good to edification; for even Christ pleased not himself; but as it is written, the reproaches of them that reproached theo fell on me." (Rom. xv. 1-3.)

Such an exhortation would have been meaningless, unless the Church had been in possession of a well-known delineation of the actions of Jesus, which exhibited Him as the model of self-sacrificing disinterestedness.

Again: "Now the God of patience and consolation grant you to be like minded one toward another, according to Christ Jesus, that ye may with one mind and one mouth glorify God, even the Father of our Lord Jesus Christ." (Rom. xv. 5-6.)

From this it follows that a delineation of Him must have been well known by the members of this Church, on which it was possible to found an exhortation to unity. Portions of the contents of St. John's Gospel correspond to this idea.

The Apostle further writes to the same Church: "And that, knowing the time, that now it is high time to awake out of sleep, for now is our salvation nearer than when we believed. The night is far spent: the day is at hand. Let us therefore cast off the works of darkness, and let us put on the armour of light. Let us walk honestly, as in the day, not in rioting and drunkenness, not in chambering and wantonness, not in strife and envying. But put ye on the

Lord Jesus Christ, and make not provision for the flesh, to fulfil the lusts thereof." (Rom. xiii. 11-14.)

Similar exhortations are found in the Epistle to the Galatians :

"As many of you as have been baptized into Christ have put on Christ." (Gal. iii. 27.)

"My little children, of whom I travail in birth again until Christ be formed in you." (Gal. iv. 19.)

The exhortation to "put on Christ," can only mean, "incorporate His character into your own;" and in order to do this it is obviously necessary that we should possess an account of the actions of Him whom we are directed to imitate on an extensive scale.

Further: the Apostle tells the Romans that the thing to be put off was the whole range of Pagan vice, as summed up in the expression, "the works of darkness;" and the new character which was to be assumed by Christians, as the opposite to this, consisted in "putting on the Lord Jesus Christ." From this it follows that the character of Christ which was to be made the subject of imitation, must have been a many sided one, as it is depicted in the Gospels.

As these three last precepts are addressed to a Church which St. Paul had neither visited nor taught, it is evident that not merely the churches of Pauline origin, but the whole Church, must have been in possession of such a delineation as the foundation of its common Christianity.

Several passages in the Epistles to the Corinthians illustrate the same subject. Thus the Apostle writes: "Though ye have ten thousand instructors in Christ, yet have ye not many fathers, for in Christ Jesus I have begotten you through the Gospel. Wherefore I beseech you be ye imitators of me." (1 Cor. iv. 15, 16.)

The expression, "ten thousand instructors in Ch ist" is of course a pleonasm ; but the whole passage clearly proves that the entire body of Christian teachers held up the actions of Christ as examples for imitation.

The Apostle continues:

"For this cause have I sent unto you Timotheus, who is my beloved son, and faithful in the Lord, who shall bring you into remembrance of *my ways which be in Christ*, as I teach everywhere in every Church." (1 Cor. iv. 17.)

Here the Apostle affirms that he had certain "ways in Christ," and that one of the purposes for which he had sent Timothy was to remind the Corinthians of them. These "ways in Christ" he likewise affirms that he taught everywhere in every Church. What were these ways? Clearly the instruction in Christ above referred to, which the Apostle exhibited in his own conduct, and which he exhorted those to whom he wrote, to make the subject of imitation. "His ways in Christ," of which Timothy was to remind them, could not have been details of his own actions, for he calls the Corinthians to witness that he had not preached himself, but Jesus Christ the Lord. It follows, therefore, that they must have consisted of details of the actions and teaching of his Master.

A delineation of Our Lord must have been well known to the members of this Church, which enabled the Apostle to plead His example as a motive for a liberal contribution for the relief of the poorer members of the Jewish Church. Then he writes:

"Therefore as ye abound in faith, and utterance, and knowledge, and in all diligence, and in your love to us, see that ye abound in this grace also. For ye know the grace of our Lord Jesus Christ, that though he was rich, yet for your sakes he became poor, that ye through his poverty might be rich." (2 Cor. viii. 7, 9.)

Similarly also, they must have been in possession of an account of his actions, which depicted him as an example of meekness and gentleness.

"Now I Paul," says the Apostle, "beseech you by the meekness and gentleness of Christ, who in presence am base among you, but being absent am bold towards you;

and I beseech you that I may not be bold, when I am present with that confidence, wherewith I think to be bold against some, who think of us as if we walked according to the flesh." (2 Cor. x. 1, 2.)

It follows therefore that this Church must have been in possession of a delineation of Jesus Christ, which exhibited Him as a perfect embodiment of gentleness and meekness; and as the reference occurs in the most controversial portion of the Epistle, that it must have been acquiesced in by his opponents. The delineation therefore must have been precisely similar in character to that in our Gospels.

A similar exhortation is contained in St. Paul's earlier Epistles. Thus he writes:

"Remembering without ceasing your work of faith, and labour of love, and patience of hope in our Lord Jesus Christ, in the sight of God, and our Father. . . For our Gospel came not in word only, but also in power, and in the Holy Ghost, and in much assurance, as ye know what manner of men we were among you for your sake; and ye became followers (imitators, $\mu\iota\mu\eta\tau\alpha\iota$) of us and of the Lord. . . . And how ye turned to God from idols to serve the living and true God; and to wait for his Son from heaven, even Jesus, who delivereth us from the wrath to come." (1 Thess. i. 3-10.)

This passage is of considerable importance, for it proves that the body of this Church consisted of converted heathen. The expression, "How ye turned to God from idols," proves that most of its members, previously to his preaching, had been ignorant alike of Jesus, and of the idea of the Christ. This must have rendered it necessary for him to give a large number of explanations as to the meaning of the Christ, and of details of the life of Jesus, sufficient to prove that he was the Christ. The Epistle makes it clear that they were now well informed on both subjects. They were perfectly familiar with the idea of the Christ, and they knew sufficient about Jesus to make him the subject of love, trust, and patient hope: They were also acquainted with sufficient details of his life to make him the subject of imitation. "Ye became imitators of us, and of the Lord;" and the whole announcement had produced so powerful a moral influence on them, that they "had turned to God from idols, to serve the living and true God," and were filled with the strongest missionary zeal to spread the knowledge of it through the neighbouring cities. In fact, a personal Jesus stands out prominently in both these Epistles. It follows therefore, as the persons addressed had been heathens, that the Gospel preached among them by the Apostle must have been rich in details respecting the person, ministry, and teaching of Our Lord; in other words, that it consisted of what I have above referred to, viz. " his ways in Christ Jesus which he taught every where in every Church."

Two passages from his later Epistles bear witness to the same facts. Thus he writes to the Ephesians:

"This I say, therefore, and testify in the Lord, that ye henceforth walk not as other Gentiles walk, in the vanity of their mind, having the understanding darkened, being alienated from the life of God through the ignorance that is in them, who being past feeling have given themselves over unto lasciviousness, to work all uncleanness with greediness. But ye *have not so learned Christ, if so be ye have heard him, and have been taught by him as the truth is in Jesus.*" (Eph. iv. 17-21.)

Similarly also he writes to the Colossians:

" As ye have therefore received Christ Jesus the Lord, so walk ye in him, rooted and built up in him and stablished in the faith, as ye have been taught, abounding therein with thanksgiving." (Col. ii. 6, 7.)

Both these passages occur in the Epistles which contain the Apostle's most advanced Christology; and as this was accepted by these Churches it follows that he must have communicated to its members a number of facts which justified that Christology, for as a large proportion of them consisted of heathen converts, the whole subject must otherwise have been beyond their comprehension. The

Ephesians are here described as having "learned Christ," as having "heard him," *i.e.* his teaching, (for they had not heard him personally) and as having been taught by him, "as the truth is in Jesus." This had led them to renounce their old pagan character, and to put on the new man created after God in righteousness and true holiness. So the Colossians are directed to walk in him as they had been taught. It follows therefore that they must have possessed a delineation of Jesus Christ which they had been in the habit of studying, corresponding to this description; or, in other words, one which resembled in its great outlines that contained in our Gospels, and formed part of the ordinary teaching of the Church.

Such is the evidence furnished by the Pauline epistles that the various Christian Churches were in possession of an account of the actions and teaching of Our Lord, analogous in its main features to that which is contained in our Gospels, and was accepted by its various sects and parties as the basis of their common Christianity.

I adduce a single passage from the Epistle to the Hebrews, which, although we cannot claim it as Paul's, is unquestionably a writing of primitive antiquity; and if not by him, must represent the views of a different section of the Church. After stating the advanced Christology of the first chapter, the author writes:—

"Therefore we ought to give the more earnest heed to the things which we have heard, lest at any time we should let them slip. For if the word spoken by angels was steadfast, and every transgression and disobedience received a just recompense of reward, how shall we escape if we reject so great salvation, which at the first began to be spoken by the Lord, and was confirmed unto us by them that heard him, God also bearing them witness, both with signs and wonders, and with divers miracles and gifts of the Holy Ghost according to his own will."—Heb. ii. 1—4.

This passage renders it incontestable, that the writer was

in possession of an account of what he considered to be the great salvation spoken by the Lord, which had been confirmed to those to whom he wrote by the testimony of eyewitnesses; and that this had received a miraculous attestation.

The only remaining point for our consideration is the evidence which these epistles furnish of the truth of the Resurrection. All the great facts to which they testify have been definitely brought out in the foregoing Lecture; and to quote and comment on all the various passages which refer to it would make this Supplement needlessly prolix. So evident are the facts on the surface of the Epistles that the student cannot fail to recognize them for himself; and so numerous are they, that it is impossible to find any two pages in which the truth of the Resurrection is not either distinctly asserted, or assumed as the foundation on which the Christian Church was erected. The Christ, who was essential to the Church, was not a dead Christ, but a living one; one who could be the object of devoted love; one who could kindle the affections; one who could claim the allegiance of the heart on account of what he had done for man; who could recognize devoted service, and reciprocate love. He must be not merely one who could excite the fond reminiscence of departed worth, but who was capable of recognizing the acts of self-sacrifice which he evoked in the hearts of those who loved him. Every mention of the Christ of these epistles either affirms or implies that it was the belief of the whole Church, and of every section in it, that Jesus had risen from the dead; and every reference to him makes it clear that, apart from this belief, the Church would have perished in its Founder's grave. The belief in the fact of the Resurrection was entwined around every association of the Christian heart. It was not only accepted as a fact, but felt to be a great moral power, which imparted to the Church its religious life. One citation will be sufficient, and it shall be from the epistle to the distant Church at Rome, which St. Paul had neither visited, nor taught. He writes:

"Know ye not that so many of us as were baptized into Jesus Christ, were baptized into his death? Therefore we are buried with him by baptism into death; that like as Christ was raised up from the dead by the glory of the Father, even so we also should walk in newness of life. For if we have been planted together in the likeness of his death, we shall be also in the likeness of his resurrection. Knowing this, that our old man is crucified with him, that the body of sin might be destroyed, that henceforth we should not serve sin, for he that is dead is freed from sin. Now if we be dead with Christ, we believe that we shall also live with him: knowing that Christ being raised from the dead dieth no more, death hath no more dominion over him. For in that he died, he died unto sin once, but in that he liveth, he liveth unto God. Likewise reckon ye yourselves to be dead indeed unto sin, but alive unto God, through Jesus Christ our Lord."—(Rom. vi. 3—11.)

Thus the Pauline epistles render it indubitable, that the resurrection of Jesus was accepted as a fact by every section of the Christian Church; and that the Church was reconstructed on the basis of its truth within a few days after the Crucifixion, in the very place where he had been publicly executed. Whether this belief could have originated in any form of mental hallucination must be determined on other grounds than those of simple attestation.

LECTURE VII.

"Brethren, be not children in understanding; howbeit in malice be ye children, but in understanding be men."—1 Cor. xiv. 20.

I HAVE proved in the last two Lectures that within a very short interval after the crucifixion of Our Lord the Church was in possession of an account of His life and actions analogous in all its chief outlines to that which is contained in our present Gospels, and that this must have been the same as that which was handed down by His primitive followers. This being so, the theories which affirm that a large portion of their contents consists of myths and legends, which gradually sprung up in the Church during the first century of our era, are deprived of all possible *locus standi*. I have further proved, by the aid of the Pauline Epistles, that within a very brief interval after the Crucifixion the Church was reconstructed on the basis of the Resurrection. This being indubitable, it is incumbent on those who deny its objective reality to offer a theory which will afford a rational account of the origin of the belief in the Resurrection, and of the reconstruction of the Church on its basis. For this purpose the theory of visions has been propounded. It will now be my duty to inquire into its validity.

In order to impart the semblance of plausibility to this theory, it is necessary to assume that the original followers of Jesus consisted of a body of men who were in the highest degree enthusiastic, credulous, and superstitious, whose enthusiasm created a number of visionary appearances of Jesus risen from the dead, and whose credulity mistook them for external realities.* But as it is impossible to credit St. Paul with excessive credulity or superstition, the only way of discrediting his testimony is to affirm that he had been wrought up to so high a degree of enthusiastic exaltation, that he was unable to distinguish between his own subjective imagination and the realities of the external world. This charge against the Apostle I have disposed of in my last Lecture, by the evidence afforded by the three chapters connected with the text, which it seems to me to be impossible to examine carefully and not to arrive at the conclusion that it is invalidated by the facts.

In a similar manner the affirmation which has been so

* The mode in which this charge is attempted to be established is a noteworthy specimen of the reasoning which has been adopted in this controversy. Every instance of superstition which can be found in any Jewish writer for several centuries preceding the advent, or in any writer, whether Jewish or Christian, for several centuries after, has been carefully collected together; and the whole charged on the followers of Jesus. This is as unreasonable as it would be to credit Lord Bacon with all the superstitions which were held by Englishmen during the three centuries before his birth, or with believing in the Spiritualism of the present day. If we wish to ascertain how far a particular author is superstitious, it is absurd to credit him at once with all the superstitions which may have been prevalent for centuries before, and after his birth. The only correct course is to examine his own writings for the purpose of ascertaining the actual superstitions they contain. Thus in the case of the Gospels, the only accurate measure of the degree in which their writers were superstitious is the superstitions which are patent in their pages. It follows, therefore, that to charge the disciples of Jesus with a degree of credulity or superstition beyond that which is clearly displayed in the pages of the New Testament, is to draw a conclusion which the premisses will not warrant. If, on the other hand their excessive credulity is assumed, because they belived in miracles, this is not to reason, but simply to assume the point at issue. It may be objected that they believed in demoniacal possession. Let the objection be accepted for as much as it is worth. But this is certainly no distinctive mark of credulity or superstition, for numbers of men of highly cultivated minds and of sound judgments have entertained the same belief.

freely made, that the primitive followers of Jesus and the Christians of the first century were credulous and superstitious beyond the average of mankind is an assumption, of which the historical evidence is wanting. I say *beyond the average of mankind*; for unless it is taken for granted that they were so, the theory of visions cannot be made to bear even the semblance of plausibility. If the Resurrection was unreal, the credulity of the followers of Jesus must have been extreme; for it is evident that no ordinary amount of it would afford any adequate account of the origin of the belief. But if the question is asked, How do we know that His followers were credulous to the extent demanded by the exigencies of the positions taken by unbelievers? the only possible answer, in the absence of all adequate historical evidence of the fact, is that they believed in the reality of miracles and in the truth of the Resurrection. This, however, involves a plain begging of the entire question. The requisite degree of enthusiasm, credulity, and superstition, must be proved and not merely assumed.

The following facts must be accounted for before we can accept the theory of visions as affording an adequate ground for the belief in the Resurrection.

1. The possibility of reconstructing the Church on the basis of this belief within a very brief interval after the Crucifixion.

2. That not only individual disciples, but disciples when assembled in bodies, were firmly persuaded that they saw Jesus alive after His crucifixion, and had interviews with Him.

3. That these interviews were not casual apparitions, but they were fully convinced that they had conversations with Him, in which they received His definite instructions as to the mode in which the Church was to be reconstructed, and that in consequence they did actually reconstruct the Church on the basis of His spiritual Messiahship.

4. The rapid diffusion of the belief among those who were not original followers of Jesus, as is proved by the

growth of the Christian Church during the thirty years which followed the Crucifixion.

5. The great change wrought in St. Paul from the most violent persecutor into the most devoted missionary of the Christian faith, as is proved by his own testimony.

6. The mighty power which has been exerted by Jesus Christ during eighteen centuries after the termination of His earthly life, as has been shown in the second Lecture of this course.

Of these unquestionable facts of history the Church has always given the following solution, which no unbeliever can deny that a sound philosophy must pronounce to be fully adequate : Jesus Christ rose from the dead : He had several interviews with His followers, in which He directed them to reconstruct the Church on the basis of His spiritual Messiahship : He endowed them with supernatural powers according to a promise made to them in these interviews, which enabled them to accomplish the work in question : They obeyed His commands. The result has been the creation of the Catholic Church, and the mighty influence which it has exerted on the destinies of man during the last eighteen centuries.

Let us now hear the solution which the theory of visions propounds as a philosophical explanation of these astounding facts. Jesus Christ never rose from the dead; but while His body was turning to corruption in the grave, some one or more of His enthusiastic followers fancied that they saw Him alive, and mistook the creations of their distempered imaginations for an actual resurrection. They forthwith, without further inquiry, accepted it as a fact, and succeeded in persuading the other disciples that He was risen from the dead. These in turn took to seeing visions of the risen Jesus, which they mistook for objective realities. In the height of their fanaticism, they not only fancied that they had interviews with Him, but that they received His orders to reconstruct the Church on the basis of His resurrection. As, however, He intended to withdraw Himself from public view, the happy thought occurred to some of them them that they heard Him direct them to change the basis of His Messiahship from that of a present and visible into an absent and spiritual one. The attempt was made; the Church was reconstituted; the new faith spread; and the result has been the erection of the greatest of institutions, and all the mighty effects which it has exerted in the history of man, on the foundation of the baseless delusions of a few credulous fanatics.

Such is the theory. Its entire plausibility is derived from the general form in which it has been propounded. The moment we confront it with the facts of history and the realities of human life, it crumbles to pieces. Thus as a matter of mere speculation in the study, nothing is easier than to assert that some enthusiastic disciple of Jesus fancied that he saw Him alive after His crucifixion, mistook an apparition for a resurrection, and communicated his enthusiasm to the rest. But these last words hide whole mountains of difficulty. How was it possible under the circumstances of intense discouragement in which the disciples were placed by the blasting of all their Messianic expectations, through the crucifixion of their Master, to breathe into them the enthusiasm requisite for seeing visions of the risen Jesus; and on the strength of such a delusion to found an institution which has stood the test of eighteen centuries? How, I ask, are a body of men to be made to believe that a person who was only a short time previously publicly executed has risen from the dead, while his body must be still somewhere at hand in the grave in which it has been interred? Has anything analogous to this occurred in the history of fact, or in the dreams of fiction? Such a theory hopelessly breaks down when it is tested by the stern realities of life and the historical conditions of the case. Let us proceed to subject it to this test.

I. The starting-point of all reasonings on this subject must be the night of the Crucifixion; for the affirmation that the belief was a gradual growth, which sprang up at a distance from the scene of the Passion is effectually disposed of by the testimony of the Pauline epistles. In what state of mind then must that evening and the following days have found the disciples of Jesus? A high state of mental exaltation is indispensable for seeing visions, and mistaking them for realities. Such visions are inconsistent with a state of mental depression which might have induced some disciple to fancy that he saw an apparition of the spirit of the murdered Jesus, but could not have suggested to the most credulous fanatic the idea of a resurrection.*

What then were the facts? It is certain that His followers had been induced to believe in Him as the Messiah of popular expectation; and that the public execution of one who laid claim to this character must have been destructive of the idea of His Messiahship. Their history, it is true, had familiarized them with the idea of murdered prophets; but although this had frequently happened, their

* The whole range of Grecian and Roman mythology may be quoted as a case in point. Rich as it is in ideal creations, in stories which involved the current beliefs in the supernatural, and in accounts of the apparitions of the spirits of the departed, it impresses us with the fact that the idea was all but universal, that from death there was no return. An inexorable fate demanded the death of man; the powers of the world below firmly grasped their prey: Jupiter himself was unable to avert from his children this inevitable doom. The two or three stories of heathen mythology which bear a resemblance to resurrections, are not only extremely grotesque, but are relegated to the distant ages of the past. The whole aspect of heathen literature proves, that although belief in the appearance of the spirits of the departed was strictly in accordance with the popular ideas of the possible; yet the return to life of one who had really died was believed to be impossible. I make this observation, because it has been often asserted in connection with this discussion, that in certain ages of the past the popular mind has not recognized the existence of such a thing as order in nature. Their order may not have been our order, but whenever the human mind advances beyond the lowest stages of barbarism, it is impossible but that it should recognize an order of some kind as existing in nature; but of this order even in the most mythical periods, the belief in the possibility of a genuine resurrection has never formed a portion.

death had never once been vindicated by a resurrection; and the Messiah was not to be a murdered prophet, but a King who was to reign in the Kingdom of God. Whatever respect therefore they may have entertained for the character of their Master; and although it is within the limits of possibility that they should have believed that He was a prophet,* His crucifixion must have convinced them that He had been labouring under a delusion in claiming to be the Christ. Their mental condition therefore must have been that of men whose hopes and expectations were utterly blasted, the very opposite of that which would have suggested the idea of a resurrection, and induced them to see visions of their Master risen from the dead. The necessary conditions of doing so, I will consider presently.

It may perhaps be urged, for the purpose of obviating this difficulty, that Jesus may have foreseen that the exasperation of His enemies would probably result in His death, and that for the purpose of encouraging His disciples, He told them that if this should happen, He would be raised again from the dead; by which He only meant that His cause would be resuscitated; and that they mistook this for a prediction of an actual resurrection; and that this raised so strong an expectation of it, as to cause them to see visions of Him returned to life again, which they mistook for realities. To this I reply that our only information that Our Lord predicted His death and resurrection is derived from the pages of the Evangelists. But if their testimony is valid to prove that He did so, it must be equally valid to prove that the disciples did not attach to His words the meaning which they literally have, and that they certainly

---

* I make this admission on the strength of the words of Cleopas recorded in Luke xxiv. 19. "Concerning Jesus of Nazareth, who was a prophet mighty in deed and word before God and all the people." These words were spoken on the evening of the Resurrection. It is impossible that even His most devoted followers could have long continued to believe in the prophetical character of one who had been self-deceived in believing Himself to be the Messiah.

did not suggest to them the idea of an actual death, or an
actual resurrection.* It would therefore have been impossible for this to have produced the state of expectancy
requisite for seeing visions and mistaking them for realities.†

* This habit on the part of opponents of accepting the testimony of
the Gospels when it favours their own theories, and of rejecting it
when adverse, is one which cannot be too strongly deprecated; for
however it may help to confirm preconceived notions, it can lead to no
result favourable to truth. Apart from their testimony that Jesus
predicted His death and resurrection, the idea that He foresaw the
high probability of His death, and expressed the hope that His cause
would revive afterwards, and designated this revival a resurrection,
and on the strength of this to propound such a theory as a true
account of the most important event in the history of the world, is to
build on a foundation of sand. When criticism accepts possibilities
for probabilities, and probabilities for certainties, all it does is to construct history out of its own subjective consciousness, a practice which
can only result in substituting our own notions for the realities of
things.

† It may be urged that the institution of the Holy Communion was
a distinct intimation made by Our Lord to His followers of His impending death. No doubt it was so; but it is very remarkable that
in the account given by the Evangelists, there is no hint of His
impending resurrection. If we take the accounts as they stand, not
one word spoken by Our Lord on this occasion could have produced an
expectation of it. The institution itself is one of the most remarkable
facts in the world's history, and is without precedent in the history of
martyrdoms. A man in anticipation of being put to death on the
morrow, directs his followers to perform a very peculiar rite for all
future time in remembrance of his death. He tells them that they are
to take a piece of bread, to break and eat it, and to drink of a cup of
wine, in remembrance that his body had been broken for them, and
his blood shed for the remission of sins. What is the only possible
inference? Either that the person who instituted the rite was fully
conscious that he was about to perform an act pre-eminently divine in
thus surrendering his life; and that that act had an intimate connection with the remission of sin; or that he was labouring under such a
degree of hallucination as to amount to disorder of the intellect.
There is no alternative between these. The world's history contains
instances enough of martyrdoms; but the enthusiasm of no martyr
has ever impelled him to do an act at all resembling this. Yet
nothing can be more calm, impressive, and devoid of the smallest trait

Still less could such an effect have been produced by the utterances of a few vague expressions, such as that God would vindicate His cause after His death; and that He would live again in its renewed life. The supposition that an utterance of this kind could have produced in the minds of the disciples such a state of expectancy as would have been requisite to enable them to see visions of Him risen from the dead, to hold imaginary conversations with Him, which they mistook for realities, and in consequence of his supposed instructions, to proceed to the work of reconstructing the Church, is too incredible to require serious argument.

The theory of visions is compelled to assume two things, both of which under the historical conditions of the case involve such difficulties as amount to impossibilities.

First.

That the followers of Jesus, both individually and conjointly, took to seeing visions of their Master risen from the dead.

Secondly.

Not only must they have mistaken these visions for realities, but they must have believed that they had conversations with Him in which they received His definite instructions as to the new basis on which they were to reconstruct the Church. It is simply incredible that they would have ventured on making such a change if they believed that Jesus had risen from the dead, unless they

of enthusiasm than the account of the institution as it is given by the Evangelists. The whole scene is one of the profoundest solemnity. Yet the act in question has received a perpetual series of commemorations from the night of the Paschal Supper to the present hour; certainly without the intermission of a single week, probably not of a single day, during a period of eighteen hundred and forty-seven years. This renders the fact of the Institution one of the most indubitable in history; and constitutes an incontestable proof that Jesus claimed to be something very different from an ordinary man, however wise or good. Still, as I have observed, there was nothing in the institution itself to suggest to His desponding followers the idea that after a few days they would see Him risen again from the dead.

were persuaded that they had received His definite instructions to do so.

This necessity of accounting not only for the belief in the Resurrection, but for the reconstruction of the Church on the new Messianic basis, involves those who propound this theory in a difficulty so overwhelming as to be subversive of the preconditions on which it necessarily rests. According to well-established principles of mental physiology, three mental states are necessary to enable even the most enthusiastic and credulous persons to mistake subjective impressions for external realities. These are Prepossession, Fixed Idea, and Expectancy; and unless they had been most energetically present in the minds of his followers, no amount of enthusiasm or credulity would have sufficed to create the necessary visions. But supposing that under the influence of these principles they had visions of a risen Jesus, it would have been impossible that visions generated by either prepossession or fixed idea could have suggested the reconstruction of the Church on a new basis.

Yet the fact that the Church was so reconstructed is unquestionable. It follows therefore that the minds of the disciples must have undergone a change as to the nature of the Messianic character during the interval which elapsed between the crucifixion of Jesus and the proclamation of His resurrection. How then will the principles of prepossession, fixed idea, or expectancy, account for their seeing such visions as could have led to the reconstruction of the Church? As for expectancy, I have already shown that it was non-existent. Prepossession and fixed idea are principles of the most conservative description. Under their influence it is impossible for a set of new ideas to be generated in the mind. It follows therefore, if these principles had induced the followers of Jesus to mistake visionary appearances and conversations for realities, they could neither have suggested the requisite change in the Messianic conception nor the consequent reconstruction of the Church.

On the contrary, they would certainly have gone on on the old lines.

II. But for the purpose of bringing these theories to the test of the facts of history, let us suppose all these difficulties to be non-existent, and that such a state of enthusiastic exaltation existed among His disciples on the days immediately following the Crucifixion, that some one of them fancied that he saw Him alive, and spread among the others the report that He was risen. Let us further assume that this enthusiast was Mary Magdalene ;* and that she mistook the gardener for Jesus. Is it credible, I ask, that a woman so enthusiastically attached to him, went away to report His resurrection to the disciples, without asking Him a single question? If she had done so, her delusions must have been instantly dissipated. But let us assume that what she fancied she saw was not the gardener, but a visionary creation of her own disordered imagination. Did she make no attempt to speak to her beloved Master? Some questions under the circumstances must have been inevitable. If she put them, did she get visionary answers, and fancy herself charged with some message to the disciples? Surely, if she did, it must have contained some promise to meet them. If so, was the promise kept? Or did He promise to meet her again? If he did so, and the appointment was not kept, her delusions must have ended. If however she fancied that she had subsequent interviews with him, she must have had a whole series of visions and ideal conversations, and mistaken them for realities. Such things may be conceivable in theory, but they become absolutely incredible when tested by the realities of this world of fact.

* I make this assumption because it is the most plausible form in which the theory of visions can be presented, it being far easier to conceive the possibility of a single person mistaking apparitions of the risen Jesus for realities, than that many did so separately and conjointly. As however it contradicts the most unquestionable facts of history, as proved by the testimony of the Pauline epistles, I do so under protest.

Let us however assume that she at once started off to tell the disciples that she had seen her crucified Master risen from the dead. Are we really to be invited to believe that in their state of despondency, occasioned by the blasting of all their expectations, they received such an announcement with open-mouthed credulity? Nothing is easier than to affirm with M. Renan that she communicated her enthusiasm to the rest. But how was it possible to do so? Does all history contain anything analogous to it? While there is no great difficulty in persuading ignorant people that a spirit has appeared, it is a wholly different thing to persuade even the profoundest credulity and the most greedy appetite for the marvellous, that a person once dead has risen again in bodily reality. As I have said, the history of fictions, while it abounds with accounts of departed spirits, regards stories of resurrections as lying outside the regions of the possible. This difficulty however is greatly increased when the person said to have been raised had been only a few days before publicly executed, and his body was close at hand corrupting in the grave. It is beyond the power of belief, that such a piece of information was accepted even by the most credulous of men, on the bare word of the informant. But let us further assume that she brought them a promise of an interview, which specified both the time and place. Was the promise kept? If not, there must have been an end of the delusion. But if they supposed that it was kept, then the whole body of the disciples must have taken to seeing visions together. Is this conceivable, while the body was close at hand, either in the custody of his friends or his foes?

It may perhaps be urged that they were satisfied with the allegation that it was necessary that he should retire out of the reach of his enemies. To this I answer, that such an excuse would have involved an open renunciation of his Messiahship, and rendered the reconstruction of the Church impossible. No amount of credulity could have accepted as a Christ one who declined to have an interview with his friends because it was necessary for him to withdraw out of the reach of his enemies, and that too after he had proved the reality of his Messiahship by his resurrection from the dead.

III.—This brings us to the very centre of the difficulty, viz., the necessity of grappling with the unquestionable facts instead of bare assumptions. Common sense affirms, and the Pauline epistles prove beyond all doubt, that these apparitions, if such they were, must have been seen not merely by a single follower of Jesus, but by many of them, separately and conjointly; and not only so, but during these apparitions they must have had conversations with him, in which they received their Master's directions as to the reconstruction of the Church on its new basis. I invite especial attention to this latter point as involving the theory of visions in the necessity of assuming the existence of these imaginary interviews and conversations, for in no other way can it account for the undeniable fact that the disciples did actually proceed forthwith to reconstruct the Church on this new basis, since it is incredible that they should have done so unless they had been fully persuaded that they had received their Master's definite instructions as to the course they were to adopt.*

Unless therefore those who propound the theory of visions

* I am aware that those who have propounded this theory maintain that the Church was reconstructed with the smallest possible deviation from the old Messianic basis; and that the persuasion of the early followers of Jesus was that He had only withdrawn from earth for a short time; and would soon return to assume the old Messianic character, and to take vengeance on His foes. But whatever might have been their belief respecting His speedy return, it is an obvious fact that the Church was reconstructed on the basis of an absent Messiah; and that this differed very materially from the old one. As I have said, if Jesus was still to continue to be the Messiah of the Church after His crucifixion, the idea of a visible Messiah was no longer tenable, unless He had exhibited Himself openly to public view after His resurrection; and consequently the Messianic conception had to be changed from that of a visible Christ who was to overcome all opposition, and to enter into His glory, to that of a Christ who had asserted his Messianic claims before the Jewish people, had been rejected, and crucified by them, and who, although He had risen

as a rational account of the origin of the belief in the Resurrection can solve these and other difficulties which are forced on them by the unquestionable facts of history, it must perish under the weight of its inherent absurdity. We know on the authority of the Epistle to the Corinthians, that the Apostles believed that they had at least two interviews with Him, when assembled together, that two of their number had private interviews with Him ; that it was the universal persuasion of the primitive believers that He appeared to more than five hundred in a body, more than half of whom were surviving when Paul wrote the letter ; and that Paul was firmly persuaded that he himself had seen Him.* There is no reason to believe that the Pauline list of appearances is meant to be exhaustive of all he had been informed of ; but for obvious reasons, I do not refer to any mentioned in

from the dead, had taken no steps to crush His enemies, but had retired out of danger into heaven, from whence He had promised at some future time to return and take possession of His kingdom, but who in the meantime delegated to His followers the work of making converts, and the danger of asserting His Messiahship on this new basis. This is evidently the smallest possible change which the Crucifixion must have rendered necessary in the Messianic conception, if the claims of Jesus to be the Christ were still to be asserted. This change, however, is a very great one, and amply sufficient for the purposes of my argument. It is one which it is impossible to believe that His followers would have ventured on unless fully convinced that they had received His definite instructions during their interviews with Him after He had risen from the dead. Men had now to be urged to accept as Christ one who had been rejected and crucified by the heads of the Jewish nation, who had withdrawn Himself out of the reach of their animosity, and who had put off to some future day the work of vindicating His Messianic claims and taking vengeance on His foes. It is impossible to deny that this was a very onerous undertaking, and that it involved a fundamental change in the conception of His Messianic character. Nothing is more natural than the question which the author of the Acts puts into the mouth of the Apostles, as addressed to the risen Jesus, " Lord, wilt thou at this time restore the kingdom to Israel ?" The whole thing is utterly inconsistent with expectancy, fixed idea, or prepossession.

* See Supplement I.

the Gospels.* This list, however, is quite sufficient for our purpose, as it proves that the Apostles were firmly persuaded that they saw Him alive when assembled in a body, that two of them believed that they had private interviews with Him; and that a very large number of persons believed that they had seen Him when they were assembled together. These facts St. Paul had such ample means of verifying, that unless they are true, he stands convicted of deliberate falsehood.

This being so, it is hardly possible to conceive of such a state of mental hallucination, as this theory of visions is compelled to presuppose, as an adequate explanation of the historic facts. It is nothing short of this, that a body of persons when assembled together, believed that on two separate occasions they saw a person alive in the midst of them, within a few days after he had been publicly executed; and that, too, while the body must have been close at hand, mouldering in the tomb, unless it had been removed by the hands of his friends, in which case they must have known of its removal; or of his enemies; in which case it must have been a matter of public notoriety.

Such a species of hallucination exceeds the capacity of lunatics; for although individual lunatics often mistake visions for realities; yet concurrence among a body of them in believing that they see the same object is unknown.†

But let us even assume that such impossibilities are possible. Here again we encounter all the difficulties to

* Their historical character, as well as that of the earlier chapters of the Acts of the Apostles, being denied by unbelievers, forbids me to quote them here as authorities in discussing the question of the truth of the Resurrection.

† It is doubtless a well established scientific fact that certain abnormal conditions of the mind can produce in individuals a conviction that they see certain objective realities, while what they fancy that they discern, is nothing but the subjective creation of their own disordered imaginations. I am aware of the existence of a few cases of spiritualistic manifestations which are alleged to have produced in a number of persons when assembled together, the impression that they all saw the same imaginary object, but there are no cases on

which I have already alluded, and with aggravated force. Is it credible, I ask, that a number of friends would have asked him no questions? If so, did they get answers? Such answers must have been all as visionary as the apparition itself—the result of a common delusion. But under the peculiar circumstances of the case, we may be sure what some of these questions must have been. They must have related to points stirring in their minds of the profoundest interest. What about the future? Was He going to withdraw Himself from the public view? Where, and when should they see Him again? Would He confront His enemies? What about His Messianic claims? What course were His followers to adopt? These, or similar questions, must have been inevitable. Did they believe that they got answers to them? If they did, all the answers must also have been visionary, the result of a common delusion; but if they got none, the illusion must have been dissipated.

But let us assume that they did receive visionary answers, which contained promises of future interviews. If these promises were believed to have been fulfilled, then there must have been a whole series of visionary interviews and

record in which a number of persons have believed that they received collectively from a visionary object an extensive body of instructions for the regulation of their future conduct, and have proceeded to act on their reality. At any rate it is quite certain that not one of the abnormal mental conditions which are referred to by Dr. Carpenter in his work on " Mental Physiology," would suffice to produce in a number of persons the belief, that on more than one occasion when they were assembled together, they saw a person who had been recently executed, alive in the midst of them; that they conversed with him, and heard him give definite instructions in reference to their future conduct, altogether different from their former views and ideas, and that on the strength of their persuasion that all this was an objective reality, they founded an institution which has had an historic existence for eighteen hundred years. Such hallucinations lie beyond the regions of the possible; and even if they could be conceived to be possible, that the attempt to erect a mighty institution on their basis should have proved a great success, is inconceivable.

conversations. If they were not fulfilled, the bubble of delusion must have burst. To ask us to accept such theories as affording a rational account of verifiable facts, and these the most important events in history, is to make a demand on our faith compared with which the belief in the most stupendous miracle recorded in the Gospels is a trifle.

In considering this subject it is hardly possible to overestimate the importance of the existence of the Church as a visible institution, which has lived an historic life from a brief interval after the Crucifixion to the present hour. Those who propound this theory forget that this is the most important thing to be accounted for; and treat the whole subject as if they were merely investigating the origin of a ghost story. That this great Society came into existence at a particular date, and at a particular place, is an historic fact. No less certain is it, that the Messianic conception on which it was reconstructed was wholly different in character from that which formed the original bond of union among the earliest followers of Jesus. Such a change must therefore have taken place in their ideas, as was adequate to convert the old bond of union into that on which the Church was actually reconstructed. The Crucifixion rendered the old Messianic conceptions utterly untenable, and unless new ones had been speedily adopted the little Society must inevitably have perished in its founder's grave. But it is the most certain of facts, that the present historic Church came into existence within a few weeks after this event. Consequently, during the interval which elapsed between the Crucifixion and the first attempt to reconstruct it, the disciples must have abandoned the old foundation of a visible Messiah, and adopted the new one, of an invisible and spiritual Messiah. But if the theory of visions is a rational explanation of the facts, not only must the appearances, and the interviews, have been visionary, but the instructions must have been so likewise. What does this mean? That the whole foundation on which the Church of Jesus Christ has been erected—that great Society which has acted mightily on man for good during eighteen centuries of time—is the creation of the fatuous dreamings of a number of disordered imaginations; and all this, we are invited to accept in the name of reason, and philosophy, rather than admit the reality of a miracle.

It will probably be objected that Mahometanism is a case of this description, and that as far as it is not founded on imposture, it rests on the unreal dreams of the prophet of Mecca; and on appearances of the angel Gabriel, which, unless they were deliberate inventions, Mahomet must have mistaken for realities.*

The perusal of the Koran leaves on my own mind the impression, that during the earlier portion of his career the Arabian prophet may have been a sincere fanatic. No less certain is the impression produced by that part of it which is latest in date, that his fanaticism had become united with no small amount of imposture. There are chapters in it which no one in the possession of his senses could have believed that he received from the angel Gabriel, or that they were written on the eternal tablets of the divine mind. On the whole, Mahomet seems to have belonged to that mixed and very mysterious order of character which we occasionally meet with in history and in actual life, which unites self-delusion, fanaticism, and imposture in nearly equal proportions.

But it will be urged, that on the strength of his conviction of the reality of the appearances of the angel, he laid claim to a divine Mission, and on this foundation has succeeded in erecting the Mahomedan Church, and thus a hallucination has been the means of creating a great reality.

* It is not my purpose in this place to draw a general parallel between Christianity and Mahometanism, but simply between the two systems, as far as they can be supposed to have originated in some mental hallucination, in the supposed visionary appearances of the angel Gabriel to Mahomet, those of Our Lord to the Apostles, and the erection of Christianity and Mahometanism on the basis of these delusions.

I answer, that the assertion is inaccurate, that Mahomet succeeded in erecting his Church on this basis. The utmost that can be affirmed is that he was induced to undertake his thirteen years' peaceful mission at Mecca under the persuasion that he had received a divine commission through the appearance of the angel. The results of his peaceful labours however were so inconsiderable, that the small band of believers whom he collected never succeeded in constituting a Church; and if he had confined himself to such labours the Church of Mahomet would never have been created. And no wonder, for the prophet never once made any manifestation of superhuman goodness, holiness or power which could impart credibility to his testimony. He stood in the position of a mere man witnessing to himself, precisely corresponding to what Our Lord meant when He said, "If I bear witness of myself, my witness is not true." His visions he saw alone, and whether they were pure delusions, or these united with an incipient form of that self-delusion which manifested itself in the latter portion of his career, they failed to create a Church until he grasped the sword. There are passages in the Koran which produce the painful impression that even at an early date a spirit of self-delusion was mixed up with his fanaticism. I allude to those in which he assumes a tone of deprecation, on account of his inability to perform a miracle, when his opponents challenged him to work one in attestation of his divine mission. But the real foundation of his Church dates from his advancement to sovereign power, which a fortunate combination of circumstances threw into his hands. With this event begins that portion of his career in which unquestionable self-delusion and imposture become united with the original fanaticism of his character. We cannot now trace the stages of his downward course, but it is probable that his change from fanaticism pure and simple to fanaticism combined with imposture was a gradual one. However this may have been, the contrast between the Christian and the Mahometan Churches is complete, not only in the mode of their foundation, but almost in every other particular. With the possession of royal authority Mahomet ceased to be the missionary, and grasped the sword, his successful use of which formed in the eyes of his followers the real vindication of his divine Mission, and constitutes the foundation on which his Church has been erected. Jesus renounced the sword and was crucified; His cross became His throne; His followers proclaimed Him a spiritual Messiah, who would conquer his kingdom, not by force but by persuasion; and on the basis of His resurrection found His Catholic Church, over which for eighteen centuries He has reigned as its invisible King. If then, as unbelievers allege, the Church of Jesus Christ has been founded on a body of visionary delusions, it is certain that the Church of Mahomet has been founded on the sternest of realities, the sword wielded by the conqueror's hand.

But the theory of visions breaks down at every point where it can be tested by the facts of history. Not only is it the most certain of facts that the Church was reconstructed on the basis of the Resurrection within a very brief interval after the Crucifixion, but it rapidly increased in numbers. To make converts was a necessity of its existence. How could this be effected? There was only one mode, viz. to proclaim the setting up of the New Messianic kingdom; and that the person whom the chiefs of the nation had recently crucified on the charge of being a false Christ, had risen from the dead and become its spiritual King. What did His adversaries, who had just compassed His death, say when within a few weeks they saw what they must have considered a new imposture set up, and multitudes joining the new Society? There was one simple way of crushing the movement—the production of the body. No amount of delusion on the part of the followers of Jesus could have resisted the logic of such an act. If they were unable to produce it, the only possible reason must have been that it had passed from their custody into that of His friends. But such a supposition is destructive of the entire theory of visions; for in that case the belief in His resurrection cannot have been the result of any delusion, but its sole source must have been a deliberately concocted fraud. If, on the other hand, the body was still in the custody of His enemies, it is simply incredible that when the Resurrection was publicly announced they would not have produced it. However the fact may have been, either way it is fatal to the visionary theory. Its only refuge is to suppose that some one stole the body, and thereupon the remainder of His disciples took to seeing visions of the risen Jesus; but for such a fraud it is impossible to assign any adequate motive, and that it became the basis of a set of visionary appearances which were mistaken for realities is incredible.

Pressed by this difficulty some of the adherents of this theory have affirmed that the followers of Jesus retired from Jerusalem after the crucifixion of their Master, to more friendly Galilee; and that these took to seeing visions of Him raised from the dead, and to reconstructing the Church.* The object of this is to gain time for the belief to grow; and to remove the scene of action to a distance from the place of the Crucifixion. The supposition however is not

* The only ground for this assumption is the message sent to the disciples through the women on the morning of the Resurrection: "Go and tell my brethren, that they go before me into Galilee; there shall they see me;" the assertion in St. Matthew's Gospel, that the eleven disciples did see Him in Galilee, and that of the fourth Gospel, which, while it affirms that He was twice previously seen by the Apostolic body at Jerusalem, tells us also that He was seen by seven disciples in Galilee. It should be observed that all three Synoptics concur in stating that the scene of the origin of the belief in the Resurrection was at Jerusalem, prior to any of the disciples leaving it for Galilee. This being so, it is absurd to accept their testimony in the one case and to deny its validity in the other. But, as I have shown above, it is impossible that St. Paul could have been ignorant where the belief originated. Every circumstance connected with him as a persecutor proves that it must have taken a firm root in Jerusalem shortly after the Crucifixion; and that the theory of its having gradually grown up in Galilee, has no other foundation than the imagination of those who have propounded it.

only devoid of all evidence, but directly contradicts the testimony of the Pauline Epistles. These render it certain that the Church was set up at Jerusalem within a very brief interval after the Crucifixion; and that it grew to sufficient numbers to induce the authorities, aided by Paul, to commence against it a sharp persecution. On this point, we are not dependent on the testimony of the Acts; but we have St. Paul's own direct affirmation. This being so, it is certain that both the priests and Paul must have made every exertion to discover the source of the delusion; the necessity of exhibiting the remains of the body, if it was in their possession, was therefore a thing too palpable to be overlooked. Equally certain is it, that if the body, or even its remains, could have been produced, the Church could never have made another convert. Besides, of all the means which were employed to put the Church down, and to convict the alleged witnesses of the Resurrection of delusion or fraud, Paul must have known the minute details; and as the agent of the priests in the persecution, he must have been entrusted with their secret theory as to the origin of the delusion; yet he joined the Church.

The following conclusions are established by the preceding reasonings.

First: the theory of visions totally fails to give us a rational account of the origin of the belief in the Resurrection, and of the unquestionable fact, that the Church was reconstructed on its basis.

Secondly: that if this theory be accepted as a solution of the facts of history, it involves a succession of events equally miraculous with those which it has been propounded for the express purpose of explaining away.

IV.—Against the cogency of these reasonings however an objection has been urged by an eminent modern physiologist, to which it would be a neglect of duty on my part not to give a serious consideration.* It is the more necessary

* Dr. Carpenter lays down, in an article in the *Contemporary Review*, entitled "The Fallacies of Testimony," certain principles which he

to do so, because there can be no doubt that it is one which is felt by no inconsiderable number of thoughtful men. It considers will explain the miracles of the New Testament, and states that "in regard to the New Testament miracles generally, he fails to see in what respect the external testimony in their behalf is stronger than it is for the reality of the miracles attributed to St. Columba," (I quote the entire passage in a Supplement to this Lecture, which see). The expression used is "the New Testament miracles generally." The ordinary reader can only understand that under this expression is included the Resurrection of Our Lord, which is certainly the greatest miracle recorded in the New Testament. This paper was read at a Meeting of the Clergy at Sion College shortly before its publication; and in the printed Syllabus he distinctly invites theologians to join issue with his positions. I have been informed, however, that at the Meeting in question, Dr. Carpenter admitted that some of the principles which he there laid down would not account for the belief in the Resurrection. If this be so, it is greatly to be regretted that he has not stated in his published paper that such is the case; for it is impossible for the reader to arrive at any other conclusion than that the Resurrection must be included among "the New Testament miracles generally." What Dr. Carpenter's views are respecting the Resurrection, and how he explains the origin of the belief in it, I am ignorant; but it seems to me that if he believes in its objective reality, it is inconceivable that he should put himself to the trouble of explaining away the other miracles, while he leaves the Resurrection untouched. At any rate, I can only deal with his published writings, and not with any private explanations of his views. There is no doubt that the whole tendency of the article in question is not only to shake the reader's belief in the truth of the miracles of the New Testament generally, but in the objective reality of the Resurrection. Most of the principles laid down in the article for the purpose of accounting for the belief in a number of well-attested miraculous narratives, and also for that in the phenomena of spiritualism, are unfolded at much greater length in his work on "Mental Physiology." He is of opinion that these spiritualistic phenomena, which rest on a very high form of attestation, are the result of certain abnormal actions of the mind. It is impossible to read his explanations of the origin of these and of various other delusions, without feeling that the principles employed, if true, are capable of being used to bolster up "the theory of Visions," the fallacies of which it is the object of this Lecture to expose. Thus in "the Fallacies of Testimony" we are referred to the case of twelve witnesses, who were firmly persuaded that they saw a person descend through the ceiling of a closed and darkened room. I need hardly say,

is to be regretted that in the form in which the objection has been urged, it is one against the general objective reality of the miracles recorded in the Bible, and not against the specific miracle of the Resurrection. As, however, it is useless to propound a theory, which assigns all these miracles, as far as they are not of legendary origin, to that class of phenomena in which mental hallucinations have been mistaken for external realities, while the Resurrection, the one great evidential miracle of the New Testament, is left untouched, I feel fully justified in concluding that it is intended to be equally applicable to the Resurrection, as well as to the other miracles of the Bible. Otherwise it would be simply nugatory, as it is clear that if the Resurrection was an objective reality, we do not require narrowly to scrutinise the attestation of each of the other miracles of the New Testament; but may be content with the general one which is given by the evangelists.* It cannot be too

that the story is an ugly parody of the appearance of Our Lord to the Apostles at Easter Eve. It may fairly be asked, if Dr. Carpenter's principles are true solutions of the origin of the belief in the one, why are they not equally applicable to account for the belief in the other? It has, therefore, been my simple duty, irrespective of what may be his view about the Resurrection, to point out, not only the contrast in point of evidence between that of all other miraculous narratives and of Our Lord's Resurrection, but also to show that the principles on which he accounts for the belief of numbers of men of cultivated intellects and of some men of eminent scientific attainments, in the phenomena of spiritualism and other similar species of supernaturalism, are totally inadequate to account for the origin of the belief in the Resurrection of Jesus Christ. See Supplement II., Lecture VII.

* What I mean is that even if some of the miracles recorded in the Gospels could be shown to have been incorrectly reported, or to have been the results of the action of powerful faith on the bodies of those who were cured by Our Lord or the Apostles, while the truth of the Resurrection remains unshaken, Christianity loses none of its claims to be accepted as a Divine Revelation. All that this position, if established, could effect, would be to alter our views as to the degree of supernatural assistance afforded to the authors of the Gospels. To offer specific objections against particular miracles, while the greatest

strongly impressed on both sides to this controversy, that the Resurrection is the one great crucial miracle, and with it Christianity as a divine revelation stands or falls. The objection may be briefly stated as follows :—

There are a considerable number of miraculous narratives which as far as attestation goes, rest on an exceedingly strong one; yet their objective reality is not believed by those who have investigated the subject. As however in many cases imposture is out of the question, and it is incontestable that those who have reported them were firmly convinced that they had witnessed them, the only possible mode of accounting for such beliefs is, by assuming that they are the result of mental hallucination.* That the human mind under certain well-known conditions is capable of mistaking subjective impressions for external realities is a thoroughly established scientific fact.† Equally so is it, that a powerful mental action, when concentrated on some portion of our bodily frame, is capable of producing results, which to the unskilled observer have all the appearance of being miraculous.‡ Among the mental conditions capable of producing such a state of mind are unconscious cerebration, prepossession, fixed idea, and that strong expectancy of an

of all miracles remains untouched, is to evade, not to solve, the question at issue.

* Of these, the phenomena sworn to by multitudes of credible witnesses, and accepted by intelligent judges, as objective realities in connection with the witch mania and those of spiritualism, may be cited as crucial examples.

† A large number of well-attested instances of spectral illusions, place this beyond the possibility of doubt. The remarkable fact is that such spectral illusions have been often witnessed by persons whose mental faculties are in other respects sound. The illusions of which I am speaking occur however only in individual cases; many persons do not concur in beholding the same object.

‡ While the power of the mind to act on the body is an unquestionable fact, the limits of its action are, in our present state of scientific knowledge, extremely obscure. Limits, however, certainly exist; and it is no less certain that a considerable number of the miracles recorded in the New Testament lie outside them.

event which bears no inconsiderable analogy to what Christians designate faith.* These, and other similar principles, have in numerous well-attested cases produced impressions of a purely subjective character, which have led persons in other respects possessed of a clear discriminating judgment, to mistake them for external realities. It is urged therefore that if the existence of such delusions in men of otherwise sound judgment is an unquestionable scientific fact, this forms a rational account of the origin of the beliefs in all those well-attested miraculous narratives, which it is impossible to believe to have originated in deliberate fraud. From this the inference has been drawn that it will afford an equally reasonable account of the origin of the miracles recorded in the New Testament. Such is the objection stated in a general form.

The first observation which I would make respecting it is that it makes no distinction between the various classes of miracles which are recorded in its pages. I shall not dispute that there are some which, taken by themselves, and detached from the great character who must have believed that He performed them, may be assigned to causes such as those which have been enumerated by the eminent physiologist above referred to.† But this is to overlook the main point in the Christian argument, as I have exhibited it

* I have only here enumerated the chief of those which are referred to by Dr. Carpenter in his work on "Mental Physiology," having only to do with those which bear directly on the question of the reality of the miracles recorded in the New Testament, and above all, of Our Lord's Resurrection.

† To this class would belong the expulsion of demons; such cures as were slow and gradual, as those referred to in the Epistle of St. James, when he speaks of the efficacy of the prayer of faith, and the anointing of the sick with oil in the name of the Lord; probably the cures effected by the passing of St. Peter's shadow over the sick, and the application of garments taken from St. Paul's person, and in general, those diseases whose immediate cause is disorder of the nervous system; but resurrections from the dead, restoring sight to the blind, hearing to the deaf, sound limbs to the maimed, and several others, belong to a wholly different category.

in the preceding Lectures, resolving, as it does, the whole matter into a question of simple attestation and the sincerity of the beliefs of those who supposed that they had witnessed them. I must repeat it again, that while the Christian miracles rest on a strong attestation, this forms only a portion of the grounds on which we accept them, viz., their connection with the divine Christ, and the powerful influence which has been exerted by Him for good in the moral and spiritual world during eighteen centuries of time. Events which, taken by themselves, may be difficult to believe on an extremely strong attestation, assume a wholly different character when viewed in connection with their attendant circumstances. To treat the question of the reality of the Christian miracles as a simple one of attestation, and nothing more, is entirely to overlook one of the most important points of the argument.

Next. The objection not only confounds together the miracles in the Gospel in a mass, but even complicates them with those in the Old Testament, which stand in a very different position even in point of attestation. I must insist, therefore, on confining the discussion to the real point at issue, and not allowing it to be extended over an indefinite range of subject matter; for the only question worth considering is, does it afford an adequate solution of the origin of the belief in the Resurrection? If the objection fails to account for this miracle, it is simply futile. It is deeply to be regretted that in these discussions unbelievers fail to recognize that this forms the key of the Christian position, which if it can be firmly held, carries with it all the other miracles of the Gospels; and if it cannot be retained, renders the defence or attack on them a useless expenditure of labour, for if it is a fact that Jesus Christ did not rise from the dead, Christianity must have originated in some form of mental hallucination.

I by no means wish to deny that there are narratives of miracles the evidence for which, viewed as a simple question of attestation and of the sincerity of those who have reported them, is stronger than that which we consider necessary to establish the truth of ordinary facts. As many of these are well known, I need not particularize them. They belong to times past; and the discussion of their truth or falsehood is wholly unnecessary in reference to the present controversy. We need not go for well-attested miraculous narratives to the history of the past. We have one of the best, if not the best attested instance of this form of supernaturalism in the midst of us, and occurring, I may say, before our eyes, in the phenomena of Spiritualism; and I ought perhaps to add, in the recently reported miracles in France. I will confine my observations, however, to the former, as it is a subject which has been carefully investigated by the author whose positions I am considering. I have already pointed out the strength of the attestation on which these phenomena rest, and therefore need not further allude to it.

It will be no duty of mine to discuss how far they have originated in fraud or hallucination, or have some foundation in causes hitherto unobserved. I have simply to do with their bearing on the Christian argument, and on the evidence for the objective reality of Our Lord's resurrection. I shall therefore only briefly state the conclusion at which the authority above alluded to has arrived, after having spent several years in the careful investigation of the subject. He is of opinion that after making every allowance for the existence of a large amount of fraud, there remains a considerable residuum of phenomena which cannot be referred to imposture as their origin; and when we consider the persons who have declared their deliberate conviction that they have witnessed them, and the circumstances under which they are alleged to have been manifested, that the idea that they have been the dupes of mere trickery is out of the question. If, therefore, we assume (as the author in question, in company with the majority of intelligent men, does) that they are unreal, the only way of accounting for them is to suppose that they are subjective impressions mistaken for external realities, and he proposes the mental states which I have mentioned above, viz., unconscious cerebration, prepossession, fixed idea, expectancy, and a few others, as adequate to account for the phenomena. As a result of this, we are asked to show that since it would be difficult to prove that the miracles of the New Testament rest on a stronger attestation than these phenomena, the belief in them may not be accounted for in a similar manner.

Viewing it therefore as an argument against the objective reality of the Resurrection, I shall do it no injustice if I put it as follows :—If eminent men of science, physicians, lawyers, even judges, and considerable numbers of men of cultivated intellect, and who have proved themselves not to have been deficient in common sense in other departments of thought, have, under the influence of these mental conditions, mistaken subjective impressions, the pure creations of their own minds, for objective realities, is it not equally likely that the simple minded followers of Jesus were a prey to similar hallucinations ; and, consequently, that the belief in the Resurrection may have owed its origin to delusions of this description? Or to put the same objection from another point of view :—If these phenomena are the work of cunning impostors, who have succeeded in imposing on men of highly cultivated intellects, what guarantee have we that the belief in the miracles of the Gospels, the Resurrection included, has not originated in the followers of Our Lord having been deluded by a similar imposture? If, on the other hand, we assume that they are objectively real, then miracles would cease to have any evidential value, for they would be undistinguishable from this species of natural phenomena, and would afford no evidence of the presence of a superhuman power. As however few whose opinions are of weight will adopt this alternative, it will be needless to discuss its possibility.

Although the reasonings which I have urged in the course of this Lecture against the theory of visions are virtual answers to the difficulties involved in this special form of the objection, yet as a direct challenge has been offered to theologians by an eminent man of science, to distinguish between the evidence which can be adduced for the phenomena of spiritualism and other well-attested miraculous narratives, which are no longer believed by intelligent persons, and that which can be adduced for the reality of the miracles of the New Testament, including Our Lord's resurrection, I will point out definitely in what this distinction consists.

1. The three principles, of Prepossession, Fixed Idea, and Expectancy, which have been laid down as the three chief causes, which render it possible to mistake subjective impressions for objective realities, are incapable of affording any rational account of the origin of the belief in the Resurrection. How far they may be adequate to account for the belief in other miraculous narratives, it will be no part of my duty to inquire. The defender of Christianity has to deal with the Resurrection, and the Resurrection alone. I observe therefore that neither of these three states of mind could have impelled the followers of Jesus to mistake visions of their risen Master for external realities, and this for the simplest of all reasons, viz., that as far as any fixed idea, prepossession, or expectancy of His resurrection is concerned, they must have been non-existent. Instead of expectancy, they must have been in a state of profound despondency, which prepossession or fixed idea could have had no tendency to dissipate. Nothing therefore can be more certain than, whatever influence these principles may have had in generating the beliefs in the miraculous narratives referred to by Dr. Carpenter, they can have had nothing to do with producing a belief in the Resurrection.

2. Not only are they inadequate, but as far as they could have exerted any influence at all, it would have been in a contrary direction. I have proved that not only must the disciples collectively have had visions of Jesus raised from the dead, if their belief was a delusion, but also that they must have held imaginary conversations with Him, in which they

believed that they received His instructions as to the reconstruction of His Church.* To this last fact it is impossible to attach too great importance in dealing with this question. Most certain too is the fact that the Church was reconstructed on a new basis shortly after the Crucifixion ; and the conditions of the case prove the truth of that which our documents affirm, that this reconstruction took place in consequence of the conviction of the disciples that they had received definite instructions from their Master to this effect. This being so, if the belief in the Resurrection was the result of mistaking visionary appearances for realities, the supposed instructions must have been equally visionary. Consequently, if fixed idea, prepossession, and expectancy were sufficiently potent in the minds of the disciples to have created visions of the risen Jesus, they must have created the instructions likewise. But these instructions involved the reconstruction of the Church on a new basis. It is evident, therefore, that they could not have owed their origin to the principles in question ; for if they can be supposed capable of creating a set of visionary instructions they would certainly have been in conformity with their old Messianic prepossessions, and we should have heard nothing of reconstructing the Church on a new basis. Prepossession brings out only what was previously in the mind. Fixed idea is the opposite to change. Of expectancy I have already sufficiently disposed.†

* That such instructions were believed to have been given is distinctly affirmed in Acts i. 3.

† It is simply marvellous that Dr. Carpenter should have written the following passage :—" I fail to see in what respect the external testimony in behalf of the New Testament miracles generally is stronger than it is for the reality of the miracles attributed to St. Columba." What is meant by external testimony ? Surely not the bare counting of the heads of the witnesses, and deciding by a majority without any reference to their intrinsic weight. It is impossible to separate the external testimony from the whole of the attendant circumstances. As I have observed above, the testimony which would be utterly invalid to establish a fact under one set of conditions may

3. The points which I have established in the former Lectures constitute the plainest distinction between the evidence of the miracles of the New Testament, and above all, of the Resurrection, and that of all other miraculous narratives ; for not only does that divine life furnish an adequate reason

be more than sufficient to establish its truth under wholly different ones. The affirmation, therefore, that the resurrection of Jesus Christ, or even that His other miracles rest on no stronger external testimony than those of St. Columba, is to me all but incomprehensible. Dr. Carpenter evidently allows that attendant circumstances form a portion of what he designates external testimony. "'No fewer," says he, " than thirty-two separate religious foundations among the Scots, twenty-one among the Picts, and thirty-seven among the Irish, many of which occupied conspicuous places in the monastic history of the earlier middle ages, seem to have been planted by himself or his immediate disciples. . . . The point on which I wish to lay stress is *the continuity of the history* as trustworthy as any such history can be." But surely the contrast is clear and distinct. If St. Columba and his followers have founded ninety monasteries which have since perished, Jesus Christ and His followers have founded the Christian Church, which after eighteen centuries of energetic life, is vigorous still. St. Columba has exerted some inconsiderable influence on the history of the Scots and Irish ; Jesus Christ has exerted the mightiest influence on the history of man—an influence which at the present hour is capable of verification. The miracle of the Resurrection created the Christian Church, and the proof of its falsehood would subvert it. This is the most certain of facts: but that St. Columba's monasteries rested on the simple basis of his miracles, or that they have perished because his miracles have been disbelieved, we have no evidence to prove. I therefore put the case thus, although it only imperfectly represents the reality of the contrast. Not only will the evidence for the truth of the miracles of St. Columba bear no comparison with that which can be adduced for the resurrection of Jesus Christ, but in accordance with the principle referred to in a former note, the evidence which may be powerless to prove the performance of miracles in connection with such a personage as St. Columba may be more than sufficient to prove them in connection with one who is not only the one great Catholic man, whose influence I have endeavoured to describe in the second, third, and fourth Lectures of this course, but who has exerted an influence for good "greater than that of all the disquisitions of philosophers, and than all the exhortations of moralists."

for the existence of the miracles; but the one is the counterpart of the other. I have proved that the energetic presence of a superhuman power in Christianity is a verifiable fact in the history of the past, and of the present. Of this power the miracle of the Resurrection is the foundation. However strong may be the persuasion of various intelligent persons, that they have witnessed a number of occurrences which we cannot distinguish from miracles, not one of them can produce an attestation of this description. The resurrection of Jesus Christ from the dead has operated mightily during eighteen centuries of history, and is operating mightily at this hour. To spiritualism and other kindred phenomena, the language of the old prophet, may still be applied with perfect justice: "Show us things that are to come hereafter, that we may know that ye are gods; yea, do good, or do evil, that we may be dismayed, and behold it together. Behold ye are of nothing, and your work of nought."

4. The belief in the Resurrection has created the Catholic Church of Jesus Christ and all the mighty results which it has wrought in history. The spiritualistic and other kindred marvels have created, and to all appearance will create, no institution either good or evil.

5. The resurrection of Jesus Christ has operated as the most elevating power which has been exerted on mankind. These alleged manifestations, with their kindred phenomena, instead of elevating men, degrade them.*

* Mr. Wallace is not insensible to the fact that the silliness of a large number of the communications from the spirit world forms a very serious obstacle to the belief in their objective reality. His explanation of it is very singular, I might almost say, if the subject were not so serious a one, amusing. It is as follows:—A large majority of those who die have during life habitually talked nonsense; it is therefore no wonder if, when they have entered into the world of spirits, they still continue to do so, and only raise themselves above it by slow and gradual steps. I also refer to another of his positions as showing the tendency of these views. He informs us that numerous as have been the communications from the spirit world, some of

6. While the Resurrection has changed the history of the world, the spiritualistic manifestations, including the best attested miraculous stories, have been barren of result. Yet if the former were objective realities, they must certainly have been able to produce very palpable results. It is clear that they could largely aid the administration of justice in the detection of crime; but in this respect they neither do good, nor do evil. No passion is stronger in the human mind than the love of gain. Yet if the facts reported are not delusions, these manifestations must be able to afford the means of gratifying it. But while the resurrection of Jesus Christ is the key which unlocks all the events of history, manifestations of this kind effect and have effected nothing.

7. Our judgment of the credibility of facts does not rest on mere attestation, but is largely modified by the consideration whether the actions are in conformity with the character of the agents. Here again the contrast between the miracles of Christianity and the best attested of all other miraculous narratives is complete. Those recorded in the New Testament are all worthy of the great Character to whom they are attributed. The other class are so undignified and grotesque, as to destroy the weight of the testimony which is alleged in their favour.

8. For the occurrence of the Resurrection and the other miracles of the New Testament an adequate reason can be assigned. They form a portion of a divine revelation, which is in harmony with the facts of the moral and spiritual world. But the spiritualistic phenomena are out of harmony with all the known facts of the universe; and if real, would be destructive of its moral order.

which are of an elevated character, its inhabitants, as far as these communications have yet informed us, know no more about God and Christ than we do. Yet this eminent scientific observer tells us that from a Sadducean unbelief in the existence of a spiritual world he has been converted by the stern logic of facts.

9. Even as a question of mere testimony the contrast is no less complete. The resurrection of Jesus, when it was first reported, could have been subjected to the test of verification, by the simple production of His body, by those who denied its reality. It is impossible for our opponents to subject the phenomena in question to any similar test.

10. The altered form, and the want of immediate recognition of the risen Jesus on the part of His followers has been alleged as a ground for believing that the appearance must have been visionary, and unreal; and at first sight the objection seems not devoid of plausibility. I reply however that on the contrary, it forms a proof of truthfulness, such as is possessed by no other supernatural occurrence. The fact, as stated by the Evangelists, is strictly in conformity with the conditions of the case. What is the real affirmation made? Not that Jesus was raised to die again; but with a body no longer subject to the conditions of mortality. This being so, it is not only in the highest degree probable — I may say, it is certain—if the Resurrection was an objective reality, that the body in which He rose from the dead, would have undergone some species of transformation from that which He wore previously to His crucifixion. If the Evangelists had asserted that there was no difficulty in recognizing Him, it would have cast suspicion on their entire narrative. But if the belief in the Resurrection had been the result of mistaking subjective impressions for objective realities, the last thing which would have occurred to them would have been to attribute an altered appearance to their risen Master. Neither unconscious cerebration, fixed idea, prepossession, or expectancy, can account for so remarkable a fact.

Such are the obvious distinctions between the evidence for Our Lord's resurrection and that which can be adduced in favour of the best attested of other miraculous occurrences.

Let me notice one further objection which has been adduced against the miracles of the New Testament before I dismiss this portion of the subject. It has been alleged that some of them may be accounted for as the result of the action of powerful faith or expectancy on the bodily frame, and that it is a well-known fact that such an effect is possible, and that to such a degree, as to bear to the uninitiated the appearance of a miracle. As this objection requires more space for its discussion than can be given to it here, I will offer a few remarks on it in a Supplement. For the present it will be sufficient to observe, that as an objection against the Christian miracles it is futile; for it is impossible to account for the origin of the belief in the resurrection of Our Lord on any such principle; and until this can be done, the attempt to explain away the other miracles recorded in the New Testament as the result of natural causes, is a mere waste of time and ingenuity.

V. The theory of visions being thus proved to be untenable, there only remains one alternative to the acceptance of the Resurrection as a fact which it will be necessary to discuss at length, viz., the theory which affirms that Jesus did not die from the effects of His crucifixion, but that He was taken down in a state of syncope, which was mistaken for death; that He gradually recovered; and that in some inaccurate rendering of this fact has originated the belief of the Resurrection. As this theory has been propounded by several eminent writers, it will be necessary to give it a brief consideration, although it is encumbered with many of the difficulties which attend the theory of visions, and with several which are peculiarly its own.

Respecting the chief facts on which the question must be discussed there will be no disagreement. It will be readily admitted that crucifixion did not necessarily involve the death of the crucified person. If he were taken down in time and carefully attended to, recovery was possible, although the chances were against it. This we know from the testimony of Josephus, who procured the order of Titus for taking down from the cross three of his crucified friends, after they had been suspended for several hours. By means of careful treatment one recovered, while two died. As, however, the Jews were at this time crucified by the Romans by thousands, it may be a question whether they all underwent the terrible infliction of a scourging previously to being fastened to the cross,—a point which must have an important bearing on the probability of recovery. The time too which, according to the accounts of the Evangelists, elapsed between Our Lord's crucifixion and His death, was not sufficient under ordinary circumstances to have extinguished life. It has, therefore, been affirmed that we have no evidence that He actually died; that it is highly probable that He did not, and that His recovery was in some way or other mistaken for a resurrection.

Respecting the possibility of recovery under such circumstances, the question into whose hands the body was committed is a vital one. The only authority for affirming that His friends obtained possession of it is that of our Evangelists.* But if their affirmation is good for this, it must be admitted to be so for a great deal more. To surrender the body for honorable burial would have been contrary to the Roman practice. His Jewish adversaries, who brought about His crucifixion, and the soldiers who accomplished it, and who from the frequency of such executions must have been familiar with the symptoms of that kind of death, were not likely to have allowed the body to pass out of their custody while life remained. If on the other hand the body continued in the custody of His enemies, recovery would have been impossible.

But viewed as an historical question, the supposition that the story of the Resurrection has originated in a recovery from the effects of crucifixion, is negatived by the following facts :—The theory is a purely modern invention. None of the adversaries of Christianity during the early ages, when

---

* It is very singular to observe the facility with which those against whose opinions I am reasoning quote the Gospels as authorities, when they can find any fact or allusion in them which can be made to favour their own views, while in other respects they treat them as unhistorical.

crucifixion still continued a common mode of punishment, ever expressed a suspicion on the subject. It is clear that such a suspicion never crossed the minds of His Jewish adversaries; nor had it ever occurred to the Apostle Paul, who, when he was a persecutor, must have investigated the entire subject; and after he became a Christian, must certainly have known whether Jesus was living somewhere in retirement, or had since expired from exhaustion or premature decay. Consequently, although it is not denied that a person who had been crucified might escape with his life, if carefully attended to, the facts above referred to demolish utterly the theory that it can have been the case in this particular instance.

But even, if it were not so, the affirmation that we have no evidence that Jesus really died, would be quite irrelevant to the present issue; for it is not only necessary to prove that he *may* not have died, but that he actually *did not*—and then the far more serious duty is incumbent on those who propound this theory to show how it is possible that the story of the Resurrection and the reconstruction of the Church on it as its basis, can have originated, if the only foundation on which it rested was that Jesus slowly recovered from His wounds, lived somewhere for a while in retirement, and afterwards shared the common fate of mortality.

But let us suppose, for the sake of argument, that Jesus awoke from a state of syncope or swoon in the sepulchre in which he was laid by His friends in the belief that He had expired; that He succeeded in creeping to the house of some friend,* where under careful treatment He recovered, and that He thereupon withdrew into retirement, out of the reach of His enemies. How, I ask, could such facts as these have become the foundation of the belief in His resur-

* It should be observed that this supposition is attended with difficulties which are insuperable. First: it involves the assumption that He was buried in a sepulchre, and not in a common grave. If He had been interred in the latter, no resuscitation would have been possible. But the fact that He was interred in a sepulchre we learn only from the

rection, and of the reconstruction of the Church on the basis of His spiritual Messiahship? We shall doubtless be told that such a belief might grow up after a time among a body of very credulous people.* How long, I ask, is the interval that would be required for its growth? Would it be a few days, weeks, months or years? I feel confident that if those who propound this theory will carefully consider

pages of the Evangelists. Independently of their testimony nothing would have been more improbable than that such should have been the case, as to surrender a criminal for honourable burial would have been contrary to Roman custom. Secondly: a sepulchre would have been a place very unfavourable to the supposed recovery, which must have been sufficiently complete to have enabled Him to convey Himself to the house of a friend. To aid in effecting it, the assistance of the spices used at the burial has been invoked. How far they would have been useful for this purpose I know not; but here again the fact that the body was wrapped up with them is known only from the pages of the Evangelists; and, taken by itself, would under the circumstances have been an occurrence in the highest degree improbable. Thirdly: it is difficult to imagine how a man in such a state of extreme exhaustion as that which is pre-supposed could have succeeded in freeing himself from the bandages and wrappings in which he was incased. Fourthly: if on leaving the sepulchre those who interred the body closed up the entrance, it is difficult to imagine by what means short of a miracle a man in this wounded and lacerated condition could have obtained egress from the tomb; and that the sepulchre was left open is simply incredible. Nothing is easier than to affirm that He succeeded in getting out of the sepulchre, and in taking refuge with a friend; but the, question must be answered, how was this possible under the circumstances? In this world of facts it is useless to make assumptions which conflict with the realities of things, and then propound them as a philosophical explanation of the origin of the greatest institution that has ever existed among men.

* Nothing is more common in this controversy than the vague assertion that such a belief would grow up in the course of time. The fact is, that the time at command for the growth of myths, legends, tendencies, and compromises, in short, for the whole apparatus necessary for the manufacture of the Christ of the Gospels and Epistles, out of a purely human Jesus, is very limited and definite. In this respect criticism is in a very disadvantageous position, compared with those scientific modern speculators, who seek to manufacture this

the question, the shortest interval which they will demand as necessary for the growth of such a delusion, will be vastly in excess of that which the unquestionable historical conditions of the case can concede to them.

Let us suppose that he succeeded in taking refuge in the house of a friend; in that case the matter must have been kept profoundly secret in order to prevent it from coming to the ears of His enemies; and it would have been impossible during the time of His gradual recovery, and until He had escaped to some place of safety, to breathe one word about His resurrection, lest their suspicions should be aroused. How long, I ask, did all this take? At any rate, he must either have died under cure, or slowly recovered. If we accept the former alternative, then most of the difficulties which I have discussed in connection with the theory of visions must be surmounted before it is possible to erect the belief in the Resurrection on such a basis; and in addition to these, it is impossible to advance one step without assuming that some one or more of His friends must have been guilty of a deliberate fraud. If, on the other hand, it is assumed that He recovered, how, I ask, in the name of common sense, could it have been possible to mistake a gradual recovery for a resurrection from the dead? Is it believable that Jesus Himself could have laboured under the delusion that His awakening in agony from His wounds in the tomb, His retirement to the house of a friend; His gradual recovery, and His survival in an exhausted condition, was an actual resurrection from the dead? If the real facts were such as this theory assumes them to have been, I feel confident that the overwhelming majority of those who do not desire to prop up a foregone conclusion, will agree that the only way in which it can have given rise to

Universe and all its wondrous adaptations, without the intervention of an intelligent Creator. The latter have eternity at their back; the indefinite periods of which they can play with as counters; the former are confronted at every step by the stern facts of history and the realities of human life.

the belief in the Resurrection, is that it must have been a deliberately concocted fraud ; or, in other words, that the Gospel of holiness is based on a foundation of conscious imposture.

But further, if the belief was set on foot by two or three disciples, how were the others to be got to accept it without being favoured with a sight of Him ? Some story must have been invented to make the matter plausible. What could have been the form of it ? Is it believable that the other disciples at once accepted the tale as a veritable reality without receiving any information as to what was become of Him ? Nor is this all. It must never be forgotten that the Church had to be reconstructed, and a claim of Messiahship set up on this as a new basis. Who suggested the change ? Will any one affirm that it was Jesus Himself ? Yet it is impossible to believe that His followers would venture to change His Messianic character from that of a visible to an invisible Christ, while they believed that He was living in retirement, unless they had also believed that He had given definite instructions to do so. If then we would avoid charging Jesus and His followers with a deliberately planned pious fraud, we must assume that He must not only have mistaken His gradual recovery for a resurrection, but deliberately determined to shift the basis of his Messiahship; and while living for the remainder of His life in privacy out of the reach of His enemies, to direct His disciples to propagate the belief that He was risen from the dead, and on this foundation to erect His Church.

If this be true, it is impossible to account for it on any theory which is consistent with honesty. It is impossible to believe that a man who had claimed to be the Messiah ; who by that claim had so provoked the public authorities that they had procured his crucifixion; who only slowly recovered from his wounds, and kept himself for the remainder of his life in retirement, could have believed himself to be the Christ; or that those of his followers who had access to him could have mistaken him for one.

Further: if Jesus died shortly after His supposed resurrection, some of His followers must have been cognisant of the fact. In that case it is impossible to acquit them of having invented the fiction that He had left the world, and gone up into heaven. If, on the other hand, we suppose that He remained several years in retirement, the same fiction must have been propagated while He was still living. In either case, the most liberal attribution of credulity and enthusiasm to His followers will fail to account for the origin of the delusion. The supposition of fraud is the only possible solution, a fraud which must have succeeded in removing whole mountains of difficulties, such as I have enumerated in considering the theory of visions, and which it will be unnecessary again to refer to. The truth is, that this theory could never have been suggested by those who have propounded it, if they had considered that the problem before them was not simply to put forward a possible account of the origin of a belief in a resurrection, but one which would satisfy the conditions of history, and account for the erection of the Christian Church on the basis that its Founder rose again from the dead.

One possible theory remains; but its bare statement will be its sufficient refutation. It is this. The body was committed to the custody of His friends, and interred by them; but it was removed by His enemies without their knowledge. On entering the tomb, His friends to their surprise found it empty; and in their inability to account for what had become of it, they adopted the theory that He must have risen from the dead; and thereupon they proceeded to reconstruct the Church. Such a theory, in addition to impossibilities, which are peculiar to itself, has to encounter all those which I have brought before you in the course of the foregoing argument.

The preceding reasonings therefore establish the following conclusion. The assumption that Jesus Christ rose from the dead is the only one which will satisfy the historic facts. The account therefore which the Church has always given of its origin is the only true one—He has risen from the dead. His resurrection being thus established, the Gospels take their genuine place in history; the Synoptics as three reports of the actions and teaching of Jesus Christ, as they were reported by His followers, and composed within that interval of time during which such traditionary reminiscences must have preserved all their freshness; and the fourth Gospel, as an account of the same divine life derived from an independent source of information. This in an evidential point of view is all that we require. It establishes the truth of Christianity as a divine revelation. To determine anything beyond this does not belong to that branch of theology which is strictly evidential; and to encumber ourselves with the defence of unnecessary positions tends rather to weaken than to strengthen our defence.

SUPPLEMENT I.

The appearance of Our Lord to St. Paul stands on a different basis from the appearances which I have discussed in the preceding Lecture. It will be therefore desirable to give a brief consideration to its evidential value.

The affirmation in the 15th chapter of the First Epistle to the Corinthians with respect to the interview with Our Lord on the road to Damascus puts it on a par with the appearances to the original disciples, affords decisive proof that Paul was fully convinced of its objective reality, "And last of all, He was seen of me also, as of one born out of due time." The Epistles, however, furnish us with no information respecting the circumstances, which can only be learned from the Acts of the Apostles.

Two facts, however, they establish on the Apostle's

express testimony. First, that previously to his conversion, he had persecuted the Church of God and wasted it. Secondly, that after his conversion, he became its most laborious Missionary, and that the whole of his future life was one devoted act of self-sacrifice to the service of his Master.

The Acts of the Apostles furnish us with three accounts of the circumstances attending his conversion; one the direct account of the historian, and the remaining two in speeches purporting to have been uttered by St. Paul. Putting these accounts together, the facts are as follows:—

St. Paul left Jerusalem inspired with a deadly hatred against the followers of Jesus, and in possession of letters commendatory from the High Priest to the Synagogues at Damascus, for the purpose of raising a persecution against the Christians in that city, and, if possible, bringing them bound to Jerusalem. As Paul's party approached the city, they found themselves surrounded by a light from heaven, "above the brightness of the sun." This light was seen by Paul, and his companions, who thereupon prostrated themselves to the ground. In the midst of this light, Paul saw a glorious figure, who addressed him by name, and expostulated with him for persecuting Him, and who in answer to Paul's inquiry who He was, declared that He was Jesus. Here occurs a slight variation between the narrative of the historian, and one of the Apostle's own accounts of the same transaction, the former telling us that Paul's companions "stood speechless, hearing a voice, but seeing no man," while the latter states that his companions "saw the light, and were afraid, but they heard not the voice of Him that spake to him." According to the second account of St. Paul a prolonged conversation took place between him and the person who thus appeared to him. The effect of the light on the Apostle was to strike him blind, so that he had to be led by the hand of his companions, and conducted to Damascus. During three days he continued without sight, after which he recovered it by a miraculous interposition, on which occasion something resembling scales fell from his eyes. He forthwith joined the Christian Church, and during the next twenty-five years devoted himself in an unceasing course of labour and suffering to the service of his Master.

Such are the facts. The utmost has been made of the slight variation in the accounts above referred to, as throwing suspicion on their historical accuracy; but the Greek is quite consistent with the fact that St. Paul's companions heard the sound of a voice, but did not distinguish articulate words. Even if the unhistorical character of the Acts of the Apostles were granted, it is in the highest degree improbable that a forger, and especially one who has displayed such acuteness in his forgery, would have been betrayed into so palpable a contradiction as to have affirmed in the same work that Paul's companions did, and did not hear the voice.

The following consideration fully establishes the historical character of the narrative given in the Acts. Whatever objections may be urged against the earlier chapters, the results of modern investigation have proved that no document which has been handed down from ancient times rests on a firmer historical foundation than the twenty-seventh chapter, which gives us the account of St. Paul's voyage and shipwreck. No shadow of doubt can rest on the mind of any one who studies this chapter, that the person who composed it was one of Paul's companions. The perusal of the preceding chapters renders it no less certain that the author of them had accompanied the Apostle in his Missionary travels during several years. This fact is alone sufficient to establish the authenticity of the account. It is incredible that a person who had been Paul's companion for a considerable period, did not receive from him some account of the event to which he attributed his conversion; and which had changed him from a persecutor into the most devoted Missionary of the Christian cause. This being so, it follows that the threefold account as we read it in the Acts, relates the circumstances of St. Paul's conversion as he himself believed in them.

Such then are the facts to be accounted for. Only two theories respecting them are possible. Either the facts were objective realities; or the Apostle was labouring under some species of mental hallucination.

Even unbelievers must admit that the former, if true, is a philosophical account of the facts and of the results which followed them. The question therefore arises, Can any theory of visions afford an adequate solution of them?

The following is the most plausible explanation which unbelief has propounded of the conversion of St. Paul on the supposition that the appearance of Jesus was due to mental hallucination. The Apostle was a man of that exalted and enthusiastic temperament which leads those subject to it to confound the subjective and the objective. This is said to be proved, not only by the whole tenour of his writings, but by the fact that after his conversion, he was in the habit of seeing visions, and falling into trances. This state of mind, acting on the beliefs in which he had been educated, made him an uncompromising opponent of Christianity, and led him to take a very active part in the murder of Stephen. The demeanour of the Martyr however had profoundly impressed him; and the whole scene continued to haunt his imagination. In this divided state of mind, yet with his former hatred of Jesus still in the ascendant, he started for Damascus with the commission from the Jewish priests. His journey gave him ample time for meditation. The image of the murdered Stephen, and the work of persecution on which he was about to enter, produced in him a feeling of deep distraction. As he approached Damascus, a natural phenomenon, such as a thunderstorm, and a flash of lightning occurred. Paul, already in a state approaching frenzy, fell to the earth in terror. His excited imagination created the image of Jesus himself, and made him fancy that he heard his voice saying, "Saul, Saul, why persecutest thou me," the voice which he heard being nothing but the echo of his thoroughly aroused conscience. Further meditation led him to join the Christian Church, and the same temperament which had hitherto made him its most active persecutor, converted him into its most energetic Missionary.

The theory of visions in this case is free from several of the difficulties with which it is beset when offered as a rational account of the appearances to the original followers of Jesus. In the latter case it was necessary to assume that bodies of disciples, when assembled together, saw visions which they mistook for realities. In the case of Paul the statement of the historian is express, that he alone saw Our Lord, and heard His voice, and that his companions saw only the light, and heard a sound: but that they heard no articulate words. The further difficulty in the case of the disciples, that they must have mistaken visionary conversations containing directions for the reconstruction of the Church, for realities, applies with less force in the case of the Apostle, who only believed that he received a direction in a single interview, to preach the Gospel to the Gentiles. In addition to this, the idea of the resurrection of Jesus, and his exaltation to mighty power in the kingdom of God, was now no longer a novelty; and the investigations of Paul the persecutor must have fully disclosed that such was the belief of the Christian Church.

On the other hand, St. Paul's case is encumbered with peculiar difficulties of its own. While acting as a persecutor, it is simply incredible that he did not sift the whole matter to the bottom. He must have been familiar with the account which was given by the disciples of Jesus. He must have been thoroughly acquainted with the theory propounded on the subject by the Jewish priests. As a member of the Cilician Synagogue, which disputed with Stephen, he must have urged all his objections against the arguments of the Protomartyr. Let us suppose that his reasonings broke down. Yet he was still unconvinced; and remained a furious persecutor. He must therefore have been under the influence of the strongest prepossession and fixed idea, and wholly devoid of expectancy. Consequently, his state of mind must have been altogether incompatible with seeing a vision of Jesus risen from the dead, and mistaking it for a reality.

The idea that the demeanour of Stephen had produced any powerful impression on him is not only a bare assumption, without one single atom of evidence to support it, but is contrary to his own express affirmations. Conscience had not remonstrated with him up to the time of the journey to Damascus. "I have lived," he says, addressing the Jewish Council, "in all good conscience towards God until this day." Not a single hint that he was in any sense a conscience-stricken man, or that he was in a relenting mood, occurs in any of his Epistles. On the contrary, to the Galatians he writes: "Ye have heard of my conversation in times past in the Jews' religion, how that beyond measure I persecuted the Church of God, and wasted it; and profited in the Jews' religion above many my equals in mine own nation, being more exceedingly zealous for the traditions of my fathers. But when it pleased God, who separated me from my mother's womb, and called me by his grace, to reveal his Son in me, that I might preach him among the heathen; immediately I conferred not with flesh and blood." Equally decisive is the address to King Agrippa, "Many of the saints did I shut up in prison, having received authority from the chief priests; and when they were put to death, I gave my voice against them. And I punished them oft in every synagogue, and compelled them to blaspheme; and being exceedingly mad against them, I persecuted them even unto strange cities. Whereupon as I went to Damascus with authority and commission from the chief priests," &c.

If the Apostle has correctly described his feelings in either of these passages, and the second of them is beyond all dispute written by himself, they utterly negative the idea of his being in such a disturbed state of mind at the time of the journey as could have produced the visionary appearance.

If it was simply imaginary, it can be accounted for on no principle known to mental science. The Apostle tells us that at the time of the journey, he was under the strongest influence of those kinds of prepossession and fixed idea which would have produced a precisely contrary result. "I was exceedingly zealous," says he, "for the traditions of my fathers." "Being exceedingly mad against them, I persecuted them even unto strange cities." His prepossessions and fixed ideas were therefore those of extreme Judaism and narrow-minded bigotry. If such a state of mind could generate visions at all, they must assuredly have been of a character precisely opposite to those which St. Paul imagined that he saw. Even if they could have suggested to him the appearance of the risen Jesus (which is impossible), we should never have heard one word about preaching Christianity to the Gentiles.

The thunderstorm and the lightning-flash are not only a mere guess on the part of those who have suggested them, but are directly contrary to the evidence we possess. Neither narrative says one word about darkness. The time of the appearance is definitely stated to have been at noonday, and it is implied that the sun was shining. Under such circumstances no flash of lightning could have exceeded the sun in brightness, and the brightness was seen by the Apostle's companions as well as by himself. The hypothesis of an attack of sunstroke would be far more probable under the circumstances than a flash of lightning; but even if assumptions wholly devoid of foundation can be admitted as accounting for one of the most important events in history, no principle then operating in the Apostle's mind could have produced the results with which the vision was attended, viz., a complete revolution in his ideas, and a self-devotion to an entirely new course of action, which ended only with his life.

One little circumstance mentioned by the historian is utterly incompatible with any theory that the appearance on the road to Damascus was only a subjective vision.

When Paul recovered his sight, we are told that there fell from his eyes "as it had been scales." This fact, if true (and it seems impossible to ascribe it to the inventive powers of the historian), points to an objective reality of some kind. Any theory of visions, therefore, is simply worthless until it can explain how it was that Paul was stricken with blindness, and that three days after, when he recovered his sight, scales fell from his eyes. It will hardly be urged that the scales were visionary ones, or that they could have resulted from the action of Paul's mind on his body.

So far are the contents of the Epistles from justifying the observation that St. Paul was a man of such a mental temperament as to have led him to confound between the subjective and the objective, that they point to a conclusion directly opposite. As I have observed in the sixth Lecture, if he had been a man of this temperament, the discussion respecting the supernatural gifts must have afforded ample opportunity for its display. Yet during the whole discussion we find nothing but the soundest reason and the acutest mental discrimination. As I have observed, the calm judgment exhibited by the Apostle throughout the entire discussion utterly negatives the hypothesis in question.

The Epistles unquestionably affirm that he had truth communicated to his mind by revelation. But to erect on this fact the theory that he was a man of that peculiar temperament which leads to the confounding of the subjective and the objective is to assume the point at issue. On the contrary, the Epistles abound with examples of his discriminating between the workings of his own mind and the divine illumination with which he believed himself to have been favoured; and they do not furnish us with a single instance in which the two are confounded together. The distinction between the affirmations of Paul in his human character—even those which he made, as one who had "obtained mercy of the Lord to be faithful," and "believing that he had the Spirit of God," is everywhere clearly marked off from that knowledge which he believed to have been imparted to him by express revelation.

The following is the only apparent instance to the contrary, which will therefore require a brief consideration. The Apostle writes, " It is not expedient for me doubtless to glory. I will come to visions and revelations of the Lord. I knew a man in Christ about fourteen years ago (whether in the body, I cannot tell; or whether out of the body, I cannot tell: God knoweth); such an one caught up to the third heaven. And I knew such a man (whether in the body, or out of the body, I cannot tell: God knoweth;) How that he was caught up into paradise, and heard unspeakable words, which it is not lawful (ἐξὸν, possible) for a man to utter. . . . And lest I should be exalted above measure through the abundance of the revelations," &c. (2 Cor. xii. 1-7.)

This passage is remarkable, and clearly establishes the following facts :—

First: that St. Paul somewhere near the time of his conversion believed himself to have been favoured with a preternatural illumination respecting divine truth.

Secondly : that this illumination was imparted by means of visions.

Thirdly : that in the particular vision in question, his own consciousness was unable to determine whether he was "in the body or out of it."

Fourthly : that as far as consciousness was concerned, he seemed to be translated out of this world into a higher sphere.

So far then is this passage from justifying the idea that he was in the habit of confounding the subjective and the objective, that it proves that on ordinary occasions he carefully discriminated between them. He tells us twice over, that on this particular occasion he could not tell for certain whether he was in the body or out of it. He was fully aware that it was a vision, but whether it was attended with a local transportation of his personality, he was ignorant.

The twofold affirmation therefore of his ignorance on this particular occasion proves that he was in the habit of exercising a careful discrimination between his visions and the creations of his own mind; and consequently that his mental character was the opposite of that which the propounders of the theory, that the appearance of Our Lord on the road to Damascus was a creation of his own disordered imagination, are compelled to assume.

The other visions mentioned by St. Luke in the Acts of the Apostles, such as the trance in the temple, the vision of the man of Macedonia, the subsequent vision of Our Lord after St. Paul's arrest, and the appearance of the angel during his voyage to Rome, are of a precisely similar character; and instead of affording the smallest countenance to the opinion that he could not discriminate on these occasions between the subjective and the objective, prove that he was constantly in the habit of doing so.

Let me briefly recapitulate.

Paul left Jerusalem for Damascus " breathing out threatenings and slaughter against the disciples of the Lord," " being exceedingly mad against them," " exceedingly zealous for the traditions of his fathers." Such a state of mind both philosophy and science teach us to be the direct opposite to that which would have been necessary for seeing a vision of Jesus and mistaking it for a reality, even if we assume, contrary to the conditions of the history, that the Apostle encountered a thunderstorm on the way. The Apostle and his companions believed themselves to have been encompassed suddenly by a light brighter than the sun. They fall to the earth. Paul beholds a divine appearance, which addresses him by name; expostulates with him for persecuting Him; affirms that He is Jesus, and informs him that he shall be instructed in what His pleasure is, after he has entered the city. The appearance deprives the Apostle of his eye-sight. Three days he continues in Damascus in profound meditation, after which he openly joins the Christian Church, on which occasion he recovers his sight by the *visible falling of scales from his eyes.* From this day forth to the end of his life, St. Paul became the most zealous of Christian Missionaries. That Jesus, who had been the object of his deepest hatred, became the object of his most ardent love. His narrow-mindedness and zeal for the traditions of his fathers, was changed into the most Catholic Christianity and a readiness to encounter every danger in its propagation. The subsequent life of the persecutor was one continued act of self-devotion to the cause of the persecuted, despite of all dangers and sufferings. Such are the facts. Let philosophy or science, if it can, afford any rational account of them on the supposition that they were the result of mental hallucination.

SUPPLEMENT II.

The following are Dr. Carpenter's positions as stated at the conclusion of his article on "the Fallacies of Testimony:"—

"Now I fail to see what stronger external evidence there is of any of the supernatural occurrences chronicled in the Old Testament, than that which is afforded by the assured conviction of this Jewish community as to what is taking place at the present time under their own eyes. And assuming, as I suppose most of us should be ready to do, that the testimony to these contemporary wonders would break down under the rigorous test of a searching examination, I ask whether we are not equally justified in the assumption that a similar scrutiny, if we had the power to apply it, would in like manner dispose of many of the narratives of old time, either as distortions of real occurrences, or as altogether legendary.

"In regard to the New Testament miracles generally, whilst failing to see in what respect the external testimony in their behalf is stronger than it is for the reality of the miracles attributed to St. Columba, I limit myself at present to the following questions :—

"First. Whether the 'miracles of healing' may not have had a foundation of reality in 'natural' agencies perfectly well known to such as have scientifically studied the action of the mind upon the body. In regard to one form of these supposed miracles—the casting out of devils—I suppose that I need not in these days adduce any argument to disprove the old notion of 'demoniacal possession,' in the face of the fact that the belief in such 'possession' in the case of lunatics, epileptics, &c., and the belief in the powers of 'exorcists' to get rid of it, is still as prevalent among Eastern nations as it was in the time of Christ. And I suppose, too, that since travellers have found that the Pool of Bethesda is fed by an intermittent spring, few now seriously believe in the occasional appearance of an 'angel' who moved its water; or in the cure of the first among the expectant sick who got himself placed in it, by any other agency than his 'faith' in the efficacy of the means. I simply claim the right to a more extended application of the same critical method.

"Secondly. Whether we have not a similar right to bring to bear on the study of the Gospel narratives, the same *principles* of criticism as guided the early Fathers in their construction of the Canon, with all the enlightenment which we derive from the subsequent history of Christianity, aided by that of other forms of religious belief. The early Christian Fathers were troubled with no doubts as to the reality of miracles in themselves; and they testified to the healing of the sick, the casting out of devils, and even the raising of the dead, as well-known facts of their own time. But they rejected some current narratives of the miraculous which they did not regard as adequately authenticated, and others as considering them puerile. Looking at it not only as our right, but as our duty, to bring the higher critical enlightenment of the present day to bear upon the study of the Gospel records, I ask whether both past and contemporary history do not afford such a body of evidence of a prevalent tendency to exaggeration and distortion, in the representation of actual occurrences in which 'supernatural' agencies are supposed to have been concerned, as entitles us, without attempting any detailed analysis, to believe that if we could know *what really did happen*, it would often prove to be something very different from what is narrated.

"By such a general admission, we may remove the serious difficulties to which I alluded at the outset—difficulties which must, I think, have been present to the mind of Locke, when he recorded, in the Common-place Book published by Lord King, the remarkable aphorism that 'the doctrine proves the miracles, rather than the miracles the doctrine.'"
—*Contemporary Review*, Jan. 1876.

I should in justice to Dr. Carpenter quote a brief passage from the earlier portion of the article:—

"And, moreover, I observe it to be among those, in various religious denominations, who are converging to the conclusion that the 'authority' of Christianity most surely consists in the direct appeal it makes to the hearts and consciences of mankind,—who most fully recognize in the life, teaching, and death of Christ, that manifestation of the Divine (ἀπαύγασμα τῆς δόξης καὶ χαρακτὴρ τῆς ὑποστάσεως αὐτοῦ) which constitutes him their Master and Lord,—and who most earnestly and constantly aim to fashion their own lives on the model of his,—that there is the greatest readiness to admit that the records of that life are tinged by the prepossessions, and subject to the inaccuracies, to which all human testimony is liable."

"But the Scientific Theist who regards the so-called 'Laws of Nature' as nothing else than Man's expressions of so much of the Divine Order as it lies within his power to discern, and who looks at the uninterruptedness of this order as the highest evidence of its original perfection, need find (as it seems to me) no abstract difficulty in the conception that the Author of Nature can, if He will, occasionally depart from it. And hence, as I deem it presumptuous to deny that there might be occasions which in His wisdom may require such departure, I am not conscious of any such scientific 'prepossession' against miracles as would prevent me from accepting them as facts, if trustworthy evidence of their reality could be adduced. The question with me, therefore, is simply:—'Have we any adequate historical ground for the belief that such departure has ever taken place?'"

It may fairly be assumed from this last passage, that although Dr. Carpenter holds the moral character of Jesus in the highest estimation, he does not accept His resurrection from the dead as a fact which is capable of proof. If he did, the question whether we have any historical ground for the belief that "such a departure" (viz. from that uniform reign of law which is commonly affirmed to be inconsistent with the idea of a miracle) has ever taken place, would be irrelevant. The author also seems to be of opinion, that there is no distinction between the Resurrection and the other miracles recorded in the New Testament, either as to the attestation on which it rests, or as regards its evidential value. Further: a miracle in his view is nothing but an extraordinary occurrence in the physical universe, which is brought about by the agency of forces of a wholly different kind from those at present in activity. Not one of his observations recognizes the possibility of moral miracles, such as I have referred to in the preceding Lectures. In a word, his views on the entire question are identical with those which were propounded in the evidential treatises of the last century and the beginning of the present. I draw attention to this, because such are the views generally propounded by scientific men when they attempt to deal with the question of the Christian miracles. They have probably been betrayed into this mode of handling the subject through the defective state of our evidential literature; but it is hardly too much to say that in so doing they have overlooked the real point at issue. It will therefore be my duty to offer a few observations on the mode in which the subject is here treated.

The question is argued as if the whole of the miracles

recorded in the Old and New Testaments stood on a common level in point of attestation, and were of equal evidential value. This course has been so commonly adopted that it is impossible too energetically to protest against it. Nothing can be clearer than that one miracle recorded in the New Testament, the Resurrection of our blessed Lord, holds a position in point of attestation which is occupied by no other, and is also distinctly affirmed by the sacred writers to be the foundation on which the Christian Church is built. This being so, I ask, Why do not those who deny the truth of the miracles of the New Testament, confine themselves to this one great issue? To what purpose is it to endeavour to disprove the truth of the other miracles, or to explain them away, while this one is left standing? If it is true, it will sustain all the rest; if it is not true, all the others will fall with it.

Nothing can be more unphilosophical than the mode which is generally adopted by our opponents of dealing with the miracles in a mass, and attempting to account for those which rest on an inferior attestation instead of concentrating their efforts on the centre of the Christian position. Scientific men would be the first to protest against the application of such a method to any great subject of their investigations, and their complaint would be just. Let us suppose that a body of theologians were to attack the credibility of geology, and in doing so, to mix up all the theories which have been propounded by geologists, and affirm that the best authenticated rest on no better evidence than the weakest; and having demolished these latter, were then to raise a shout of triumph, and boast that they had demolished geology as a science. They would justly denounce this course as a convincing proof of the irrational conduct of theologians. Yet this bears a close resemblance to the mode in which the question of the miracles of the New Testament has been discussed. It is the very course which has been pursued by Dr. Carpenter. His first observations are directed to the miracles of the Old Testament. Having adduced the case of a body of fanatic Jews who at the present day are persuaded of the reality of some very grotesque miraculous performances, he observes that he fails to see that the miracles which are chronicled in the Old Testament rest on any stronger attestation than the convictions of this Jewish community.

I reply, first:

In discussing this question it is absurd to begin with the miracles of the Old Testament. We readily allow that the evidence on which they rest is far weaker than that for the miracles recorded in the New. In fact, our reason for believing in their reality is, not the evidence *per se*, but the general recognition which the writers of the New Testament give to the books of the Old. To treat the subject as though the evidence for the resurrection of the dead man who was thrown into Elisha's grave was on a par with that of our blessed Lord, would be simply absurd, when the one was barren of result and the other forms the foundation on which the Christian Church has been erected, and the turning point in the history of the world. If Jesus Christ really rose from the dead, Christianity must be a divine revelation, even if we were unable to establish the historical credibility of a single miracle recorded in the Old Testament.

Secondly: the fallacy is committed of placing all the miracles of the Old Testament on the same level in point of attestation. As among the New Testament miracles there is one which holds a place of special prominence—the Resurrection—so there is a series among those of the Old Testament, which hold a similar position, the great miracles of the Exodus. It is not my duty in this place to enter into a discussion of their historical credibility, but simply to draw attention to the fact, that in point of attestation they exceed that of every other miracle recorded in the Old Testament. They are directly connected with the historical life of the Jewish nation and the foundation of the Jewish Church. From that hour to this the Jewish nation has lived a life differing in character and intensity from that of every other nation. It is an unquestionable fact that some events connected with the Exodus created this nation. Their sojourn in Egypt is historical; their sojourn in the wilderness is historical; their conquest of Canaan is historical. Rightly or wrongly, the Jewish nation have always affirmed that these events, including the foundation of the Jewish Church, were in the closest way connected with the miracles of the Exodus, and they are in the closest manner united with them in the Jewish records. I fully admit that all this does not prove that they were actually performed; but in point of attestation it clearly places them in a very different position from some of the miracles performed by Elijah and Elisha.

The same observations are even more applicable to the miracles of the New Testament. Nothing can be more illogical than to treat them in a mass as though they all stood on the same level in point of attestation. Such a mode of dealing with the question would be in itself sufficiently unscientific; but it is greatly aggravated when the writers of the New Testament have especially selected one of those miracles, and affirmed that with its truth or falsehood their case stands or falls. "If," says St. Paul, "Christ be not risen, then is our preaching vain, and your faith is also vain. Yea, and we are found false witnesses of God, because we have testified of God that He raised up Christ, whom He raised not up, if so be the dead rise not."

It is therefore an entire misapprehension of the Christian position to call upon us to adduce direct proof for each miracle recorded in the New Testament. All that is necessary is to establish the truth of the Resurrection, and to show that the followers of Jesus, who must have witnessed the events of His ministry, reported that He performed a number of actions which must have involved the possession of a superhuman power. As I have said before, if He rose from the dead, it is far more probable that other miracles were performed by Him than that none were; and this one great miracle being established, the truth of the others requires no stronger attestation than the ordinary events of history, but may be accepted without the necessity of pointing out who were the witnesses of each particular one, or proving that they were competent judges as to its really miraculous character. Even if it could be proved that some have been incorrectly attributed to Him, or that they were wrought by calling into greater activity forces which under certain known conditions energize in man, it would leave the real point of the Christian argument untouched. Scientific men should clearly understand that the Christian position is not dependent on our ability to prove the truth of every miracle which is recorded in the Bible, but of the resurrection of Jesus Christ, and the manifestation by Him of a superhuman power exerted in the moral and spiritual world during eighteen centuries of history. To discuss the question on other principles is to raise a false issue.

It appears however that Dr. Carpenter has other objections against the Christian miracles than those which have been adduced by him in the Essay which I am considering. "I limit myself *at present*," he says, "to the following questions." Whether these other objections are stronger, or weaker, than those which he has adduced, we are left in ignorance; but the reader is allowed to remain under the impression that there is yet some formidable force held in reserve with which he is prepared to fall upon the Christian position. Such a force, even when existing only in the imagination, has produced a powerful influence on the decision of many a battle in actual warfare. All that we can do on the present occasion is to guard against the influence which any unknown force of reasoning which is held in reserve may exert in our imaginations, and to point out that that which is actually employed wholly fails to touch the Christian argument.

First: we are asked to solve the question " whether 'the miracles of healing' may not have had a foundation of reality in natural agencies perfectly well known to such as have scientifically studied the action of the mind upon the body?" The meaning of this question is made sufficiently clear by another passage (p. 292). After speaking of the effects which the mind when powerfully exerted can produce on our bodily frames, (for Dr. Carpenter is of opinion that even the marks of the stigmata affirmed to have been produced on certain Medieval Saints, have been produced in this manner,) he writes:

"In these and similar phenomena a strong conviction of the possession of the power on the part of the healer seems to be necessary for the excitement of the faith of those operated on; and the healer recognizes by a kind of intuition, the existence of that faith on the part of the patient. Do not several phrases in the Gospel narratives point to the same relations as existing between Jesus, and the sufferers who sought his aid? The cure is constantly attributed to the 'faith' of the patient, whilst on the other hand, we are told that 'Jesus did not do many mighty works in his own country, because of their unbelief'—the very condition which, if these mighty works had been performed by His own will alone, would have been supposed to call forth its exertion, but which is perfectly conformable to our own experience of the wonders of mesmerism, spiritualism, &c. So Paul is spoken of as 'steadfastly beholding the cripple at Lystra, and seeing that he had faith to be healed.'"

The question here proposed for our solution, "whether "the miracles of healing may not have had a foundation in "natural agencies well known to such as have studied the "action of the mind on the body" is altogether beside the point at issue. Such might have been the case without interfering with their miraculous character. There is no reason why in the performance of a miracle, Our Lord should not have made use of forces already existing in the universe, only so modifying and combining them, as to be a special manifestation of purpose; for it is this manifestation which constitutes the great distinction between an unusual occurrence and a miracle. Dr. Carpenter however has adopted the idea that to constitute an event a miracle, its occurrence must involve either a violation or a suspension of the laws of nature; and that it would be no longer a miracle if caused by the agency of forces already existing. He seems in short to think that to constitute an event a miracle it must be brought about by the agency of the divine will *alone*, without the intervention of any secondary causes. The inaccuracy of this idea I have already pointed out in a supplement to a former Lecture. As therefore it is quite conceivable that Our Lord's miracles wrought in material nature, such as the turning of the water into wine, and the feeding of the five thousand, may have had a "*foundation*" in forces already existing, by combining and imparting to them a different direction, without involving any creative act, in the same manner He may have made use of forces energizing in man, for the purpose of effecting his miraculous cures. I do not say, that this was the real mode of their performance; but the mere possibility that it may have been so, is a sufficient answer to Dr. Carpenter's objection. He that used a strong east wind as the intermediate agent for effecting the great miracle of the Exodus may also have wrought His miraculous cures by the combination and intensifying of forces already acting in man. The event would be none the less a miracle, provided it exceeded human power to summon them into activity, and to combine and direct them in such a manner as to realize the special purpose of His will.

But Dr. Carpenter goes considerably further, and observing that Our Lord and His Apostles generally required "faith" in the patient as a condition of the exercise of their miraculous powers, propounds a theory that their miracles may have been brought about in a manner similar to the wonders of mesmerism and spiritualism; and that the operator discovered the presence of a suitable amount of faith in the patient by a kind of intuition.

Here again the reasoning is singularly unfortunate, for

unless the principle which he has laid down is capable of accounting for all the miracles recorded in the New Testament, it is valueless as affording an adequate account of the origin of any of them. Even if we admit that some of the cures could have been effected by exciting a powerful action on the nervous system, all the most important miracles lie outside its limits; but Dr. Carpenter falls into the fallacy to which I have already alluded of disposing of them all in a mass.

It will be unnecessary to discuss the truth of his position, as to the influence which a powerfully excited "faith," call it by whatever name we please, whether prepossession, fixed idea, or expectancy, can exert on our bodily frames. It is doubtless startling to be informed that mental phenomena of this description can produce the stigmata; but on general points of physiology I am ready to accept Dr. Carpenter as an authority. There can be no doubt, that not only is "faith" the mightiest power in the moral and spiritual worlds, but it can also exert a powerful influence on man's bodily structure. Of this we have all of us, in greater or less degree, had experience. But real as this power is, and although the precise limits within which it can be exerted are unknown, there are certain bounds which it cannot pass. I submit, therefore, the following reasons, which render it certain that Dr. Carpenter's position leaves the Christian argument untouched.

First: whatever power faith may be capable of exerting, it is plain that it could not have effected the Resurrection of Our Lord; and that this event, if an actual occurrence, lay wholly beyond its limits. This being so, it is simply futile to propound the action of this principle, as accounting for any number of the miracles of the Gospels, while it leaves the greatest of them unexplained.

Secondly: there are several other miracles recorded in the Gospels, such as the instantaneous giving of sight to the blind, of hearing to the deaf, speech to the dumb, the cure of lepers by a word, and others, which the principle of faith in any known condition of its action, would have been utterly unable to effect. This being so, it is useless to propound this principle as a rational explanation of the miracles in the New Testament, while it is at best only capable of accounting for a limited number of them.

Thirdly: it by no means follows, even if the action of powerful faith was one of the intermediate instrumentalities through which the miracles of the New Testament were effected, that it nullifies their miraculous character. To affirm that it does so, is quietly to assume that God cannot work miracles through the agency of forces already existing in nature and in man. I must repeat it once more, that the particular force employed in its production does not constitute an event a miracle, but the combining of forces, be they what they may, and the imparting to them such a direction as to be a manifestation of purpose. Let us take as an illustration the case of the woman who for twelve years had suffered from an issue of blood, and whose case had baffled the skill of the physicians of the time. Our Lord tells her that her faith has saved her. If we admit that her faith wrought so powerfully on her bodily frame, that it effected her instant cure, will Dr. Carpenter affirm that there are any known cases of *instantaneous* cures effected by mesmerism? If not, the principle is worthless to invalidate the reality of even the miracle in question, still more that of the miracles of the New Testament in general.

The position which I take is this. The miracles wrought by Our Lord were the natural results of the divine which dwelt within Him, just as ordinary human actions are the natural results of the forces energizing in man. Neither the one nor the other necessarily involves an interruption of the order of nature. To take an illustration: If the more intelligent animals have any perception of such an order, a large number of human actions must appear to them violations of the only order which their limited faculties enable them to conceive. At any rate, they must be to them utterly incomprehensible; nor can they have the smallest idea of the nature of the forces by which they are effected. Relatively to them therefore, they are miraculous. Yet we know that what man really does, when he performs such actions, is not to suspend or violate any natural law, but merely to give a particular direction to the existing forces of the universe, by means of his intelligent volition. In the same manner then, if our blessed Lord was really a superhuman Christ, actions which were the natural results of his superhuman working, would be miraculous to men, just as in accordance with the above illustration, many human actions must be to the highest intelligence of the inferior races. Such actions are in fact signs (σημεῖα); those which are peculiar to man, of the presence of human intelligence and power; those of the divine Christ, of divine intelligence and power. It follows, therefore, that even if Dr. Carpenter's theory is correct, it is useless for the purpose of explaining away the miracles which the Gospels have attributed to Our Lord.

As the real nature of possession is a point which is still eagerly debated, it will be unnecessary for me to express an opinion of my own. I have fully considered the position taken by the writers of the New Testament on that subject in Chapters IX. to XII. of *The Supernatural in the New Testament.* I shall only observe that Dr. Carpenter is labouring under a misconception when he supposes that the question of possession has been finally disposed of, and that the belief in its objective reality is incapable of a rational defence. Before he can arrive at this conclusion, his philosophy must give us a rational solution of those terrible manifestations of the human mind, which a most intelligent and trustworthy witness has recently described as having come under his own observation among the devil-worshippers in India;[*] and of many other of its abnormal activities. As far as the present argument is concerned, it matters not whether the persons

---

[*] See *Contemporary Review*, February 1876, "Demonolatry, Devil-dancing and Demoniacal Possession."

who were cured by Our Lord were demoniacs, maniacs, or both. In either case their cure, as described in the Gospels, would have been equally miraculous. Insanity is in many instances a complaint capable of cure by human means, under proper treatment. But the mode in which Our Lord cured demoniacs would be found utterly inefficacious in the hands of our physicians for the cure of lunacy. The successful application of their method is a sign ($\sigma\eta\mu\varepsilon\tilde{\iota}ov$) of human skill; that of Our Lord, of the power of the divine Christ.

With respect to the descent of the angel to trouble the waters at the Pool of Bethesda, I need only remark that the issue here raised is irrelevant to the point under discussion. He seems not to be aware that most recent editions of the Greek Testament, on the authority of the best manuscripts, reject the passage as a spurious addition to the Fourth Gospel.

I fully concur with Dr. Carpenter, that it is both our right and our duty to bring to bear on the Gospel narratives the same principles of criticism as guided the early fathers in their construction of the Canon, aided by all the enlightenment which we derive from the subsequent history of Christianity, and of other forms of religious belief. I would even add to what he considers necessary for the successful study of the question, and say, aided by all the light which we can derive from any quarter whatever. Those who have studied the Gospel narratives have long felt this to be both their right and their duty; and that it is so, is certainly no discovery of the author before me. But while we feel it to be a duty to bring to bear the whole enlightenment of modern times on this subject, we think that this can only be successfully done by the use of methods which are strictly logical, and in conformity with the principles of the inductive philosophy, not by the practice so generally adopted by a particular school of critical historians, of creating history out of their own subjective consciousness; nor by assuming that everything which is possible is probable; and that everything which is probable, so long as it corresponds to our own ideas of what things ought to have been, is a certainty on which we may erect any amount of theories, however contradictory they may be to all the realities of life. This method has been very extensively employed by modern critics, and not unfrequently by the students of physical science, when they attempt to deal with questions which affect the inner life of Christianity. This is not to import modern enlightenment but modern darkness into the study of the subject; and instead of basing our beliefs on the firm foundation of scientific knowledge, to erect them on the sandy foundation of conjecture.

The following passage in the Essay before me is a dangerous approach to the use of some of these darkening processes in dealing with historical questions.

"I ask whether past and contemporary history do not afford such a body of evidence of a prevailing tendency to exaggeration and distortion in the representation of actual occurrences, in which 'supernatural' agencies are supposed to have been concerned, as entitles us, without attempting any detailed analysis, to believe that if we could know *what really did happen,* it would often prove to be something very different from what is narrated."

In one sense, these last words are very like a truism; and we shall all of us unanimously agree with the author that "if we could know what really did happen, it would often prove to be something very different from what is narrated." This is not only true of many miraculous narratives, but of not a few of the most ordinary events of life. This disposition to amplify and to misrepresent facts, and occasionally even to invent them, is unfortunately but too prevalent; but our duty in all such cases is carefully to sift out the truth; and not to take refuge in a universal Pyrrhonism.

The principle here laid down by Dr. Carpenter amounts to this:—"Because there has been a prevailing tendency to exaggeration and distortion in the representation of actual occurrences in which supernatural agencies are supposed to have been concerned;" therefore, "without attempting any detailed analysis of them," we may deal with them in a mass, and arrive at the conclusion "that, if we knew what really did happen, it would often prove something very different from what is narrated." He uses the word "often," but it is evident that what he really had in his mind was not "often" but "always;" for if this were only *often* the case, the observation would be inapplicable to the point at issue; because the Gospel miracles, crowned as they are by the Resurrection of Our Lord, which rests, as we have seen, on the highest form of historical attestation, would have the strongest possible claim to stand among the excepted number. But this wholesale method of dealing with extensive classes of occurrences, which vary greatly in the attestation on which they rest, without any detailed analysis of the particulars, is alike unphilosophical and unhistorical. Whenever such processes are employed, they indicate the presence, not of calm philosophical inquiry, but of a foregone conclusion.

What would be said by our men of science if theologians had applied the same method four or five centuries ago to every fresh discovery as it occurred? I admit that unhappily there have been times when theologians employed the same methods as those adopted by Dr. Carpenter in respect to the miracles of the Gospels; and none are more stern in their denunciations of them than the writers in question. Let us suppose, for example, that when Columbus returned from the discovery of America, and related the wonders he had seen, he had been met by the following reasoning: "Does not past and contemporary history afford such a body of evidence of a prevalent tendency to exaggeration and distortion in the representation of actual occurrences of distant voyages and travels as entitles us, without any detailed analysis of the evidence, to believe that if we could know what really did happen, it would prove something very different from what you have told us?"

Of Dr. Carpenter's work on "Mental Physiology" I wish

to speak with the greatest respect. While I am far from accepting all his principles and conclusions, I have to thank him for his successful analysis of many of the abnormal phenomena of the human mind, and above all, for the devotion with which he, almost alone of scientific men, has attempted to investigate the nature of the phenomena of Spiritualism, that greatest of all the delusions of modern times. Whether he is right in all his explanations of these phenomena may be still open to dispute; but it is certainly high time that both religious and scientific men should investigate them to their foundation, when we consider that the belief in their objective reality has been accepted not only by the multitude, but by no inconsiderable number of cultivated minds. But on carefully considering the explanations which he has given of these phenomena, and of various other delusions of the past, I could not help feeling that some of them were capable of being used for the purpose of invalidating the evidence of Our Lord's Resurrection, and that they were almost certain to produce this effect on those who have not made the whole subject a matter of careful inquiry. I by no means wish to imply that Dr. Carpenter, in propounding them, intended them to be used for this purpose. But the fact remains that they can be so used, and that ordinary readers are very likely so to use them. I have therefore felt it a duty to point out, as I have done in the foregoing Lecture, that even if they are the true solution of the phenomena in question, they have no real bearing on the attestation of that great miracle, on the objective reality of which the Christian Church is erected. With respect to his observations on miracles generally, Dr. Carpenter has only shared the fate of a large number of persons who have entered on the discussion of questions which lie outside their own special studies; and I cannot help thinking, despite his own belief to the contrary, that what he has written on the subject of miracles has been really due to the unconscious presence in him of that form of "prepossession" or "fixed idea" which is the "eidolon" of scientific men, that miracles are so highly improbable that to inquire into their evidence in any particular instance is a superfluous task; and it is greatly to be feared that no inconsiderable portion of this prepossession has been occasioned by his assuming the position which has been taken by many eminent theologians as true, that the idea of a miracle necessarily involves either a suspension or a violation of the laws of nature.

LECTURE VIII.

"That which I speak, I speak it not after the Lord, but as it were foolishly, in this confidence of boasting."—2 Cor. xi. 17.

THERE is no one thing which at the present day is occasioning a greater amount of difficulty to a number of inquiring and deeply religious minds than some of the theories that have been propounded respecting the nature and extent of the inspiration under the influence of which the different books in the Bible have been composed. These theories have been identified in the popular mind, and by not a few students of science, with the truth of Christianity itself. I have been informed by Christian men who have devoted themselves to the study of physical science, that nothing so heavily presses on their faith as the persistency with which the truth of revelation has been identified with these theories of inspiration. On the other hand, it is certain that many of the sharpest attacks of unbelief derive their chief strength from the idea that Christianity is pledged to their truth. On one point I can speak with something like authority as to the effect which they produce on the unbelief of the working-classes of this country. I have during the last six years been present at discussions at which I have heard not less than one hundred addresses, made by unbelievers who belong to this class of society, on points which they consider to involve the truth of Christianity. Taking these objections as a whole, I feel convinced that at least two-thirds of them owe their entire plausibility to their identification of that particular form of inspiration, which is usually designated verbal or mechanical, with a divine Revelation. To this theory they believe Christianity to be pledged, and consequently that every objection which can be urged against the Old Testament on the ground that its statements or its language are not scientifically correct; or that its moral teaching is imperfect; or that it attributes to God the passions of humanity; or against the New Testament, on the ground that discrepancies exist in the Gospels which are difficult to reconcile; in a word, that everything in the Bible which is at variance with mechanical verbal accuracy is fatal to its claim to be considered a revelation from God.

Nor are these opinions confined to the classes in question, but with various modifications there is also among educated men a wide-spread belief that Christianity must answer with its life for our inability to reconcile every statement in Scripture with the discoveries of modern science; and not only so, but with the popularly accepted views of what Scripture affirms. The same thing is true with respect to its historical statements, even to the extent of maintaining the accuracy of the commonly accepted system of Chronology, and a vast number of other points which it is needless here to particularize. The same principle has been applied to the New Testament, and it is hardly too much to affirm that no inconsiderable number of the objections which are popularly urged against the truth of the Gospel narrative generally, are founded on the assumption that each of them must belong to that class of historical writings which rigidly follow the sequences of time and place; and that any deviation from this is fatal to their historical character. All this has been quietly assumed in the face of the fact that two of the Gospels affirm in definite language that they are not histories in the strict sense of that term, but memoirs, compiled for the purpose of teaching a religion; and the other two, if they do not assert this in express words, plainly imply it.

On similar principles the demand is frequently made to defend the entire morality of the Old Testament, or to renounce our Christianity, as though it were inconceivable that God's revelations can have been of a progressive character. In fact, turn where we will, we are confronted with similar objections, most of which owe their validity to the assumption that the truth of Christianity is dependent on our ability to show that all its facts and phenomena are consistent with the theory that the divine assistance which was imparted to the writers of the sacred books, must have been of such a character as to guard them from the possibility of error on all subjects alike, whether religious, philosophical, scientific, or historical; and that to concede the possibility of error on any one of these points, is to surrender the claims of Christianity to be accepted as a Revelation from God. From this has resulted, not only an extensive diffusion of actual unbelief, but (what is worthy of our deepest attention) a large number of religious men have been greatly shaken and disquieted in their faith.

This evil has been intensified by several of the efforts that have been made to counteract it. Many zealous but injudicious defenders of Christianity have propounded solutions of these difficulties of so inadequate a character, that they can be accepted by none but those who are pledged to the maintenance of a particular hypothesis.* The effect of solu-

* I adduce one of a very extreme character from a recently published work, as an illustration of the danger of such methods. Common sense for eighteen centuries has read the account of the Crucifixion as affirming that Our Lord was crucified between two robbers. A recent writer, whom it will be unnecessary to name, has made the notable discovery, that he was crucified between four. St. Luke designates the persons who were crucified with him as κακοῦργοι (malefactors); the other evangelists λησταί (robbers). This writer therefore thinks it necessary to maintain that a κακοῦργος and a λῃστής were crucified on each side of him. This is, I own, a very exaggerated instance, but it will serve my purpose of illustrating the mischief which has resulted from propounding inadequate solutions of difficulties, for the purpose of bolstering up a favourite theory. Unhappily such forced explana-

tions of this kind has been to create a great deal more unbelief than they have removed, producing as they do the impression on unbiassed minds that the defenders of Christianity are reduced to the utmost straits by the objections which have been urged.

I am deeply sensible of the responsibility attending any attempt to handle this question. I feel however that its importance is so great in reference to the present aspects both of scientific and popular thought, that to pass it over in silence would be an evasion of a plain duty. I by no means wish to affirm that all the difficulties which are agitating men's minds at the present day, have originated in the supposed necessity of maintaining a particular theory of inspiration. Many of them are closely connected with questions of Theism, and in the higher regions of thought we are undoubtedly approaching a great crisis between the principles of Atheism and Pantheism on the one side, and those of Theism on the other. Yet it cannot be denied that no small number of them have arisen from the cause I have mentioned, and from that which is closely allied to it, the

---

tions have not been adopted only by persons who have to maintain a particular theory of Inspiration. We have a remarkable instance of one in Paley, who was quite free from prejudices of this description, in his attempt to solve the difficulty about Cyrenius and the taxing. No scholar at the present day will for a moment accept his translation of αὕτη ἡ ἀπογραφὴ πρώτη ἐγένετο ἡγεμονεύοντος τῆς Συρίας Κυρηνίου; "This was the first assessment (or enrolment) of Cyrenius, Governor of Syria;" the words "Governor of Syria" being used after the name of Cyrenius as an addition or title, just in the same manner as an inaccurate modern writer might have said that a particular act was done by "Governor Hastings," although in truth it had been done by him before he was advanced to the station from which he received the name of "Governor." The simple fact is that the words ἡγεμονεύοντος τῆς Συρίας Κυρηνίου never could have borne the meaning which Paley has here ascribed to them. Whether St. Luke was right or wrong in his statement as to the fact, there is only one possible interpretation of his words, namely, "*while Cyrenius was Governor of Syria.*" Such forced explanations are far more dangerous than a candid admission of a difficulty.

desire of maintaining the traditionary interpretations of certain passages in the Bible as the only admissible ones. This is unquestionably the case with many of the difficulties which have been suggested by modern science, of which no small number would disappear if the popular theories on this subject were abandoned for one which is strictly in conformity with the facts and phenomena of the Bible itself. If, for example, we assume that inspiration was not a general but a functional endowment, and consequently limited to subjects in which religion is directly involved, and that in those which stand outside it the writers of the different books in the Bible were left to the free use of their ordinary faculties, a large number of the objections which are popularly urged against Revelation from the standpoint of physical science and modern criticism would become simply nugatory.

I am aware that it has been urged that it is impossible to separate the religious element in the Bible from the various other subjects that are closely interwoven with it, and consequently that the accuracy of all must stand or fall together. So far, however, is it from being the fact that there is any real difficulty in the idea that God may have seen good to enlighten particular men on religious subjects and to leave them on others to their own unassisted powers, that it is strictly analogous to the mode in which He has communicated to us our ordinary knowledge, and therefore it affords a strong presumption that He has adopted the same course in communicating a Revelation. Thus not only has each man special mental powers which qualify him for grappling with particular subjects, and leave him on others in comparative ignorance; but the information conveyed to us by any one of our senses conveys to us no knowledge on subjects which belong to the special function of another. This is an unquestionable truth, although we are not always conscious of it in our actual experience, as, for example, in the case of vision. In the fully educated state of this faculty we judge of distance instinctively; though the power to do so is not any portion of our original sense of sight, but is derived from the combination of vision with the sense of touch. While in the present condition of our consciousness the two acts are undistinguishable, we know that the function of the eye itself is strictly limited to the perception of coloured objects; and that in the proper subject-matter of the other senses it leaves us destitute of information.* In this respect then the idea of special functional enlightenment is analogous to the mode of the divine acting in nature; and the difficulties which it involves are precisely of the same kind as those which we experience as to the source of some of the perceptions of our senses. If therefore God has adopted the same mode of communicating supernatural and natural knowledge; and consequently, if inspiration did not confer a general enlightenment on every subject which came within the mental horizon of the inspired man, but only a functional one, we are at once freed from a host of difficulties which are at this moment grievously harassing no inconsiderable number of inquiring minds, and which form the armoury from which the weapons employed in the attack on Christianity are drawn.

In considering the present aspect of the controversy between Science and Revelation, it is of the highest importance that we should discern clearly what constitutes the real source of our danger. It has arisen in no small degree from theologians under the influence of particular theories of inspiration having put in claims to occupy provinces of

* That the human eye only acquires the faculty of discriminating distance by means of a gradual education of the organ is proved not only by the fact that infants are apparently unable to discriminate distance until some time after birth, but also by the unquestionable fact that grown persons who have been blind from their birth and in after life obtained the use of their eyes, are at first devoid of all perception of distance, which they only gradually acquire by the aid of experience derived from the other senses. Yet in the fully educated state of the faculty the perception of distance is not only united with that of vision, but we are incapable in consciousness of separating the one from the other.

thought to which theology had no legitimate right. That this has been the case in past times is undeniable. The story of Galileo is a striking case in point. Theologians of his day were firmly persuaded that to assert that the earth moved round the sun, and not the sun round the earth, and the earth on its axis, was to contradict the Bible. We now know that what it really contradicted was not the Bible itself, but the Bible interpreted in accordance with a particular theory of inspiration. The result has been that theology has had to retreat from an untenable position. But to come nearer to our own times. Theologians did not take warning by this great disaster, and proceed to inquire whether the principles which led them into it rested on an adequate foundation, but clung as closely as possible to their former theories. The science of geology has come into existence almost in our day. Again was it affirmed that this new science contradicted the Bible; and consequently it was denounced as anti-Christian. Many of us can well remember when a great number of things which are now held as truths by most of those whom I am addressing, would have been denounced as of the most dangerous character. The positions once taken on this subject are sufficiently exemplified by the earliest editions of Hartwell Horne's *Introduction to the Study of the Bible*, which some of us used almost as a text-book; and yet they were liberal compared with the popular views of their day. What has been the result? New ground has had to be occupied; old theories have had to be modified, and we have now arrived at the conclusion that the defence of the former positions was not vital to Christianity.

Nor are indications wanting that similar consequences are likely to ensue from other subjects of modern scientific investigation; to instance one of them—the antiquity of man. In using this term, I am not referring to his enormous antiquity as deduced from his supposed existence in the first stone age, or during the preglacial period; I allude to the evidences furnished by the early history of civilization, and by the science of language. It has been very generally held by theologians, that the Bible is pledged to a definite chronology; and that the supposition that the interval which separates us from the first man can exceed seven thousand years is inconsistent with its claim to be accepted as a divine revelation. So strong has been this conviction that to this hour no inconsiderable number of Bibles continue to be printed with this chronology in their margins, a practice which has led many people to view it as of equal authority with the sacred text. But the investigations which have recently been so successfully prosecuted in the early history of civilization, and the discoveries which have been made in the science of language, have gone a great way to show that this position will also prove as untenable as those which have already had to be abandoned; for the period which the received chronology lays down as separating the date of the building of Solomon's temple from that of the Deluge seems inadequate to meet the demands that are made upon us by the growth of civilization and of language.

I by no means wish to imply that scientific men in their controversies with theologians have been always in the right. On the contrary it has recently been made painfully evident, that no inconsiderable number of them, when they pass beyond the special subjects of their studies, have propounded theories which rest on a very slender basis of fact, and endeavoured to impart to a number of crude speculations, the justly earned weight of their own scientific reputations.*

* We have a remarkable instance of this in Mr. Darwin's work entitled *The Descent of Man*, in which he attempts to show how the moral nature of man may have been produced by a process of slow and gradual evolution out of the instincts of the lower animals. Great as are his attainments as a naturalist, this work shows clearly that he has not mastered even the elements of the science of man's spiritual and moral nature. It is much to be regretted that so many scientific men, while they are loud in their denunciation of the dogmatism of theologians of past ages, imitate them in this worst aspect of their conduct in giving utterance to dogmatical assertions on

Still it is an undeniable fact that science steadily advances; and that in so doing, it has compelled the abandonment of positions which were once held to be essential to the defence of Revelation; and it is no less clear that other similar positions are in considerable danger. It cannot be denied that the recurrence of retreats of this description is a thing which in the interests of religion is pre-eminently undesirable. It is not only fraught with danger but is exercising the most injurious influences at the present moment. Scientific men who are hostile to revealed religion are never wearied with taunting us with the abandonment of positions which theologians once declared to be essential to the Christian faith; and in consequence they venture to predict our ultimate expulsion from our own proper territories. What then is the plain duty of theologians under these circumstances? I answer, thoroughly to investigate the principles which have led to the occupation of positions which have thus proved to be untenable, and to abandon those which rest on no adequate foundation.

My first inquiry must therefore be directed to ascertain the cause of that warfare which is now raging between the believers in Revelation and the students of science. I am not now speaking of those forms of scientific thought which are essentially atheistic or pantheistic, for their opposition to Revelation rests upon principles which it is impossible for me to discuss in these Lectures; but of those which are consistent with the principles of theism. My remarks must be confined to those grounds of offence which have been given by believers in Revelation; for my space would wholly fail me if I were to attempt to discuss those which have been given by the students of science. I make this remark solely in order to guard against the supposition that I hold them blameless.

What then, is the cause, as far as theologians are concerned, of this unhappy and dangerous warfare which is

subjects which lie outside the limits of their special investigations. Such dogmatism seems to be the original sin of the human intellect.

now proving so trying to the religious faith of multitudes? To this question there can be only one answer. Theologians have claimed for theology departments of thought which form no legitimate portion of its domains, but which really belong to the students of science. This course they have been led to adopt under the influence of certain *à priori* theories respecting the nature and extent of inspiration, and to adopt modes of interpretation, the inevitable result of which has been to bring theology into collision with the progress of modern thought. My position is, that this mode of determining on mere abstract principles what inspiration must have been, and then assuming that it actually has been so, is a method which is utterly faulty; and is precisely identical with those methods of studying physical science which for so many ages rendered it barren of result. I contend that the only mode of arriving at any theory of inspiration which will rest on a foundation of reality, is not by assuming what inspiration must have been, but by inquiring what it actually has been; or in other words, by founding it on a rigid induction of the facts and phenomena of the Bible.

In taking this ground I shall at once proceed to shelter myself behind the authority of one whose name will be heard with reverence in this place, the greatest of all English theologians, Bishop Butler. The positions which have been laid down by him in Chapter III. Part II. of his *Analogy* seem to me to be quite adequate to meet all our wants at the present day. When we consider that a great portion of our present scientific and critical difficulties were unknown when he composed his great work, the principles which he has enunciated on this subject are a striking proof of his profound insight into the realities of things. It may be said of Butler, as St. Paul said of Luke: " His praise is in the Gospel in all the Churches," yet it is surprising to what a degree his positions have been disregarded even by his professed disciples. If his warning voice had been heeded, we should have been spared much of that bitter contest in which theology has been involved with modern science. Yet by the eager defenders of popular theories of inspiration against the progress of scientific thought, the principles which were laid down more than a century ago by the greatest defender of Christianity, whose orthodoxy none have ever ventured to impeach, are not even referred to in this controversy; and they still persist in affirming to be vital to Christianity, what he has shown to be unessential to its defence. The words of the old Roman Satirist may be almost quoted here: "Virtus laudatur et alget."

Stated generally, the position taken by Butler amounts to the denial of the validity of all theories of inspiration which are erected on merely *à priori* principles, and to the affirmation that the only firm foundation on which to erect any theory on this subject is the careful application of the principle of induction. But it will be desirable that I should briefly state his special positions. His text is subjoined in a note.*

---

* "Now if the natural and revealed dispensations of things are both from God, if they coincide with each other, and together make up one scheme of providence, our being incompetent judges of the one, must render it credible that we may be also incompetent judges of the other. Since upon experience the acknowledged constitution and course of nature is found to be greatly different from what before experience would have been expected, and such as men fancy there lie great objections against, this renders it beforehand highly credible, that they may find the revealed dispensation likewise, if they judge of it as they do of the constitution of nature, very different from expectations formed beforehand; and liable in appearance to great objections; objections against the scheme itself, and against the degrees and manners of the miraculous interpositions by which it was attested and carried on. . . . These observations, relating to the whole of Christianity, are applicable to inspiration in particular. As we are in no sort judges beforehand, by what laws or rules, in what degree, or by what means, it were to have been expected that God would naturally instruct us; so upon supposition of His affording us light and instruction by revelation, additional to what He has afforded us by reason or experience, we are in no sort judges by what methods, or in what proportion it were to be expected that this supernatural light and instruction

1. As *à priori* principles are inadequate guides to the knowledge of the realities of the Universe; and as they lead

would be afforded us. We know not beforehand what degree or kind of natural information it were to be expected that God would afford men, each by his own reason and experience; nor how far He would enable, and effectually dispose them to communicate it, whatever it should be, to each other; nor whether the evidence of it would be certain, highly probable, or doubtful; nor whether it would be given with equal clearness and conviction to all. Nor could we guess, on any good ground I mean, whether natural knowledge, or even the faculty itself by which we are capable of attaining it, reason, would be given us at once or gradually. In like manner we are wholly ignorant what degree of new knowledge it were to be expected God would give mankind by revelation, upon supposition of His affording one; or how far, or in what way He would interpose miraculously to qualify them to whom He should originally make the revelation, for communicating the knowledge given by it; and to secure their doing it to the age in which they should live, and to secure its being transmitted to posterity. We are equally ignorant whether the evidence of it would be certain, highly probable, or doubtful; or whether all that should have any instruction from it, and any degree of evidence of its truth, would have the same, or whether the scheme would be revealed at once, or gradually unfolded. Nay, we are not in any sort able to judge whether the revelation would have been committed to writing, or left to be handed down, and consequently corrupted by verbal tradition; and at length sunk under it, if mankind so pleased, and during such time as they are permitted, as they evidently are, to act as they will.

"But it may be said, that a revelation, in some of the above circumstances, one, for instance, which was not committed to writing, and thus secured against the danger of corruption, would not have answered its purpose. I ask, what purpose? It would not have answered all the purposes it has now answered; and in the same degree; but it would have answered others, or the same, in different degrees. And which of those were the purposes of God, and best fell in with His general government, we could not at all have determined beforehand. . . . . And thus we see that the only question concerning the truth of Christianity is, whether it is a real revelation; not whether it is attended with every circumstance which we should look for. And concerning the authority of Scripture, whether it is what it claims to be, not whether it be a book of such a sort, and so promulgated as weak men are apt to fancy a book containing

us, when we yield ourselves to their guidance, to erroneous views of its actual constitution, so they must be equally invalid guides as to what must be the contents of a revelation, or the mode of its communication.

2. They afford us no reliable information respecting the amount of knowledge which God would be pleased to communicate in any given revelation, supposing that it has been His pleasure to impart one.

3. We are equally unable to determine what method He would employ in the communication of such knowledge; and by consequence we are ignorant of the nature and extent of the divine assistance which would be imparted to those who would be employed in its communication. Of only one thing we have à priori certainty, that if God gives a revelation, it will realize the divine purposes in giving one, but the precise nature of those purposes we can only learn from the contents of the revelation itself.

4. We have no means of determining in what degree or proportion supernatural illumination would be afforded; and consequently, our à priori knowledge fails to enable us to determine to what extent an element of human frailty would be permitted to underlie the record of that revelation.

5. Equally invalid is our à priori knowledge to determine how far, or in what way, "God would interpose miraculously to qualify those to whom he should impart a revelation, for communicating the knowledge of it to others; or to insure their transmission of it to posterity."

6. We are equally ignorant, if a revelation were communicated, whether the record of it would be committed to writing, or left to be handed down, and consequently, "cor-

---

a divine revelation should. And therefore neither obscurity, nor seeming inaccuracy of style, nor various readings, nor early disputes about the authors of particular parts, nor any other things of the like kind, though they had been much more considerable in degree than they are, could overthrow the authority of Scripture, unless the prophets, apostles, or Our Lord, had promised that the book containing the divine revelation should be secure from these things."

rupted by verbal tradition, and at length sink under it, if mankind so pleased."

7. We are equally ignorant as to the degree in which "obscurity, or inaccuracy of style, or various readings, or disputes about the authors of particular parts of it, or any other thing of the like kind," would become mixed up with its contents; and consequently we have no right to assume that the presence of such things is inconsistent with the idea that the book which contains them, contains also the record of a divine revelation.

8. If it be objected, that the presence of such imperfections would be inconsistent with the purpose of God in communicating a revelation, the answer is, that we have no knowledge of what are the divine purposes, beyond the facts of a given revelation; and that such facts (be they what they may) are certain to be consistent with those purposes. Hence the only mode of forming any theory as to the nature and extent of the inspiration that guided the human authors of the Bible, must be by a careful investigation of its contents.

9. The only mode in which our knowledge of the contents of a revelation can receive enlargement is, by a careful study of its facts and phenomena, in precisely the same way as we acquire increased knowledge of the Universe; and there is no valid *à priori* objection against the possibility of such increase in knowledge.

Such are the principles which were laid down by this profound thinker more than a century ago, as to our inability to determine on mere abstract principles the extent of knowledge which would be communicated in a revelation, the degree of divine assistance which must be vouchsafed to those through whom it is communicated, or the extent to which an element of human imperfection would be allowed to enter into its record. These principles, if they are correct, and if they had been firmly adhered to, would have been sufficient to have guarded theologians, not only from the danger of taking many false positions, which they have since had to abandon, but are adequate to meet nearly all the difficulties which have been suggested by the progress of scientific and critical investigation. Would that theologians had taken their ground in conformity with his cautious foresight!

The want of attention which the principles thus laid down by the great defender of revealed religion receive at the present day is not a little remarkable. Eager combatants rush into the field in total disregard of them; and while there is scarcely a writer on any theological question who has not been proud to refer to the name of Butler, whenever it can be quoted in his favour, yet on this subject his principles, though bearing in the closest manner on the theological controversies of the present day, are simply ignored, while no one ventures openly to impugn them. But if they can be proved to be unsound, surely some voice ought to have been raised to warn the student of his danger. The time was when the writings of the great Bishop were profoundly studied in this University; and although controversies have since assumed an atheistic or pantheistic, rather than a theistic form, may the day be far off when they will cease to be subjects of deep interest to the student. Probably every Bishop on the Bench has during the present century recommended to candidates for holy orders the study of *The Analogy*; yet surely it would have been only right, in the case of a work which has been thus widely accepted by Christians of all denominations, either that positions of such importance should be fully accepted, or the inaccuracy of his reasonings, if such there be, pointed out. But neither has been done, and ardent disputants are rushing into the contest, and proclaiming that unless their own particular theories of inspiration are accepted, the truth of Christianity is imperilled. Need we wonder if scientific men have taken them at their word?

If Butler's principles are correct (and I own that I cordially accept them), all our current theories of inspiration err in being based on *à priori* assumptions or on expressions found in particular books, as to the degree of divine assistance which was afforded to prophets and Apostles on special occasions, and applied to Scripture as a whole, instead of on a careful induction of the facts and phenomena of the Bible. A brief statement of their nature will make this plain.

1. The verbal and mechanical theories and their various modifications. I shall treat these two theories as one, because except as to some minute points of difference they are practically the same.

This theory, though now scarcely held by any theologian of note, embodies in some of its modifications most of the popular views on the subject. Of all the theories of inspiration this is the most thoroughgoing and consistent. Yet so completely is it at issue with the facts and phenomena of the Bible that few of its advocates venture to carry it out with logical consistency.* Its central idea is the denial of

* There is one point at which the most rigid adherents of this theory hesitate to carry it out to its logical consequences. Yet it is evident that if it has any value at all, it is impossible to stop where they do. If the words of Scripture are throughout the dictation of the Divine Spirit, the style of its different books must be His style, and not that of their human authors. This would render it necessary to assume that their style is the most perfect and perspicuous possible ; and that the sacred books, as they issued from their writers' hands, must have been free alike from errors in grammar and orthography. If this was not the case, it would involve the admission of some human element of imperfection (it may be a very small one, but still it is a real one) into the sacred volume, the very idea, in fact, which this theory has been invented for the purpose of excluding. It is moreover essential to the validity of the theory that the style should be clear and perspicuous, for obscurity of style is not only a human imperfection but a very fruitful source of error. Here, however, the facts of the Bible are too palpable for the most thoroughgoing of systematizers. No one can pretend that it does not contain obscurities of expression ; and in fact every one who reads its pages instinctively recognizes the modes of thought of its different authors. Those who hold this theory therefore shrink from carrying it out to its logical conclusion. In this respect Mahomet was more consistent. He held a theory of inspiration analogous to the verbal and mechanical one ; and therefore he

the presence of any human element in the Bible. The sacred writers were in fact the mere penmen of the Divine Spirit, and accordingly not only ought no trace of human imperfection to exist in the book, but its statements on every point, whether of philosophy, science, or history, must be infallibly correct. Such a theory, I need not say, exposes us at every point to the attacks of unbelief, and constitutes one of the most dangerous weapons which it brings to bear on the popular mind.

2. The dynamical theory. This theory is, I believe, held almost exclusively by professed theologians, being one difficult of comprehension to ordinary men. One of its chief objects is to recognize that human element in the Bible, the presence of which is too obvious to be denied. Yet it assumes that the human element is so completely interpenetrated by the divine, that the two become inseparably united.* It will be at once seen that this theory is of a

appeals to the perfection of his style as a proof of its divine origin, and challenges angels and men to produce its like. The whole theory is, however, so completely at variance with the facts and phenomena of the Bible as to constitute a striking proof of the length to which even intelligent men will go under the influence of *à priori* prepossessions. In fact, with the Gospels, the Acts of the Apostles, and the Pauline Epistles in our hands, it is simply marvellous that such a theory should ever have been propounded; and still more so, that it should have been so extensively accepted. It forms one of the many proofs of the eagerness with which men seek for an infallible guidance which God has denied them, instead of pursuing truth by the aid of those faculties which He has imparted to them. Thus one party hope to find such guidance by assuming the infallibility of a man; and the opposite party by assuming that of a book.

* Some of those who hold the dynamical theory of inspiration have illustrated it by affirming that the divine and human elements are united in the Bible in the same manner as in the person of Jesus Christ. This illustration, however, throws no real light on the subject. As we are completely ignorant of the mode of this latter mystery, such a comparison is only an attempt to illustrate a dark subject by one still darker. It is not my duty, however, to discuss the merits of this theory, which is certainly far more moderate and rational than those which are popularly current, but to draw attention to the fact that

purely *à priori* character, and it will be unnecessary to speak further of it here, as the influence which it exerts on present controversies is very inconsiderable.

3. The theory of plenary inspiration. Not only is this theory also based on purely *à priori* principles, but its vagueness is its sufficient condemnation. It defines nothing. Plenary inspiration means full inspiration, but this leaves entirely open the question, What constitutes full inspiration? To answer this, we must ascertain what were the divine purposes in communicating it; and this, as Butler tells us, can be known on no *à priori* principle. To say that if God communicates supernatural assistance he will realize His own purposes in giving it, is little better than a platitude. The question is, what are those purposes? Are they to communicate all truth, or only religious truth? or how far, to use Butler's language, is it the divine purpose to exclude from the record of Revelation every conceivable form of human imperfection? All these points must be determined before such an expression as "plenary inspiration" can have any definite meaning. The plain fact is, that every person who holds that the Scriptures have been given by inspiration from God in any sense whatever, must hold that the inspiration imparted to their authors must have been "plenary" in reference to the purposes of God in giving it. To use this term, therefore, as a designation of a particular form of inspiration can serve no other purpose than to hide from ourselves our own confusion of thought.*

although it has been formed for the purpose of finding room for that human element which beyond all contradiction exists in the pages of the Bible, yet in all other respects it rests on an *à priori* basis, and is not the result of the application of the principle of induction.

* The following is Dean Alford's account of plenary, as distinct from verbal inspiration, which he heartily rejected: "If I understand *plenary inspiration* rightly, *I hold it to the utmost,* as entirely consistent with the opinions expressed in this Section. The inspiration of the sacred writers I believe to have consisted in the fulness of the influence of the Holy Spirit, specially raising them to and enabling them for their work—*in a manner which distinguishes them from all*

4. The theory of superintendence. The object of this theory is to account for the fact, which is patent to every reader of the Bible who does not blind his eyes to palpable realities—the presence of a human element in its pages, but at the same time to guard it from the possibility of that error to which everything human is liable. To effect this purpose, a theory has been propounded which assumes that while the various writers made use of their ordinary faculties in the composition of the sacred books, such a controlling influence was exerted over them by the Divine Spirit, as to preserve them from the possibility of error, not only on points connected with religion, but on every other subject which came within their mental horizon. I say this because, unless it goes to this extent, the expression is equally vague with that of "plenary inspiration," and really defines nothing; for unless the superintendence extended to the entire contents of the Bible, it would leave us utterly in the dark as to the limits within which it was exerted. The *à priori* character of this theory is at once manifest, for it makes no pretence of having been arrived at by an induction of the facts and phenomena of Scripture. On the other hand, every one who believes in inspiration at all, must likewise believe that a superintendence of some kind was exerted

other writers in the world, and their work from all other works. The men were full of the Holy Ghost,—the books are the outpouring of that fulness through the men—the conservation of the treasure in earthen vessels. The treasure is ours in all its richness; but it is ours, as only it can be ours, in the imperfections of human speech, in the limitations of human thought, in the variety of incident, first to individual character and then to manifold transcription, and the lapse of ages." (Alford, *Prolegomena to the New Testament.*) While agreeing with the author in many of his general conclusions, I cannot help thinking that this passage fully bears out the remarks which I have made in the text, as to the confusion of thought involved in this theory of inspiration; while professing to define it, it leaves us in the region of vagueness and uncertainty to such a degree, that it is only in a very qualified sense that it can be called a theory at all. Several of his previous reasonings on this subject are also vitiated by resting on an *à priori* basis.

over the human authors of the Bible. But unless we lay down its nature and limitations, we determine nothing.

5. One more theory must be noticed; that which affirms that a special inspiration was vouchsafed to the authors while they were engaged in the composition of the various books, different from the ordinary inspiration, under the influence of which they acted and taught. We know as a matter of fact that apostles in their ordinary actions were not possessed of any infallible guidance. The author of the Acts of the Apostles tells us that Paul and Barnabas separated one from another because they could not agree about taking Mark as their companion; and Paul expressly informs us that serious doctrinal errors were legitimate deductions from the inconsistent conduct of Peter. Hence has arisen the supposed necessity for a theory which will discriminate between the ordinary inspiration of an apostle, and that which he possessed when composing a letter or a Gospel for the instruction of the Church. But not only does this theory contradict the express assertions of St. Paul, that his oral teaching was quite as authoritative as his written teaching (2 Thess. ii. 16), but it is compelled to assume that if one of the converts had copied down an ordinary discourse delivered by an apostle, or an affirmation made by him on a religious subject in the course of common conversation, it would not have been equally inspired with a letter dictated by an amanuensis. Not only does such a theory rest solely on à priori assumption, but it contradicts the express assertions of the New Testament. The influence, however, of these latter theories on existing controversies is comparatively small. Most of them are only known to professed students of theology. But the "verbal" theory, with its various modifications, continues to exercise a very powerful influence on the public mind, and thereby exposes us to the sharpest attacks of scientific unbelief, and forms the chief stumbling-block in the way of a large number of anxious inquirers.

I now proceed to examine the value of all theories of

inspiration which are founded on *à priori* assumptions. My position is as follows. The abstract principles on which they are based, when applied to the facts of the universe, utterly break down as explanations of its realities. If they are carried out to their logical conclusions, they leave us in the presence of two alternatives, viz., the necessity of either denying or explaining away the facts, or of denying that the universe is the work of a creator who is all-powerful, all-wise, and all-good. Many eminent modern unbelievers have assumed the truth of these principles, and have arrived at this conclusion as the result. If we admit the premisses, the conclusion beyond doubt logically follows. A few illustrations of this mode of reasoning will suffice.

1. It has been laid down as a self-evident proposition, that if the universe be the work of a being who possesses infinite power, it ought to be free from every conceivable defect which unlimited power could have removed. But in the universe as it actually exists, there are unquestionable instances of imperfection. The inference has been therefore drawn, that if a God made the universe, his power must be limited. So far the conclusion legitimately follows from the premisses, and the only mode of breaking the force of the argument is to deny the reality of the assumption which lies at its foundation.

2. On similar principles it has been argued, that if a Being who is possessed of infinite power, and infinite wisdom has made the universe, it is impossible that he can have made the imperfect structures which are frequently found in the bodies of men and other animals. It is argued that such imperfection, if due to an intelligent creator, can only have resulted from some defect in his power or his wisdom. Yet the fact is unquestionable that such imperfections do exist.* The inference therefore is drawn, that if the

---

* Among the many striking illustrations of this is the unquestionable fact that parents not only transmit to their children particular diseases, of which lunacy and idiotcy are distressing examples, but even a tendency to particular vices.

universe is the work of a God, he must be one who in these respects is subject to limitations.

3. On similar principles it has been inferred, that the being who has made the universe, if he is possessed of infinite power and wisdom, cannot be perfectly benevolent, for a being perfectly benevolent must will the perfect happiness of his creatures. Yet the existence of both physical suffering and moral evil is unquestionable. The attempt is therefore made to impale us on the horns of the following dilemma :—If the Creator is perfectly benevolent, then his wisdom or his power must be limited; or if these are without limits, he cannot be perfectly benevolent.

4. A similar inference has been drawn from the conception of perfect justice. It is unquestionable that the present moral order of the universe is not a perfect manifestation of this attribute. Hence it is inferred that the Being who has made it must be imperfect either in justice, in wisdom, or in power.

These conclusions are inevitable if we admit the truth of the premisses. Mr. Mill has urged them in his posthumous essays with an unsparing logic. The only mode of escaping from the inference which he draws is one which will be accepted by every theist, namely, by denying the validity of his assumption that the impress of perfection must of necessity be stamped on all the works of a perfect Creator.

From these reasonings I draw the following conclusion. It is impossible that the same *à priori* principles which are unsound when applied to the structure of the universe can be safe guides as to the nature and extent of the supernatural assistance which God must have vouchsafed in the communication of a Revelation. In each case an abstract theory has been laid down that God must act in this or that particular manner. In the one it is assumed that if a God of infinite power, wisdom and benevolence has made the universe, He was bound to realize our highest conception of those attributes in every portion of His creative work. This we know, as a matter of fact, that He has not done, and hence it has been inferred that if the evidence justifies our recognizing the existence of a God at all, it is only of one who is subject to limitations. On the other hand, it has been assumed that if a God, who is perfectly wise and veracious, has made a revelation, he was bound to exclude from its record every vestige of human imperfection, and to impress on every portion of its contents the stamp of infallibility.

At this point the two arguments, while continuing to rest on the same abstract principles, diverge in opposite directions. It is assumed that the Bible is such a revelation. On the principles above stated the inference is justly drawn, that no trace of error or imperfection can exist in any portion of its contents. This being so, the advocates of this theory are compelled to adopt one of the two following courses, either to deny the truth of every discovery in science, history, or criticism, which is at variance with the received opinions respecting the contents of Scripture; or to adopt some mode of interpretation which shall bring the Scriptures into harmony with the new facts. The adoption of the latter course is perfectly legitimate, except when theologians are compelled by the exigencies of their position to put interpretations on Scripture which are inconsistent with the obvious meaning of its writers. Still the principle is a correct one, for if the Universe and the Bible are both Revelations from the same God, it may fairly be assumed that fresh discoveries in the one would throw light on the meaning of the other. The only danger of it arises from the temptations to which it exposes theologians to put non-natural interpretations on the Bible.

Still however it is in the highest degree desirable that we should take our stand on principles which will save us from the danger of having to make any more retreats from untenable positions before the steady advance of scientific knowledge. The only sure mode of accomplishing this is to adopt the principle laid down by Butler, that all theories of inspiration, as far as they are based on *à priori* principles, are unsafe guides to the realities of things, and that the only way in which light can be thrown on this question is, not by laying down how God must have acted, but by inquiring how He has acted, and thus bending our theories of inspiration into conformity with the facts and phenomena of the Bible, and not the latter into conformity with our theories. By pursuing this course we shall be able to welcome truth from whatever quarter it may come.

Assuming therefore that the *à priori* principles above referred to are utterly invalid as guides to the realities of things, it follows that the only mode of throwing light on this difficult question is,

First,

To ask the sacred writers whether they have made any such general assertions as to the nature of their own inspiration as would enable us to construct a theory which would be applicable to the entire Bible.

Secondly,

In the absence of any such definite affirmations on their part to apply the principle of induction to its contents, in precisely the same manner as we do to any other subject of investigation, and to propound a theory which will cover the existing facts. Other road to truth on this subject there is none.

Such a method is in conformity both with common sense and with sound philosophy. Surely nothing is more absurd than on mere abstract principles to attribute to the writer of a Book of Scripture such a degree of divine assistance as he himself apparently disclaims. Let me take an illustration from St. Luke's Gospel. If the verbal or mechanical theory, or any of its modifications, is correct, every word in this Gospel must be the dictation of the Divine Spirit. Yet in the preface the information as to the sources whence the author derived his materials is of a most definite character. He tells us that he instituted a careful investigation into the truth of the facts which he has narrated; and that while he was not an eye-witness of them himself, he has compiled his narrative from the testimony of those that were; and he adds that the purpose he had in view was that his readers might know the certainty of the things in which they had been instructed.* Yet notwithstanding these affirmations, the exigencies of theory have induced persons to affirm that the contents of this Gospel were dictated by the Divine Spirit. I fully admit that there is nothing in his assertions which is inconsistent with the idea that its author was possessed of one or more of the supernatural endowments referred to in the Pauline epistles, as extensively bestowed on the members of the Apostolic Church, and which may have aided him in his inquiries and imparted additional strength to his natural faculties; but it is plain that it cannot have been of such a nature as to have superseded their use or rendered human sources of information unnecessary.

It becomes therefore a matter of the greatest importance in reference to this inquiry to ascertain whether the Bible contains any such definite assertions as to the degree of the supernatural assistance afforded to its authors as will enable us to found on them a theory which will accurately define the extent of their inspiration. Such an inquiry may safely be confined to the New Testament, because it distinctly affirms that the enlightenment which was possessed by the apostles and prophets of the New Dispensation was greatly in excess of that possessed by the most enlightened men of the old. Now although the writers of the New Testament habitually cite the Old Testament as a divine book, and affirm that God spake in it on various definite occasions, yet not a single passage exists in it which lays down the degree of supernatural enlightenment possessed by its authors, or informs us how far a human element

---

* Ἐπειδήπερ πολλοὶ ἐπεχείρησαν ἀνατάξασθαι διήγησιν περὶ τῶν πεπληροφορημένων ἐν ἡμῖν πραγμάτων, καθὼς παρέδοσαν ἡμῖν οἱ ἀπ' ἀρχῆς αὐτόπται καὶ ὑπηρέται γενόμενοι τοῦ λόγου, ἔδοξεν κἀμοὶ, παρηκολουθηκότι ἄνωθεν πᾶσιν ἀκριβῶς, καθεξῆς σοί γράψαι, κράτιστε Θεόφιλε ἵνα ἐπιγνῷς περὶ ὧν κατηχήθης λόγων τὴν ἀσφάλειαν.—(Luke i. 1-4.)

entered into its composition.* Several writers of the Old
Testament also distinctly appeal to historical documents which

* It may be objected that the assertion is very common that the
Holy Spirit spake in and by the prophets, as in such passages as
"who by the mouth of thy servant David hath said" (Acts iv. 25);
and "Well spake the Holy Ghost by Esaias the prophet unto our
fathers," &c. (Acts xxviii. 25); and many others. These passages
unquestionably affirm that in each specified instance the prophets
spake under a divine influence, yet they leave us without information
as to its precise character or limits. Still less is it possible from such
passages to construct a theory of inspiration which shall be applicable
to the entire Bible. Besides, a great number of these passages leave
us without any means of accurately judging whether in each case the
prophet spake by special suggestion or from a general enlightenment
pervading his mind, by which he was able to penetrate into the mind
of God. Still further, such assertions leave us without any information on the point which is all-important in reference to modern controversies, viz., how far the divine influence conveyed an illumination on
points which were only collateral to, and not of the essence of, the
prophetic utterance. But whatever opinion we may form as to the
extent of divine illumination which such passages attribute to the
prophets on particular occasions, it is evident that to infer from them
that the same illumination presided over the composition of every part
of the Bible, including the whole of the historical books—Proverbs,
Ecclesiastes, and the Canticles—is to erect a pyramid of theory on an
apex of fact. But still further, the quotations from the Old Testament which are made by the writers of the New have a very important bearing on the entire subject. They afford the strongest proof
that they only attributed the general sense, and not the words in
which it is conveyed, to the influence of the Divine Spirit. This is
proved by the great freedom of quotation which is used in such references. The extent of this can only be fully estimated by an actual
comparison of the cited passages with their originals in the Old Testament. If one thing connected with this subject is more certain than
another, it is that the mode in which the Old Testament Scriptures
are referred to and quoted in the New, is fatal to all theories of
mechanical or verbal inspiration. Various theories have been propounded for the purpose of evading this difficulty, but all are destitute
alike of foundation and of proof. I will only notice one of them,
that which affirms that the passages as cited in the New Testament
are the genuine utterances of the prophets of the Old, and that the
variations from them in our present Old Testament are due to corruptions in the text. This is not only a bare assumption made for the

have since perished as the authorities for their statements, in the same manner as St. Luke grounds his assertions on the testimony of eye-witnesses. Even if we understand the disputed passage in Timothy as asserting that "all scripture was given by inspiration from God," this still leaves us in complete darkness as to the nature or extent of the divine influence.*

The most important passages in the New Testament bearing on this question are Our Lord's promises made to His followers of such supernatural enlightenment as was necessary to qualify them for propagating His religion and found-

---

express purpose of supporting a theory, but it creates far greater difficulties than it would solve. The following inference would be its logical result. If errors have crept into the text of the Old Testament to the extent which they must have done in the instances in question, it follows that an equal amount of error must be diffused over the entire volume, of which these quotations form but a small portion. The theory therefore, if true, would shake our confidence in the text of the Old Testament to its centre.

* Even if in accordance with the authorized version, we admit that in 2 Tim. iii. 16 the word θεόπνευστος forms a portion of the predicate instead of the subject of the sentence, it leaves the question as to the mode and degree in which this divine influence acted altogether undetermined. Our version, however, has represented the Apostle as making a nearer approach to laying down a theory of inspiration than the Greek does, when it renders the word θεόπνευστος "given by inspiration from God." But its only legitimate meaning is, "breathed into by God," and this leaves the extent of the influence indeterminate. Thus we can only make it affirm what modern theories require, by first assuming that it does so. Not one word does it assert as to inspiration conferring a divine enlightenment on points of science, philosophy, history, or criticism; in fact, it implies that it did not extend to such subjects, for it affirms that Scripture is "profitable for doctrine, for reproof, for correction, for instruction in righteousness, that the man of God may be perfect, throughly furnished unto all good works." As to its profitableness to their light on subjects of philosophy, science, history, or criticism, it is not only utterly silent, but by its silence implies that such points formed no legitimate portion of its subject-matter, and it would be quite consistent with the presence of a fallible human element in the Bible in connection with all these and many other subjects.

ing His Church. That He promised them a supernatural assistance fully adequate to enable them to accomplish this work is expressly affirmed; but nowhere does He define its nature or extent. His three most definite promises are*—

First. That the Divine "Spirit should guide them," not into all truth generally, but into all *the* truth, which the context plainly limits to religious truth.

A second assures them that the Spirit should teach them all things, and refresh their memories as to His utterances.

A third that He would impart to them a knowledge of the future.

There is yet one more, but it has no bearing on the present question, that when they should be summoned to answer before the established tribunals, the Spirit would suggest to them the proper materials for their defence.

These constitute the whole of Our Lord's promises on the subject, and it is evident that they are inadequate to form the basis of a general theory as to the nature or extent of that divine assistance which was afforded to the human authors of the Bible. All that we can affirm is that it was adequate to qualify His disciples for the work which He directed them to perform, but it is impossible to erect upon them a general theory of inspiration, or to determine how far an element of human imperfection would be permitted to enter into its record.

* The following are the express promises of Our Lord: "But the Comforter, which is the Holy Ghost, whom the Father will send in my Name, he shall teach you all things, and bring all things to your remembrance, whatsoever I have said unto you." (John xiv. 26.) "But when the Comforter is come, whom I will send unto you from the Father; even the Spirit of truth, who proceedeth from the Father, he shall testify of me: and ye also shall bear witness, because ye have been with me from the beginning."—(John xv. 26, 27.) "Howbeit when he, the Spirit of truth is come, he shall guide you into all truth εἰς τὴν ἀλήθειαν πᾶσαν, all *the* truth, i.e., all the truth alluded to, not into every department of truth), for he shall not speak of himself, but whatsoever he shall hear, that shall he speak, and he shall shew you things to come. He shall glorify me, for he shall receive of mine, and shall shew it unto you."—(John xvi. 13, 14.)

Nor do the assertions in the Epistles enable us to get beyond this. St. Paul has several times informed us that his knowledge of Christianity was communicated by direct revelation from Jesus Christ; but he nowhere defines the nature of that divine guidance under which he acted, or claims a general infallibility. Not a single passage can be adduced from his writings which implies that he considered himself more under the influence of the Spirit when he wrote his Epistles than he was in his ordinary teaching; but, on the contrary, they make it clear that he considered both to be of equal authority. Several passages also make it certain that he was capable of discriminating between those utterances which were due to divine enlightenment and those which were the result of his mere human judgment. Of these the passage which I have chosen for my text, with its entire context, forms a very remarkable example. Still the extent of the influence is left undetermined, and we have nothing else to guide us except his oft repeated assertion that his knowledge of Christianity was complete, and that it was communicated to him by revelation. But all this does not give us a hint that he considered himself possessed of a supernatural enlightenment on any subject which was merely collateral to Christianity, and in which Christian truth was not directly involved. On several points also the Apostle claims to speak with the full authority of Christ; but in some of these there seems to be a reference to Our Lord's own personal teaching, which he evidently considered to be of a higher authority than his own.* It is

---

* Of this the following are examples: "And to the married, I command, yet not I, but the Lord, 'Let not the wife depart from her husband,' . . . and 'Let not the husband put away his wife.'" (1 Cor. ix. 10, 11.) Here the Apostle is directly referring to the teaching of Jesus Christ; and he evidently places his own on an inferior level in point of authority. Again: "Now concerning virgins, I have no commandment of the Lord, yet I give my judgment as one that hath obtained mercy of the Lord to be faithful." (1 Cor. vii. 25.) Here again the distinction is drawn between his own Apostolical judgment and the express commands of Our Lord. The context shows

also worthy of remark that any equivalent to the formula, "Thus saith the Lord," with which the prophets of the Old Testament introduce their utterances, is only to be found on one or two occasions in the pages of the New.*

that his own decision on the points in question was not intended to have the force of invariable law; but to be subject to modification in conformity with the peculiar circumstances and character of the individual. So again, after recommending abstinence from marriage under certain circumstances, he still enforces his judgment with hesitation, as though it might be influenced by the peculiarities of his own mental temperament, in the following words: "But she is happier if she so abide after my judgment; and I think also that I have the Spirit of God." (1 Cor. ix. 40): the Greek is δοκῶ. This is evidently the language of a man who considers that his judgment is entitled to the highest deference in consequence of the illumination of the Divine Spirit which he possessed; but who yet feels that he does not on such a subject speak with an infallible authority. This is strongly contrasted with the mode in which he speaks elsewhere in this same epistle. "If any man think himself to be a prophet or spiritual, let him acknowledge that the things that I write unto you are the commandments of the Lord." (1 Cor. xiv. 37.)

* The habit which has so extensively prevailed, of designating the entire Bible, and even our own interpretations of it, as "the Word of God," has no doubt greatly contributed to the diffusion of the popular views on the nature and extent of the supernatural guidance imparted to its writers. The very form of the expression conveys to ordinary minds the idea that every word in it is the dictation of the Divine Spirit. Hard language has been applied to those who have endeavoured by the use of a greater accuracy of expression, in saying that the Bible *contains* the Word of God, to bring about a greater accuracy of thought. Those who make use of the denunciations to which I allude, seem either to be ignorant of the fact, or to have forgotten it, that that great defender of the Christian faith, Bishop Butler, must be included among those whom they thus condemn. Throughout the chapter, to which I have so often referred, he carefully distinguishes between the book which contains the revelation and the revelation itself. Thus in the passage above quoted, he writes, "Unless the prophets, apostles, or Our Lord, had promised that the book containing the divine Revelation should be secure from these things." It is hardly possible to overestimate the confusion of thought which has originated from this inaccurate use of language. To say that the Bible contains the Christian revelation is accurate; to say that it *is* the Christian revelation, the reverse.

The only portion of the New Testament which can be regarded as propounding a theory of inspiration is St. Paul's description of the nature of the enlightenment which was conferred by "the Supernatural Gifts" and of the mode of their action. To these I have already alluded for a different purpose. As far as this description goes, it affirms in direct terms that the influence was not a general one, extending to every faculty of the mind, and conferring an absolute infallibility, but a limited and functional one. It establishes the following points as certain.

In like manner, to affirm that it contains the Word of God is accurate; but to affirm that it is the Word of God is misleading; for if every separate portion of it is so, not only must my text, with its entire context, which the Apostle affirms that he uttered, "not after the Lord, but as it were foolishly, in the confidence of boasting;" but such expressions as "the salutation by the hand of me, Paul; Remember my words," and a large number of others, of a precisely similar import, which are evidently the utterances of the human Paul, be so. It should be observed, once for all, that the use of this expression is not justified by one single passage in the New Testament; for although its writers affirm that God spake by prophets, and generally in the Scriptures of the Old Testament, yet nowhere does it apply this designation to the entire Bible. I am aware that it will be replied, that it is very convenient to designate the Bible thus for popular purposes; and that the idea has become so fixed in the popular mind, that to do otherwise would shake the belief in its divine character. Its convenience I shall not dispute; but matters have come to that point, where questions of convenience must be sacrificed, when their result is to impress on the public mind theories of inspiration, which imperil the belief in Christianity. As to the plea that to use more accurate language would shake the faith of the people in Christianity, the first question to be determined is, Is it true? and if it be not, a saying of Our Lord has an intimate bearing on the point in hand, "Every plant which my heavenly Father hath not planted must be rooted up." The charge of rationalism may be made with far greater justice against those who propound *à priori* theories out of their own subjective consciousness as to how the Bible must have been written, if it really contains a divine revelation, rather than against those who reverently inquire of its authors what was the nature and extent of that superhuman guidance under the influence of which they wrote.

1. The supernatural gifts conferred a special enlightenment on a definite subject-matter only.

2. That the enlightenment which was conferred by one gift conferred none on the special subject-matter of another.

3. That the enlightenment was not general, but functional.

4. That the gift operated, when once conferred, according to the analogy of the ordinary faculties of the human mind.

5. That it was so completely functional, that the gift did not secure its possessor from the danger of abusing it.

6. That several of these gifts were occasionally united in one individual, in which case they conferred a more extended enlightenment; and that their object was to qualify their possessors for the discharge of certain offices in the Church.

7. Even the highest gifts did not convey a knowledge which was perfect.

The importance of the Apostle's description of these gifts is very obvious. The conferring of them was the distinct fulfilment of Our Lord's promises of supernatural guidance which he would afford to the apostles in the conduct of their mission. This is repeatedly affirmed in the pages of the New Testament.* Taking these gifts therefore as a whole, they must be considered as constituting the inspiration which was possessed by the Apostolic Church. Consequently the Apostle's description of them constitutes the only theory

---

* Not only is this rendered certain by the assertions in the earlier chapters of the Acts, but we have St. Paul's repeated affirmation to the same effect, of which the following is an example :—" Wherefore when he ascended up on high, he led captivity captive, and gave gifts unto men. . . . And he gave some apostles, and some prophets, and some evangelists, and some pastors and teachers, for the perfecting of the saints, for the work of the ministry, for the edifying of the body of Christ." (Ephes. iv. 8, 11, 12.) Writing to the Corinthians, he says, " I thank my God always on your behalf, for the grace which is given you by Jesus Christ, that in every thing ye are enriched by him in all utterance, and in all knowledge ; even as the testimony of Christ was confirmed in you; so that ye come behind in no gift, waiting for the coming of our Lord Jesus Christ."—(1 Cor. i. 4-7.)

of inspiration which can be found in the New Testament. As such, it stands in striking contrast to all those which have been laid down on *à priori* principles, and which have obtained so wide a currency in the Church. It follows therefore that as this constitutes the only direct light which the New Testament throws on the subject, any further information which we require can only be obtained, as Butler affirms, in the same way as we acquire it in all other subjects of human inquiry, by a careful and reverent exercise of those rational faculties which God has given us on the investigation of the facts and phenomena of the Bible.

I now proceed to apply the principles which have been laid down by Butler to the solution of some of our chief scientific difficulties. The only thing which would render them inapplicable, would be some distinct affirmation in the New Testament bearing on the question. But as we have seen, the only thing which it contains resembling a theory of inspiration, instead of being opposed to the principles of Butler, is one which is strictly in conformity with them. The shortness of the space remaining at my command, compels me to confine my observations to a few of the most important points in dispute.

First: as to the difficulties suggested by Geology in connection with the first chapter of Genesis.

It will be no duty of mine to enter on the vexed question of the interpretation of this chapter. This has already been so thoroughly discussed, that it would hardly be possible to say anything fresh on the subject. One point may, at all events, be considered settled, viz., that the meaning which has been universally attributed to it until comparatively recent times, and which the exigencies of a particular theory of inspiration naturally suggested, is in direct opposition to the scientific facts. It is beyond question that the passage has produced a very general belief, that the entire created universe was brought into its present form in a period of six natural days. This is obviously the meaning which would be attached to it by a reader unacquainted with the facts of science. But it is no less certain, that when the passage is closely scrutinized, uninfluenced by any particular theory as to the nature of inspiration, it is capable of bearing, without offering any violence to it, a different interpretation. All modes of interpretation however, which endeavour to accommodate it to the scientific facts, are founded on the assumption that the narrative is couched in language which is not scientifically correct, but pre-eminently popular; and possibly, that the entire representation was seen in vision.

Adopting then one or more of the modern modes of interpretation which have been applied to it under the influence of the light of geological discoveries, how stands the case? Let it be observed that a great peculiarity attaches to this passage of Scripture. Other narratives are founded on the testimony of eye-witnesses. This one cannot; for Creation, from the nature of the case, could have had no witness. There are only two alternatives as to its origin. Either the facts must have been made known by Revelation, or its statements must have been the result of a lucky guess of some one in the primitive ages of the world; for the idea that the knowledge could have been the result of scientific investigation in those times is out of the question.* The question then is a very important one, how do the statements in this chapter, when interpreted in accordance with modern critical methods, stand in relation to the unquestionable facts of geological science? The answer of even the most determined opponents of Revelation must be, that while in some minute points they are not absolutely consistent with the scientific facts, yet they make a marvellously near approach to them. This is the more remarkable

---

* Some of the recent discoveries in connection with the pyramids may possibly suggest the idea of a lost scientific age. How far this may be true with respect to the mathematical and astronomical data in question, I would not venture to express an opinion, but that such knowledge could have extended to geological science there is not one particle of evidence.

when we compare it with the numerous cosmogonies of the ancient world. These, with one or two exceptions, are not only unspeakably grotesque, but bear no kind of resemblance to the facts disclosed by geological science.

One additional fact requires notice. I have no wish to express an opinion whether Creation may have been effected in conformity with any modern theory of evolution; but I ask attention to the singular fact, that there are two expressions in this chapter, which an evolutionist, who believes in theism, might accept as a popular exposition of his theory. The first of these occurs in the description of the creation of the marine animals; and the second, in that of the land animals. In both cases the creation is ascribed, not to an immediate, but to a mediate agency. Thus we read, "And God said, *Let the waters bring forth abundantly*, the moving creature that hath life, and fowl that may fly in the open firmament of heaven." The next verse affirms that this actually took place; and adds that "*the waters brought them forth abundantly*." In a similar manner the earth is commanded to produce the land animals. It cannot be denied, that as far as the language goes, it is quite consistent with such a theory of evolution as affirms that the Creator has acted through a principle of this kind as the intermediate agent in effecting his creative work.*

---

* It is not within my province in these Lectures to enter into discussions respecting questions of Theism. Still I cannot help expressing an opinion that the attempt which has been made in certain quarters to denounce all theories of evolution as essentially Atheistic or Pantheistic, is pre-eminently unwise. Theories of evolution which assume the possibility of creating the universe and its present order by the action of the blind forces of nature, without the intervention of an intelligent Creator immanent in and directing and controlling them, are undoubtedly of this character, and have imparted in the eyes of many a plausibility to atheistic and pantheistic theories of the origin of the universe of which they were previously destitute, and it is undeniable that this has been one of the results with which Mr. Darwin's theories have been attended. But it is no necessary consequence of a theory of evolution that it should exclude

Still, close as is the resemblance between the geological record and this chapter, thus interpreted, it must be candidly

the conception of an intelligent Creator. Rather, when such theories are closely scrutinized, they are found to be powerless to produce any result without one. As regards the Bible, it is beyond question that it teaches not only that God is distinct from and above the universe, but that He is immanent in it, and constantly energizing in its forces. This being so, there is no more difficulty in supposing that the Creator, after having given existence to the substance of the universe, has used some process of evolution as one of the means through which He has carried on His creative work than that He has called each separate species into existence by what is called direct and immediate creation. As to what immediate creation is, we are utterly ignorant, and our *à priori* knowledge entirely fails to determine the *modus operandi* in which God must have carried on His creative work. If the knowledge of this is ever attained, it will be, not by the abstract speculations of theologians, but by a careful study of the facts of the universe. One thing is certain upon any theory of creation, that in the production of each individual of a species, God acts in conformity with a principle of evolution, and not of direct creation, every individual man having been in this manner unquestionably produced from the first parents of the human family through a process, part of which is known to us, but the remainder is buried in impenetrable obscurity. Consequently, it is in the highest degree unwise to affirm that the idea that God has used a principle of evolution as one of the means through which He has effected his creative work, is essentially atheistic or pantheistic. One thing is certain. While this theory has obtained an extensive acceptance among scientific men, the data which are as yet in our possession are inadequate to justify a positive and dogmatical affirmation on the subject. Our duty is therefore to hold ourselves in a state of expectancy, free from all *à priori* theorizing, and ready to accept the truth from whatever quarter it may come. If we keep ourselves steadily in this position, we shall avoid the danger of having to beat any further retreats before the advance of scientific knowledge. In whatever way it may be ultimately proved that the universe has been constructed, it will never be discovered to have been built by the sole action of the blind forces of nature, without the interposition of an intelligent Creator. In speaking of theories of evolution, it should ever be kept in mind that there are many others besides the Darwinian in conformity with which the Creator may have partially energized in His creative work. Scriptural Theism unquestionably affirms that the forces of the uni-

admitted that the geological facts do not exactly correspond in all their minuter details with the events as they are here narrated. Are we then, in conformity with some *à priori* theory of inspiration, to put a strain upon the language of the chapter, which it will not bear, or deny the scientific facts; or, if we can do neither, abandon our belief in Christianity as a divine revelation? I reply, that there is a more rational alternative, viz., to apply Butler's principles to the case before us.

First: the leading idea of the entire chapter is not a scientific but a religious one; its object being to affirm that the Universe is the work of one almighty and intelligent Creator. This being its obvious aim, it is strictly in conformity with the above principles, that the scientific arrangement being entirely subordinate to the main purpose, may have been accommodated to the religious one. Butler's principles firmly establish the fact, that we have no *à priori* certainty that a revelation, whose one great object is the communication of religious truth, must be minutely accurate on points of scientific knowledge in the record which contains it, on pain of forfeiting its character as a revelation from God.

Secondly: the narrative nowhere affirms that its contents were communicated by immediate revelation to the author of the Book of Genesis. There is nothing whatever to imply that it was not in existence long prior to his time, or that the writer did not find it already in existence, and incorporate it into his work. He is in fact very particular

verse are a constant manifestation of the energies of God. That theory which contemplates the universe as a self-acting machine which was once constructed by God, but the forces of which, when once brought into existence, continue their everlasting operations independently of His immanence in them, and grind out a succession of results with faultless precision, independently of His intelligent control, may be abstractedly consistent with Theism, but hardly with the Theism of the Bible, which contemplates God, not only as a perfect mechanist or chemist, which this theory represents Him to be, but as a Father.

in informing us what parts of the Pentateuch were communicated to him by special revelation; but he gives us no hint whatever that he derived his knowledge of any part of the book of Genesis in this way. As, however, it is certain that the contents of this chapter, unless they were the results of a lucky guess, must have been the subject of some primitive revelation, it follows that during some period the vehicle of its transmission must have been a traditionary one. A careful perusal of the different ancient cosmogonies proves that they possess many points in common, and therefore renders it highly probable that they are as many different versions of some primeval account, of which the grotesque elements are subsequent interpolations, which they have undergone in the course of oral transmission.* Here then we may invoke Butler's principle, that we have no *à priori* certainty that God would interfere to prevent the account from undergoing some degree of corruption in the course of such transmission; and consequently, that this may have been the source of its minuter divergencies from the strict accuracy of scientific facts. If this be so, it follows on the same principles, that we are unable to affirm that a supernatural enlightenment must have been imparted to the author of the book of Genesis, to enable him to correct them. The principle therefore which has been adopted by numerous defenders of Christianity, of representing that its truth must stand or fall with our ability to reconcile every statement of this chapter with the minutest accuracy of scientific facts, cannot be too strongly reprobated. If the writer had expressly affirmed that he had received every word in the chapter by immediate revelation from God; and that such revelation was intended to be scientifically correct, the presence of errors in his narrative would have

---

* This is strongly confirmed by the discovery of the genuine Chaldean cosmogony by the late Mr. G. Smith. Its close resemblance to that in Genesis is unmistakable, the latter being the monotheistic account of Creation, and the former being the same account exhibited in a polytheistic dress.

been inconsistent with his pretensions. But as Butler has well observed, the presence of errors of this kind would only invalidate a revelation if the record of it contained a definite promise that it should be exempt from them.

Secondly : as to the antiquity of Man. According to the popularly accepted theories of inspiration, the Scriptures are considered to be pledged to a system of Chronology which affirms that the creation of man cannot be separated from the present time by an interval of more than about seven thousand years, and the Flood by more than about five thousand; and that any alleged discoveries of science which prove that man has existed on the earth for a longer period are inconsistent with the claims of the Bible to contain a divine Revelation.*

I am not here alluding to the demands made by a particular School of Geologists for millions of years since the first appearance of man on this planet, but for a longer interval of time than that which according to the received system separates the deluge from the present day as rendered absolutely necessary by the evidence which has been adduced of the gradual growth of civilization and of language. The facts may be briefly stated. We are now in the possession of data which prove the existence of an advanced state of civi-

* Thus the question has been eagerly debated as to the exact time of the Israelites' sojourn in Egypt, or whether the interval of 450 years which St. Paul assigns in his address to the Jews in the synagogue at Antioch in Pisidia, is correct, as though the life of Christianity depended on the issue. As we have seen, we have neither à priori nor à posteriori knowledge that an apostle must have received supernatural illumination on the subject of Chronology. Why might not St. Paul have adopted that which he knew to be currently accepted by those whom he addressed? If he had done otherwise, he would have incurred the danger of diverting their attention from the all-important question of the Messiahship of Jesus to the discussion of his new and previously unheard-of Chronology. To determine the true Chronology of Scripture is in itself a study of great interest; but to do so as though the accuracy of every statement in it was vital to Christianity, is to place a needless stumbling-block in the way of both believers and unbelievers.

lization at a very early period, say, between three and four thousand years before Christ. This civilization, as in the case of Egypt, is united with a very complicated system of theology. The proof is incontestable that neither of these came into existence spontaneously, but that both have been gradually developed. Whatever theory we may adopt as to whether man originated in a highly civilized or in a savage state, the evidence which has been adduced proves that the condition of things which the remains of antiquity disclose, could only have grown up during a long interval of time, which must be added on to our earliest historic date. Thus, if man began as a savage, he must have elevated himself to that state of civilization which the earliest monuments of Egypt and other countries disclose, by a gradual growth which must have required a long interval of time. If, on the other hand, he began in a highly civilized condition, and was possessed of a pure theology, a very considerable period must have elapsed before the complicated, and in many respects, degraded Egyptian theology could have grown out of this. I select this merely as a single illustration of the large mass of evidence which is daily accumulating upon us.

These considerations acquire an increased force which is becoming irresistible by the investigations which have been made into the origin and growth of language. Not only is it certain that the Sanskrit, the Latin and the Greek, and several others originated out of a common language at a period of very remote antiquity, but this common language and all the other primitive languages have had a long history of their own, during which they have gradually diverged from some original and common stock. The evidence of all this, which is accumulating on us with a rapid pace, is incompatible with the popularly accepted theories about the date which must be assigned to the deluge, or even to the creation of man, on the supposed authority of the Scriptures of the Old Testament. Nor will the confusion of tongues at Babel free us from the difficulty, as the evidence is incontestable that after the formation of the original varieties these various languages have passed through a long period of gradual growth.

On the other hand, when we consider the data which they furnish for the construction of a system of chronology, it is evident that they are of an extremely meagre character, and have little or no value independently of a particular theory of inspiration. The date of the building of the Temple by Solomon is tolerably certain, but beyond this we get involved in obscurity and mists, which gradually thicken into intense darkness. Not only are the numbers subject to grave suspicion, but for a long interval the sole authority is a list of persons, who are said at a certain age to have begotten their sons, some of whose names bear every appearance of not being the designations of individuals but of nations. Still it cannot be denied that if it is necessary to accept the theories of inspiration of which I have been speaking, as vital to Christianity, the conclusion that a period of little more than 5000 years must separate us from the second beginning of the human race, and 7000 years from the first origin of man, logically follows from the premisses.*

It cannot be denied that the present state of this controversy is causing anxiety to a large number of inquiring and deeply religious minds. Under the influence of current theories of inspiration, the opinion has been widely diffused that if the dates of the creation of man and of the deluge must be carried up several thousand years higher than those which have hitherto been commonly assigned to them, the position of Christianity as a divine revelation is seriously

* The absurdity of the popular theories of inspiration is exhibited in a striking light by the fact that each of the three copies of the Old Testament which we possess furnishes us with a different system of Chronology; and it is now impossible to ascertain for certain which was the one adopted by the author of the book of Genesis. They cannot be all true, and may be all false.

This being so, nothing can be more unwise than to discuss this question as though the truth of Christianity was in any way dependent on the mode of its solution.

imperilled. On the other hand, opponents taking advantage of this state of thought, loudly proclaim that the disproof of the received system of Chronology is nothing short of the demolition of the claims of the Bible to be a record of a divine revelation.

What, then, is the remedy? I reply, the cordial acceptance of the principles laid down by Butler. These difficulties, and the unedifying discussions between theologians and men of science might have been avoided if his warnings had been heeded, and theories of inspiration had not been propounded as vital to Christianity, whose sole ground of validity is that they correspond with the *à priori* conceptions of those who have invented them. The whole difficulty vanishes as soon as it is fairly recognized that we have no evidence whatever that the divine enlightenment which was imparted to the human authors of the Bible must have extended to questions of Chronology and other kindred subjects. The fact is certain that the author of St. Matthew's Gospel has omitted three links in the genealogy of Jesus Christ, so that a person whom he designates as the son of another was in reality his great grandson.* If such an omission has taken place where we can verify it by a reference to the Book of Kings, it is impossible to be sure that protracted intervals of time may not have been omitted in the scanty materials which constitute the chronological basis of the Book of Genesis. The proper reply to all difficulties of this kind is that we have no certainty derived either from an *à priori* or an *à posteriori* source that the writers of the Bible possessed a superhuman guidance on subjects of this

* The three omitted names are Ahaziah, Joash, and Amaziah. Various reasons have been assigned for the omission, but these are utterly inconsistent with the theory of verbal inspiration or any of its modifications. This however is far from being the only difficulty connected with the genealogy. The fact of the omission is not removed by any possible explanation of its cause; and this renders it highly probable that in the genealogies of the Old Testament, especially in those of remote times, other omissions, and extending over far greater intervals of time, may have taken place.

description; and our duty is not merely to hold such opinions secretly within our own bosoms, but openly to announce and act on them, in order that the many stumbling-blocks which now endanger the faith of thousands may be removed out of their way.

Thirdly: a similar course of reasoning may be applied to the numerous questions which have been so eagerly debated about the deluge and its alleged universality, as though the life of Christianity was involved in the issue. Here again, if a rigid *à priori* theory is assumed which requires absolute accuracy of expression in the record of Revelation, there can be no doubt that the Book of Genesis affirms its universality; and renders it necessary to assume the performance of a number of stupendous miracles by means of which the different animals of whose existence the narrative does not give us the smallest hint, were conveyed into the ark. In a similar manner it throws on Revelation the weight of a whole mass of difficulties connected with questions of physical science, under which the faith of multitudes has been made to stagger. We cannot wonder, when such principles have been laid down by popular writers on theology, if a large number of the students of science have taken them at their word, and boldly announced that their discoveries are inconsistent with the claims of Christianity to be accepted as a divine revelation. But if we apply to this subject the principles which were laid down by the great defender of Christianity more than a century ago, the difficulties in question cease to have any real existence. They may still remain subjects of profound interest; but whichever way they may ultimately be determined by the increase of our scientific knowledge, they will no longer be regarded as vital to the acceptance of Christianity as a divine revelation.

Fourthly: the same principle is applicable to a numerous class of critical questions as to the date and authorship of the sacred books. I by no means wish to deny the deep interest of many of these questions, or for one moment to deprecate their study, but only to correct the popular idea that the life of Christianity is involved in their solution. Thus we have had endless discussions about the Pentateuch, its authorship and date, and the number of documents out of which it has been composed.* Questions of this kind, which are involved in deep obscurity, and of which the evidence at best is small, seem to have a particular attractiveness to a numerous class of learned men. In many cases the uncertain character of the evidence is only surpassed by the boldness of the theories which have been erected on it. A late eminent writer, who holds it to be a composite work, has with the most astounding self-confidence boldly affirmed that he can discriminate the portions which have been derived from these different documents, and ascribe them to their respective authors. It is admitted however on all hands that considerable portions of the Pentateuch, if not written by Moses, are genuine representations of his teaching and institutions. This being so, I fall back on the position taken by Butler, as inherently sound, which lays down that, "Neither disputes about the authorship of different parts of the Bible, nor any other things of the like kind, though they had been much more considerable than they are, could overthrow the authority of Scripture unless the prophets, apostles, or Our Lord had promised that the book containing the divine revelation should be secure from these things." If the principle thus enunciated by this great defender of

---

* I may add that questions about the accuracy of the Biblical numbers, especially of those contained in the Pentateuch, are often eagerly debated as though the truth of Christianity was dependent on the result. I observe, in the first place, that nothing is more likely to get corrupted in transmission than numbers. Secondly, if Butler's principles are correct, we have no à *priori* knowledge that supernatural enlightenment would be afforded on such subjects to those through whom a revelation was communicated. Thirdly, we have no promise of Christ that such knowledge should be imparted, nor is there any affirmation of prophet or apostle bearing on the subject. This being so, when theologians discuss the subject in the way to which I have referred, they not only place a false issue before unbelievers, but pursue a course which endangers the faith of believers.

Christianity is correct, it ought to have been accepted as their guide by all those who have engaged in modern controversies on these and kindred subjects.

Fifthly. My space will only allow me very briefly to apply the same principle to the discrepancies which are alleged to exist in the Gospels. These have been magnified to an extent that is absurd. A large number of them admit of an easy reconciliation under the guidance of common sense. Others arise from the fragmentary nature of the narrative and our ignorance of the entire facts. Not a few of the remainder owe their origin to the fact that the events have been grouped in reference to the religious purpose of the author rather than in the order of strict historical sequence. Of a few the reconciliation is difficult. Of these the threefold account of the miracle at Jericho may be mentioned as an example, St. Matthew's Gospel affirming that two blind men were cured, while it is the obvious meaning of St. Mark's narrative that one only was cured at the entrance to the city, and of that of St. Luke, that a single blind man was cured by Our Lord after he had passed through the city. This difficulty is increased by the fact that words and actions so closely alike are attributed to Our Lord and to the blind men, that it is hardly possible to believe that they were repeated twice over in the manner in which they are given in St. Mark's and St. Luke's Gospels; and even this would leave the statement in St. Matthew unexplained, that two blind men were cured by Our Lord as He departed from Jericho. The attempted reconciliations of this discrepancy are all very forced and unnatural, and do far more mischief to the historical character of the Gospels than the candid admission of its reality. With respect to difficulties of this description (and they are very few*),

---

* Another very striking instance is the apparent disagreement between the Synoptics and St. John as to the day on which Our Lord celebrated the Last Supper, and its Paschal character. Every effort of ingenuity has been exhausted on this controversy, and the mass of literature which has grown out of the attempts to solve the difficulty

the best solution will be found in the principle laid down by Butler, that it is impossible to affirm that if the contents of the Gospels were left to be handed down by tradition during the first thirty years of the existence of the Church, inaccuracies may not have been introduced in the process. A careful study of the parallel narratives will impress the student with the conviction that they have certainly passed through some period of oral transmission. To this all their phenomena point. It is therefore quite rational to affirm, if any of the alleged discrepancies are real, that this is the source in which they have originated, and that we have neither any *à priori* certainty, nor promise of Our Lord, nor assertion of His Apostles, that the writings of the New Testament must be free from errors of this description, which after all are powerless to affect its general historical character. The only wonder is, not that they exist, but that their numbers are so few.

A large majority of the other difficulties which arise in connection with the present aspects of modern thought, as far as they are not Atheistic or Pantheistic, may be solved on the same principles. The following proposition, which goes to the root of the entire difficulty, seems so self-evident as to require simply to be stated to insure its acceptance as true. Principles of investigation which, when applied in past ages to the study of the constitution of the universe, have not

---

is large. Still, if after perusing the most elaborate disquisitions on the subject one reads the simple narrative of the Evangelists, one cannot avoid feeling that the difficulty remains. It seems far more satisfactory, therefore, to have recourse to the principle of Butler, that it has been occasioned by the Synoptics having passed through a period of oral transmission before they were committed to writing. A similar principle is the best solution of an apparent discrepancy between the Synoptics themselves as to the precise day on which the different events in Passion Week occurred, and of those other apparent discrepancies on the reconciliation of which so much ingenuity has been expended. They have only a real importance when the truth of Christianity is complicated with that of a particular theory of inspiration.

only been barren of good result, but have led to positive errors, cannot be safe guides to truth when applied to the study of Revelation. Let these then be abandoned; and let those which have unfolded to us what is the real constitution of the universe be substituted in their place. This will lead to an enlarged view of the realities of Revelation, and enable both revelations of God—the one made in the created universe, and the other in the person of Jesus Christ our Lord—to be studied in harmony.

I conclude with the words of the great Bishop, which cannot be too deeply impressed on the mind of every student:—"And as it must be owned that the whole scheme of Scripture is not yet understood, so if it ever comes to be understood before the restitution of all things, and without miraculous interpositions, it must be in the same way as natural knowledge is come at—by the continuance and progress of learning and liberty, and by particular persons attending to, comparing, and pursuing intimations scattered up and down in it, that are overlooked and disregarded by the generality of the world." What is the inference? Both must be studied, not under the guidance of abstract and unverifiable theories, but by the light of patent and incontrovertible facts. If this course be pursued, the three great revelations of God—in the material universe, in the moral nature of man, and in the person of Jesus Christ our Lord—will constitute one harmonious whole, each throwing light on the other during the ages of the future, until in the dispensation of the fulness of time all things are gathered together in Christ in one, whether they be things on earth or things in heaven.

SUPPLEMENTARY NOTE.

The foregoing Lectures were composed, and the larger portion of them in type, before the publication of Professor Mozley's Lectures entitled "Ruling Ideas in Early Ages." It was impossible therefore for me to notice the positions taken in them on the subject of miracles, which apparently present some points of divergency from those adopted by him in his Bampton course. I will state the points laid down in his Lecture on the Sacrifice of Isaac, as to the evidential value of miracles, and then offer some observations on their bearing on the views propounded in the present volume. The very interesting discussions on the alleged imperfection of the moral teaching of the Old Testament, and Professor Mozley's mode of meeting the difficulty form no legitimate portion of the present argument. I shall therefore confine my observations to the subject of miracles.

The propositions laid down in the Lecture on the Sacrifice of Isaac are as follows :

1. That the general rule laid down in Scripture is, that miracles are evidences of the divine will ; and that a command which has the warrant of a miracle may be regarded as coming from God.

2. While this is the general principle, a collateral principle is recognized in Scripture, that miracles may be permitted by God for the purpose of trial.

3. When a miracle contradicts any clear knowledge we have of the divine will, in such cases it does not bear its primary and most natural interpretation as an evidence of the divine will ; but the secondary interpretation as a trial of moral strength in resisting that apparent evidence of the moment, and from without, in favour of the more real evidence of His will which we have from antecedent sources and from within.

4. A miracle cannot authorise the acceptance of any doctrine manifestly opposed to the Gospel revelation.

5. The rule of Scripture in substance is, that no great moral or religious principle or law of conduct, of which we are practically certain on general antecedent grounds, can be upset even by a real miracle; but that when the two come into collision, as evidence, the miracle must give way, and the moral conviction stand; that no miracle in short can outweigh a plain duty; and that a real miracle might be wrought, and yet it would be wrong to do the act which the miracle enjoined.

6. A miracle may be evidence of a divine command to do a particular act to a man whose moral conceptions are low, and yet be no evidence to one in whom they are of a more elevated character. Consequently, miracles may have been evidence of divine commands to former ages, which would wholly fail to prove such commands at the present day. From this it follows that a miracle may in some former age of the world have formed an adequate attestation of a supposed divine command to kill a son; but if it were wrought at the present day in attestation of a similar command, it would be our duty to reject it.

If these are accurate accounts of the Scripture doctrine of the evidential character of miracles, it seems to me that the only effect of their performance would be to throw a plain man into a state of hopeless uncertainty as to what they really substantiated, or what line of duty they prescribed to him. In this note I shall draw attention to a few only of the difficulties involved in the views thus enunciated.

As Dr. Mozley considers that miracles may be performed not only as evidences of a divine command, but for the purposes of trial, it becomes a matter of the highest importance to ascertain whether miracles wrought for this latter purpose are performed by the finger of God, or by the power of Satan. He admits that real miracles may be performed which we are bound to disobey by rejecting the doctrine or the command which they have been performed for the purpose of substantiating. But if any such are alleged to be performed by God, it brings us face to face with a question of the greatest difficulty, viz., whether it is consistent with His character to perform miracles of this description. If on the other hand they are alleged to be Satanic, this opens the all-important question, how are such miracles to be distinguished from the miracles of God, for nothing can be more certain than, if there is no clear mode of discriminating between them, that the evidential value of miracles would be utterly destroyed. Yet no hint is given us how these important questions are to be determined.

But further: if miracles are performed for the purposes of trial, they cannot be the sole and adequate attestations of a revelation. In such a case a person who witnesses a miracle may justly entertain a doubt whether it was wrought to prove a doctrine, or to justify a command; or to test his religious or moral principles, as to whether, despite of the miracle, he would follow the dictates of his own conscience. It is impossible that miracles can subserve the two opposite purposes of being evidences of a divine command, and tests of faith, unless those wrought for the latter purpose bear some mark which clearly distinguishes them from the former.

Let us now consider Dr. Mozley's third position. Assuming its truth, it follows that the evidence afforded by a miracle cannot overbear the clear dictates of our conscience, but whenever it runs counter to them, we are bound to reject the miracle as being a trial of moral strength; or, in other words, a temptation. But the consciences of many earnest men are frequently misinformed. Thus St. Paul tells us that he was acting strictly in conformity with his conscientious convictions, when he persecuted the Christians to the death. If Dr. Mozley's position therefore is correct, he was justified in rejecting the miracles wrought by the apostles in attestation of Our Lord's resurrection, as permitted for the purpose of testing the firmness of his adhesion to the Mosaic dispensation.

So with respect to the fourth proposition, that a miracle cannot authorise the acceptance of any doctrine manifestly opposed to the Christian Revelation. This must have been equally true of the Jewish Revelation. But who is to be the judge when doctrines manifestly contradict either of them? There can be no other court of appeal but the conscience of the individual. Now as the obligation to obey the Jewish ceremonial law rested, according to the general principles laid down by Dr. Mozley in his Bampton Lectures, on the evidence of miracles, it follows that a Jew would have been justified in coming to the conclusion that the miracles wrought in attestation of a system, such as Christianity, which was intended to supersede it, were merely trials of his moral strength, and therefore that it was his duty to reject them. This being so, it follows that the Judaizing Christians of the Apostolic Churches were not without substantial reasons for rejecting the validity of St. Paul's Apostolical Commission, notwithstanding his plea that he possessed a miraculous attestation, for they could plead against them, not only the fact that Our Lord was circumcised, but that he himself was an observer of the Jewish rites, and never directed their abolition during the whole course of his ministry. Consequently, as the Pauline doctrine of the abolition of circumcision was, to use the words of Dr. Mozley, "a manifest contradiction" of the fundamental teaching of the Old Testament, and received no support from the direct teaching of Our Lord, the Judaizing Sections of the Church were fully justified in denouncing St. Paul as a false apostle, notwithstanding the miracles which it was admitted that he performed. They were in fact on this theory only trials of faith, and as such, worthy of rejection.

But further: Dr. Mozley affirms in his first Bampton Lecture, that the only thing which would justify any rational man in accepting the truth of many of Our Lord's declarations respecting himself, is the evidence of miracles. But according to the principles laid down in the Lecture we are now considering, would not those who witnessed Our Lord's miracles have been justified in rejecting them as affording evidence of such "incredible assertions" on the ground that they were intended for the purposes of trial in resisting that "apparent evidence of the moment, and from without, in favour of the more real evidence from antecedent sources, and from within?"

I fully agree with Dr. Mozley, that no miracle can justify us in the breach of a plain duty, for the simple reason that there is no ground for supposing that God would ever allow one to be performed for such a purpose. If an apparent miracle is performed which commands us to commit an act which we believe to be immoral, the legitimate conclusion is, that it is an act of legerdemain, a fraud, or the result of some mental hallucination on our part. The supposition that real miracles are wrought for the purposes supposed by Dr. Mozley, would involve simple-minded men in such a mass of difficulties as would deprive them of all evidential value. The miracles recorded in the Gospels were not performed for the benefit of the select few who constitute a kind of spiritual aristocracy, but of the masses of mankind.

With respect to the general proposition that miracles may be a justification of particular acts, to an age when the moral standard is low, while they would fail to afford any such justification to a more elevated one, it must be remembered, that even in ages of deep moral degradation, all are not sunk to the same dead level. To such, miracles would not be evidences of a divine command, but trials of moral strength. To take an illustration from modern times. War does not violate the general conscience of the Christian Church at the present day. A miracle therefore, according to the principles laid down by Dr. Mozley, might justify a particular war as an actual divine command to wage it. But a section of the Christian Church, the Quakers, believe war to be contrary to the principles of the Gospel. To such therefore a miracle wrought for the purpose of sanctioning it, would be simply a trial of moral strength. It follows therefore, that if the evidential character of miracles is correctly set forth in the positions I am considering, it is of a nature so vague and indefinite, as to be valueless for the purposes of proof.

There is one sound principle, and only one, which affords an adequate explanation of the imperfections of portions of the morality of the Old Testament. It is to be found in an utterance of our Blessed Lord himself: " Moses, for the hardness of your hearts, wrote you this precept."

As far as the Sacrifice of Isaac is concerned, the question whether miracles will justify such commands is simply irrelevant, for the narrative in Genesis does not contain a hint that a miracle was wrought for its justification. All that it tells us is, that an intimation was conveyed to the patriarch (of the precise mode in which the communication was made we are not informed), to offer his son as a burnt sacrifice, and that Abraham recognized in it a divine command. But not one word is said about the performance of a miracle in attestation of its reality. This idea can be only introduced into it by assuming that the command itself constituted a miracle. I fully admit that when God commands us to perform a particular act, He can give us the fullest assurance that the command is from Him. But to class together supernatural communications made to individuals, and Our Lord's miracles under a common term, is to invite confusion of thought. In no ordinary sense of the term can it be said that Abraham's sacrifice of Isaac was authorised by the evidence of a miracle wrought as an attestation that the command came from God. I can only again express my conviction that if the positions laid down by Dr. Mozley in these Lectures are accurate accounts of the functions which miracles perform in connection with Christianity, they are simply destructive of their evidential character.

www.ingramcontent.com/pod-product-compliance
Lightning Source LLC
Chambersburg PA
CBHW021415300426
44114CB00010B/495